The Impact of Digital Transformation and FinTech on the Finance Professional

Volker Liermann · Claus Stegmann
Editors

The Impact of Digital Transformation and FinTech on the Finance Professional

palgrave
macmillan

Editors
Volker Liermann
ifb AG
Grünwald, Germany

Claus Stegmann
ifb Americas, Inc.
Charlotte, NC, USA

ISBN 978-3-030-23718-9   ISBN 978-3-030-23719-6   (eBook)
https://doi.org/10.1007/978-3-030-23719-6

© The Editor(s) (if applicable) and The Author(s), under exclusive license to Springer Nature Switzerland AG, part of Springer Nature 2019
This work is subject to copyright. All rights are solely and exclusively licensed by the Publisher, whether the whole or part of the material is concerned, specifically the rights of translation, reprinting, reuse of illustrations, recitation, broadcasting, reproduction on microfilms or in any other physical way, and transmission or information storage and retrieval, electronic adaptation, computer software, or by similar or dissimilar methodology now known or hereafter developed.
The use of general descriptive names, registered names, trademarks, service marks, etc. in this publication does not imply, even in the absence of a specific statement, that such names are exempt from the relevant protective laws and regulations and therefore free for general use.
The publisher, the authors and the editors are safe to assume that the advice and information in this book are believed to be true and accurate at the date of publication. Neither the publisher nor the authors or the editors give a warranty, expressed or implied, with respect to the material contained herein or for any errors or omissions that may have been made. The publisher remains neutral with regard to jurisdictional claims in published maps and institutional affiliations.

Cover illustration: Sergey Nivens, Shutterstock
Cover design by eStudio Calamar

This Palgrave Macmillan imprint is published by the registered company Springer Nature Switzerland AG
The registered company address is: Gewerbestrasse 11, 6330 Cham, Switzerland

Preface

Digitalization has gained substantial recognition in a broad range of very different areas. Drastically reduced prices for both on-premise and cloud storage combined with an extreme increase in IT performance have served to make artificial intelligence (AI) including machine learning and deep learning more and more part of our daily lives. Younger kids will not remember a time without personal assistants like Alexa and Siri, or commands like "Hey Google" or "Hey Mercedes". The technology sector led by Google, Apple, Facebook, Amazon (GAFA) is investing heavily in these technologies as well as blockchain for their software, services, analytics and devices. The automotive, logistics and health-care sectors as well as many others are currently undergoing massive change processes and will be entirely different 10 years from now.

This book takes an in-depth look at how digitalization is affecting players in the financial sector including banks and insurance companies. Moreover, within the finance sector, this work is explicitly focused on analytical topics including finance, accounting, regulatory reporting and client-related aspects. In the wake of the financial crisis, the finance industry had to invest heavily in data integration, processing and data lineage to comply with a long list of new regulatory requirements. Basel III was internationally agreed in 2017 and new regulations are on the way. The coming regulations will likely be less extensive and less costly than what banks have had to deal with in the past few years. On the other hand, banks and insurance companies must use the data generated for regulatory purposes to optimize analytical processes, accelerate reporting for decision-making and, most importantly, improve prediction of client behavior. The demand for the abovementioned advanced analytical methods will increase sharply in the risk and finance departments of financial institutions.

This will change the financial professionals' perspectives and require their ability to understand AI, deep learning, machine learning or blockchain technology. In addition to this, the architectures and infrastructures will have to mirror these method-driven improvements. Of course, the financial professionals will not be required to invent these methods themselves. They already exist and, combined with cloud services, are being offered by the big technology players or flexible fintech companies on the market. Financial professionals will be required to evaluate, tailor and implement these methods whenever they can leverage the available processes. They can even present entirely new opportunities in holistic financial planning or simulation.

Regulators also have to take these technologies into account. On the one hand, they have to evaluate whether neuronal networks, for example, can amend common risk methods. Another example described in this book consists of using blockchain technology for syndicated loans. Regulators will have to approve applications and processes like this in the future.

This book is intended to provide a full spectrum of information, from the fundamental principles of digitalization to concrete examples of how new methods and infrastructures can be applied and implemented in the existing bank and insurance IT architectures. A central focus here is on the area of bank management, in which risk management, planning, data integration and data lineage will be improved dramatically in coming years.

The authors have created a comprehensive work of broad yet in-depth content, which will benefit risk managers, finance managers, managers for regulatory and internal reporting and IT managers alike.

I hope this book helps and encourages all readers to embark on a successful, albeit demanding, digital journey.

Frankfurt, Germany

Dr. Andreas Dombret
Former Board Member of Deutsche
Bundesbank (2010–2018)

Disclaimer

The information contained in this book is provided for information purposes only. The information is of a general nature and is not intended to address the circumstances of any particular individual or entity. Ifb International AG assumes no responsibility for errors or omissions in this document and shall not be responsible for any damages arising out of the use of, or otherwise related to, this book. Nothing contained in this book is intended to, nor shall have the effect of, creating any warranties or representations from ifb International AG or any affiliate of ifb group. Furthermore, the information on this document is not a commitment, promise or legal obligation to deliver any material, code or functionality. No one should act on such information without appropriate professional advice after a thorough examination of the particular situation.

The information contained herein is being furnished solely for information purposes and may not be reproduced, redistributed, passed on or published, in whole or in part, to any other person for any other purpose.

The names and/or logos of actual companies and products mentioned herein may be trademarks of their respective owners.

Contents

1 Introduction   1
Volker Liermann and Claus Stegmann

Part I   Automation, Distributed Ledgers and Client Related Aspects

2 Batch Processing—Pattern Recognition   13
Volker Liermann, Sangmeng Li and Norbert Schaudinnus

3 Hyperledger Fabric as a Blockchain Framework in the Financial Industry   29
Martina Bettio, Fabian Bruse, Achim Franke, Thorsten Jakoby and Daniel Schärf

4 Hyperledger Composer—Syndicated Loans   45
Gereon Dahmen and Volker Liermann

5 The Concept of the Next Best Action/Offer in the Age of Customer Experience   71
Uwe May

6 Using Prospect Theory to Determine Investor Risk Aversion   79
Constantin Lisson

x   Contents

Part II   Bank Management Aspects

7   Leveraging Predictive Analytics Within a Value Driver-based Planning Framework   99
Simon Valjanow, Philipp Enzinger and Florian Dinges

8   Predictive Risk Management   117
Volker Liermann and Nikolas Viets

9   Intraday Liquidity: Forecast Using Pattern Recognition   139
Volker Liermann, Sangmeng Li and Victoria Dobryashkina

10   Internal Credit Risk Models with Machine Learning   163
Markus Thiele and Harro Dittmar

11   Real Estate Risk: Appraisal Capture   177
Volker Liermann and Norbert Schaudinnus

12   Managing Internal and External Network Complexity: How Digitalization and New Technology Influence the Modeling Approach   193
Stefan Grossmann and Philipp Enzinger

13   Big Data and the CRO of the Future   225
Richard L. Harmon

Part III   Regulatory Aspects

14   How Technology (or Distributed Ledger Technology and Algorithms Like Deep Learning and Machine Learning) Can Help to Comply with Regulatory Requirements   241
Moritz Plenk, Iosif Levant and Noah Bellon

15   New Office of the Comptroller of the Currency Fintech Regulation: Ensuring a Successful Special Purpose National Bank Charter Application   259
Alexa Philo

Contents xi

Part IV   Methods, Technology and Architecture

16   Mathematical Background of Machine Learning   271
Volker Liermann, Sangmeng Li and Victoria Dobryashkina

17   Deep Learning: An Introduction   305
Volker Liermann, Sangmeng Li and Norbert Schaudinnus

18   Hadoop: A Standard Framework for Computer Cluster   341
Eljar Akhgarnush, Lars Broeckers and Thorsten Jakoby

**19   In-Memory Databases and Their Impact on Our (Future)
Organizations**   357
*Eva Kopic, Bezu Teschome, Thomas Schneider, Ralph Steurer
and Sascha Florin*

**20   MongoDB: The Journey from a Relational to a Document-
Based Database for FIS Balance Sheet Management**   371
Boris Bialek

21   Summary and Outlook   381
Volker Liermann and Claus Stegmann

Notes on Contributors   385

Index   399

List of Figures

Chapter 1

Fig. 1	What can competitors do better?	3
Fig. 2	The path of benefit	4
Fig. 3	Impact of digitalization on earnings and costs	5

Chapter 2

Fig. 1	Pattern recognition process	14
Fig. 2	System architecture—schematic representation	16
Fig. 3	A simple batch process	17
Fig. 4	Structure of a trained Bayesian network	22
Fig. 5	Test data set	22
Fig. 6	Reconstruction error	24

Chapter 3

Fig. 1	Distinction between virtual machines and containers	32
Fig. 2	Schematic workflow of an endorsed transaction	39
Fig. 3	Private channels in Hyperledger Fabric. Every peer participates in the main chain (gray), but can also have several side-channels with different participants (white, black)	40
Fig. 4	Private data hidden from an unauthorized peer	41
Fig. 5	blockToLive setting in the configuration	42
Fig. 6	Zero-knowledge proof identity mixer	42

xiv   List of Figures

Chapter 4

Fig. 1	Involved parties	49
Fig. 2	Business process domains	50
Fig. 3	Components of the Hyperledger Composer modeling language	56
Fig. 4	Hyperledger Composer Playground online login	59
Fig. 5	Modeling language example (participants)	61
Fig. 6	Modeling language example (loan types)	62
Fig. 7	Modeling language example (loan substructures)	62
Fig. 8	Sample data (transaction)	63
Fig. 9	Sample JavaScript code (generate loan)	64
Fig. 10	Sample data (participants)	65
Fig. 11	Sample data (transaction)	65
Fig. 12	Sample data (collateral)	66
Fig. 13	Generated loans for syndicate members	67
Fig. 14	Example query (all loans)	67
Fig. 15	The primary decision—on or off the blockchain	68
Fig. 16	A typical Hyperledger Composer solution architecture	68

Chapter 6

Fig. 1	An empirically valid value function exhibiting concavity (risk aversion) over positive values and convexity (risk-seeking behavior) over negative values	86
Fig. 2	Choice between a risky asset and a fixed deposit with the same expected return, in which the worst possible scenario is a negative return, so that uncertainty aversion over losses influences the outcome	89
Fig. 3	Choice between a risky asset and a fixed deposit with a zero expected return, where the worst possible scenario is a zero return, so that only uncertainty aversion over gains influences the outcome	90
Fig. 4	Choice between a risky asset and a fixed deposit with a positive return less than the expected value of the risky asset's return; The fixed deposit's return has been increased relative to the previous question, so as to determine whether the investor still prefers the fixed deposit	91
Fig. 5	Investor decision following a downturn; This question is used to evaluate investor temperament	92

Chapter 7

| Fig. 1 | Example of overall planning framework | 101 |
| Fig. 2 | Value driver trees embedded within the planning framework | 102 |

Fig. 3	Value driver tree design principle	103
Fig. 4	Process-oriented illustration of the inclusion of external value drivers	106
Fig. 5	Example of a linear model	108
Fig. 6	Available living spaces in The City	110
Fig. 7	Total building costs in The City	110
Fig. 8	Regression results	112
Fig. 9	Mortgage market development	113
Fig. 10	Market share prediction	113

Chapter 8

Fig. 1	Overview of the risk management pyramid—goals of risk management	119
Fig. 2	Scenario-based planning including value driver modeling by ABM	121
Fig. 3	Transversal risks	122
Fig. 4	General mechanics of transversal risks	123
Fig. 5	Process of transversal risk calculation	124
Fig. 6	Simulation of the impact of climate legislation on a company's risk profile	125
Fig. 7	The effect of the reduced demand for office space	126
Fig. 8	The effect of increasing e-commerce market share	126
Fig. 9	Projection of the risk situation—motivation for change	130
Fig. 10	High-level example—is risk developing in line with the strategy?	131
Fig. 11	Projection of the risk situation in the future—general	132
Fig. 12	Credit risk example (simplified)	133
Fig. 13	Projection of the risk situation vs. scenario-oriented risk planning	134
Fig. 14	Financial risk management—evolution in three steps	136

Chapter 9

Fig. 1	Analysis framework	143
Fig. 2	Intraday liquidity—regulatory stress test (example)	143
Fig. 3	Stress test requirements overview	146
Fig. 4	Example of cumulative cash flows	147
Fig. 5	Evaluation of clustering result	148
Fig. 6	Clustering result based on global alignment kernel distance and 13 clusters	149
Fig. 7	Z-normalized vs. original time series of cluster No. 3	149
Fig. 8	Subclustering: grouping cluster members according to mean and variance	150
Fig. 9	Subclustering of cluster No. 3	150

xvi　List of Figures

Fig. 10	Forecasting the target time series	151
Fig. 11	Clustering result	152
Fig. 12	(1) Nearest cluster based on nearest neighbors; (2) Nearest cluster based on cluster center	152
Fig. 13	R Shiny—loading data	153
Fig. 14	R Shiny—preprocessing data	154
Fig. 15	R Shiny—extraction clusters	154
Fig. 16	R Shiny—clustering member filtering with FX = EUR and Client = Deutsche Bundesbank	155
Fig. 17	R Shiny—brush the cluster members	155
Fig. 18	R Shiny—load actual time series and search for the nearest cluster	156
Fig. 19	R Shiny—select additional time series of "Deutsche Bundesbank" by "Expert"	157
Fig. 20	R Shiny—add the selected time series into the group of forecasting candidates	157
Fig. 21	R Shiny—forecasting the actual time series using the forecasting candidates	158
Fig. 22	R Shiny—load actual time series and search for the nearest cluster	158
Fig. 23	R Shiny—add additional time series of the same currency "EUR" by "Expert"	159
Fig. 24	R Shiny—forecasting the actual time series using the forecasting candidates	159
Fig. 25	R Shiny—blockwise aggregation	160
Fig. 26	R Shiny—aggregate the forecast time series with 3 blocks	160
Fig. 27	R Shiny—aggregate the forecast time series with 6 blocks	161

Chapter 10

Fig. 1	Differences between the traditional mode and a machine learning based mode of modeling	166
Fig. 2	The impact of splitting data into a training set and a test set on the performance of the resulting artificial neural network. The AUC after 1500 training steps for the test set of the DNN_10.20.10 model (boxes), the LogReg model (circles) and for the training set of the DNN_10.20.10 model (triangles)	173
Fig. 3	Comparison of the performance of three different artificial neural networks: the AUCs for the test set (circles = predictive power) and for the training set (triangles = fit effectiveness) of the DNN_2.2 (inner lines), DNN_10.10 (outer lines), and DNN_10.20.10 (blue). The benchmark result of the logistic regression is shown as a gray line. The inner and outer curves simply serve as visual guides	174

Chapter 11

Fig. 1	Modularized approach	180
Fig. 2	Substance and dynamic data	181
Fig. 3	Example scheme for an application built to extract information from appraisal documents	187
Fig. 4	Example German real estate appraisal	189
Fig. 5	Structure of extracted data	190

Chapter 12

Fig. 1	Recent models of systemic risk	194
Fig. 2	Taxonomy of network complexity	196
Fig. 3	Setting up trait matrices	202
Fig. 4	Self-organizing map	202
Fig. 5	Multi-layered network representation of interbank financial links	205
Fig. 6	Overview of process mining	207
Fig. 7	Process mining use case—handling event stream data	212
Fig. 8	Process mining use case—cloud resource allocation for business processes	213
Fig. 9	Process mining use case—distributed application architectures	213
Fig. 10	Overview of agent-based modeling	215
Fig. 11	Agent-based modeling use case—financial services industry	218
Fig. 12	Agent-based modeling use case—new product launch	219
Fig. 13	Agent-based modeling use case—bond market participation	219
Fig. 14	Meta-process coping with network complexity	222

Chapter 13

Fig. 1	Traditional data warehouse	227
Fig. 2	Modern data warehouse	228
Fig. 3	Agent-based model—Example	235

Chapter 16

Fig. 1	Domains of machine learning	272
Fig. 2	Components of a machine learning system	273
Fig. 3	Classification graph	275
Fig. 4	Linear classification	275
Fig. 5	Nonlinear classification	276
Fig. 6	Clustering	277
Fig. 7	Steps in centroid-based models	282
Fig. 8	Normalization	284
Fig. 9	Example of three time series X, Y and Z	285

xviii   **List of Figures**

Fig. 10	Dynamic time wrapping	286
Fig. 11	Alignment path	287
Fig. 12	Example of cross-correlation	289
Fig. 13	Example Bayesian network	290
Fig. 14	Example Bayesian network	290
Fig. 15	Examples of conditional independence	291
Fig. 16	Example Bayesian network—creditworthiness	292
Fig. 17	Markov blanket	293
Fig. 18	Bayesian network parameter learning	293
Fig. 19	Decision tree	294
Fig. 20	Random forest	296
Fig. 21	K-fold cross-validation procedure	298

Chapter 17

Fig. 1	Deep learning in the artificial intelligence context	306
Fig. 2	Perceptron and feedforward network	307
Fig. 3	Perceptron—weights and activation functions	308
Fig. 4	Simple feedforward neural network (FF or FFNN)	308
Fig. 5	Feedforward neural network (FF or FFNN)—architecture	310
Fig. 6	Overview—activation functions	312
Fig. 7	Gradient descent algorithms	313
Fig. 8	Back propagation	314
Fig. 9	Deep feedforward network (DFF)	315
Fig. 10	Recurrent neural network (RNN)	316
Fig. 11	Translation of a recurrent cell	316
Fig. 12	Simple recurring cell	317
Fig. 13	Memory cell in detail	317
Fig. 14	Structure of long-/short-term memory (LSTM) and gated recurrent unit (GRU)	317
Fig. 15	Gated recurrent unit—memory cell	318
Fig. 16	Autoencoder (AE)	319
Fig. 17	Spare autoencoder (SAE)	319
Fig. 18	Variational autoencoder	319
Fig. 19	Denoising autoencoder	320
Fig. 20	Boltzmann machines	321
Fig. 21	Restricted Boltzmann machines	321
Fig. 22	Deep belief networks (DBN)	322
Fig. 23	Deep convolutional network (DCN)	322
Fig. 24	Deconvolutional network (DN)	323
Fig. 25	Deep convolutional inverse graphics network (DCIGN)	323
Fig. 26	Generative adversarial network (GAN)	324
Fig. 27	Extreme learning machine (ELM)	324

Fig. 28	Liquid state machine (LSM)	325
Fig. 29	Echo state machine (ESM)	325
Fig. 30	Deep residual network (DRN)	326
Fig. 31	Kohonen machine (KM)	326
Fig. 32	Support-vector machine (SVM)	327
Fig. 33	Neural turing machine (NTM)	327
Fig. 34	Autoencoder	329
Fig. 35	Distributed representations	332
Fig. 36	Word analogies	332
Fig. 37	A simple CBOW model with one word in the context	333
Fig. 38	CBOW model with multiple words for one context	334
Fig. 39	Skip-gram (SG) model	335

Chapter 18

Fig. 1	FsImage	345
Fig. 2	MapReduce	346
Fig. 3	SparkContext within the Apache Spark Framework	350
Fig. 4	DAG Visualization	350
Fig. 5	Overview of built-in libraries in Apache Spark	351
Fig. 6	Relationship and processing in and between the Apache Spark libraries (Das, 2015)	352
Fig. 7	Overview over graph analytics pipeline in GraphX	352

Chapter 19

Fig. 1	Big data or computationally intensive operations relocated to in-memory computing	359
Fig. 2	Adapted system environment	360
Fig. 3	Traditionally separated online transaction processing (OLTP) and online analytical processing (OLAP)	361
Fig. 4	SAP HANA time line	363
Fig. 5	SAP HANA platform overview	364
Fig. 6	Cash Flow Generator (CFG) and Query Creator (QC)	367

Chapter 20

Fig. 1	MongoDB web interface	376
Fig. 2	OS server entity	378
Fig. 3	Server overview	378

List of Tables

Chapter 2

Table 1	Data set examples	18
Table 2	Data categorization	21
Table 3	Conditional probability per feature	22
Table 4	Reconstruction error per feature	24
Table 5	Cross validation results of random forests	26
Table 6	Cross validation results of Bayesian network	26
Table 7	Cross validation results of autoencoder	26

Chapter 10

Table 1	Overview of different models that were used	171

Chapter 18

Table 1	Price development of hard disk storage	342

Chapter 20

Table 1	Example of a MongoDB representation of a financial position	375

1

Introduction

Volker Liermann and Claus Stegmann

1 Introduction

1.1 Why This Book?

The financial sector and in particular the banks are in a state of upheaval. Haven't they been continuously for the past twenty or thirty years? Digitalization as a megatrend with all its sub-aspects is hitting all industries and many of the templates for better business generation[1] and cost optimization look quite similar across these industries.

What are the fundamental differences between the financial services sector and other industries? The business environment surrounding banks has the additional load of excessive regulation requirements and technology-driven competitors (fintech companies or GAFA[2]). Depending on the region,

---

[1]Generating better business based on better contact with clients and a better understanding of clients' needs.

[2]GAFA—technology companies—Google Amazon Facebook Apple.

V. Liermann (✉)
ifb AG, Grünwald, Germany
e-mail: volker.liermann@ifb-group.com

C. Stegmann
ifb Americas, Inc., Charlotte, NC, USA
e-mail: claus.stegmann@ifb-group.com

© The Author(s) 2019
V. Liermann and C. Stegmann (eds.), *The Impact of Digital Transformation and FinTech on the Finance Professional*, https://doi.org/10.1007/978-3-030-23719-6_1

other challenges like geopolitical uncertainties, increasing credit risk driven by the end of a long economic cycle or a low-interest rate phase must be added to the business environment.

Before delving further into the details of the banking business environment, we would like to introduce you to the focus of this book, namely the impact on financial professionals. Does the storm taking place in the financial industry effect the financial or risk management department? Will the cacophony of "blockchain, fintech, AI, Zettabyte Era, RPA, …" spouted out by consultants, tech evangelists and other prophets affect the accountant and risk manager? The answer is yes, but to a different extent than other parts of a financial institution are affected.

In this introduction and the first part, we will be looking at aspects of digitalization and fintech companies in more detail to explain the impact on the financial industry. The second and main part of the book will illuminate those aspects from the perspective of a financial department and cover the bank management matters involved. Given the importance of regulation to the industry, we address the regtech dimension in part three. The final part summarizes new and different methods being applied within the environment of financial professionals as well as the technology and architecture considerations. The book ends with summary and outlook in the final chapter.

1.2   Setting the Scene

So again, why is digitalization affecting and frightening stakeholders in the financial industry differently than those in other industries? First of all, the competitors (fintech or technology companies) are by nature better in leveraging technology to decrease costs and satisfy customers. Secondly, most competitors focus only on parts of the value chain. Thirdly, the outdated IT landscapes and encrusted organizational structures in traditional banks prevent quick changes. And lastly, the scaling effect of digital business models poses an overwhelming threat.

When it comes to digitalizing business models, there is no guaranteed success if gone alone. Application programming interfaces (APIs) enable traditional banks to compete with new competitors along the entire value chain. The idea behind this consists of establishing a digital financial platform/ecosystem. This is referred to as platform banking, API-based banking or open banking. Platform banking is to some extent driven by the European Payment Services (PSD 2) Directive (EU) 2015/2366

Fig. 1 What can competitors do better?

(see The European Parliament and the Council of Union, 2015), which forces European banks to provide access to client's payment data (naturally only with the client's consent). Figo is a well-known example of such an API provider (see Figo GmbH, 2019). PSD 2 opens up business opportunities for new market participants, as it makes it much easier to switch banking service providers (Fig. 1).

Many of the traditional banks, however, have accepted this challenge and are doing well in adopting the strengths of their competitors. The gap in organizational flexibility is being closed using agile methods, albeit only to a minor extent. Technological advance is being absorbed to some extent by way of co-innovation, investment or copying the best parts. The competition is driving banks to rethink their core bands and competencies to focus and reshape their business model. However, outdated IT landscapes and legacy systems are slowing innovation and transformation.

Talk of leveraging technology leads to the question: What will drive the business models of banks in the future? In 2015, Lloyd C. Blankfein, CEO Goldman Sachs, called the company a "technology company" based on the fact that Goldman Sachs has 9000 programmers. David McKay CEO Royal Bank of Canada responded by saying, "If a bank thinks it is a tech company, then it is wrong. We are still business-to-consumer and business-to-business companies, trying to meet customer needs. Banks are using technology to anticipate those needs and meet them in a creative way, but we don't derive our income from technology" (RBC CEO Dave McKay looks to stay ahead of technology, 2017) (Fig. 2).

Fig. 2 The path of benefit

With regard to technology, the cloud and various cloud strategies[3] require mention. The primary benefits of the cloud include scaling based on changing requirements (timing and changing resources) as well as the associated cost advantage and efficiency. The financial sector still has certain reservations regarding the cloud due to the sensitive data involved and the reputational impact a data leak would cause. Cloudera has an interesting approach to accompany clients from an on-premise environment to a private or public cloud in development over time.

Robert Solow stated in 1987, "You can see the computer age everywhere but in the productivity statistics" (Solow, 1987, July 12). A deeper look at digitalization's impact on financial institutions could lead to a similar assessment today. The main question is: Do we serve the customer better by using this technology?

To a certain extent, Dan Ariely already summed up big data in 2013 in a way that could now be applied to AI, machine learning, deep learning and blockchain: "Big data is like teenage sex: everyone talks about it, nobody really knows how to do it, everyone thinks everyone else is doing it, so everyone claims they are doing it" (Ariely, 2013, January 6). Banks have to decide if their business model is technology or customer-centric. The latter will be the future!

Design thinking (Brown, 2008, June) puts the client first from the initial stages of the product development process. Concepts like Customer Journey (CJ) and Context Driven Banking (CDB) focus on being there for the customer at the right time.

Fintech companies and technology companies (GAFA) are by far more dynamic (in terms of organizational structure and innovation speed) than traditional financial institutions. Fintech companies are most successful in picking well-chosen parts of the value chain and providing better

---

[3]Private cloud, public cloud, … .

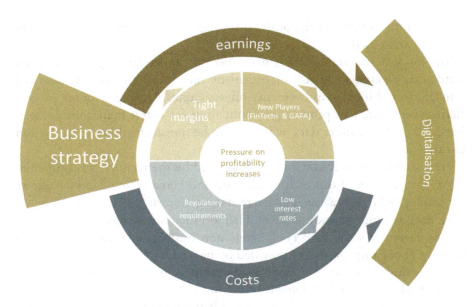

Fig. 3 Impact of digitalization on earnings and costs

(i.e., cheaper or more convenient) services. However, these companies are restricted due to their limited capital. A bigger threat is posed by the GAFA companies due to their deep pockets and the ability to change the playing field of a whole industry, like Apple did with the music industry or Google with maps. The impact is already being felt in the payment context in the form of Apple Pay, Google Pay and Alipay.

1.3 Impact on Financial Professionals

Financial and risk management professionals can only contribute to the client-centric business models on a small scale. But they could be less restrictive on business than is currently the case. Financial and risk management have to become more dynamic, adoptable or, to use the digitalization buzzword, "agile."

The cost saving aspect driven by optimization and automation up to automated decision-making, can significantly improve banks' stability and agility. The templates for this do not differ much from those applicable to other industries.

The twofold impact of digitalization is illustrated in Fig. 3. Banks in Europe are suffering from an enormous pressure to increase profitability.

Digitalization can impact the business strategy on both ends of the spectrum (earnings and costs).

The model's and architectures developed for understanding the customer better, can be applied to risk management and, to a lesser extent, financial management. Model improvements offer significant enhancements in predicting the future and providing a foundation for better management decisions. All of this requires data, which has to be transformed into information and then knowledge.

New technological foundations are adopted by the technology companies (GAFA). Examples of this include Hadoop and Hana. While Hadoop allows for scaling, SAP Hana can accelerate aggregation at the database level to drive data analysis on another level. Hadoop incurs reasonable implementation cost even at scale. SAP Hana offers new business applications resulting from the speed improvements provided by new technology.

The predominate business model in the financial sector centers around risk, which implies an excellent knowledge of the risks taken and an outstanding ability to manage these risks. Data ["Data is the fuel of the digital economy" (HM Treasury, 2018)] turned into information has always been the main ingredient for the financial sector's risk-based business models. Incorporating new previously unavailable data or more detailed (i.e., more granular and interconnected) data provides the potential to improve risk analysis.

The distributed ledger technology opens up a wide space for optimizing internal processes as well as improving customer satisfaction by speeding up communication and by increasing commitment. The syndicated loan use case is a good example for both (internal and client-oriented) potential improvements.

Literature

Ariely, D. (2013, January 6). *Big data is like teenage sex* ... [Twitter].

Brown, T. (2008, June). Design thinking. *Harvard Business Review.*

Figo GmbH. (2019, January 29). figo homepage. *figo.io* [online]. https://www.figo.io/.

HM Treasury. (2018). *The economic value of data.* London: HM Treasury.

RBC CEO Dave McKay looks to stay ahead of technology. Macknight, J. (2017). s.l.: The Banker.

Solow, R. (1987, July 12). We'd better watch out. *New York Times Book Review*, p. 36.

The European Parliament and the Council of Union. (2015). *Payment services in the internal market—Directive (EU) 2015/2366.* Strasbourg: s.n. Directive (EU) 2015/2366.

Part I

Automation, Distributed Ledgers and Client Related Aspects

The world is changing and so is the financial services industry. Bill Gates said, "banking is necessary, banks are not"—a disruptive statement to say the least. That was all the way back in 1994. But will it become true in our age? Although most American banks are quite profitable,[1] fear of disruptive change has been significant in recent years. In 2014 banks started fearing the fintech companies and their ability to disrupt the banks' business models. In 2015 and 2016, it became clear that they are "only" ripping out certain parts of the bank's value chains. Due to their focused approach, many fintech companies were quite successful in doing so to a certain extent. Robo-advisors are a good example of this.

Other fintech companies have proven that they understand the customer needs better than the traditional financial institutions. N26[2] is an example of a start-up that at first simply sought to provide a digital wallet for young people. The company then realized that parents showed interest in a more digitalized bank. Based on this, they developed a purely smartphone-based bank by decomposing the classical services in a user-friendly way. The higher grade of digitalization produces a significant amount of data, which can be used to understand what customers need in new depth. Examples of this approach are NBO,[3] CJ[4] and context driven banking.

---

[1]Especially in contrast to the German banks.

[2]N26 (formerly known as Number 26 until July 2016) is a German direct bank, headquartered in Berlin, Germany [see (N26 Inc., 2019)].

[3]NBO—Next Best Offer

[4]CJ—Customer Journey.

8   Part I: Automation, Distributed Ledgers and Client Related Aspects

Bitcoin is a well-known application of the distributed ledger technology. While it first targeted sanctions-free transfer of value, bitcoin has now developed into a currency-like payment alternative [see (Nakamoto, 2008)]. Driven by the architecture, the intermediators (normally financial institutions) are cut out of the process, thus restricting traditional financial institutions' customer contact to a minimum.

Even some central banks like the Monetary Authority of Singapore (MAS) [Project "Ubin" see (Singapore Exchange, 2018)], the Bank of Canada [Project "Jasper" see (Chapman, Garratt, Hendry, McCormack, & McMahon, 2017)] and the German Bundesbank ["Forschungsprojekt Blockchain" in (Bundesbank, 2017)] are experimenting with distributed ledger technology. In a research project conducted by the German Bundesbank in 2017, they mirrored bonds into a distributed ledger using Hyperledger. This same pattern can be found with regard to so-called security tokens. In addition to the distributed ledger implementation, security tokens promise to exchange the token with things in the real world (goods or money). This type of asset-backed or Bretton-Woods-style[5] cyber-currency could push this kind of distributed ledger to a new level.

While the world of tokens and public blockchain is continuously transforming, the distributed ledger technology with private blockchains is opening up interesting new applications. This includes we.trade in the area of trade finance and digital replicated bonds using blockchain technology (LBBW and Daimler Benz) as well as Everledger in the diamond certification domain.

A core aspect of digitalization that covers almost all areas is robotic process automation (RPA)[6] and workforce automation. Over the long term, RPA aims to replace manual decisions using robots that can identify decision patterns. This transformation is rarely done with a big bang, especially in traditional financial institutions, but rather performed incrementally. The different levels of process automation are shown in Fig. 1. The six levels indicated here span from manual decisions to autonomous decision-making.[7]

Robotic Process Automation (RPA) is intended to relieve people of performing dull repetitive tasks in front of their computer screens all day long. RPA replaces human labor but also minimizes the risk of human error. RPA

---

[5]The Bretton Woods system of monetary management established among the United States, Canada, Western Europe countries, Australia and Japan in 1944. One key element was that the exchange rate between the dollar and an ounce of gold was fixed.

[6]RPA—Robotic Process Automation.

[7]The 5-step decision automation model is dealt with in detail in (Bitcom, 2017).

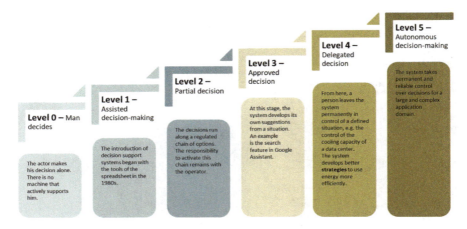

Fig. 1 5-step decision automation model

helps rethink and redefine financial services processes. A decision has to be made, as to which parts of the process can be fully or partially automated and when. Simply put, RPA is software that uses artificial intelligence (AI) and has machine learning capabilities to handle repetitive high-volume tasks.

Workforce virtualization using robotics has the potential to fundamentally change the way financial institutions tackle multiple areas of process execution while providing significant business benefits. While its rapid introduction is almost inevitable, leading companies will use it as a way to not only reduce costs, but also to improve controls and improve employee effectiveness, make them more productive and evaluate them within the organization. The coverage of digitalizing processes differs significantly between traditional non-digital banks and challenger banks.

While Fig. 2 shows the primary steps of process automation (on the left), it is important to understand that the early steps only contribute minor growth in efficiency. The real boost happens when decision-making is automated.

Aspects like standardized processes and process industrialization are necessary milestones on the road to full digital transformation. In recent years, companies in the US and Europe have sought to reduce their operating costs and increase their overall efficiency by standardizing, centralizing and sometimes outsourcing a wide range of processes. These processes were initially of high volume but with little added value, e.g., Accounts Payable, Accounts Receivable, General and Subledger bookings, expense reports and other activities once performed at the company's headquarters. Over time,

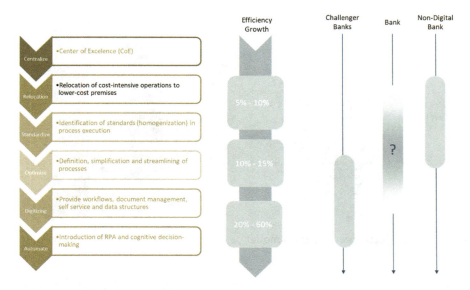

Fig. 2 Automation of Location Determination

more complex and sensitive "industrialization" processes have been introduced through standardization and the use of third-party platforms. These include compliance, compensation reviews and policies, contract management, and a variety of other corporate functions, many of which relate to risk management.

Examples of this transformation include risk reports and batch processes. Extensive, time-consuming risk reports are perfect candidates for automation that allows for timely, accurate and comprehensive data quali<ty reviews and remedial actions as indicated. Batch processes can be separated into two tasks: (A) monitoring and validation of already automated processes (e.g., data transfer) and (B) automated decisions on whether processes should be restarted or whether manual steps are necessary.

Chapter 2 "Batch Processing—Pattern Recognition" (Liermann, Li, & Schaudinnus, 2019) describes a practical application of monitoring and data-pattern recognition. The chapter introduces the necessary framework for such tasks, including data lakes and methods like Bayesian networks, random forest and autoencoders.

The next subsection focuses on private blockchains and introduces the Hyperledger framework that is part of the Linux project. The two chapters focus on different aspects of the Hyperledger framework. As stated earlier, the blockchain applications can generally be split into two kinds of domains: the public blockchains (e.g., bitcoinand Ethereum) and the private blockchains (e.g., Hyperledgerand Corda). This book focuses on private blockchains, because we see more potential and applications here for financial services companies.

Chapter 3 "Hyperledger Fabric as a Blockchain Framework in the Financial Industry" (Bettio, Bruse, Franke, Jakoby, & Schärf, 2019) introduces the main components and concepts of Hyperledger Fabric. The chapter provides an in-depth description and can be seen as a summary of the documentation for the Hyperledger project. Concepts like nodes of a blockchain, permissions and blockchain channels are explained as well as the consensus mechanism and design possibilities Hyperledger Fabric offers on this side. Chapter 4 "Hyperledger Composer—Syndicated Loans" (Dahmen & Liermann, 2019) describes the Hyperledger Composer tool and a practical application for syndicated loans. Hyperledger Composer is a tool used to develop rapid prototypes based on the Composer modeling language.

The last two chapters of this part address client-related aspects like NBO, context-driven banking [see "The concept of the next best action/offer in the age of customer experience" (May, 2019)] and prospect theory within the context of wealth management documenting the client-oriented approach of a Robo advisor [see "Using prospect theory to determine investor risk aversion in digital wealth management" (Lisson, 2019)].

Literature

Bettio, M., Bruse, F., Franke, A., Jakoby, T., & Schärf, D. (2019). Hyperledger fabric as a blockchain framework in the financial industry. In V. Liermann & C. Stegmann (Eds.), *The impact of digital transformation and fintech on the finance professional*. New York: Palgrave Macmillan.

Bitcom. (2017). *Künstliche Intelligenz verstehen als Automation des Entscheidens Leitfaden*. Berlin: Bitcom Bundesverband Informationswirtschaft, Telekommunikation und neue Medien e.V.

Bundesbank, D. (2017). *Monatsbericht September 2017*. Frankfurt: Deutsche Bundesbank.

Chapman, J., Garratt, R., Hendry, S., McCormack, A., & McMahon, W. (2017). *Project Jasper: Are distributed wholesale payment systems feasible yet?* Ottawa: Bank of Canada—Financial System Review.

Dahmen, G., & Liermann, V. (2019). Hyperledger composer—Syndicated loans. In V. Liermann & C. Stegmann (Eds.), *The impact of digital transformation and fintech on the finance professional*. New York: Palgrave Macmillan.

Liermann, V., Li, S., & Schaudinnus, N. (2019). Batch processing— Pattern recognition. In V. Liermann & C. Stegmann (Eds.), *The impact of digital transformation and fintech on the finance professional.* New York: Palgrave Macmillan.

Lisson, C. (2019). Using prospect theory to determine investor risk aversion in digital wealth management. In V. Liermann & C. Stegmann (Eds.), *The impact of digital transformation and fintech on the finance professional.* New York: Palgrave Macmillan.

May, U. (2019). The concept of teh next best action/offer in the age of customer experience. In V. Liermann & C. Stegmann (Eds.), *The impact of digital transformation and fintech on the finance professional.* New York: Palgrave Macmillan.

N26 Inc. (2019). *N26.* Retrieved February 15, 2019, from N26: https://n26.com/en-us/.

Nakamoto, S. (2008). *Bitcoin—A peer-to-peer electronic cash system.*

Singapore Exchange, M. A. (2018). *Delivery versus payment on distributed ledger technologies—Project Ubin.* Singapore: Singapore Exchange, Monetary Authority of Singapore.

2

Batch Processing—Pattern Recognition

Volker Liermann, Sangmeng Li and Norbert Schaudinnus

1 Introduction

1.1 The Manual Aspects of a Batch Process

Key risk indicators (KRI) and key performance indicators (KPI) are the figures banks use to manage themselves on a quantitative basis. In many cases, internal and regulatory key figures are calculated using a number of steps, which are often bound together and monitored as a batch process. The whole process includes data extraction in the core banking system, calculation and transformation into the business intelligence system. This part of the process takes place with almost no human interaction unless something goes wrong, which happens more or less often depending on the situation.

While the batch process in itself is automated, verification and inspection of the results still require many manual steps. The error log analysis, process monitoring, quality checks and plausibility checks associated with deducing

---

V. Liermann (✉) · S. Li · N. Schaudinnus
ifb AG, Grünwald, Germany
e-mail: volker.liermann@ifb-group.com

S. Li
e-mail: sangmeng.li@ifb-group.com

N. Schaudinnus
e-mail: norbert.schaudinnus@ifb-group.com

© The Author(s) 2019
V. Liermann and C. Stegmann (eds.), *The Impact of Digital Transformation and FinTech on the Finance Professional*, https://doi.org/10.1007/978-3-030-23719-6_2

KRIs and KPIs largely still involve manual processes. Ideally, monitoring is partly based on business rules, which also implies manual adjustments.

1.2 Why Monitoring of a Batch Process Is a Good Application for Artificial Intelligence (AI)

In many cases, the error analyses and plausibility checks performed as part of generating KRIs and KPIs are a complex but repetitive and structurally similar sequence of steps. The repetitive and structurally similar nature of the manual performed tasks, in particular, makes these tasks an ideal application for machine learning and deep learning.

1.3 Structure of the Chapter

In the following sections, we will be describing all the components required for a meaningful prototype. In Sect. 2 we describe the general structure of processing a high-level architecture. Section 3 introduces a simple example of a batch process within the domain of market risk management. The models used in the prototype are described in Sect. 4. Application of the model is described in Sect. 5. Section 6 compares the models used, which is then followed by a summary in Sect. 7.

2 General Setup

In this section, we lay out the general components of the required architecture and steps to be performed to find patterns in the processed data as well as the repetitive structures in error messages produced by the transformation and calculation step of the batch process.

2.1 General Process for Pattern Recognition

The three main steps are illustrated in Fig. 1. Data first has to be collected throughout the performed batch process. The collected data should be as

Fig. 1 Pattern recognition process

granular as possible. This provides the algorithms with the best foundation for detecting repetitive structures and patterns in the processed data as well as in error or warning messages. The collected data is mass data and therefore best stored in cold data storage. Transfer to cold data storage should be asynchronous in order not to slow down the original batch process.

When using supervised learning, the data collection process includes defining and capturing labels. These labels perform one or more of the following tasks: (a) condense the error situation, (b) identify the cause of a collection of errors or (c) identify an uncommon situation. The labels should also indicate actions for correcting or resolving the error.

The next step consists of training the model. This implies data analysis in combination with a model selection process. Some examples of appropriate models within the context of batch processing are described in Sect. 4.

The final step consists of applying the model in a productive environment (discussed in detail in Sect. 5). In this step, the trained model is applied to the data produced by a batch process (error messages and result data). The model then makes predictions regarding the quality and plausibility of the produced KRI/KPI. These predictions can be used as an improved starting point within the context of error analysis. In some situations, the aggregated information can be used to automatically initiate steps to adjust or restart mislaid transformations and calculations. The general approach to fitting and testing a model is also explained in Sect. 6.

2.2 System Architecture

Figure 2 shows the three steps (collect data, analyze data and apply model) mapped to a system landscape. The upper section indicates two examples of batch processes that produce data. Before step 1, for example, the nominal volume is stored by transaction and, after step 1, the present value by transaction is stored in the data lake.

The center of Fig. 2 represents the analysis performed on the data stored in the data lake. Model development often includes ready-to-use frameworks implemented in Python, R or other suitable languages. The result of the analysis is a model that can be applied to a new batch process.

Application of the model to a new performed batch process is illustrated in the lower area of the figure. The model receives the input in the same structure as during model training. Based on the input data provided by the batch processes (error messages and result data), the model will predict starting points for error analysis or, in some situations, the model can even automatically initiate steps to adjust or restart misguided transformation and calculations.

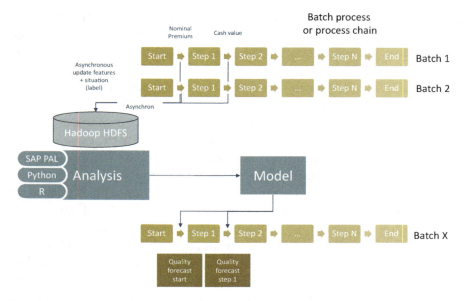

Fig. 2 System architecture—schematic representation

3 Illustrative Example: Present Value Calculation

In this section, we provide numerical experiments on self-generating data, in which the machine learning methods Bayesian network and autoencoder are used to extract error patterns.

3.1 Process Description Detail

We generate data by considering the following simple batch process, which only consists of two steps (as shown in Fig. 3).

To perform one process, we need the following:

- A business date (effective date)
- A list of business contracts with corresponding necessary business conditions and nominal values.
- An interest rate curve.

In the first step, the process computes the present value of all business contracts on the given business date and the interest rate is used for discounting

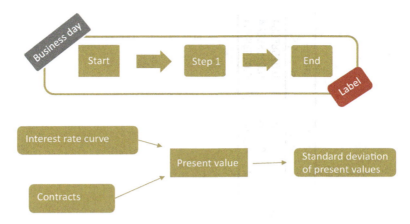

Fig. 3 A simple batch process

the cash flows. The second step consists of computing the standard deviation of present values.

3.2 Data Generation, Features and Label Mapping

According to the process presented above, the following values are collected as features:

- Nominal value of each business contract;
- Each interest rate point on the interest rate curve;

We develop the following three different types of processes, which are represented by variable "label":

- Label = 0; normal/correct data sample;
- Label = 1; suspicious data sample with incorrect nominal values, in which two nominal values are switched "by accident".
- Label = 2; suspicious data sample with incorrect interest rate, in which the number after and before the decimal point are switched "by accident" (e.g., 2.8% -> 8.2%);

Some examples of data samples are provided in the following figure. "Nominal_3" and "Nominal_4" are switched in data set No. 9, while "interestrate_6" and "interestrate_7" are detected in data set No. 10 (Table 1).

Table 1 Data set examples

	Nomina1_l	Nomina1_2	Nominal_3	Nominal_4	intere-strate_1	intere-strate_2	intere-strate_3	intere-strate_4	intere-strate_5
8	10000	50000	1e+05	2e+05	0.01796151	0.02043887	0.02284754	0.02545518	0.02585884
9	10000	50000	2e+05	1e+05	0.01796151	0.02043887	0.02284754	0.02545518	0.02585884
10	10000	50000	1e+05	2e+05	0.01796151	0.02043887	0.02284754	0.02545518	0.02585884

	intere-strate_6	intere-strate_7	intere-strate_8	intere-strate_9	intere-strate_10	Label
8	0.02896003	0.02924513	0.03375989	0.03245982	0.03572923	0
9	0.02896003	0.02924513	0.03375989	0.03245982	0.03572923	1
10	0.08296003	0.09224513	0.03375989	0.03245982	0.03572923	2

The data is generated by iteratively repeating the following algorithms:

Algorithms: generating data samples for a list of business dates.

Require: a list of business dates;
    Initialize the interest rate curve on the first business date;
    For each business date in the list do the following:

- Generate label based on a Bernoulli distribution with parameter p
- Update the interest rate by adding a normal distributed "change", which is proportional to the difference to the previous business date
- If the label is not equal to zero, include the corresponding anomaly in the data
- Compute present values of contracts and standard deviation of present values
- Move on to the next business date

Twenty business dates are chosen and the algorithms above are repeated 20 times. This results in around 400 data samples. In addition to this, the parameter p is set to 0.8, so that 20% of the data samples are suspicious. Note that the error or warning messages of the batch process are not taken into consideration in the numerical experiment.

4   Model Selection and Training

4.1   Set of Reasonable Models

The specific task in the setup for pattern recognition is to detect anomalies in a defined process. Anomaly detection is a vast field of research involving statistical analysis and machine learning techniques. In our application, we aim to identify fraudulent sets of features using a model, which is able to learn from recent observations.

One task of the model is to predict suspicious processes and specify the error (i.e., assign a label). Many classic machine learning algorithms are capable of this task. In a realistic process situation, however, nonlinear correlations between different features and a complex interplay of several sub-processes have to be mapped correctly. A network structure is therefore an adequate representation for a model. We consider two different network-based models in the following section—Bayesian networks and autoencoders.

Bayesian networks are probabilistic models, which assign probabilities to different states and relate between different states using conditional probabilities as edges. By construction, Bayesian networks assume independence of states that are aligned in parallel. Hence, their structure can be aligned with the workflow diagram of the original process. The structure can be easily interpreted.

Autoencoders, on the other hand, are based on neural networks. They consist of an encoding and a decoding layer and aim to reproduce the input features by applying an internal representation. This representation is specific for different kinds of fraudulent processes. In contrast to Bayesian networks, autoencoders don't require labels for training. Their structure is self-assembling and the model is a black box. Typically, autoencoders require larger amounts of training data to perform like an aligned Bayesian network. This also depends on the number and size of hidden layers. Both models have the advantage that the source of an error can be traced back through the network to the responsible input feature. They allow for computation of scores that relate to probabilities of fraudulent behavior.

In order to rank the two suggested models within the context of machine learning approaches, we use a simple random forest classifier as a benchmark. Each decision tree will try to achieve maximal selectivity by applying binary decisions for each feature separately. The core of the random forest algorithm is to harmonize these separately achieved results. We therefore know that this classical model is not capable of performing in the same way.

4.2 Anomaly Detection Based on Bayesian Networks

The work presented below is implemented using the R package "bnlearn". In addition to this, a compact introduction in Bayesian networks can be found in Liermann, Li, and Schaudinnus, Mathematical background of machine learning (2019b).

4.2.1 Data Preprocessing for Bayesian Networks (Categorization)

As part of the work with Bayesian networks, it is common to discrete the data to speed up the training process. Data discretization ensures that all the nodes of the network are discretely distributed. Within the context of this

2 Batch Processing—Pattern Recognition

Table 2 Data categorization

	presentvalue_1	presentvalue_2	presentvalue_3	presentvalue_4	interestrate_1	interestrate_2	interestrate_3	interestrate_4	interestrate_5	interestrate_6
1	183.7016	400.4973	1977.573	3955.145	0.01792628	0.02049871	0.02329589	0.02488051	0.02663047	0.02900508
2	185.2018	409.8442	1997.908	3995.816	0.01762572	0.02024520	0.02331923	0.02475960	0.02655662	0.02866718
3	188.7141	423.5519	2027.017	4054.035	0.01783356	0.02019858	0.02291768	0.02501550	0.02621764	0.02926027
4	184.7419	400.3113	1977.574	3955.147	0.01756371	0.02031896	0.02267955	0.02513194	0.02596181	0.02903491
5	191.6304	438.6482	2059.801	4119.601	0.01740357	0.01981723	0.02273709	0.02516067	0.02547259	0.02931362

	interestrate_7	interestrate_8	interestrate_9	interestrate_10	var	label
1	0.03119444	0.03261420	0.03399232	0.03455710	3043520	0
2	0.03140241	0.03258988	0.03363363	0.03432253	3102494	0
3	0.03085079	0.03246221	0.03354268	0.03498420	3186293	0
4	0.03071973	0.03259911	0.03348289	0.03521805	3042674	0
5	0.03055047	0.03250813	0.03295890	0.03494464	3283363	0

Categorization ⬇

	presentvalue_1	presentvalue_2	presentvalue_3	presentvalue_4	interestrate_1	interestrate_2	interestrate_3	interestrate_4	interestrate_5	interestrate_6
1	1	3	3	3	1	1	1	2	1	2
2	1	3	3	3	1	1	1	2	1	2
3	1	3	3	3	1	1	1	2	1	2
4	1	3	3	3	1	1	1	2	1	2
5	1	3	3	3	1	1	1	2	1	2

	interestrate_7	interestrate_8	interestrate_9	interestrate_10	var	label
1	2	2	2	2	1	0
2	2	2	2	2	1	0
3	2	2	2	2	1	0
4	2	2	2	2	1	0
5	2	2	2	2	1	0

work, the data generated as shown above has to be categorized before providing it as training data for a Bayesian network. An integer N has to be provided as a parameter, which determines the number of categories to be built[1]. For each feature, we generate N equidistant increments between the maximum and the minimum value. The data, which belong to the corresponding increment, will be replaced by a numerical value. The following is a simple example of categorization (Table 2).

4.2.2 Model Selection and Training

We train a Bayesian network using data generated as shown above. The structure of the Bayesian network is illustrated in the following Fig. 4.

Given a new data set as follows (without variable "label", see Fig. 5).

We are able to predict the "label" variable using the Bayesian network trained as shown above.

```
> predictedlabel
[1] 2
```

The fraudulent features can be detected according to the corresponding conditional probabilities (Table 3).

The features "interestrate_1", "interestrate_3", "interestrate_6" and "interestrate_7" have the highest probability of being suspicious due to their lower conditional probability.

---

[1]In this work, we always build the same number of categories for all features. This can be extended to assign the number of categories for each feature specifically.

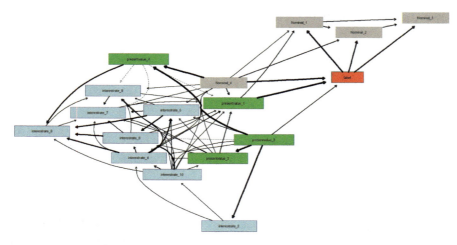

Fig. 4 Structure of a trained Bayesian network

```
  Nominal_1 Nominal_2 Nominal_3 Nominal_4 presentvalue_1 presentvalue_2 presentvalue_3 presentvalue_4 interestrate_1 interestrate_2 interestrate_3 interestrate_4
59    10000    50000    1e+05     2e+05      695.7155       3063.07        7610.643       15221.29       0.08113033     0.02104775    0.03205502    0.02236439
   interestrate_5 interestrate_6 interestrate_7 interestrate_8 interestrate_9 interestrate_10    var
59    0.05298552    0.07233794     0.09299732     0.03422363     0.02390978     0.03392938   40903114
```

Fig. 5 Test data set

Table 3 Conditional probability per feature

	name	conditionalProbability
1	Nominal_1	0.92761051
2	Nominal_2	0.92967570
3	Nominal_3	0.94405842
4	Nominal_4	0.92558086
9	interestrate_1	0.00000000
10	interestrate_2	1.00000000
11	interestrate_3	0.00000000
12	interestrate_4	1.00000000
13	interestrate_5	0.01292158
14	interestrate_6	0.00000000
15	interestrate_7	0.00000000
16	interestrate_8	1.00000000
17	interestrate_9	1.00000000
18	interestrate_10	1.00000000

4.3 Anomaly Detection Using Stacked Autoencoders

The *h2o* framework[2] provides an implementation of stacked autoencoders that can be used via an API in R and other high-level programming languages. The model can be customized with regard to the size and number of hidden layers. The larger the network structure, the more samples are required to train a reliable model. For our toy model, we chose an architecture with three hidden layers, each of which obtains five neurons.

A brief introduction to autoencoder neural networks is provided in Sects. 3.3 and 4.1 in Liermann et al., Deep learning—An introduction (2019a).

4.3.1 Model Selection and Training

The reconstruction error is used to quantify the chance of an anomalous sample. Since our training data set mostly consists of "successful" samples, internal representation of our autoencoders is targeted to reconstruct these samples. Large reconstruction error values indicate anomalies.

Figure 6 shows the reconstruction for each sample, sorted by size of the reconstruction error along the abscissa. For each sample, the respective labels are also listed using circles. Except for a single sample, the model reliably shows a separation between successful and fraudulent runs with a reconstruction error of 0.01.

Using k-fold validation, this reconstruction error can be used to construct a model that can detect fraudulent data. We achieve a mean precision of … and a mean recall of … for our toy system with the setup mentioned above. The model is also robust, having negligible standard deviations:

The autoencoder model facilitates returning reconstruction errors per input feature. The figure below shows an example of this output for a sample with the label 2. In this case, interest rate curves 6 and 7 are swapped. Consequently, large reconstruction errors occur. The sorted list returns these two features as the most fraudulent contributions (Table 4).

---

[2]H2O is an open-source software framework for big-data analysis, see H2O.ai (2019)

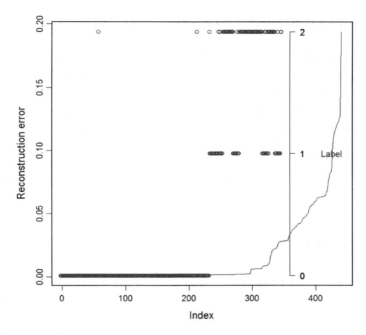

Fig. 6 Reconstruction error

Table 4 Reconstruction error per feature

	name	reconstruction error
1	reconstr_Nominal_1.SE	1.236751e-03
2	reconstr_Nominal_2.SE	1.488634e-04
3	reconstr_Nominal_3.SE	6.229904e-03
4	reconstr_Nominal_4.SE	2.232449e-03
5	reconstr_presentvalue_1.SE	1.339410e-03
6	reconstr_presentvalue_2.SE	2.006953e-02
7	reconstr_presentvalue_3.SE	4.846460e-02
8	reconstr_presentvalue_4.SE	1.070595e-02
9	reconstr_interestrate_1.SE	1.248218e-01
10	reconstr_interestrate_2.SE	5.756057e-06
11	reconstr_interestrate_3.SE	1.073211e-02
12	reconstr_interestrate_4.SE	5.098603e-03
13	reconstr_interestrate_5.SE	1.017413e-01
14	reconstr_interestrate_6.SE	1.840531e-01
15	reconstr_interestrate_7.SE	4.691191e-01
16	reconstr_interestrate_8.SE	1.646276e-02
17	reconstr_interestrate_9.SE	1.729365e-02
18	reconstr_interestrate_10.SE	1.479954e-03
19	reconstr_var.SE	9.527660e-02

5 Applying the Model and Model Deployment

Once the model has been trained and produces meaningful support for batch process analysis, it can be deployed for use in the production environment. Such a deployment should be conducted step by step from support processes and semi-automated actions through to automated correction in the final state.

The support processes could be that the algorithm identifies the error source and determines the person or organization responsible for resolving this issue based on the data pattern. The relevant person or organization receives an email with context information (e.g., the affected transactions or business partner).

The information and context provided by the email is an aggregation of the error messages and pattern identified to supply the relevant information to resolve the issue. This provides the opportunity to identify the tasks with a high frequency and a low or medium amount of effort in implementing an automated resolution.[3] A semi-automated response of the algorithm could be (automated) actions, which require manual approval by a user and the request for approval could be an email or any other workflow-based communication.

Depending on the algorithm's accuracy and the impact of a false alarm, the organization can then decide when to move toward a fully automated resolution of the issue raised by the algorithm. Even in the final state, certain manual tasks will remain given the automation complexity and effort associated with the rare frequency of occurrence.

6 Model Comparison

6.1 Performance Comparison: Autoencoder vs. Bayesian Network vs. Random Forests

As a benchmark, we have chosen random forests, which is a standard classification algorithm introduced in Chapter 16 "Mathematical Background of Machine Learning" (Liermann et al., Mathematical background of machine

---

[3]In some cases, the complexity and the range of possible solutions is so huge, that automation is not reasonable.

Table 5 Cross validation results of random forests

	iterationNr	validationresult
1	1	0.8318182
2	2	0.8340909
3	3	0.8250000
4	4	0.8340909
5	5	0.8318182
6	6	0.8363636
7	7	0.8363636
8	8	0.8272727
9	9	0.8295455
10	10	0.8272727

Table 6 Cross validation results of Bayesian network

	iterationNr	validationresult
1	1	0.8636364
2	2	0.9068182
3	3	0.8863636
4	4	0.8931818
5	5	0.8977273
6	6	0.9045455
7	7	0.9000000
8	8	0.8931818
9	9	0.8909091
10	10	0.8848653

Table 7 Cross validation results of autoencoder

	iterationNr	validationresult
1	1	0.9068182
2	2	0.9068182
3	3	0.9068182
4	4	0.9045455
5	5	0.9090909
6	6	0.9068182
7	7	0.9090909
8	8	0.9090909
9	9	0.9113636
10	10	0.9068182

learning, 2019b). We iteratively perform k-folds cross-validation with $k = 10$ for random forests, Bayesian network and autoencoder ten times, whereby the data are split randomly into 10 subsets in each new iteration. The results are collected in the following three figures. Bayesian network and autoencoder both perform better than random forests (Tables 5, 6 and 7).

6.2   Individual Model Strengths and Weaknesses

The validation results presented in the previous section are specific to the task at hand and cannot be broadened without care. For the task at hand, the autoencoder has the most predictive power, followed by the Bayesian network. The conventional machine learning algorithm random forest has the lowest predictive power, but it is still not bad.

The clear advantage of the Bayesian network is the comprehensibility, while the autoencoder remains a black box to some extent. Deeper analysis of the random forest can provide more insight, but requires a willingness to delve deeply into the random forest structures.

7   Summary

The chapter describes the general and universal issues of identifying error sources and causes in batch processes used during the estimation of key indicators in many financial or risk management tasks. A blueprint shows how to implement a framework to analyze error messages and to derive error sources and causes by including data patterns. Collated error messages and data patterns can indicate error sources/causes. Once the sources/causes are identified, resolution can be achieved using various levels of automation (from manual and semi-automated to fully automated resolution).

The chapter explains the approach by applying three models (random forest, Bayesian network and autoencoder) to a simple risk management calculation process.

The universal nature of the issue opens up the opportunity to save costs by automating the detection of high-frequency error causes. Looking at the business cases and the costs for the required infrastructure, it will be challenging to get a quick return on investment (ROI) with an initial simple use case. The potential provided by the universal nature of the task and the number of processes to be automated clearly opens up the possibility of quick amortization of the infrastructure costs.

Those currently involved in the purely manual resolution process are not likely to miss these repetitive and boring tasks. They can invest more time in tasks that match their intellectual potential, which could include more complex error situations or further process and method optimization.

Literature

H2O.ai. (2019, January 29). *h2o.ai overview*. Retrieved January 29, 2019, from h2o.ai documentation http://docs.h2o.ai/h2o/latest-stable/h2o-docs/index.html.

Liermann, V., Li, S., & Schaudinnus, N. (2019a). Deep learning—An introduction. In V. Liermann & C. Stegmann (Eds.), *The impact of digital transformation and fintech on the finance professional*. New York: Palgrave Macmillan.

Liermann, V., Li, S., & Schaudinnus, N. (2019b). Mathematical background of machine learning. In V. Liermann & C. Stegmann (Eds.), *The impact of digital transformation and fintech on the finance professional*. New York: Palgrave Macmillan.

3

Hyperledger Fabric as a Blockchain Framework in the Financial Industry

Martina Bettio, Fabian Bruse, Achim Franke,
Thorsten Jakoby and Daniel Schärf

1 Blockchain in the Financial Environment

Blockchain and distributed ledger technology are being discussed in many contexts in the financial services industry. There are generally two main perspectives, from which to look at these technologies:

A. focus on the payment options enabled by coins and tokens in the blockchain
B. focus on smart contracts and the distributed nature of the technology.

M. Bettio (✉) · F. Bruse · A. Franke · T. Jakoby · D. Schärf
ifb AG, Grünwald, Germany
e-mail: martina.bettio@ifb-group.com

F. Bruse
e-mail: fabian.bruse@ifb-group.com

A. Franke
e-mail: achim.franke@ifb-group.com

T. Jakoby
e-mail: thorsten.jakoby@ifb-group.com

D. Schärf
e-mail: daniel.schaerf@ifb-group.com

© The Author(s) 2019
V. Liermann and C. Stegmann (eds.), *The Impact of Digital Transformation and FinTech on the Finance Professional*, https://doi.org/10.1007/978-3-030-23719-6_3

The first route is taken by Bitcoin and Litecoin, for example, which are both public blockchains with a focus on the sanction-free transfer of values. Given the dynamics raised by the blockchain hype, Bitcoin and Litecoin could become fiat-money type currencies in the future. Transparency and the public nature of the coding (functional-technology), the blockchain (data-technology) and to some extent restriction-free access for the users are essential to these blockchains. The underlying technology has immersive disruptive potential to change the payment processes and payment infrastructure by taking intermediaries out of the money transfer equation. Technical (speed) and reputational (trust in the long-term value of the coins/tokens) repercussions have restricted incursion of the disruptive potential into the financial sector and payment processes in particular.

The second perspective focuses more on the functional aspects in a distributed ledger, namely smart contracts and the opportunity to manage privacy and access rights. Smart contracts can be used to implement business logic inside a distributed ledger and define processes as standards for all participating parties. Due to the digital nature of these implementations, smart contracts have the potential to speed up processes and achieve better adherence to contracts by algorithmically defining the intentions of processes. By design many business-driven applications are not accessible to the public. This is partly driven by regulatory requirements like AML and CTF and the assigned know-your-customer (KYC) process and partly by the intention to only do business with invited and known participants. Privacy is also required for price-related issues like user individual pricing or for general privacy requirements arising from the discreet nature of the business.

Blockchains with the ability to implement smart contracts can generally be either private or public. The most prominent example for the latter is Ethereum, a public blockchain that can also carry smart contracts, which subsequently enables other blockchains to be built on top of the Ethereum blockchain with their own rules and methods (so-called ERC-20 tokens). On the other hand, Ethereum itself permits payment between different parties and is therefore also part of the first perspective mentioned above.

1.1 How Does the Financial Sector Feel About Blockchain?

Although people are talking a lot about Bitcoin and there are blockchain-related articles in the media almost every day, there are two very different points of view on this topic in the business world and especially in the financial sector.

On the one hand, there are almost obsessively progressive customers, who are trying various approaches to implementing blockchain in almost every conceivable line of business, although the benefits of using blockchain in a particular case may be miniscule or even nonexistent. These customers are testing various frameworks from Ripple to Corda or the Hyperledger frameworks, weighing their best options and designing one proof of concept after the other. Some of them have already built more than 40 prototypes and are using several of them in a productive environment.

On the other hand, there are lots of more conservative banks, which are completely ignoring the topic and not even considering the advantages of blockchain-based systems at all. "Why should we do something with Bitcoin?" is a sentence we have heard numerous times. (Mixing up Bitcoin (a cryptocurrency) and blockchain (a distributed database technology) along other misconceptions about the way how blockchain works are common issues.)

We are not in favor of either of these extremes, keeping in mind Amara's law: "We tend to overestimate the effect of a technology in the short run and underestimate it in the long run" (Ratcliffe, 2016). For us, it makes sense to stay informed about what is possible with blockchain, think about possible business applications and decide whether blockchain could be a valuable addition to your system environment. Don't write off blockchain for your company too quickly. It is not without reason that the blockchain technology is spreading like wildfire.

1.2   Should Banks Use Blockchain?

The strengths of blockchain-based applications are diverse:

Worldwide transactions with untrusted third parties and transactions that require perfect anonymity are the primary selling points. Blockchain's protection against forgery due to hash keys and certificate-based encryption bundled with its customizable agreement and endorsement policies to determine whether a transaction is valid makes it suitable for many applications. Another important point is the immutability of the blockchain itself, meaning it is impossible to delete or alter a transaction after it has taken place without everyone knowing it.

So why should banks and the financial sector keep track of new developments in the blockchain space?

Among the many possible use cases are cross-border payments, which are currently expensive and slow due to the need of involving several banks and currencies. This leads to remittance fees of about 5% of the total amount, which can be reduced with the blockchain to 1% while also providing for real-time transactions (FinTech Futures, 2019). Other use cases include banking networks for syndicated loans (see section 3 in Dahmen & Liermann, 2019) using smart contracts, improvement of online identity management through the blockchain or new and better loyalty programs for banks and insurers based on the transparency and traceability that blockchain provides.

A maintained framework can be helpful for setting up your use case with blockchain and achieving results quickly. A strong competitor in this area is the open-source product Hyperledger Fabric, which can be used free of charge.

2 The World of Hyperledger

2.1 Technologies and the Umbrella Approach

The Hyperledger project is a part of the Linux Foundation and hence a free, open-source project. It encompasses the general design philosophy of an open and modular approach that unifies several frameworks under a shared umbrella. Additionally, its open-source nature enables Hyperledger to access many already available tools, frameworks and programming languages, upon which it is built.

Docker is the most important in this regard. It uses containers as a flexible way of running different applications in a virtual environment (Fig. 1).

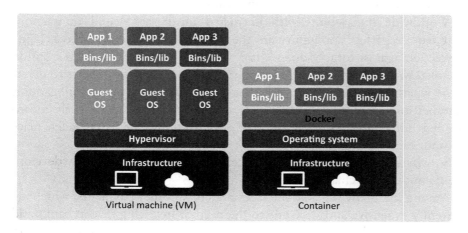

Fig. 1 Distinction between virtual machines and containers

Contrary to virtual machines, Docker sits on top of the host system and reuses its kernel and libraries. This allows Docker containers to be used to easily set up multiple instances of a software like Hyperledger (e.g., several simulated blockchain nodes), without installing a complete virtual guest operating system (OS) like Linux or Windows. The different containers can communicate with each other and the host system. They can also be copied easily for backups, testing and deployment, especially in the cloud.

Another important piece of open-source technology you will encounter in the Hyperledger ecosystem is Node.js, which is based on JavaScript. While JavaScript is primarily used for client-side applications like websites, Node.js was developed for server-side applications such as web servers. It can be used to create a blockchain application and access it with the Hyperledger Node.js SDK, but also to design smart contract logic (alongside Go and Java).

2.2   Various Hyperledger Framework Projects

There are an increasing number of blockchain frameworks available under the Hyperledger umbrella. Three of these have now reached the project status "active", meaning they fulfill certain strict Hyperledger quality criteria. The first is Fabric, which was originally contributed by IBM and Digital Asset. Fabric is distinguished from the other frameworks by its flexibility in establishing private communication channels between nodes and applying different smart contract logic using chain code. A more in-depth explanation of Fabric is provided in the next section.

To take advantage of these smart contracts in mobile applications, Hyperledger Iroha was contributed by Soramitsu. It comes with iOS and Android SDKs for creating blockchain applications for mobile devices. The third is Hyperledger Sawtooth, which was contributed by Intel. It was created with a special focus on big networks and fast consensus mechanisms by implementing the "Proof of Elapsed Time" consensus protocol.

With regard to "incubation" status projects, we would also like to mention Hyperledger Indy. It provides an ecosystem for managing digital identity information with a blockchain. Private data can remain in a customer's wallet and they can decide which of their data they are willing to share. The framework was contributed by the Sovrin Foundation.

2.3 Hyperledger Tools

In addition to the frameworks mentioned above, the lively community of developers around Hyperledger has created several tools to simplify working with the system. They have to be installed separately and are all still in a so-called "incubation" (beta) status, but they provide us with good hints as to where the future lies.

Hyperledger Composer is at the top of the list. This development framework is designed to build business networks at a business-centric abstraction level. Smart contract logic and applications with interfaces to other tools can be built using an easy scripting language and a graphical user interface. We have dedicated an entire section of this book to Hyperledger Composer to illustrate the tool's advantages (see Dahmen & Liermann, 2019). According to the information available at the time of writing, Fabric 1.4 LTS will be the last supported version of Composer and an alternative approach consists of only using its modeling language by integrating the Concerto npm package in your project.

Another helpful software tool made for monitoring a chain is the Hyperledger Explorer. As the name suggests, it can be used to explore the blockchain. Using a web app, users can view and query the chain's data blocks and transactions. All the activity within the network can be observed. It also provides an overview of the network status itself, the connected nodes, their names and communication routing.

When it comes to blockchain management and operation, Hyperledger Cello is the software of choice. It can be used to deploy customized blockchains on demand. Administrators can maintain a pool of different hosts and blockchain networks on a dashboard and provision them instantly. Generating new chains as well as setting up and invoking smart contract logic are all possible within very short time frames.

Quilt provides a solution sending values across different ledgers (distributed or non-distributed) in Hyperledger. It implements the Interledger protocol using a common namespace for accounts and a protocol for synchronized atomic swaps.

When it comes to blockchain, many customers ask us about performance based on what they heard about the slow transaction speeds of Bitcoin during the boom phase in the winter of 2017. It is always tricky to provide a precise answer to the questions pertaining to this. The Linux Foundation has therefore added a new standard for measuring performance on a blockchain. Hyperledger Caliper provides a tool for measuring performance with a set of predefined use cases. It produces a report with statistics about transactions per second, latency and resource utilization.

A newer addition to the toolbox should not remain unmentioned. To improve security and not reinvent the wheel with every framework or application, Hyperledger offers Ursa. This is a cryptographic library that includes basic crypto functions but also ways to implement zero-knowledge proofs (see Sect. 2.11.3).

All these existing tools make Hyperledger a good starting point for a journey into the world of blockchain.

3 Hyperledger Fabric (HLF)

Comprehension of the technical concept and structure of Hyperledger Fabric is important to understanding the potential of this new architecture in terms of security, privacy and performance (Kakavand, Kost De Sevres, & Chilton, 2017). The primary components of the blockchain architectures are organizations, peers, orderers, membership service providers (MSPs) and channels (Cachin, 2016). In the following subsections, we will be explaining the structure of Hyperledger Fabric blockchain networks. First, we will take a closer look at the single components that are physically part of the blockchain network. In a second step, we will connect those components and explain how they interact with one another.

3.1 Peers

The backbone of a blockchain network is a set of peers. Peers are the key elements of the network, as each of them contain a copy of the ledger. Peers also store the chain code, which is referred to as smart contracts in other ledger solutions. Those that do store the chain code can compute updates of the ledger following a predefined set of rules. The ledger and the smart contracts contain the network's information and store it in so-called blocks that make up the blockchain. Each peer is part of a single company, which enables the peer to authenticate itself to the network and thereby interact with it.

Hyperledger Fabric has two different types of peers: endorsing peers and anchor peers. Endorsing peers have a special function during the transaction. They serve as the gatekeeper of a transaction and are used to verify a transaction before it is committed. Endorsing peers execute the chain code and sign the results prior to any other peer in the network according to the defined endorsement policy. Every peer in the network is a potential endorser. The anchor peer represents a special kind of peer and serves as the gate to the blockchain network for an organization. This peer is visible to all participants of the blockchain network and routes tasks, blocks or requests from other participants in the organization's network. By doing so the anchor peer lowers the overall network load on individual peers and other components to achieve better network performance.

3.2 Orderers

Like the peers, an orderer is a physical component of the blockchain network. Its primary responsibility consists of cutting incoming transactions into blocks, which will be attached to the existing blockchain. In contrast to the blocks of the Bitcoin network, the blocks in Hyperledger Fabric do not need to be of equal size. Blocks are cut when a certain amount of time has elapsed, or a certain amount of transactions have arrived depending on which condition is met first.

3.3 Membership Service Providers and Organizations

One of the most powerful features of Hyperledger Fabric is the MSP. The identity of the different actors in the blockchain network (such as peers and orderers) should be proven by a trusted authority inside the network. This authority is provided by the MSP. The MSP in Hyperledger Fabric uses a public key infrastructure (PKI) with a hierarchical model. The PKI provides a list of identities and the MSP indicates which of these identities can join the network (Hyperledger, 2018e). The peers on the other hand use the credentials provided by the MSP to authenticate the transactions.

Organizations are a logical construct in the Hyperledger Fabric framework. The organizations manage their members under a single MSP. In some cases organizations can also require different MSPs if the members of the organization have very different functionalities (Hyperledger, 2018f). MSPs can be divided into channel MSPs and local MSPs. A channel MSP defines the channel configurations and rights and is shared between all the network participants, while a local MSP defines the permissions for peers and orderers in the system file of either of them.

Organizations can also add additional peers without requiring permission from other users of the blockchain network. Those additional peers are connected via the predefined anchor peers to the whole network. Organizations also manage their own certificates and therefore can issue and revoke certificates, which are needed to gain access and interact with the blockchain (Wahab, 2018).

3.4 Channels

Channels are used In Hyperledger Fabric to create private connections between different members of the network. A channel can include various peers, members and a defined set of transactions, which can only be executed in that channel (Androulaki et al., 2018). When a new channel is created, a so-called genesis block is generated. It contains information about the channel, the policies and the list of members and anchor peers that can join the channel. When a new member is added, the channel information is transferred to the new member in the form of a block (Hyperledger, 2018c).

3.5 Consensus Mechanisms and Transactions

The consensus algorithm is quite different than that of blockchains like Bitcoin or Ethereum. While Bitcoin and Ethereum use the Proof of Work (PoW) concept, Hyperledger Fabric uses an endorsement approach. For each transaction there is a predefined set of endorsing peers, which need to sign the transaction. Configuration of which endorsing peers are required is defined using the endorsement policy (explained later in this chapter in Sect. 2.10).

The following steps are performed to successfully submit a transaction and to add it to the blockchain. The user sends a transaction request to one peer. This request is broadcast to the endorsing peers, which simulate the transaction and generate a read/write set. This set contains the result of the simulation. If the endorsing peer approves the result, it will be signed and sent back to the user's blockchain client. After the client has received the read/write sets, they will be forwarded to the orderer. The orderer takes the transaction along with the other transactions in the network and cuts them into a block. This block is transferred to all peers in the channel using the gossip protocol. Each of these peers validates the block and determines whether the read/write set is correct and endorsed by the right peers. Only following this final validation will the block will be appended to the blockchain.

3.6 Certificates

Hyperledger Fabric uses digital certificates based on the X.509 standard with elliptical curve encryption. These certificates are used to develop a PKI. One or more certificate authorities (CA) handle access and identities in a Hyperledger Fabric blockchain network. A PKI comprises several "Certificate Authorities" (CAs), whereby so-called root CAs and intermediate CAs form a chain of trust. The root CA at the top of this chain of trust is usually, but not necessarily, a commercial certificate provider. The intermediate CAs can obtain their certificate from the root CA or another intermediate CA and then sign new intermediate certificates with their own certificate. This forms a tree-like structure, in which each of the CAs can issue and verify user identities. Each CA has a so-called certificate revocation list, for cases in which an identity is no longer needed. This list includes the revoked identities that must no longer have access to the network. Hyperledger Fabric includes an optional built-in CA. This makes Fabric easy to use for enterprises because the necessary features are already implemented.

3.7 Endorsement Policies

Endorsement policies define which users have to approve and validate a transaction to insert it in the ledger. The Validation System Chaincode (VSCC) is invoked from a peer as a part of the transaction flow. The VSCC is used to determine the validity of all transactions and to prove that the sources of endorsement are reliable (Hyperledger, 2018d). Blockchain peers have a prespecified set of endorsement policies referenced by a deploy transaction that installs specific chain code. Endorsement policies can be parametrized, and these parameters can be specified by a deploy transaction (Hyperledger, 2018b).

Endorsement policies are used in Hyperledger Fabric during the transaction flow as described in the following example:

- HLF starts a transaction proposal and it is sent to the endorsing peers for verification. The transaction proposal includes a client ID, the chain code ID, a timestamp and the client signature.
- The endorsing peers can simulate the transaction, executing the chain code. If the transaction is valid, the peer will sign the transaction and return it to the proposer (Rilee, 2018).

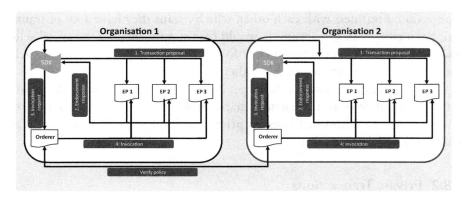

Fig. 2 Schematic workflow of an endorsed transaction

- The proposer waits until a sufficient number of required approving messages are sent back. A collection of authorized transactions is called an endorsement.
- Once the proposer has received enough signatures according to the policy, it can submit the transaction to be added to the ledger through the ordering services (Fig. 2).

3.8 Privacy Methods

One important consideration when using a blockchain-based solution is how to ensure privacy where needed, either to provide compliance with the General Data Protection Regulation (GDPR) or to keep certain transaction information hidden from other participants in a business network.

GDPR compliance has become an important factor in Europe since it took effect in May 2018. GDPR compliance includes the right to be forgotten, which stipulates that every subject in the network has the right to request deletion of their personal data (European Commission, 2018).

It is often desired or necessary to keep certain details of a transaction or the entire transaction hidden from the public or even from other participants in the network. Hyperledger Fabric therefore provides a set of different tools to comply with these requirements.

3.8.1 Channels

A channel is a virtual blockchain on top of the main chain, which has its own set of rules and access policies. Channels are used as a subnet by larger groups doing business with each other, which means they have a lot of transactions in common. One example would be a supply chain with several sellers, resellers and buyers, in which information about prices between each party should not be known to each other (Fig. 3).

One constraint of channels, however, is that every participant in the channel has insight into all transactions happening on the channel. To address this problem, an additional layer of privacy called Private Transactions was added to Hyperledger Fabric.

3.8.2 Private Transactions

To provide the ability to hide certain information from other peers in a channel, a second layer of privacy was implemented in Hyperledger Fabric 1.2 (Fig. 4).

The so-called private data collection (Hyperledger, 2018a) can contain one or more participants and consists of 2 parts.

The actual private data, which is stored in a second side-database (SideDB) next to the main database and a hash, which is written to every ledger of the main database. All data from this SideDB is therefore connected to the blockchain via a hash, which is only decipherable by the owner of the private key to that database. These hashes can be used for auditing purposes and serve as evidence of a transaction. Thus, everyone can still see changes in the private database reflected by the hash, but not the content

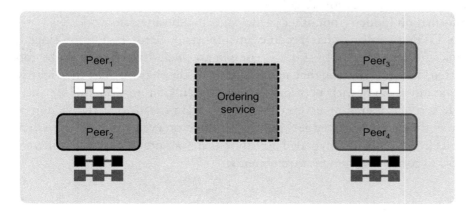

Fig. 3 Private channels in Hyperledger Fabric. Every peer participates in the main chain (gray), but can also have several side-channels with different participants (white, black)

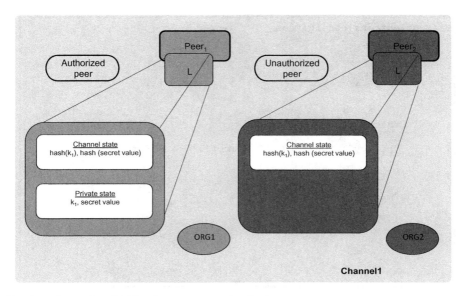

Fig. 4 Private data hidden from an unauthorized peer

of the change. The aforementioned right to be forgotten can be enforced in private transactions, as anyone can delete their own SideDB at any time. The hash pointing to the underlying data would still exist, but the data itself is deleted irreversibly.

An additional concept implemented with private transactions is called limitation of usage. It is possible to define a blockToLive policy for every private data collection, which defines an amount of time (in number of blocks) after which the underlying SideDB is automatically deleted. One possible implementation of this policy can be seen in Fig. 5.

Private transactions can be used in the main chain and within channels.

3.8.3 Zero-Knowledge Proof

The third and most restrictive privacy mechanism Hyperledger Fabric has to offer is zero-knowledge proof via a special CA called identity mixer. Zero-knowledge proof denotes a method used to prove a fact without revealing any additional information beyond this fact. One application of a zero-knowledge proof could be age-verification, in which someone could prove their age to be over 18 without revealing their actual age (Fig. 6).

```
// collections_config.json


[
    {
        "name": "collection1",

        "policy": "OR('Org1MSP.member','Org1MSP.member')",

            "requiredPeerCount": 0,

        "maxPeerCount": 3,

            "blockToLive":10000

    }

]
```

Fig. 5 blockToLive setting in the configuration

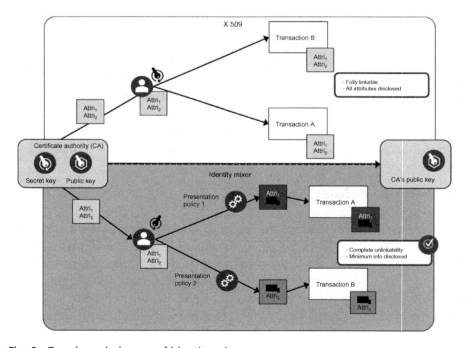

Fig. 6 Zero-knowledge proof identity mixer

The identity mixer can be used as a CA in HLF to determine the attributes one wants to disclose for each transaction. This is performed using flexible public keys called pseudonyms, which point to the same secret key, such that a different pseudonym can be used each time one needs to verify an identity. Therefore, the identity mixer ensures complete unlinkability between different certificates without knowledge of the original certificate.

However, as auditability is a requirement in many blockchains, it is also possible to assign special parties that are able to break the unlinkability under certain circumstances.

4 Perspectives

At the beginning of the blockchain hype, financial organizations were very skeptical about using the new technology. However, it is increasingly obvious how much money could be saved by processing the enormous amounts of transactions faster and more secure with less dependency on paper. Old communication processes by mail and fax for setting up syndicated loans or in the trade finance area, for example, could vanish with the help of blockchain. Interbank and cross-border payments and settlements could take advantage of high transaction speeds with less intermediates by using cryptocurrencies.

However, we do not see the biggest potential of blockchain as a "new" fiat money, but rather as an intermediatiory platform for creating trust between different parties. Counterparty verification, which is another crucial component in the banking business, could be simplified and made more secure. It will benefit from KYC and anti-money laundering algorithms implemented in smart contract logic combined with blockchain's security protocols for data protection. With regard to GDPR, data could even remain private in a customer's private blockchain "wallet" if necessary. In summary, the next five years promise to be very exciting, innovative and perhaps even game-changing.

Literature

Androulaki, E., Manevich, Y., Muralidharan, S., Murthy, C., Nguyen, B., Sethi, M., … Laventman, G. (2018). *Hyperledger Fabric: A distributed operating system for permissioned blockchains.* Cornell University Library.

Cachin, C. (2016). *Architecture of the hyperledger blockchain fabric*. Zurich: IBM Research.

Dahmen, G., & Liermann, V. (2019). Hyperledger composer—Syndicated loans. In V. Liermann & C. Stegmann (Eds.), *The impact of digital transformation and fintech on the finance professional*. New York: Palgrave Macmillan.

European Commission. (2018, October). *2018 reform of EU data protection rules*. Retrieved from https://ec.europa.eu/commission/priorities/justice-and-fundamental-rights/data-protection/2018-reform-eu-data-protection-rules_en.

FinTech Futures. (2019, February). *How blockchain could change the global remittance industry*. Retrieved from https://www.bankingtech.com/2018/06/how-blockchain-could-change-the-global-remittance-industry/.

Hyperledger. (2018a, October). *Hyperledger Fabric key concepts: Private data*. Retrieved from https://hyperledger-fabric.readthedocs.io/en/release-1.2/private-data/private-data.html.

Hyperledger. (2018b, October). *Hyperledger Fabric: Architecture explained*. Retrieved from https://hyperledger-fabric.readthedocs.io/en/release-1.2/arch-deep-dive.html.

Hyperledger. (2018c, October). *Hyperledger Fabric: Channels*. Retrieved from https://hyperledger-fabric.readthedocs.io/en/release-1.2/channels.html.

Hyperledger. (2018d, October). *Hyperledger Fabric: Endorsement policies*. Retrieved from https://hyperledger-fabric.readthedocs.io/en/release-1.2/endorsement-policies.html.

Hyperledger. (2018e, October). *Hyperledger Fabric: Identity*. Retrieved from https://hyperledger-fabric.readthedocs.io/en/release-1.2/identity/identity.html.

Hyperledger. (2018f, October). *Hyperledger Fabric: Membership*. Retrieved from https://hyperledger-fabric.readthedocs.io/en/release-1.2/membership/membership.html.

Kakavand, H., Kost De Sevres, N., & Chilton, B. (2017, January). *The blockchain revolution: An analysis of regulation and technology related to distributed ledger technologies*. SSRN.

Ratcliffe, S. (2016). Roy Amara 1925–2007, American futurologist. In S. Ratcliffe (Ed.), *Oxford essential quotations* (4th ed.). Oxford: Oxford University Press.

Rilee, K. (2018, October). *Understanding Hyperledger Fabric—Endorsing transactions*. Retrieved from https://medium.com/kokster/hyperledger-fabric-endorsing-transactions-3c1b7251a709.

Wahab, A. (2018, October). Retrieved from extending Hyperledger Fabric network: Adding a new peer. https://medium.com/@wahabjawed/extending-hyperledger-fabric-network-adding-a-new-peer-4f52f70a7217.

4

Hyperledger Composer—Syndicated Loans

Gereon Dahmen and Volker Liermann

1 Introduction

1.1 Two Approaches Considering Distributed Ledger Technology

Blockchain and distributed ledger technology are being discussed in multiple contexts throughout the financial services industry. In general, two primary approaches are being taken to these technologies:

- focus on payment and coins/tokens or
- focus on smart contracts and the distributed nature of the technology.

These two approaches are discussed in detail in the introduction in (Bettio, Bruse, Franke, Jakoby, & Schärf, 2019).

The first approach is for example taken by Bitcoin and Ethereum, both public blockchains with a focus on sanction-free transfer of values.

G. Dahmen (✉)
ifb Lux S.A, Luxembourg, Luxembourg
e-mail: gereon.dahmen@ifb-group.com

V. Liermann
ifb AG, Grünwald, Germany
e-mail: volker.liermann@ifb-group.com

© The Author(s) 2019
V. Liermann and C. Stegmann (eds.), *The Impact of Digital Transformation and FinTech on the Finance Professional*, https://doi.org/10.1007/978-3-030-23719-6_4

Ethereum is a public blockchain with the capability to implement smart contracts and, as such, one might consider Ethereum to be located somewhere in between the two approaches but, due to its public nature, we classify Ethereum as belonging to the first approach.

1.2 Motivation for the Use Case—Why Syndicated Loans?

This chapter focuses on smart contracts, the distributed nature of the technology and the possibility of limiting access to information and processing to selected groups of involved participants.

Loan syndication is currently a highly manual process for all involved parties. This includes

- the loan initiation process,
- the invitation of syndicate members by the syndicate leader,
- the exchange of information about the borrower and about the loan to be syndicated between the syndicate leader and the syndicate members,
- the out-payment of the loan by the syndicate members to the syndicate leader and by the syndicate leader to the borrower,
- the transfer of the incoming interest and capital payment from the borrower to the syndicate members by the syndicate leader,
- the information about payments due but not paid by the borrower and
- last but not least, the processes of restructuring and write-off.

There are three main reasons why it makes sense to introduce Hyperledger technology:

1. Digitally defining business requirements using algorithms or coding.
2. A certainty of integrity of the data exchanged between the involved parties.
3. Different access rights for the different participants.

As can be seen, syndicated loans have process requirements in all three areas mentioned above as reasons for introducing Hyperledger technology: (1) Automation of the highly manual processes and introduction of a single platform for all participants using blockchain technology, (2) Trust and transparency in the data exchanged between the involved parties, and (3) implementing the proper access rights to the data and processes according to business requirements. The details and the nature of syndicated loans will be discussed in more detail in Sect. 2.

1.3 Possible Frameworks and Tools

The potential of distributed ledger technology can be best illustrated by a sample application with a selected set of functions and processes within the context of syndicated loans. Implementation could be started without any tools or existing code-snippets but, given the compact format of this chapter and the business focus, only a high-level modeling tool is appropriate.

Two distributed ledger frameworks are possible candidates for illustrating an implementation approach: Corda from R3 or Hyperledger Fabric from The Linux Foundation. Although R3 is a profit-oriented company/consortium, it provides open-source components for distributed ledger development. R3 focuses on the financial industry and is well established in this sector (see B3i, 2018). In Bettio et al. (2019), we already introduced the Hyperledger framework and presented the concepts of this technology. Hence, in this chapter, we will refer to the framework and concepts presented therein. Most notably, we will use the tool Hyperledger Composer to exemplify how quickly and easily a distributed ledger can be designed and implemented.

For the sake of simplicity and comprehensibility in terms of the underlying business process and the technology, this chapter only presents some exemplary structures and processes necessary for a syndicated loan sample. It should not be understood as a full, business-ready description of how to implement all required syndicated loan processes using distributed ledger technology. In addition, thorough discussion should be conducted as to whether full implementation of all syndicated loan structures and processes within the distributed ledger technology is reasonable.

1.4 Structure of the Chapter

This chapter focuses on the possibilities of digitally implementing (smart) contracts, processing and clearing between several parties in the financial industry using blockchain and distributed ledger technology. In the introduction, we indicated the advantages of this technology in such settings and pointed out syndicated loans as a very good use case for improving contract and process digitalization particularly because several financial institutions are involved.

In Sect. 2, we outline in more detail the use case of syndicated loans with a focus on the interactions between the involved parties and the processes that need to be implemented in the blockchain.

In Sect. 3, we explain how to implement the necessary distributed ledger technology using Hyperledger Composer.[1] As can be seen, Hyperledger Composer provides very useful tools for implementations in a financial business environment. For the syndicated loans use case, however, entities and transactions have to be defined in a specialized way to meet the business requirements. We show that such entities and transactions can be defined quite easily in the Hyperledger Composer environment.

In Sect. 4, we work out in detail a sample transaction of the syndicated loans use case, showing at code level the entities and transactions needed as well as the relation to the business events. In addition, we show how such an implementation can be integrated into the existing environments of the participating financial institutions and which Hyperledger Composer tools can support such integration.

In Sect. 5, we provide a summary and outlook.

2 Syndicated Loans—Introduction

A syndicated loan is a loan provided by a group of lenders and can be structured.[2] In most cases, a syndicated loan is arranged and administered by one or more banks. A single arranging bank is called the lead arranger and when a group of banks arranges the loan, they are referred to as joint-lead managers (or co-lead managers).

This section provides a brief overview of the benefits for borrowers and lenders, and outlines the main business requirements needed to digitalize syndicated loans. The legal issues of such implementation will not be discussed here. There are other substantiated publications on the legal implications of smart contracts and data stored or transferred in a public or semipublic way [for more details see (Bernhard Steinrücke, 1956); (Derleder, Knops, & Bamberg, 2003); (Rösler, Mackenthun, & Pohl, 2002); (Taylor & Sansone, 2007)].

---

[1]Hyperledger Composer is one of the projects in the Hyperledger Greenhouse.
[2]In terms of different tranche types (junior, mezzanine and senior tranche).

2.1 Business Origin

The origin of this common bank product can be traced back to the renowned Fugger bankers of the fifteenth century. There are several motivations for syndicating a loan:

- Risk sharing: The total credit amount does not comply with the internal or external credit risk limits [e.g., the European Union's large exposure requirement, see Part Four—Large Exposures in European Parliament and of the Council (2013)].

 – Capital requirements: The capital requirements for the full volume is unbalanced in comparison to the bank's other business activities.
 – The borrower wants all his core bank connections to participate in the loan.

However, the risk sharing aspect for lenders is usually the main motivation for syndicating a loan.

2.2 Involved Parties

In Fig. 1: Involved parties, the borrower is indicated on the left and the syndicate members on the right. Both are connected through the lead manager, which is sometimes also called the sole-lead manager.

The lead manager has the prime contact to the borrower and is usually the initiator of the syndication. The lead manager maintains the contracts, pricing and communication with the borrower. In most cases, the syndicate

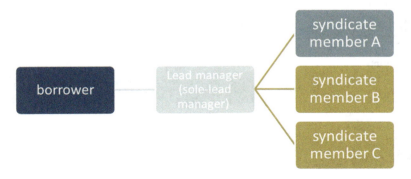

Fig. 1 Involved parties

members pay a fee to the lead manager for the service provided. If more than one institution is part of the contract with the client, the group of such institutions is called Joint-Lead Managers.

2.3   Types of Syndicated Loans

There are two types of syndicated loans, which differ in the type of commitment the lead manager makes to the borrower:

A. Best-effort syndication: The commitment of the syndicate leader for the total amount of the syndicated loan is subject to the commitment of the syndicate members to underwrite the syndicate shares of the syndicated loan as outlined in the contract with the borrower (best effort).
B. Underwriting: The commitment of the syndicate leader for the total amount of the syndicated loan is unconditional irrespective of the amount of syndicate shares underwritten by potential syndicate members; in this case, the lead manager takes the risk of having to disburse the entire amount of the loan out of his own book in the worst case.

2.4   Business Process Domains

The three primary processes for managing a syndicated loan are illustrated in Fig. 2. The upper part of the figure represents business or transaction initiation. This process is mainly driven by the lead manager interacting with the borrower. Disbursement in the center of the figure represents the start of business processing of the syndicated loan.

Fig. 2 Business process domains

The lower part of the figure indicates the processes surrounding interest payments and repayments (including amortizable loan). This figure illustrates how the business is processed.

2.4.1 Business Initiation

On the one hand, the lead manager negotiates the loan contract and the collateral to be provided with the borrower during initiation of the syndicated loan. The payments (redemption schedule, interest payment frequency) and the price (interest rate, initial discount) of the loan are also agreed on. On the other hand, the lead manager also negotiates with the (potential) syndicate members pertaining to the loan conditions and the volume share[3] plus the fee paid to the lead manager for arranging the syndicated loan.

Therefore, the syndicate members are involved in the negotiation with the borrower but always through the lead manager. The degree of involvement differs by the type of syndicated loan (best-efforts syndication or underwriting). Once the contracts are signed with both the borrower and the syndicate members, the lead manager collects the disbursements from the syndicate members and disburses the total loan amount to the borrower.

2.4.2 Business Processing

Interest and repayment cash flows are paid by the borrower to the lead manager. The lead manager transfers them to the syndicate members according to the agreed share of the syndicated loan and the fee. Late payment information is to be communicated to the syndicate members due to the required processes regarding payment defaults.

In case the syndicated loan defaults, the lead manager and the syndicate members may agree on restructuring of the loan or a partial or total write-off. Impairment is not part of the business processing between the lead manager and the syndicate members, however, as impairment is only an internal evaluation by the bank with no effects on the contracts or the payment obligations.

---

[3]A special product variation consists of splitting the transaction into tranches like a CDO instead of a percentage share.

2.4.3 Business Approval Requirements

As a blockchain for syndicated loans is not a public blockchain like Bitcoin or Ethereum, the business approval requirements are very different and depend strongly on who owns the blockchain. However, it is important to distinguish between the blockchain's technical consensus algorithms to ensure all participants agree on the technical integrity of the blockchain, and the business approval requirements derived from the business functions as well as ownership of the blockchain processes or entities and ownership of the blockchain itself. The business approval requirements include those related to blockchain administration on the one hand, which are mainly derived from ownership, and requirements related to business functions on the other hand, which are primarily derived from approvals needed for conducting the business. When implementing the blockchain, the business approval requirements have to be added to the consensus algorithms, which ensure the blockchain's integrity. On the other hand, it has to be guaranteed that the consensus algorithms used to ensure integrity are not misused to introduce inappropriate business approval requests.

In this section, we only examine the business approval requirements and not the technical consensus algorithms used to ensure integrity. There are basically three scenarios for implementing a syndicated loans blockchain and each of these results in different business approval requirements:

1. Single sole-lead manager blockchain:
   In this case, the blockchain is created and owned by only one bank, which seeks to make streamline its processes for syndicating loans as a sole-lead manager, particularly regarding initiation and processing by automating the necessary data exchange and approval interactions between the sole-lead manager and the syndicate members. Only the owning bank acts as a sole-lead manager. All other participating banks are just syndicate members, but they also have the advantage in this scenario of increased efficiency regarding data exchange and approval interactions. Both the sole-lead manager and the syndicate members benefit from the ensured integrity of the exchanged data and approval actions resulting from use of the blockchain technology. The borrower does not participate in the blockchain.
   With regard to blockchain administration, approval is not generally required as the owning bank provides the blockchain as its own system for syndicated loans to be used by the syndicate members. If the syndicate

members don't want to use the sole-lead manager's system for handling syndicated loans, they simply have to decline usage at the very beginning. The approval of a syndicate member (but not that of the others) is only required when the data of a participating bank itself changes.

With regard to the business functions, the sole-lead manager is responsible for the data and transactions of the syndicated loan. The syndicate members have to approve the actions but only to the extent that the business requires it, as these actions effect the volume of their syndicated loan share, loan conditions or write-off, for example.

2. Joined syndicated loan blockchain:

   In this case, the blockchain is created and owned by several banks. The owners may act as sole-lead managers or as syndicate members. There may be further participating banks, which do not own the blockchain and act only as syndicate members. The advantages of the owners possibly acting as sole-lead managers and of the syndicate members are the same than mentioned in item (1) above. The borrower does not participate in the blockchain.

   With regard to blockchain administration, approval is required from all banks that own the blockchain but not from other participants, for which the rules of item (1) apply.

   With regard to the business functions, the sole-lead manager is responsible for the data and transactions of the syndicated loan. The syndicate members have to approve the actions but only to the extent that the business requires it, as these actions effect the volume of their syndicated loan share, loan conditions or write-off, for example. Other owners of the blockchain, who are not part of the loan syndicate, do not have to approve any actions regarding the syndicated loan.

3. Semipublic borrower-including syndicated loan blockchain:

   In this case, the blockchain is created and owned not only by banks acting as sole-lead managers or syndicate members, but also by the borrowers. This means that the borrower can use the blockchain to ask for bids of syndicated loans and choose the best one. There may be further participating banks, which do not own the blockchain and act only as syndicate members as well as further borrowers who do not participate in the blockchain.

   With regard to blockchain administration, approval is required from all banks and borrowers that own the blockchain, but not from other participants.

   With regard to the business functions, not only the sole-lead manager but also the borrower is responsible for the data and transactions of the syndicated loan considered as the borrower has the choice to accept the offered syndicated loan or not. Therefore, both the borrower and the sole-lead manager have to approve all actions of the syndicated loan. As in the other two scenarios, the syndicate members have to approve the actions but only to the extent that the business requires it, as these actions effect the volume of their syndicated loan share, loan conditions or write-off, for example. Other owners of the blockchain, who are not part of the loan syndicate and not the borrower, do not have to approve any actions regarding the syndicated loan.

It is not very likely that banks will want to put money into the administration of such a blockchain, as it could possibly reduce their profits by making their competing loan conditions much easier to compare for potential borrowers, who may force the banks to adjust their conditions to those of the lowest bidder. This type of blockchain is therefore more likely to be introduced by large companies, which can urge their banks to participate in it.

3 Hyperledger Composer

Hyperledger Composer is one of the six tools provided under the Hyperledger umbrella as of 2018. Hyperledger Composer is designed to rapidly develop a blockchain using the underlying Hyperledger Fabric framework [for more details on the Hyperledger Fabric framework see Bettio et al. (2019)]. Hyperledger Composer uses the API[4] provided by Hyperledger Fabric and proves a highly efficient tool for use in Proof of Concepts (PoC) and prototypes (for details see Hyperledger, Key concepts in Hyperledger composer, 2018d).

3.1 General Overview

In mid-2018, rumors have it that Hyperledger Composer would receive less support from IBM, because the company would be shifting its focus toward improving the underlying Hyperledger Fabric framework. Nonetheless, it was announced that Hyperledger Composer will support Hyperledger Fabric

---

[4]API—application programming interface.

version 1.4.[5] The concerto modeling language will live on in the accord project (Accord Project, 2018).

According to our knowledge as of the beginning of 2019, Convector framework (WORLDSUBU, 2019) will take the place of the Hyperledger Composer as a rapid development tool for prototypes and PoCs. The additional benefit of Convector framework is that it will support more than just the Hyperledger Fabric framework. The basic objects in Hyperledger Composer and Convector differ, but they are transferable to a certain extent. Due to the current uncertainty in this regard (Hyperledger Composer is already widely used by business-oriented users) we are using Hyperledger Composer in our description.

The three main components of Hyperledger Composer are:

1. the modeling language which is used to define the participants and the assets,
2. the transactions which interact with the participants and the assets, and
3. the rights to access data and transactions.

Queries should also be mentioned in this context as they are used to obtain information on more than one participant/asset, which includes filtering data in the blockchain.

There are some more objects like Connection Profiles, Identities and Business Network Cards, which are required to set up a Hyperledger Composer network. We will not go into further detail on these interesting subjects, as we intend to focus on the modeling aspects (transforming the business use case into the Hyperledger Composer structures) here. The core aspect in this context, however, is that you can map identities to participants in the network.

3.2   Modeling Language

The Hyperledger Composer modeling language is an easy to use programming model. With a minimal knowledge of JavaScript and JavaScript Object Notation (JSON), even business staff without sophisticated IT expertise can develop and deploy tiny prototypes or contribute to PoCs. Of course this will even be a much easier task for trained developers.

---

[5]The Hyperledger Composer supports Hyperledger Fabric 1.4, but does not use the new 1.4 functionalities (see Hyperledger, github, 2019).

Fig. 3 Components of the Hyperledger Composer modeling language

The provided structure of Participants/Assets/Transactions offers a perfect grid for mapping the acting business people, the business rolls, the business items and the actions into the Hyperledger Composer world. The main predefined objects are summarized in Fig. 3.

The three main predefined objects are explained in the following subsections. When developing one's own network, inheritance of these objects is used to model the requirements specific to the use case.

Further details on the modeling language can be found under Hyperledger, Hyperledger composer modeling language (2018c).

3.2.1 Participants

The members of a business network are called participants. By submitting transactions or owning assets, for example, they are the acting individuals in the network. The participants are identified by an ID and can have all the properties required by the business use case. The participants can be mapped to a Hyperledger Composer network identity.

Examples are a buyer/seller, a car owner, a regulator or—in the syndicated loan use case—a borrower, a lead manager and a syndicate member.

3.2.2 Assets

The assets are the physical or nonphysical items, which are stored in and handled by the network. They can represent almost anything. Like the participants, the assets have an identifier and can be transformed by transactions. They can be assigned to participants or related to other assets.

Examples include a house, a car, a device or—in the syndicated loan use case—a syndicated loan, a share on a syndicated loan and collateral.

3.2.3 Transactions

The transactions define the mechanisms of how participants interact with the assets. Common actions include transfer of ownership, offering a bid in an auction or updating characteristics like the price of an asset.

Selling an asset or approving certain features by a third person are also common examples. In the syndicated loan context, transactions include deriving the syndicate member loans from the sole-lead manager loan by the syndicate member share or distributing an incoming interest payment to the syndicate members.

3.2.4 Permissions

The permissions are a core component of a private network and quite a tricky one. In most business use cases—especially when pricing in a non-transparent market is involved—the opportunity to share just the required information is an incessant characteristic.[6]

The opportunities to model permissions for participants, assets and trans-actions are manifold. The implementation practice shows that access control is a crucial aspect that should be addressed at an early stage of the implementation project. More details can be found in (Hyperledger, 2018b).

3.2.5 Queries and Events

Queries are used to retrieve multiple data entries from the blockchain. For example, a query can be used to obtain all the network's participants or assets. The data received can be filtered using WHERE-statements, as used in SQL.

---

[6]In Corda from R3, the approach is formulated from another point of view: "The only parties who should have access to the details of a financial transaction are those parties themselves and others with a legitimate need to know" (Brown, Carlyle, Grigg, & Hearn, 2016). In Hyperledger, this task is performed by channels or permissioned transactions.

Events are triggers set for certain business events. A Node.js application can subscribe to an event and perform defined actions depending on this event.

3.2.6 Consensus Algorithms in Hyperledger Composer

In contrast to bitcoin where "proof of work" is the defined consensus, the consensus algorithm in Hyperledger Fabric can be customized depending on the structure and purpose of the consortium running the network.

The consensus algorithm in Hyperledger Fabric (and hence in Hyperledger Composer) has two components: The "principal" and the "threshold gate". A "principal" (P) identifies the entity, whose signature is expected in the consensus process. A "threshold gate" (T) requires two inputs: an integer t (the threshold) and a list of n principals or thresholds, which can themselves include other threshold gates.

Example: (Node.js notation): A, B, C are peers in the network.
T (2, 'A', 'B', 'C') requests a signature of 2 principals (66%) from A, B or C.
T (1, 'A', T (2, 'B', 'C')) requests either a signature of originator A or a signature of B and C.

As shown here, the consensus can be adapted to the needs and the network structure. The consensus structure normally reflects the trust in the network.

Example: (CLI notation): A, B, C are peers in the network.
AND ('A', 'B', 'C') requests a signature from each of the three peers.
OR ('A', 'B') requests a signature from one of the two peers.
OR ('A', AND ('B', 'C'))requests either a signature of A or a signature of B and a signature of a member of C.

This technical flexibility allows it to set up a sophisticated consensus rule set to fulfill the business approval requirements necessary to conduct business as described in Sect. 2.4.3.

3.3 Business Network Archive

Business network definitions consist of one or more model files, JavaScript files and an access control file. Basically, it is a zip file containing the model files (defining participants/assets/transactions), the JavaScript files

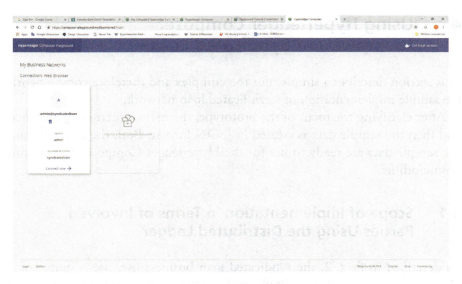

Fig. 4 Hyperledger Composer Playground online login

(containing the chain code for the transactions) and the access control file (defining the permissions in the network). For further details see (Hyperledger, 2018a).

3.4 Composer Playground

Composer Playground can be used as an online or offline tool to rapidly develop and test Hyperledger Composer networks. Using the Hyperledger Composer business network concept, it is even possible to roll out a business network archive to Microsoft Azure or Amazon Web Services (AWS).[7] Details on how to use Composer Playground can be found in (Hyperledger, 2018e) (Fig. 4).

The business network cards concept allows for working on various projects.

---

[7]Other cloud providers like Google Cloud could work as well, but we have not tested them yet.

4 Using Hyperledger Composer to Implement Syndicated Loans

This section describes a simple, not too complex and therefore comprehensible sample implementation of a syndicated loan network.

After clarifying the focus of the prototype, the main structures are defined and then the sample data is created in JSON format. Both the structure and the sample data are ready to use for the Hyperledger Composer Playground online/offline.

4.1 Scope of Implementation in Terms of Involved Parties Using the Distributed Ledger

As described in Sect. 2, the syndicated loan business use case is quite complex. To keep this sample simple and emphasize the structural modeling aspects, only one transaction is described here: splitting of the sole-lead managers loan into the syndicated member loans based on the syndicated member shares. We have also implemented a simple link to collateral here. The collateral split is not shown as a transaction.

One can easily think of many extensions especially in the area of contract initialization. The potential is extremely high if a consortium of sole-lead managers and syndicate members (and possibly even borrowers) manage to establish a platform to exchange loan contract, business partner and collateral information in a predefined structured form. Ideally, it would be established with a direct link into the participating banks' core or legacy systems.

4.2 Simplified Data Model Structure

First, we define the core elements of our business network. The acting organizations (participants), the loan contracts and the collateral (assets) as well as the actions operating on the assets or, in some cases, on the participants (transactions).

4.2.1 Participants

The structure of the acting organizations is defined in Fig. 5. A network member is defined first. Members, borrowers and creditors are then derived

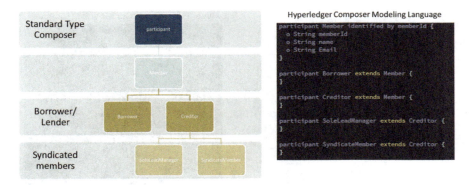

Fig. 5 Modeling language example (participants)

based on this. Furthermore, sole-lead managers and syndicate members are derived from the creditors.

Obvious possible extensions to the borrower include rating and payment information such as the account number and bank sorting code.

4.2.2 Assets

In the first step, we define the loan as an inheritance of the standard Hyperledger Composer type "asset". The loan contains common features such as information on the borrower, the start and end date, and the loan conditions or cash flow information (see Fig. 6). Please note that the link to the borrower is optional. The link to the participant points to the borrower structure in the business network.

The syndicated loan structure is derived from the loan structure by adding a link to the syndicated members from the business network and includes the syndicate member's share of the syndicated loan.

The loan's substructures are defined in Fig. 7. The loan derived from the standard Hyperledger Composer asset structure is linked to three array structures:

A. loan conditions,
B. cash flows, and
C. collateral information.

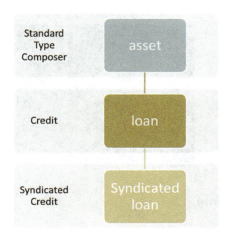

Fig. 6 Modeling language example (loan types)

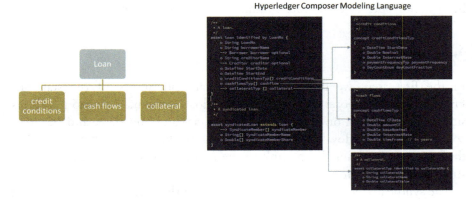

Fig. 7 Modeling language example (loan substructures)

Even though the first two seem to be redundant, a potential transaction in the business network could be a cash flow generator that generates the loan cash flows according to the loan conditions.

The collateral information includes the collateral value that can be used to calculate the unsecured portion of the loan (in this example, we will use a transaction only to split the cash flows but not the collateral values, so the calculation only makes sense for the sole-lead manager).

4.3 Transaction Example (Function)

The sample transaction we describe here performs the splitting of the sole-lead manager loan into the loan volumes of the loan's syndicate members. Splitting is performed based on the syndicate member shares. The parameters passed to the business network include the transaction to be executed (generateLoans) and the loan number of the sole-lead manager's loan (see Fig. 8).

As can be seen in Fig. 9, the transaction generateLoans() loops through the syndicated members and generates new loans in the business network based on the shares of the syndicate members in the loan contract with the borrower.

As already mentioned, the collateral value (and the collateral as an asset) is not split here.

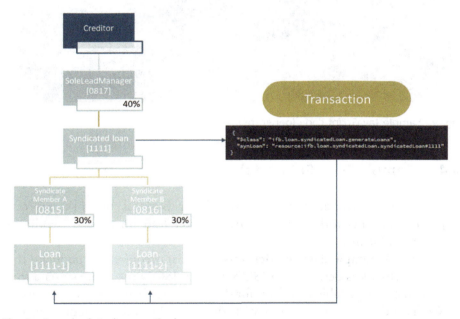

Fig. 8 Sample data (transaction)

```
1
2    /* global getAssetRegistry getParticipantRegistry getFactory */
3
4    /**
5     * generate the loans für the syndicate members by the syndicate Members share
6     * @param {ifb.loan.syndicatedloan.generateLoans} tx syndicated Loan number
7     * @transaction
8     */
9
10   async function generateLoans(tx) {
11       const factory = getFactory();
12       const NS = 'ifb.loan.syndicatedloan';
13   //  Loop over all syndicate members
14       for(var i=0; i < tx.synLoan.SyndicateMemberName.length; i++) {
15           var subLoan = factory.newResource(NS, 'loan', tx.synLoan.getIdentifier()+'-'+i);
16           subLoan.LoanNo = subLoan.getIdentifier();
17           subLoan.borrowerName = tx.synLoan.borrowerName;
18           subLoan.borrower = tx.synLoan.borrower;
19
20           subLoan.creditorName = tx.synLoan.SyndicateMemberName[i];
21           subLoan.creditor = tx.synLoan.syndicateMember[i];
22
23           subLoan.StartDate = tx.synLoan.StartDate;
24           subLoan.StartEnd = tx.synLoan.StartEnd;
25           subLoan.creditConditions = [] //tx.synLoan.creditConditions
26           // copy original cashflow
27           var CashflowCopy = Object.assign({}, tx.synLoan.cashflow);
28           subLoan.cashflow = tx.synLoan.cashflow
29           // Adjust Cash flow according the individual share
30           for(var j=0; j < subLoan.cashflow.length; j++) {
31               subLoan.cashflow[j].amountCF = CashflowCopy[j].amountCF * tx.synLoan.syndicateMemberShare[i];
32               subLoan.cashflow[j].baseNominal = CashflowCopy[j].baseNominal * tx.synLoan.syndicateMemberShare[i];
33           }
34           // set collateral values
35           subLoan.collateral = tx.synLoan.collateral
36           let SubLoanRegistry = await getAssetRegistry(NS + '.loan');
37           await SubLoanRegistry.add(subLoan);
38           // copy back |
39           for(var j=0; j < subLoan.cashflow.length; j++) {
40               tx.synLoan.cashflow[j].amountCF = CashflowCopy[j].amountCF / tx.synLoan.syndicateMemberShare[i];
41               tx.synLoan.cashflow[j].baseNominal = CashflowCopy[j].baseNominal / tx.synLoan.syndicateMemberShare[i];
42           }
43       };
44   }
45
```

Fig. 9 Sample JavaScript code (generate loan)

4.4   Sample Data Set (Data)

Once we have defined the structure of our business network, we can populate this network with borrowers, sole-lead managers, syndicate members and loans.

In Fig. 10: Sample data (participants), the data required to populate the business network is described in JSON format. JSON is a compact data format in an easily readable text form for data exchange between applications.

We have defined the borrower with the ID 4711 and the creditor in the creditor role with the ID 0817-C. The ID of the sole-lead manager role is 0817 and the IDs of the two syndicated members are 0815 and 0816 accordingly.

Each business network attendee is assigned a name and an email address in addition to their ID, as required in the business network participant structure model.

4 Hyperledger Composer—Syndicated Loans

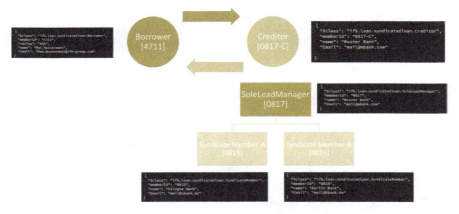

Fig. 10 Sample data (participants)

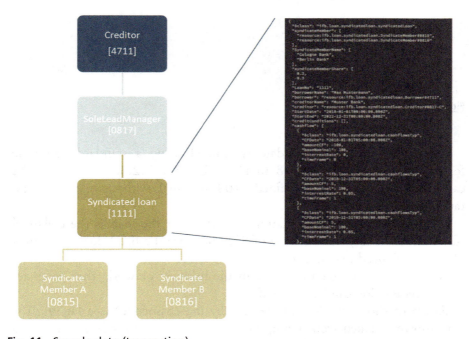

Fig. 11 Sample data (transaction)

Figure 11 shows part of the loan data in JSON format. This includes the link and the ID of the syndicated members (0815 and 0816) as well as their respective shares of the borrower loan (30% each). Supplementary information about the borrowers and links to the business network participants are passed on to the loan.

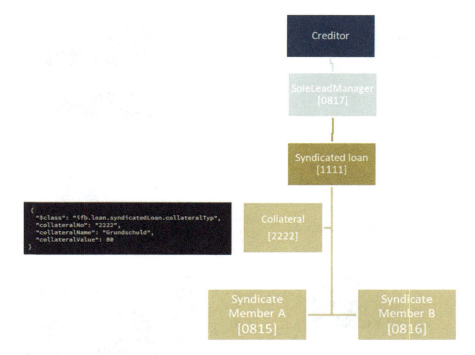

Fig. 12 Sample data (collateral)

The loan's start and end date is defined using a standard date-time format (from January 1, 2018 to December 31, 2022). In the end, the cash flow information is defined (100 nominal with a yearly interest rate of 5%).

In Fig. 12, the final information we define for the loan is the collateral (fundamental debt) with a value of 80. Therefore the blank loan portion is 20 at the sole-lead manager level.

Now, with all the data available in the business network, the "generate-Loans" transaction can be executed.

Figure 13 shows the loans generated by the chaincode[8] (see Fig. 9). The data shown is taken from Composer Playground. The syndicate loan data can now be exported to the syndicate member's legacy system for further processing.

The newly generated data can also be retrieved via query. A query that retrieves all (split) loans in the network is shown in Fig. 14.

---

[8]Transaction written in JavaScript.

Fig. 13 Generated loans for syndicate members

```
1  /** Sample queries for Syndicated Loan business network
2   */
3
4  query selectCLoans {
5    description: "Select all Loans"
6    statement:
7        SELECT ifb.loan.syndicatedloan.loan
8  }
```

Fig. 14 Example query (all loans)

4.5 Integration in the Bank Architecture

To increase the optimization potential, the banks must work on a smooth connection and integration of the distributed ledger network in the bank's IT infrastructure.

In Fig. 15, the important question is addressed: Where should a functionality be developed? Should it be in the distributed ledger or in the bank's individual environment? From a general perspective, the answer is simple. Functionality applicable to all members should be implemented by chaincode in the business network. Bank individual functions and processes should be implemented independently using the Hyperledger API.

In practice, the question must be answered within and along the covered processes. In terms of cost efficiency and standardization, it is desirable to place as much as possible in the centralized business network. However, if the bank's policy regarding the process in question requires the ownership of the IT code of the process, the bank may want to develop and maintain the IT process on its own even if it is inefficient.

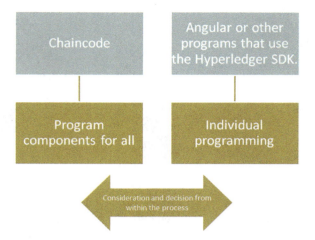

Fig. 15 The primary decision—on or off the blockchain

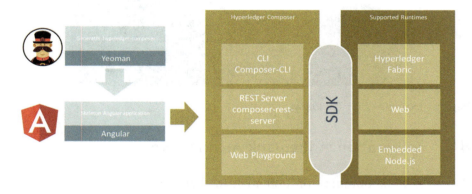

Fig. 16 A typical Hyperledger Composer solution architecture

Hyperledger Composer offers tools to automatically generate interfaces (Yeoman) that can be used for testing and further enhanced up to an individual user interface (see Fig. 16). To some extent, this functionality is also offered by Hyperledger Composer Playground.

The generated Angular application skeleton can be used as a starting point for the bank's individual function and process development.

As the Hyperledger Composer offers a REST Server interface (composer-rest-server), integration into the bank's core[9] systems (e.g., SAP's

---

[9]Core—centralized online real-time exchange.

S4Banking, Flexcube Banking Solutions by Oracle, T24 by Temenos Group, etc.) can be achieved using common middleware architectures. This smooth integration ensures that the potential gains in efficiency of this automation are substantially lifted.

5   Summary and Outlook

Hyperledger Composer is a flexible business-oriented tool that can implement quick and easy prototypes and PoCs for distributed ledger technology. Even though the environment is still dynamic in terms of changes in the tool sets, Hyperledger Composer has proven that the distributed ledger technology can be used for many financial use cases and be implemented in a smooth and pragmatic way. Hyperledger Composer's modeling language is straight forward to learn and easily understood. The interfaces can be automatically generated.

However, detailed definition of a rule set for access rights is one of the keys to an accepted and successful distributed ledger implementation.

The media (and hence the world) is talking about public blockchains like Bitcoin and Ethereum, whereas the great potential of the private distributed ledger technology established by a consortium is mostly being overlooked, at least until it becomes widely successful.

At the end of 2018, it was announced that IBM will no longer support the Hyperledger Composer project and shift their capacities toward improving Hyperledger Fabric by working on a high-level API for it. Nonetheless, Hyperledger Composer has a good reputation for prototypes and PoC implementations. The modeling language will definitely maintain its relevance, as it is being used in other projects like the "Accord Project" (see Accord Project, 2018).

Literature

Accord Project. (2018). *Accord Project*. Retrieved from Github https://github.com/accordproject.

B3i. (2018). *B3i Home*. Retrieved from B3i https://b3i.tech/home.html.

Bernhard Steinrücke, H. S. (1956). *Das Konsortialgeschäft der deutschen Banken*. Berlin: Duncker & Humblot.

Bettio, D. M., Bruse, F., Franke, A., Jakoby, T., & Schärf, D. D. (2019). Hyperledger Fabric. In V. Liermann & C. Stegmann (Eds.), *The impact of digital transformation and fintech on the finance professional*. New York: Palgrave Macmillan.

Brown, R. G., Carlyle, J., Grigg, I., & Hearn, M. (2016). *Corda: An introduction*.

Derleder, P., Knops, K.-O., & Bamberg, H. (2003). *Handbuch zum europäischen und deutschen Bankrecht*. Berlin and Heidelberg: Springer.

European Parliament and of the Council. (2013). *Regulation (EU) No 575/2013 of the European Parliament and of the Council*. Brussels: European Parliament and of the Council.

Hyperledger. (2018a). *Business network definition*. Retrieved from Hyperledger Github https://hyperledger.github.io/composer/latest/business-network/businessnetworkdefinition.

Hyperledger. (2018b). *Hyperledger composer access control language*. Retrieved from Hyperledger Github https://hyperledger.github.io/composer/latest/reference/acl_language.html.

Hyperledger. (2018c). *Hyperledger composer modeling language*. Retrieved from Hyperledger Github https://hyperledger.github.io/composer/latest/reference/cto_language.html.

Hyperledger. (2018d). *Key concepts in hyperledger composer*. Retrieved from Hyperledger Guthub https://hyperledger.github.io/composer/latest/introduction/key-concepts.html.

Hyperledger. (2018e). *Using playground*. Retrieved from Hyperledger Github https://hyperledger.github.io/composer/latest/playground/playground-index.

Hyperledger. (2019, January 11). *github*. Retrieved from Hyperledger composer—Release notes https://github.com/hyperledger/composer/releases.

Rösler, P., Mackenthun, T., & Pohl, R. (2002). *Handbuch Kreditgeschäft*. Berlin: Springer.

Taylor, A., & Sansone, A. (2007). *The handbook of loan syndications & trading*. New York: McGraw-Hill.

WORLDSUBU. (2019, February 12). *Hyperledger development tools—Convector suite*. Retrieved from WORLDSUBU https://worldsibu.tech/convector/.

5

The Concept of the Next Best Action/Offer in the Age of Customer Experience

Sales Management/Forecasting in Financial Services in the Age of Artificial Intelligence

Uwe May

1 Introduction

This chapter aims to bridge the gap between the concept of the next best offer (NBO) and the forecasting derived from it. The NBO or next best action (NBA) concept is concisely explained and special features are highlighted here.

Application of this concept in the financial services industry is also described briefly. In addition, this chapter highlights the special features of the banking sector compared to other sectors characterized by high-volume transactions. Customer experience is a holistic approach to customer management. Classification is carried out here against the backdrop of the current state of customer experience implementation. This also includes topics such as omnichannel management and artificial intelligence.

Finally, possible effects on the interdependencies between forecasting and implementation of the NBO concept are discussed and options for action identified.

U. May (✉)
maihiro, Ismaning, Germany
e-mail: uwe.may@maihiro.com

© The Author(s) 2019
V. Liermann and C. Stegmann (eds.), *The Impact of Digital Transformation and FinTech on the Finance Professional*, https://doi.org/10.1007/978-3-030-23719-6_5

2 Next Best Action/Offer Concept

Sales management has included the concept of NBA or NBO for many years now. Historically, it can be assigned to the AIDA approach (see Rawal, 2013; Riedl, 1992). AIDA stands for Awareness/Attention, Interest, Desire and Action.

Awareness in this context means becoming aware of or attracting attention for a specific product. After awareness, an information phase follows, in which the interest in a product arises and is satisfied. However, only in the presence of desire does the purchase (action) ultimately take place.

NBA enable you to increase customer retention, strengthen upselling and cross-selling initiatives, and optimize the customer experience with every interaction. This is based on historical data, snapshots of a customer's current situation and static customer data, which can originate from corporate systems and external sources, in order to derive forecasts that are as accurate as possible and link them to suitable offers.

Basically, it is an attempt to predict the future behavior of a customer or prospective customer using various approaches. This model focuses on individual transactions.

Transactionality can be both a blessing and a curse. It is a curse in that it always leads to a SINGLE next activity, and it is a blessing in that the additional information available is used for the specific context. This allows for the use of recognized methods of predictive analytics when implemented correctly. This specific context becomes all the clearer the more one delves into the concept of the customer journey, a much-discussed topic, which is explained in a subsequent section. Within the context of a customer journey, various points of contact with the customer are collected in various media/channels as data points and displayed as a whole (see Wolny & Charoensuksai, 2014). In short, a lot of information, transactions and channels provide an exact picture of customer behavior which allows for assessing future behavior as well.

The NBO can then be seen as the most targeted form of action. The transaction is understood as an offer and thus as an additional business opportunity. There are different requirements for the action as well as for the offer. On the one hand, actually having all the information available is critical. This raises questions about the day-to-day business. For example, who is allowed to have and see which information? How is technical availability solved? Is the data integrated and consistent? On the other hand, the question arises as to how the short-term objectives of a company (or even a sector) fit in with the findings derived from the analysis of the information.

For example, product A should be sold because inventory stocks are too high, but the predominant recommendation based on the results of NBO analytics is product B. Now what?

In the past, everyone was able to answer this question to some extent based on their own experience. Oftentimes, it was the operational requirements rather than the analytical findings that determined the NBO.

But what does this look like in banking?

3 NBO in Banking

In principle, the banking sector provides the ideal conditions for the application of the NBA/NBO concept. Customer relationships consist of high-volume transactions in the vast majority of cases (retail banking, asset management, SME). As a result of these transactions, banks have a very intimate and secure knowledge of their customers—account data provides a very accurate reflection of their lives—and fewer illusions. On the one hand, this enables banks to know precisely what the customer is already doing, and on the other, what they may not be doing yet compared to others. An example of this is the support provided to SMEs. Due to the higher level of transparency resulting from a lower number of account connections, a relatively high level of information security is generated regarding whether the customer already uses certain services (outsourcing, facility management, etc.) or products (factoring, leasing) and what this looks like in comparison to other SMEs.

In addition, banks usually have a large number of employees who are in contact with a large number of customers through various channels. Furthermore, banking products are generally not subject to any capacity restrictions or delivery difficulties.

As a result, it is not surprising that there are quite a number of examples that explicitly reflect the application of the NBA/NBO concept in the banking sector.

So is it "all systems go" at the banks? To answer this, we just have to look at the issues of the recent past: credit certificates for bad real estate loans, borderline interpretation of tax laws on product design (CUM/EX), prioritization of products with high commissions, high turnover rates in security accounts for high handling commissions.

An incomplete list of headlines from the past few years gives way to the suspicion that the results of analytics have not always prevailed in these cases, and suggests that sales pressure and the like have gained the upper hand.

It therefore comes as no surprise that the sector is a top target for financial advisory start-ups. The aforementioned fundamental suitability of the sector for such data-driven approaches in connection with technical and methodical expertise, and the simultaneous historical levels of freedom almost seem to be an invitation.

If the NBO approach is implemented correctly, financial institutions have numerous opportunities to regain lost trust. Could it be possible to learn something from other industries?

4 Banking, NBO and Other Industries

The NBO concept is used in various industries. These industries, such as commerce and telecommunications, are characterized by high customer numbers, high transaction figures and low earnings contributions per customer/transaction. The intention therefore consists of achieving the highest possible accuracy in the most cost-effective way.

Amazon is always cited as a prime example from the commerce sector. The company is an incredible success story and the website offers many well thought-out features to solve customer problems. One example of this is returns management. With regard to NBO, however, everyone has probably already had their own experiences. After buying a television set, you will be offered many additional products such as wall mounts, sound systems, etc., but also other television sets. Is it really likely that you will buy another television set in this situation? This little example illustrates difficulties in successfully implementing the concept. Even a recognized top company has its problems.

Other industries are facing additional challenges. Alongside logistical challenges such as product availability and possibly insufficient IT skills, there is another critical factor: comprehensive customer information. On the one hand, this includes internal information. Banks have a clear advantage in this regard in that they have a complete overview of each individual customer's history based on account information. They also have a database of other accounts or customers at their disposal as well as the ability to create corresponding profiles. This fulfills the two core requirements, i.e., historical data and reference data that can be used in forecasting, and underlines the special suitability of banks as a field of application for the NBO concept. On the other hand, comprehensive information now also includes a multitude of external information from different channels and social media. Thus it is quite possible to deduce which newspapers or television broadcasts are consumed by individuals based on their comments on Twitter and the like. Here again, the aforementioned customer experience/journey comes into play.

5 NBA and CX (Omnichannel, Customer Journey and AI)

Another important aspect when considering the NBA is adaptation to the current technical conditions. As mentioned at the beginning of this chapter, the NBA concept was established several years ago and was one of the first approaches taken to predictive analytics.

Customer management as such naturally continues to pursue the same goals as it did many years ago. Making the right offer to the right customer at the right time is still the top priority. However, tools have developed and therefore the options have increased. This can be illustrated quite well by the following three factors that impact the foundation for making a decision:

1. Observation time
2. Scope of observation
3. Recommendation algorithm

In the past, the time period most focused on was the period leading up to the decision point. The behavior of other customers was only considered at a much later phase of the sales process. In the current context, the entire life cycle of the customer/interested party must be taken into account. In the past, of course, this was mainly due to limitations on information collection and storage. The necessary technology was not available or not usable, at least in part due to cost/benefit analysis.

These technical framework conditions also apply to the scope of observation. In this context, scope indicates the number of different contact channels. Whereas this included only very few channels (call center, affiliated branches, possibly e-mail marketing) in the past, it has since become critical to observe and evaluate all channels in the interplay outlined above. This is not only technically demanding, but also requires comprehensive management of data protection regulations, and cannot be achieved without comprehensive systems for customer (experience) management in combination with coordinated processes in the areas of marketing, sales, service and data management/protection.

Both factors—time and scope—determine the information content that can be derived from the observed customer behavior (customer journey). However, the customer journey comprises significantly more content than just a concrete offer. It is necessary to accompany the customer through a multitude of coordinated actions, at the end of which or during the course of which offers are made from time to time. From this, one can hypothesize that only advanced technology allows for the actual implementation of the NBA concept.

The third influencing factor also lies in the technical environment. The use of artificial intelligence is increasingly finding its way into these systems. Even though AI has already been incorporated in the systems to some extent, it is imperative to understand these procedures. Although a data scientist qualification is very important, it is not yet very widespread in the market and in the relevant specialist areas.

The development of these three influencing factors over time illustrates the rapid development of requirements for the correct and complete implementation of the NBA concept. However, it also becomes clear that the quality of the recommendation must have improved overall due to the significantly larger foundation for decision-making.

6 NBO and Forecasting

What do all these findings in connection with the NBA have to do with forecasting? The intention of the NBO concept has always been to better assess future transactions. NBA is superimposed on this as an overall concept. If a bank succeeds in gaining the trust of its customers by means of consistent, customer relevant information (actions), an NBA approach implemented in line with the current possibilities should not only increase the number of actions for the various points of contact throughout the customer journey, but also the accuracy of the offers. This should have a positive effect on the accuracy of the forecast.

However, an indispensable prerequisite for this is the trustworthy handling[1] of customer data. Within this context, trustworthy refers to both the physical handling (where the data is stored and whether it will be resold, for example) as well as the psychological handling (whether relevant actions can be taken and relevant offers made) of customer data.

---

[1] Bill McDermott: "We all know trust is built in drops, but lost in buckets" (SAP SE, 2019).

In any case, correct implementation also means that individual influences—referred to above as sales pressure—are less likely to occur. Long observation periods and large amounts of data in conjunction with automated algorithms are more difficult to influence. Clear rules of conduct have emerged in connection with the greatly increased mistrust of customers toward companies with regard to data handling. Most likely, these rules will not only be monitored internally, but also by customers and their actions or even through comments in social media.

7 Summary

Banks are in a constant state of upheaval, and it is easy to see that current issues are considerably accelerating this effect. In addition to market requirements and historical as well as ever-increasing current regulatory requirements, topics such as technological change and digitalization are also being addressed. As a result, entry barriers for competitors from the non-banking sector have never been so low. This is partly due to the fact that many banking products are interchangeable. What's more, the value of the advice received by customers does not always live up to expectations.

Within this context, the NBA or NBO concept in conjunction with consistent implementation represents an approach to regaining lost trust. Consistent implementation means using the latest technology, but above all creating offers that are precisely aligned with customer needs. This results in context-based positioning of the corresponding bank products. Whenever customers have the feeling that a product fits their individual context, the probability of buying increases. This increased probability can be measured and leads to improved forecasting. A positive side effect is that, by recognizing the needs and contexts, ideas for new and even better fitting products can arise, thus completing the learning cycle.

Literature

Rawal, P. (2013). AIDA marketing communication model: Stimulating a purchase decision in the minds of the consumers through a linear progression of steps. *International Journal of Multidisciplinary Research in Social Management, 1,* 37–44.

Riedl, R. (1992). AIDA-Formel. In G. Ueding (Ed.), *Historisches Wörterbuch der Rhetorik* (pp. 285–295). Tübingen: Walter de Gruyter GmbH.

SAP SE. (2019). *Why customer experience is everything*. Retrieved January 28, 2019, from SAP News Center https://news.sap.com/2018/11/bill-mcdermott-sap-select-customer-experience-everything/.

Wolny, J., & Charoensuksai, N. (2014). Mapping customer journeys in multi-channel decision-making. *Journal of Direct, Data and Digital Marketing Practice, 15*(April), 317–326.

6

Using Prospect Theory to Determine Investor Risk Aversion

Constantin Lisson

1 Introduction

While technological innovation can enable new forms of value creation, much of the hype about emerging technologies is backed by little genuine innovation. Though all start-up companies claim that their products and services are disruptive, they are often little more than existing services embellished through the liberal use of technical vocabulary. This is especially true of the asset and wealth management industry.

Unlike the proverbial silver bullet, the use of technology alone is not a sufficient condition for adding value (Frederick P. Brooks, 1995). Instead, innovative technologies must be used to solve well-defined problems from within a domain of application. We present a practical application of prospect theory in an investment management setting as an example of how digital technology can facilitate a novel solution to an old problem: Determining investor risk aversion in an empirically valid manner. The importance of a reliable method for estimating investor risk aversion becomes especially apparent in times of increased market volatility, when investors are tempted to liquidate their assets after a downturn, realizing their losses and forfeiting participation in a subsequent market recovery.

C. Lisson (✉)
LIQID, Berlin, Germany
e-mail: constantin.lisson@liqid.de

© The Author(s) 2019
V. Liermann and C. Stegmann (eds.), *The Impact of Digital Transformation and FinTech on the Finance Professional*, https://doi.org/10.1007/978-3-030-23719-6_6

Traditional approaches to estimating investor risk aversion often rely on a combination of qualitative reasoning and imprecise strategy descriptions ("Do you prefer our 'balanced' or our 'moderately dynamic' portfolio?") and the implicit assumption of expected utility maximization. This assumption is empirically questionable and leads to investment decisions that may not be in the investor's best interest. Such approaches typically underestimate the frequency with which extreme outcomes occur, the sensitivity with which investors evaluate these outcomes, and the dependency of the investor's evaluation of a given outcome on whether a positive or a negative return has materialized.

Although the prospect theory model of Kahnemann and Tversky is now widely recognized as the most empirically valid available description of decision-making under uncertainty, it has yet to find widespread adoption in the investment management industry (Kahnemann & Tversky, 1979). One of the reasons for this lack of adoption of prospect theory is its higher complexity than that of approaches based on expected utility maximization. It is difficult, if at all possible, systematically to incorporate practical decision support tools based on prospect theory into a traditional, paper-based investor onboarding process.

Furthermore, prospect theory lacks the formal microeconomic foundations that underpin expected utility theory. These theoretical foundations are crucial to a normative theory of choice under uncertainty. Whether they are crucial in a practical setting depends on whether one aims at achieving perfect rationality or at accounting for the ways in which real-world agents deviate from it. We will argue that empirical validity is more important in an industry setting than axiomatic foundations.

1.1 Scope of This Chapter

To provide a backdrop against which to discuss practical applications of prospect theory, we first revisit the assumptions underlying the expected utility maximization paradigm that is used—implicitly or explicitly—at many investment management firms. We describe how an assessment of investor risk aversion can differ from such a traditional approach and how its digital implementation can make it easier to account for findings from prospect theory. We conclude with a case study on how such a procedure is implemented and successfully used on a daily basis at the digital investment management firm LIQID.

1.2 Structure of This Chapter

Section 2 outlines the theoretical reasoning underlying traditional approaches to evaluating investor risk aversion. We present the axioms underlying the von Neumann-Morgenstern (vNM) utility theorem, discuss their validity in experimental settings and thought experiments, and investigate the empirical validity of the strictly concave utility functions that are typically associated with vNM utility theory. We show that prospect theory may offer a more reliable way of evaluating investor risk preference than vNM utility theory because an investor's cognitive biases materially affect her investment results, so that they must be accounted for. Section 3 presents a practical implementation of prospect theory-based risk assessment at LIQID.

2 Traditional and Prospect Theory-Based Approaches to Explaining Decision-Making Over Uncertain Outcomes

According to the vNM utility theorem, decision-makers who adhere to the four vNM axioms will act as though they are maximizing the expected value of a utility function in a setting of choice under uncertainty. These axioms have to be cumulatively valid for the implications of expected utility to hold in a real-world setting. We will see that the strictly concave utility functions typically associated with vNM rationality are empirically questionable and that the axioms themselves are violated in experimental settings and thought experiments (Briggs, 2017).

2.1 von Neumann-Morgenstern Utility Theory

The expected utility paradigm of vNM defines a preference ordering over outcomes A and B as

$$A \prec B \leftrightarrow u(A) < u(B),$$
$$A \succ B \leftrightarrow u(A) > u(B),$$
$$A \sim B \leftrightarrow u(A) = u(B).$$

Equation 1: Preference ordering.

An outcome A is strictly preferred to an outcome B if the utility derived from outcome A is strictly greater than that derived from outcome B. We can define the preference relations $\preccurlyeq$ and $\succcurlyeq$ for weak preference analogously using $\leq$ and $\geq$ in the definition.

As was shown by von Neumann and Morgenstern (1953), this preference relation based on a utility function is equivalent to the assumption that the decision-maker's preferences adhere to the axioms of **completeness, transitivity, continuity** and **independence**. Such a decision-maker is said to be vNM rational.

While we will see that these axioms are intuitively reasonable, there are theoretical and empirical counterexamples, in which decision-makers do not act in accordance with them. As preparation for the prospect theory model of decision-making under uncertainty, we now review the four axioms and discuss how two of them—the completeness axiom and the transitivity axiom—can lead to empirical and theoretical problems. Recall that the axioms must be collectively valid for the vNM utility theorem to hold. A single credible counter-example is sufficient to cast doubt on the empirical validity of vNM expected utility theory.

Axiom I: Completeness

Let L and M be any two lotteries. A vNM-rational decision-maker will always either prefer one lottery to the other or be indifferent between them, that is

$$L \prec M, M \prec L, \text{or} L \sim M.$$

Equation 2: Axiom I: Completeness.

As a hypothetical counterexample, consider the problem of choosing a career path. This can be seen as a lottery, since a given choice will lead to monetary and nonmonetary outcomes that are uncertain at the time of choosing a career. The agent's utility will depend on these outcomes. An agent may not fulfill the completeness axioms because she may not have evaluated the utility of all of her options, as this is not empirically necessary for making a career choice. Consider an individual who is currently pursuing a given career A and who has never seriously considered the alternative careers B and C. It may be the case that $B \prec A$ and $C \prec A$. It is then conceivable that

$$B \not\prec C \text{ and } C \not\prec B,$$

which by the completeness axiom requires that

$$B \sim C$$

So that the decision-maker is indifferent between the two options. However, indifference would imply that, as soon as an additional reward is added to either B or C, that career option would automatically become preferred over the other. This may not be an accurate representation of the decision-maker's preferences.

Briggs (2017) proposes the example of an electrician who has never seriously considered becoming a singer or an astronaut. Because neither a career as a singer nor a career as an astronaut was ever seriously considered by her, it is accurate to say that she neither prefers becoming a singer to becoming an astronaut, nor does she prefer becoming an astronaut to becoming a singer. In this situation, the completeness axiom implies that, if an additional monetary reward of 100 dollars were added to the career choice of becoming a singer, that career choice would necessarily become the preferred one over becoming an astronaut. It is doubtful that a real-world decision-maker would agree with this statement, which casts doubt on the empirical validity of the completeness axiom.

Axiom II: Transitivity

A decision-maker whose utility function is a transitive order relation and who prefers an outcome M to an outcome L, and outcome N to outcome M, will always prefer outcome N to outcome L, that is

$$L \prec M \text{ and } M \prec N \rightarrow L \prec N.$$

Equation 3: Axiom II: Transitivity.

While this axiom is intuitively reasonable, it can be shown both empirically and theoretically that it is not a requirement for decision-making behavior that may be considered rational. A theoretical counterexample is the thought experiment by Quinn (1990). In this admittedly contrived example, there is a person who receives a monetary reward for inflicting pain on themselves through electric current. This is done using a device with an intensity setting ranging from 0 (off) to 1000 (extreme pain). Suppose that the dial can only be moved up, but not down and that the individual does not feel an increase in intensity from s to $s + 1$, but that they would feel an increase in larger increments. The decision-maker's utility function is increasing in money and decreasing in pain inflicted. In this situation, the agent is confronted with the optimal choice of intensity. The optimal level here is that which best solves the trade-off between the positive contribution to utility received from monetary compensation and the negative contribution to utility from pain inflicted.

In such a situation, it is rational to prefer the higher of any two adjacent levels of intensity, such that $s + 1 \succ s, \forall s \in [0, 1000 - 1]$. However, because increments greater than one inflict significant pain on the decision-maker, she may not prefer a higher level of intensity directly to a lower one that is not immediately adjacent to it, so that for $s' < s''$,

$$\begin{cases} s' \prec s'' \, if \, |s'' - s'| = 1 \\ s' \succ s'' \, if \, |s'' - s'| > 1 \end{cases}$$

Under the premises of the thought experiment, such a preference ordering is not irrational, but it directly contradicts the transitivity axiom.

Axiom III: Continuity

For lotteries $L \preccurlyeq M \preccurlyeq N$, for which we assume that they can be linearly combined, there is a value of $p \in [0, 1]$, for which

$$pL + (1 - p)N \sim M$$

Equation 4: Axiom III: Continuity.

That is, if M is located between L and N within the preference relation, the agent is indifferent between M and an appropriately weighted average of N and L. This axiom appears largely uncontroversial.

Axiom IV: Independence

If $L \preccurlyeq M$, that is, a decision-maker weakly prefers outcome M to outcome L, an alternative outcome N, no matter how strongly weighted, should not matter for the existing preference relation between L and M, as long as N does not affect L and M, that is

$$qL + (1 - q)N \preccurlyeq qM + (1 - q)N$$

Equation 5: Axiom IV: Independence.

for $q \in [0, 1]$. A counterexample to the axiom of independence is the Allais paradox, which is not re-stated here. The interested reader is referred to Allais (1953).

2.2 Shape of the Investor Utility Function

Traditional expected utility theory admits three types of curvature for the utility function:

1. If u is linear, $u(E[X]) = E[u(X)]$ and the agent is risk-neutral; she is indifferent between a certain payoff and a stochastic payoff with an identical first moment;
2. If u is concave everywhere, $u(E[X]) \geq E[u(X)]$ and the agent is risk-averse; she prefers a certain payoff to a stochastic payoff with first moment identical to it;
3. If u is convex everywhere, $u(E[X]) \leq E[u(X)]$ and the agent is risk-seeking; she prefers a stochastic payoff to a certain payoff with identical first moment.

Of these options, concave utility is by far the most commonly chosen one. The assumption of concave utility is based on the empirical observation that people generally display risk-averse behavior when presented with the choice between a gamble and a certain payoff. This is especially true when all outcomes are positive.

When the outcomes of the gamble are negative, however, so that we are concerned with uncertainty surrounding losses, people's behavior changes. When confronted with the choice between a certain negative payoff and an uncertain negative payoff with the same expected value, people will tend to choose the uncertain payoff, even if the maximum loss that can be incurred by this gamble is significantly higher.

This indicates that the more appropriate model for the decision-maker's utility function should be concave for payoffs > 0 and convex for payoffs < 0. This empirical observation was already recognized by Harry Markowitz and more recently formalized and popularized by Kahnemann and Tversky (1979), culminating in the development of prospect theory, which earned Daniel Kahnemann the 2002 Nobel Memorial Prize in Economic Sciences (Fig. 1).

Expected utility theory does not easily admit such a utility function. Prospect theory, on the other hand, proposes value functions with just such curvature but lacks a theoretical foundation. The question then becomes whether theoretical foundations or empirical validity are more important for practical application. We will return to this question after discussing probability weighting under expected utility theory and prospect theory.

2.3 Linear Probability Weighting

Traditional expected utility theory assumes that decision-makers weight the outcomes of a stochastic event according to the objective probabilities

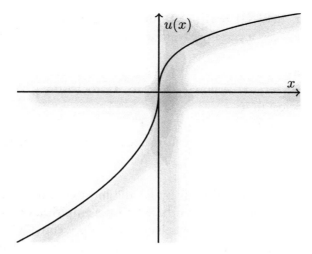

Fig. 1 An empirically valid value function exhibiting concavity (risk aversion) over positive values and convexity (risk-seeking behavior) over negative values

$p_i, i \in [1, \ldots, n]$ with which they occur. In some situations, the assumption that the objective probability of a given event is known may be more appropriate than in others, but there are some interesting situations in which the probabilities are arguably known or at least available.

Consider, for instance the purchase of a lottery ticket. The probability of earning a positive return on a lottery ticket is known, as it is often communicated by the lottery itself. It can therefore be assumed that people are aware that the expected value of a lottery is negative. Why is it, then, that people purchase lottery tickets nonetheless?

According to Kahnemann and Tversky (1979), investors transform probabilities using a weighting function π, even if the true probabilities associated with the outcomes are objectively known, as in the lotto example, where regulators often require some measure of disclosure. This weighting function is purported to have an inverse sigmoidal shape and to lie above the weighting function implied by linear probability weighting for low-probability events and below it for high-probability events. People thus systematically over-weight low-probability outcomes and under-weight high-probability outcomes. Total utility under prospect theory is then given by

$$V = \sum_{i=1}^{n} \pi(p_i) u(x_i).$$

Equation 6: Total utility under prospect theory.

This explains a number of empirically observable behaviors that cannot be explained using expected utility theory. The purchase of lottery tickets is only one of them. As people systematically overestimate the probability of a win, they prefer the purchase of a lottery ticket. Over-insurance is another such phenomenon. As decision-makers systematically overestimate the probability of rare events such as severe disease, accidents, and the like, buying insurance becomes more attractive than not buying insurance.

2.4 Is Utility Theory a Positive or a Normative Enterprise?

The primary strength of vNM utility theory is that it allows us to show that a utility function can be defined using axiomatic foundations, the concavity (or less frequently, convexity, resp.) of which is the same throughout its domain. However, as we saw above, both the strictly concave utility functions typically assumed in vNM utility theory and the axioms themselves are incompatible with decision-making behavior observed in an experimental or observational setting.

We can interpret the incompatibility or vNM utility theory with empirically observed decision-making behavior in two ways. Interpreting utility theory as a purely positive or descriptive enterprise, the work of Kahnemann and Tversky leads us to conclude that vNM utility theory is not an accurate representation of actual decision-making behavior and is therefore not a suitable model (Kahnemann & Tversky, 1979). If, however, we see utility theory as a normative or prescriptive endeavor, it is possible to think of vNM rationality as an ideal that is not empirically verified because real-world agents act irrationally.

In an applied setting, the issue is not which theory is inherently better than the other, but which is useful in modeling the behavior of real-world decision-makers. To return to the example of investment management, which is applied decision-making under uncertainty in its perhaps purest form, it is not reasonable to treat investors as rational decision-makers in the face of overwhelming evidence that they are not. This is the case especially if investors' deviations from rationality have an impact on their realized investment performance, as is the case with liquid securities and investment management solutions in which liquidation can be triggered by investors at any time if their psychological risk tolerance has been exceeded.

In an investment management setting, one of the largest risks to long-term investment performance is an investor's premature liquidation following a market downturn. Historically, downturns in capital markets have been followed by relatively swift recoveries. A premature liquidation decision triggered by an investor is rooted not in the foundational assumptions of microeconomics, but in the prospect theoretical concept of loss aversion. Even under the assumption that vNM rationality is an ideal for decision-making, an investment management service must not assume such behavior because this would underestimate the probability of detrimental early liquidation, which the client can trigger at any time. In this way, liquidity undermines the ability of an investment management service to leverage the advantages that a rational decision-making process may entail. Prospect theory and its applications are thus not a tool for perfectly rational decision-making, but for decision-making that leads to outcomes that are in line with the investor's own view on risks. It is therefore not at all contradictory to conclude that vNM rationality may best describe an ideal decision-maker, while at the same time concluding that prospect theory is more appropriate in an industry setting because it evaluates risks in accordance with the way investors perceive them.

The mean-variance portfolio selection paradigm of Harry Markowitz assumes that investors maximize an objective function that is increasing in expected portfolio return and decreasing in portfolio return volatility (Markowitz, 1952). In other words, investors are assumed to, ceteris paribus, always prefer more return and always prefer less risk. While this seems reasonable, it does not account for the empirical observation that people often exhibit convex utility (i.e., risk-seeking behavior) over negative outcomes, which occur over the short and medium term in almost any portfolio.

An approach that seeks to identify those types of risk aversion that investors actually exhibit should capture not only the investor's sensitivity to volatility (i.e., the annualized standard deviation of the portfolio's returns). Instead, such an approach should include **uncertainty aversion on gains**, **loss aversion** and **investment temperament** to reduce the probability of losses exceeding the investor's psychological ability to bear them. To incorporate these forms of risk aversion, they must be evaluated for each new client in the most objective and user-friendly possible manner. This is the focus of the following section.

3 Case Study: Using Prospect Theory to Select Optimal Portfolios

LIQID Asset Management is a fast-growing German digital investment management firm based in Berlin and focusing on affluent clients. In close cooperation with HQ Trust, a leading German family office, LIQID offers active and passive investment management solutions and access to alternative asset classes like private equity.

One of the cornerstones of LIQID's approach is the prospect theory-based determination of an optimal risk profile for each investor's portfolio. Considering the deviations of the empirically observed behavior of decision-makers from vNM rationality, LIQID, together with BhFS Behavioural Finance Solutions GmbH (BhFS), has implemented a risk assessment test that accounts for the different ways in which investors will respond to outcomes in their portfolios. BhFS is a thought leader in applications of behavioral finance to financial industry problems. The reader is referred to the excellent Bachmann, De Giorgi, and Hens (2018) for a more formal treatment than can be provided here.

3.1 Investor Risk Assessment Test

Figure 2 presents the section of the LIQID risk test that estimates investor loss aversion. The investor is presented with the prospect $(\frac{1}{2}, +3\%; \frac{1}{2}, -3\%)$, corresponding to a risky asset and a risk-free fixed deposit, which earns no

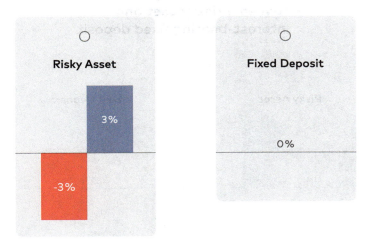

Fig. 2 Choice between a risky asset and a fixed deposit with the same expected return, in which the worst possible scenario is a negative return, so that uncertainty aversion over losses influences the outcome

return. A loss-averse investor will opt for the fixed deposit. In the subsequent iterations of the question, the loss in the negative scenario of the risky asset is progressively reduced until the investor prefers the risky asset to the fixed deposit. This point of preference for the risky asset is used to obtain an estimate of the investor's loss aversion. The later the investor switches from the fixed deposit to the risky asset, the more loss averse she is.

Figures 3 and 4 present the part of the LIQID onboarding process that estimates uncertainty aversion on gains. This question initially presents the user with the prospect ($\frac{1}{2}, 0\%; \frac{1}{2}, +3\%$), corresponding to a risky asset and a risk-free fixed deposit, which earns no return. The difference between this question and the previous one is that now there are no negative outcomes. Even a risk-averse investor will typically prefer the risky asset when the return on the fixed deposit is no more attractive than the worst possible outcome for the risky asset (as in Fig. 3). The return on the fixed deposit is then progressively increased over the subsequent iterations of the question until the investor prefers the fixed deposit. The point at which the fixed deposit becomes preferred is used for calibrating the investor's uncertainty aversion on gains. This point of preference for the fixed deposit may be reached, for example, for the prospect shown in Fig. 4, where the certain outcome for the fixed deposit is now higher than the worst possible outcome for the risky asset. An investor with low uncertainty aversion on gains, however, may

Fig. 3 Choice between a risky asset and a fixed deposit with a zero expected return, where the worst possible scenario is a zero return, so that only uncertainty aversion over gains influences the outcome

Imagine that you are given the choice between a risky asset and a fixed deposit with an annual interest of 1%

Fig. 4 Choice between a risky asset and a fixed deposit with a positive return less than the expected value of the risky asset's return; The fixed deposit's return has been increased relative to the previous question, so as to determine whether the investor still prefers the fixed deposit

continue to prefer the risky asset for a larger number of iterations before switching to the fixed deposit.

As mentioned above, one of the most important nonmarket risks to successful long-term investment is premature liquidation following a downturn. This is captured by the investor's investment temperament. The question shown in Fig. 5 displays a simulated series of cumulative portfolio returns that is presented to the investor. Even in a situation in which the risk-return profile of an investor's portfolio still corresponds to her long-term objectives, it is likely that temporary downturns will make her nervous. In the situation displayed in Fig. 5, it is clear that the total return over the investment period is still positive. Depending on the duration and magnitude of the downturn, this situation may trigger premature liquidation. The investor's answer to this question allows the algorithm to derive an estimate of her ability to tolerate losses psychologically.

Based on the investor's answer to the questions shown above, LIQID uses a proprietary model to map the three parameters of loss aversion, uncertainty aversion on gains, and investment temperament to an optimal risk class. Risk classes map to the percentage of equities and similarly volatile securities in the portfolio and the mapping accounts for the impact of the portfolio's composition on the three measures of risk aversion discussed

Fig. 5 Investor decision following a downturn; This question is used to evaluate investor temperament

above. In this way, the probability of loss events too severe for the investors' risk tolerance is reduced.

4 Summary

We have seen that risk measures that treat gains and losses as equally important to investors fall short of providing a realistic model for decision-making under uncertainty. We discussed the difference between normative models, such as the expected utility maximization paradigm of von Neumann and Morgenstern, and positive models that lack sound theoretical foundations, but are more empirically valid, such as the prospect theory model pioneered by Kahnemann and Tversky (1979). In an investment management setting, one of the largest nonmarket risks to satisfactory long-term portfolio performance is premature liquidation after temporary downturns. In order to appropriately assess the impact of different types of risk on investor behavior, we argued that empirical validity of a decision model is more important in industry applications than axiomatic foundations. We discussed how prospect theory can enable investment management firms to more accurately assess investor risk tolerance, which should lead to better recommendations and improved long-term portfolio performance, as investors are less frequently confronted with downturns of magnitudes they cannot tolerate. We concluded by illustrating how prospect theory can be used in an industry setting while maintaining an intuitive user experience in a digital investor onboarding process.

Literature

Allais, M. (1953). Le Comportement de L'Homme Rationnel Devant Le Risque: Critique Des Postulats et Axiomes de L'École Americaine. *Econometrica, 21,* 503–546.

Bachmann, K. K., De Giorgi, E. G., & Hens, T. (2018). *Behavioural finance for private banking: From the art of advice to the science of advice* (2nd ed.). Hoboken: Wiley.

Briggs, R. (2017). Normative theories of rational choice: Expected utility. In *Stanford encyclopedia of philosophy* (Spring 2017 ed.). Stanford: Metaphysics Research Lab, Stanford University.

Frederick P. Brooks, J. (1995). No silver bullet—Essence and accident in software engineering. In J. Frederick P. Brooks (Ed.), *The mythical man-month, anniversary edition with 4 new chapters* (pp. 1069–1076). Amsterdam, NL: Elsevier Science B.V.

Kahnemann, D., & Tversky, A. (1979). Prospect theory: An analysis of decision under risk. *Econometrica, 47*(2), 263–292.

Markowitz, H. M. (1952). Portfolio selection. *Journal of Finance, 7,* 77–91.

Quinn, W. S. (1990). *The puzzle of the self-torturer.* Cham: Springer.

von Neumann, J., & Morgenstern, O. (1953). *Theory of games and economic behavior.* Princeton, NJ: Princeton University Press.

Part II

Bank Management Aspects

The impact of digitalization and fintech is primarily seen in the domains of CRM[1] or, more generally, in customer interaction as a whole, payments (which could be seen as a part of customer interaction) and crime prevention (e.g., fraud prevention KYC,[2] AML,[3] CTF[4] and cybercrime).[5] The two first domains were introduced and addressed in Part I. In this part, we aim to discuss practical applications of methods, technology and architecture to the important field of bank management

The impact of digitalization on bank management and its different aspects are manifold. Digitalization is used in multiple ways, but there are no real standards or approaches covering all aspects. Nonetheless, there are patterns that can be applied to many domains of bank management.

We grouped the chapters in this part into three domains: (A) improvements in planning, (B) applications in financial risk management, (C) outlook and vision. Naturally, there are other domains that could be addressed as well (e.g., non-financial risk management[6]) but we have focused on these three here. The following statements from the chapters are highlighted by domain.

---

[1]CRM—Customer Relationship Management.

[2]KYC—Know Your Customer.

[3]AML—Anti-Money Laundering.

[4]CTF—Counter-Terrorist Financing.

[5]Which can be summarized under non-financial risk management.

[6]The aspects of non-financial risk management are covered with a minor score in (Harmon, 2019).

96   Part II: Bank Management Aspects

First, we address innovations in the planning process and the ongoing dovetailing of risk management and planning. Chapter 7 "Leveraging Predictive Analytics Within a Value Driver Based Planning Framework" introduces the idea of the "driver-based planning" (Valjanow, Enzinger, & Dinges, 2019). In a nutshell, this consists of identifying the value drivers of the business, thus making planning more strategic. Chapter 8 "Predictive Risk Management" adds planning as a new ingredient in a long-term risk management process (Liermann & Viets, 2019), aiming to avoid the situation the mice are confronted with in Franz Kafka's "A Little Fable" (German: "Kleine Fabel").

"Alas", said the mouse, "the whole world is growing smaller every day. At the beginning it was so big that I was afraid, I kept running and running, and I was glad when I saw walls far away to the right and left, but these long walls have narrowed so quickly that I am in the last chamber already, and there in the corner stands the trap that I am running into."

"You only need to change your direction", said the cat, and ate it up.

Both chapters show the importance of planning and the shift taking place in the controlling department from backward-looking analysis toward more strategic evaluation of options. The trend is to centralize knowledge and interrelations for a holistic view of the financial institutions business model by aligning and connecting individual developments and market developments.

As already mentioned, non-financial risk management is not covered in this part, as they evolved many years ago from operational risk designs. Nevertheless, some domains are touched on in Part III "Regulatory Aspects" of this book (Plenk, Levant, & Bellon, 2019). The level of awareness of the various domains of crime prevention is high because, if a case occurs, the impact (reputational and financial) could be massive. By analyzing behavioral patterns, deep learning algorithms can provide major improvements.

The second domain includes the applications to financial risk management. The methods for the estimations of future developments have evolved. An interesting field in this regard consists of liquidity risk management. A well-established use case in liquidity risk management is the prediction of deposit volumes[7] incorporating cyclical and seasonal effects [see (Ahmadi-Djam & Nordström, 2017) and (Kreynen, Olieman, Doorn, & Spanoghe, 2016)]. While this aspect is widely discussed, we focus on intraday liquidity in Chapter 9 "Intraday Liquidity: Forecast Using Pattern Recognition"

---

[7]The change in deposit volumes is one of the main uncertainties a bank has to deal with in liquidity management (given the bank is active in this product domain).

(Liermann, Li, & Dobryashkina, 2019). The chapter shows how high-frequent cash flow data can be used to detect patterns in the client's payment behavior and how to drive these patterns forward to predict the liquidity situation by currency.

Chapter 10 "Internal Credit Risk Models with Machine Learning" (Thiele & Dittmar, 2019) provides a practical example of rating system implementation using deep learning algorithms. The chapter also compares the standard methods (e.g., linear regression and random forest) used for rating systems regarding their power of prediction. It shows how easy such a rating system can be implemented using open source deep learning frameworks.

The final chapter in this domain picks up on a special aspect in the implementation of real estate risk. Due to the narrowed profitable investment opportunities, volumes in the real estate asset class grew quickly. An integrated risk management and view of the portfolio is still difficult, because of the gap in detailed structured information regarding individual properties. This detailed structured information is key to setting up meaningful integrated risk management for real estate. While the information is available in appraisals, Chapter 11 "Real Estate Risk: Appraisal Capture" (Liermann & Schaudinnus, 2019) introduces a framework for extracting the required information from real estate appraisals using classical NLP[8] approaches like NER[9] and Word2vec.

The last domain of the part consists of two forward-looking and visionary chapters. One chapter describes the importance of network structures and their growing application in financial management while the other chapter depicts a vision of how a CRO[10] can use the new architectures, methods and tools.

Chapter 12 "Managing Internal and External Network Complexity: How Digitalization and New Technology Influence the Modeling Approach" delineates the variety of applications of networks in the financial and risk management field (Enzinger & Grossmann, 2019). Network structures have recently become important in modeling complex interactions and time dependencies such as second-round effects. These methods include neural networks like SOMs,[11] multi-layered networks and ABM.[12]

---

[8]NLP—Natural Language Processing.
[9]NER—Named Entity Recognition.
[10]CRO—Chief Risk Officer.
[11]SOM—Self-Organizing Maps.
[12]ABM—Agent-Based Modeling.

98 Part II: Bank Management Aspects

The final chapter in this part "Big Data and the Cro of the Future" (Harmon, 2019) looks into the mid-term and long-term perspectives of an architecture and methods set to meet the future challenges facing CROs.

Literature

Ahmadi-Djam, A., & Nordström, S. B. (2017). *Forecasting non-maturing liabilities.* Stockholm: Royal Institute of Technology, School of Engineering Sciences.

Enzinger, P., & Grossmann, S. (2019). Managing internal and external network complexity. In V. Liermann & C. Stegmann (Eds.), *The impact of digital transformation and fintech on the finance professional.* New York: Palgrave Macmillan.

Harmon, R. (2019). The CRO of the future. In V. Liermann & C. Stegmann (Eds.), *The impact of digital transformation and fintech on the finance professional.* New York: Palgrave Macmillan.

Kreynen, B., Olieman, C., Doorn, F. v., & Spanoghe, M. (2016). *Time series predictions for bank.* Delft: TU Delft.

Liermann, V., & Schaudinnus, N. (2019). Real estate risk—appraisal capture. In V. Liermann & C. Stegmann (Eds.), *The impact of digital transformation and fintech on the finance professional.* New York: Palgrave Macmillan.

Liermann, V., & Viets, N. (2019). Predictive risk management. In V. Liermann & C. Stegmann (Eds.), *The impact of digital transformation and fintech on the finance professional.* New York: Palgrave Macmillan.

Liermann, V., Li, S., & Dobryashkina, V. (2019). Intraday liquidity—forecast using pattern recognition. In V. Liermann & C. Stegmann (Eds.), *The impact of digital transformation and fintech on the finance professional.* New York: Palgrave Macmillan.

Plenk, M., Levant, L., & Bellon, N. (2019). How technology (or algorithms like deep learning and machine learning) can help to comply with regulatory requirements. In V. Liermann & C. Stegmann (Eds.), *The impact of digital transformation and fintech on the finance professional.* New York: Palgrave Macmillan.

Thiele, M., & Dittmar, H. (2019). Credit risk models and deep learning. In V. Liermann & C. Stgemann (Eds.), *The impact of digital transformation and fintech on the finance professional.* New York: Palgrave Macmillan.

Valjanow, S., Enzinger, P., & Dinges, F. (2019). Digital planning—driver-based planning levraged by predictive analytics. In V. Liermann & C. Stegmann (Eds.), *The impact of digital transformation and fintech on the finance professional.* New York: Palgrave Macmillan.

7

Leveraging Predictive Analytics Within a Value Driver-based Planning Framework

Simon Valjanow, Philipp Enzinger and Florian Dinges

1 Introduction

1.1 Introduction to the Subject

The impetus provided by the continuing high competitive pressure in the financial institutions sector, triggered among other things by agile new fintech companies and the low-interest environment on the one hand, and the disruptive innovations of digitalization on the other, will inevitably assert itself in the further development of bank management and financial controlling departments. This impetus results in the further development of controlling concepts as well as the use of new technologies and can build on an increasingly wider availability of data. One of the predestined and most promising concepts for further development is value driver-based planning, which uses predictive analytics as part of data mining to obtain

---

S. Valjanow (✉) · F. Dinges
ifb AG, Grünwald, Germany
e-mail: simon.valjanow@ifb-group.com

F. Dinges
e-mail: florian.dinges@ifb-group.com

P. Enzinger
ifb International AG, Zurich, Switzerland
e-mail: philipp.enzinger@ifb-group.com

© The Author(s) 2019
V. Liermann and C. Stegmann (eds.), *The Impact of Digital Transformation and FinTech on the Finance Professional*, https://doi.org/10.1007/978-3-030-23719-6_7

a broad spectrum of methods for forecasting and opens up new possibilities for optimizing planning. The use of predictive analytics methods provides transparency and traceability in the identification and validation of causal relationships as well as the estimation of the materiality of individual value drivers, so as to consistently support systematic inclusion of macroeconomic and market parameters in the value driver models or trees, while also significantly increasing the sustainability of these parameters. However, conceptual extensions and delimitations as well as a systematic approach are required to raise the optimization potential, i.e., to transfer it from theoretical considerations to concrete line operation applications. This chapter focuses on these conceptual considerations as well as the transition to further development of value driver-oriented planning.

1.2 Structure of the Chapter

We will first provide an overview of the required technical basics and then present the use of R for realizing and programming the algorithms necessary for mapping and testing causal relationships. We will subsequently examine an application case for deriving market volumes by forecasting future sales opportunities for mortgage loans using regression of market parameters. The last section includes a recapitulation of the key technical and implementation-oriented issues as well as a conclusion regarding the potential and the outlook for this concrete area of predictive analytics application.

2 Main Part

2.1 Technical Principles

2.1.1 Scope of Integrated Value Driver-Oriented Planning

Planning is not a clearly defined term and can be found in various forms. A project or company result can be planned. Budgeting and planning are sometimes used synonymously and qualifiers such as integrated or advanced result in local or company-specific interpretations. As such, it is important that we first define and delimit the integrated and value driver-oriented planning described here.

All plans have the aim of abstracting a future state based on expectations at the time the plan is created, thus involving an allocation of resources to achieve the target state. Planning is therefore a forecast, thus requiring a decision to be made under uncertainty (Wild, 1982).

The subject of planning in the following analysis is a medium-term or multi-year plan for a company or financial institution. The forecast thus includes investment and allocation of resources to achieve a targeted P&L result and balance sheet status, while not exceeding defined risk limits. Within this context, the term integrated indicates that all necessary components for mapping the future result, cost and risk scenarios are technically consistent in themselves and in relation to each other (Fischer, 2015), and mapped in a comprehensive framework (see also Fig. 1), i.e., the data lineage (from local branch sales to the consolidated income statement) is ensured and uniform definitions and use of data and methods are enforced. Value driver (Rappaport, 1986; Copeland, Koller, & Murrin, 1998) based means that planning values are not defined at the level of a financial statement item, such as the net interest margin (NIM) contribution, but based on variables that drive the NIM contribution or significantly influence it (Schäfer, 2009). The profit/loss item is thus determined based on the causal relationship between the variables (for example, new business volume in lending business in connection with the expected margin) and the profit/loss item (NIM contribution).

In summary, integrated and value driver-oriented planning must cover the following key issues to make an effective contribution to bank management:

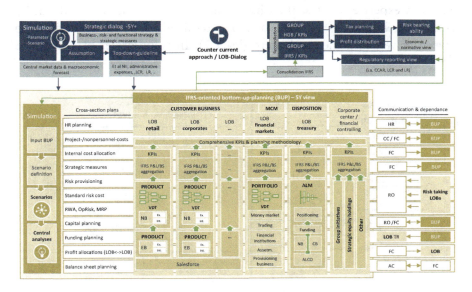

Fig. 1 Example of overall planning framework

- Operationalization of the strategy in terms of profit target and risk appetite
- Medium-term view of operational development of the business segments
- Resource allocation (equity, human capital and IT)
- Transparency with regard to sources of income, costs and risks
- Benchmark in plan/actual comparison reporting
- Goal setting and incentive function for plan implementation

For simplification purposes, the synonym value driver planning is used in the following for integrated and value driver-oriented planning.

2.1.2 The Value Driver Model Concept and Design

As part of value driver planning, the causal relationships are to be defined conceptually and summarized in a model. Mapping to value driver trees (model) has become an established means of illustrating the defined causal relationships. Individual value driver trees are in turn integrated into the overall framework, resulting in implementable value driver planning (see Fig. 2).

A top–down approach can be used to design a value driver tree (see figure below). Modeling is based on the result item here. This means the result item is broken down in alignment with the drivers. The drivers are initially selected as expert estimates, then historically validated and adjusted until a sustainable relationship is established. The result is a functional relationship between drivers and the result item (level 1). In value driver planning, the

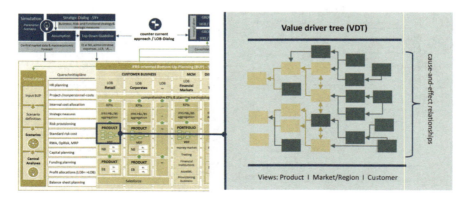

Fig. 2 Value driver trees embedded within the planning framework

defined drivers of the first level can be used as planning objects. If drivers of the first level are themselves subject to a causal relationship, the top–down procedure can be further used, so that the driver of the first level becomes an intermediate result, which in turn results from drivers of the second level. The value driver tree is developed successively with each further level or branch. The defined tree can then be used for planning. Planning objects are thus all drivers in the tree and determined for the years of medium-term planning by the respective planner (planned value per driver and per planning year). The resulting item for the planning year is therefore mathematically derived from the function of drivers and intermediate results (Fig. 3).

A basic distinction must be made between internal and external drivers. If the institute is itself capable of designing the driver (e.g., number of employees in sales), it is an internal driver. If, on the other hand, the institute cannot influence the driver (e.g., development of the gross domestic product), it is an external driver. External drivers should particularly be modeled if, in addition to medium-term planning (base case), alternative scenarios (deviation from base case) are also to be determined, as scenarios can be linked to different points of departure from the macroeconomic forecast (base case). To be able to derive the effect of the changed initial situation on the result item, the external drivers affected must be integrated into the value driver tree (Kappes & Schentler, 2015).

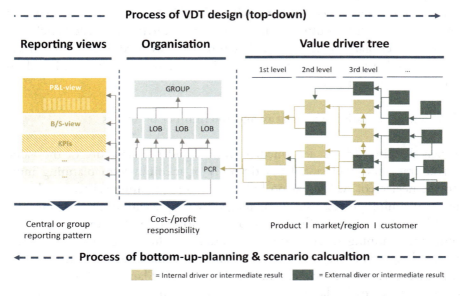

Fig. 3 Value driver tree design principle

In practice, several value driver trees should be defined along with the business model. Alignment with products, customers and markets or regions has proven worthwhile in this regard to map specific driver combinations. This alignment is also helpful in the planning process, as the relevant value driver trees can be released to the profit center for planning.

2.1.3 Challenges

Although value driver planning represents a transparent and comprehensible instrument of medium-term planning that is already being used in its entirety or in parts by many institutes, challenges arise in development and implementation in practice, which should be taken into consideration.

Three essential success factors are:

1. Objective derivation and determination of causal relationships

As there are no generally accepted causal relationships or a generally accepted industry standard for financial institutions, this is usually based on a few intuitive drivers in the form of expert estimates. The required objective validation and testing of non-intuitive drivers and a multitude of driver combinations is rarely conducted. This is mainly due to the complex methods and effort involved. There is also a lack of automated processing, suitable tools and necessary data, with which initial quantitative tests and validation as well as routine back-testing can be carried out. The benefits of a value driver planning model are therefore not fully used. Important drivers remain unidentified, which makes deviation analysis more difficult in subsequent target/actual comparisons.

2. Operationalization: granularity and the number of drivers

When defining drivers, intermediate results and the structure of the value driver trees, the operational practicability of medium-term planning must not be neglected. As long as no fully automated planning exists, the drivers in the planning process must be managed by people with limited resources.

When the almost infinite number of drivers implies improved planning and planning security, this often leads to a high degree of granularity in the design with very many drivers. However, this is also accompanied by increased planning effort and model complexity. Planning should include each driver for each planning year, different products, regions, etc. and each additional driver increases the effort for the planning profit and cost centers. A high level of complexity leads to less acceptance outside the design team, as the planning methodology is not among the core competences at the management levels or in the profit and cost centers where planning is carried out.

Therefore, there is a trade-off between the granularity of the value driver trees and the planning effort as well as the acceptance of the planners involved (Rieg, 2015). Due to the fact that there is no benchmark or an optimal number of drivers, it is advisable to focus on a few essential drivers on the one hand and develop the value driver trees in cooperation with the planners/market units on the other hand.

3. Knowing the drivers vs. being able to plan/forecast the drivers

In addition to their significance to the result item, drivers should also be examined with regard to factual predictability (Zaich, Witzemann, & Schröckhaas, 2012). One illustrative, albeit exaggerated, example of this is the fact that internet availability has a pronounced impact on digital business models and thus, for example, on the essential sales channel for direct banking or blockchain based promissory note issuance. This would certainly constitute a driver. However, it is difficult to estimate the actual availability or restrictions over the next four to five years and the concrete impact of these parameters on online business. Therefore, it is advisable to weigh predictability when integrating an additional driver, especially if it is an external driver.

2.1.4 The Application Areas of Predictive Analytics in the Planning Process

Predictive Analytics

The term predictive analytics basically comprises all the statistical tools that allow a statement to be made about the probability of occurrence and/or the effects of certain events. These tools range from simple regression models to complex machine learning algorithms. The planning process naturally includes short and medium-term quantification of P&L, balance sheet and risk figures and it is therefore intuitive that the scope of predictive analytics tools can be extended to planning. In the planning process, macroeconomic data is, among other things, converted into economic forecasts, which are then incorporated in the planning process. Aside from expert estimates, no market standard has established itself to date for these chains of effects between macroeconomic data and planning results. The methods have been available for a long time, but the modular system architectures that have often evolved over time prevent the data from being used systematically in the planning process. The mutually reinforcing drivers of technological change and the associated regulatory innovations [BCBS 239 (Basel Committee on Banking Supervision, 2013), etc.] are causing concepts such as single source of truth and central data hubs as well as group-wide data and method glossaries to become increasingly mature in the financial sector and thus enabling more effective use of data. The idea behind value driver-oriented planning is to allow internal and external data to flow into the planning process and to provide a toolbox of methods, with which to process this data.

2.2 Value Driver Planning Use Cases—Statistical Methodology and Application

Consideration of external value drivers in the modeling of plan variables requires the establishment of causal relationships in a value driver model (e.g., Fig. 4 middle pillar). As can be seen in the figure, balance sheet and profit and loss statement items must be broken down into their individual components (top–down) to identify the value drivers. In the lending business, for example, net interest income can be divided into two components:

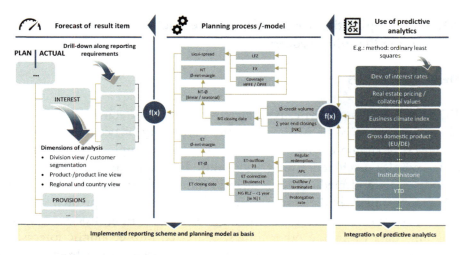

Fig. 4 Process-oriented illustration of the inclusion of external value drivers

the expected credit volume and the interest margin with which it is to be placed on the market. The dependency between credit volume and interest margin must be delimited in the model. For the credit volume, the market share can be modeled based on the institution's own history and made dependent on internal and external value drivers. The dependence on interest conditions can be taken into account in the model as an internal value driver. Alternatively, from a market perspective, the credit volume can be modeled as long as it is defined in a geographical and product-specific way. The interest conditions are then included using the market share that the institution has in the analysis.

After successful identification of the components that can be modeled (endogenous) in the value driver model, internal and external value drivers (exogenous) must be identified using the available data. In the following, the key planning figure business volume is considered first. Internal data including the industry or region are suitable for defining portfolios that have common external value drivers. In particular, new business should be distinguished from changes in the volume of existing business. Internal value drivers, such as the number of sales staff or advertising budget, can influence the volume of new business, as can external value drivers, such as unemployment rates or property prices. Statistical modeling is used to establish a causal relationship between the endogenous key planning figure and the exogenous value drivers. A natural candidate for statistical analysis consists of the group of linear models. The results of these models are accessible and easy to communicate, thus making them well suited for management and planning purposes. It is important to note here that standard linear regression models do not recognize causal relationships. Correlations can only be examined with regard to their statistical significance. Therefore, professional assessment of the chains of effects is indispensable if regression models are used to model them (Klauck & Wünnemann, 2010).

When using this methodology, several exogenous variables (internal and external value drivers) can be placed in relation to one endogenous variable (e.g., new business volume). In the analysis, variable coefficients are determined for each exogenous variable, which describe the causal relationship assuming all other things remain unchanged. An estimated linear model is shown in Fig. 5, which places the average business volume for business customers of a German bank in relation to various macroeconomic parameters. The coefficient of GDP_DE can now be interpreted as meaning that if GDP

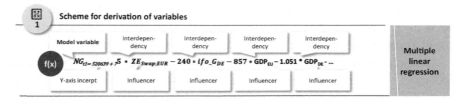

Fig. 5 Example of a linear model

per capita in Germany decreases by €100, the average business volume will increase by about €105,000.

The determined parameters can therefore be used to ensure the model sufficiently depicts the scenarios required for planning. For the business volume, external value drivers that have a significant causal relationship must be identified in the same. In a first step, standardized macroeconomic parameters are made available by the economics department or an external data provider. Algorithms are available to assess significance by analyzing a portfolio of macroeconomic parameters and their subsets to determine causal relationships with the endogenous variable. An algorithm searches for the model with the highest quality by either gradually adding new variables to the zero model or gradually reducing the full model. Alternatively, a model can be created in an initial manual process that is checked for sufficient significance as part of a process carried out at regular intervals. In this variant, a technical connection between the value drivers and the endogenous key planning figure should be devised, which is then statistically analyzed and optimized with regard to quality. There are a number of criteria for the quality of a model, the best known being the Akaike information criterion (AIC) and the Bayesian information criterion (BIC) (Davidson & MacKinnon, 1999). Within the process of quality optimization, the tendency of the coefficients should always be economically questioned, as is also the case in a traditional planning process. If trends contradict expectations, the cause should be analyzed and assumptions questioned. Once the coefficients have been determined, the forecast from the economics department (planning for internal value drivers) can be entered in the model to obtain the forecast for the key planning figure. This can serve as direct input for the planning process or as a business challenge for the expert estimate. This methodological approach also ensures the macroeconomic scenario is consistently taken into account in planning.

2.3 Real Estate Market—Use Case

For the purpose of usability and better understanding, the following use case demonstrates the value driver selection process and describes intuitive methods for modeling the correlations between value drivers and balance sheet variables. The real estate data used for modeling was collected in an urban area in Germany. A German bank's relative market share of mortgages for the area is also used as an endogenous variable, which is affected by external value drivers.

2.3.1 Value Drivers

To select values drivers in the real estate market, potential value drivers must first be identified and then analyzed for significance in terms of correlation with the endogenous variable. Value driver identification requires an in-depth understanding of what influences real estate prices, which in turn drives the demand for mortgages. The statistical tool box described above can be used to analyze the correlations. For this use case, we examine the mortgage demand in a large central German city, which we will simply refer to as "The City".

In the first step, the available living space that the municipal government assigns to housing development will be analyzed as the initial value driver for the number of mortgages. New housing developments are often built on credit and we therefore expect a positive relationship with mortgage volume.

In the second step, we will look at the total building costs incurred in The City for housing developments as a proxy for real estate spending capacity. We also assume a positive relationship with mortgage volume here.

Other candidates for value drivers include the building's micro-location (infrastructure such as schools, medical doctors, public transportation and grocery stores), macro-location (price development in the area), or population growth in The City. For the sake of simplicity, we have defined a two-factor model with the value drivers "new available living space" and "total building costs".

Some of the aforementioned drivers will be analyzed in this example. Both figures show an increasing trend for new available space and total building costs over time. We therefore predict positive development of the mortgage demand in The City (Figs. 6 and 7).

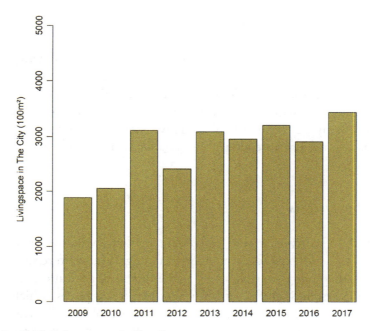

Fig. 6 Available living spaces in The City

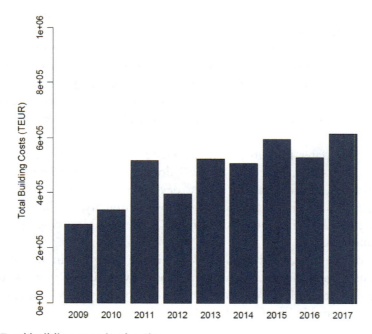

Fig. 7 Total building costs in The City

2.3.2 Simple Linear Regression on the Real Estate Market

Based on the presented data above, the real estate market in The City is surveyed using "The Mortgages Bank" as an exemplary Bank operating in The City's mortgages sector.

For modeling purposes, we need to specify a dependent variable. To estimate the market share of a particular institute, we will specify two models—one for the mortgage demand in The City and one for the mortgage volume that can be sold by The Mortgage Bank. This allows us to model the market share both endogenously and dynamically by dividing the estimated mortgage volume by the mortgage demand. If we were to model the market share directly, we would just gain a linear trend over time. Specifying the boundaries (0, 1) for the endogenous variable can also be challenging. The new available living space and the total building costs variables will be used as the exogenous variables in the following analysis.

We use the statistics software R to analyze the data for regression (an introduction to linear regression can be found in Sect. 2.1 in Liermann, Li, & Schaudinus, 2019). The following figure shows the results, which are generated using the summary function in R (Fig. 8).

As can be seen in the last figure, both value drivers are significant at a 5% level of significance for our bank and market model (Figs. 9 and 10).

As we can see, the relative market share increases over time due to the rise in mortgage demand (upper figure). At a granular level, the upper figure shows a similar trend between market and bank (upper line market, lower line bank), but the bank's development is less dynamic relative to the market. Now we will have a closer look at The Mortgage Bank's market share prediction (second figure). We generate the data using the "predict" function for 2018 and the following years, so we can see the predicted market (points) and the smoothed trend (line) in the figure over the years.

As this example shows, we can predict the relative market share for the following years using ordinary regression analysis. As described above, regression will improve as we implement more value driver data.

112 S. Valjanow et al.

```
Call:
glm(formula = real estate$Bank_vol ~ real estate$LivingSpace +
real estate$BuildingCosts, family = gaussian)


Deviance Residuals:
     Min        1Q      Median       3Q        Max
    -6356     -3718      -2498      3624      13264

Coefficients:
                              Estimate      Std. Error      t value      Pr(> | t | )
(Intercept)                 -1077.9125     19390.6485       -0.056       0.95747
real estate$LivingSpace       -81.5023        29.0927       -2.801       0.03110    *
real estate$BuildingCosts       0.6639         0.1379        4.813       0.00296   **


Signif. codes:   0 '***' 0.001 '**' 0.01 '*' 0.05 '.' 0.1 ' ' 1


(Dispersion parameter for gaussian family taken to be 52675612)

       Null deviance:     9038962572    on 8    degrees of freedom
    Residual deviance:     316053674    on 6    degrees of freedom
    AIC: 189.91

Number of Fisher Scoring iterations: 2



Call:
glm(formula = real estate$Market_vol ~ real estate$LivingSpace +
real estate$BuildingCosts)


Deviance Residuals:
     Min         1Q       Median       3Q         Max
   -7934.5     -4340.3     -577.1     1229.9     10537.2

Coefficients:
                              Estimate      Std. Error      t value      Pr(>|t|)
(Intercept)                 23211.3743     18185.3384        1.276       0.2490
real estate$LivingSpace      -100.6828        27.2843       -3.690       0.0102    *
real estate$BuildingCosts       1.2279         0.1294        9.492       7.79e-05  ***


Signif. codes:   0 '***' 0.001 '**' 0.01 '*' 0.05 '.' 0.1 ' ' 1

(Dispersion parameter for gaussian family taken to be 46330576)

       Null deviance:     6.0483e+10    on 8    degrees of freedom
    Residual deviance:     2.7798e+08    on 6    degrees of freedom
    AIC: 188.75

Number of Fisher Scoring iterations: 2
```

Fig. 8 Regression results

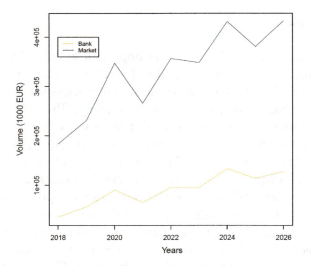

Fig. 9 Mortgage market development

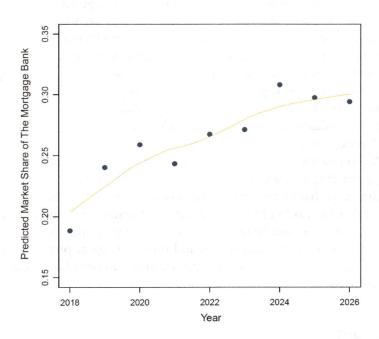

Fig. 10 Market share prediction

2.4 Conclusion

As shown, medium-term planning is an important building block in corporate management. Investments, i.e., the allocation of scarce resources, such as available capital, are allocated to the business segments based on planning and are therefore tied up for the time being. The value driver-based approach increases transparency. Causal relationships for business success serve as a foundation and provide explanations and starting points for subsequent target/actual comparison. Planning quality and significance increase significantly. Although the advantages are obvious, in practice there is often a lack of suitable tools for defining value driver trees appropriately and comprehensibly. The statistical methods used for predictive analytics are the obvious choice when it comes to closing this gap. The combination of expert knowledge and objective methods allows further potentials of value driver-based planning to be realized for practical use. However, IT support and corresponding data histories are required to increase these potentials and derive connections with external drivers. The aim here must include achieving a high degree of automation, standardization and validity. Suitable tools and programs that also offer the necessary performance are already available today.

For many financial controlling departments, introducing these tools still requires entering new terrain and therefore a goal-oriented and evolutionary approach is recommended for implementation. To achieve an appropriate cost–benefit ratio, a pilot phase should first be implemented in line with the user story. It is advisable to start with one product or business area to then roll out the findings and the methodological know-how gained across the entire planning model.

In addition to medium-term planning, other applications in financial controlling (including forecasts during the year) can be optimized using predictive analytics, so that implementation costs can be further scaled by extending them to other forecasting functions in financial controlling, and the benefits of predictive analytics can be felt across a broad range of operations.

In summary, the increasing spread and proper usage of predictive analytics can be expected to significantly optimize and improve planning in financial institutions.

Literature

Basel Committee on Banking Supervision. (2013). *Principles for effective risk data aggregation and risk reporting.* Basel.

Copeland, T., Koller, T., & Murrin, J. (1998). *Unternehmenswert. Methoden und Strategien für eine wertorientierte Unternehmensführung (2. akualisierte und erw. Auflage)*. Frankfurt/Main: Campus.

Davidson, R., & MacKinnon, G. J. (1999). *Econometric theory and methods*. Oxford: Oxford University Press.

Fischer, T. (2015). *Grundlagen, Instrumente und Entwicklungsperspektiven (2. Aufl.)*. Stuttgart: Schäffer-Poeschel.

Kappes, M., & Schentler, P. (2015). Planung mit Treibermodellen für mehr Steuerungsmöglichkeiten und Effizienz. In R. Gleich, S. Gänßlen, M. Kappes, U. Kraus, J. Leyk, & M. Tschandl (Eds.), *Moderne Instrumente der Planung und Budgetierung. Innovative Ansätze und Best Practice für die Unternehmenssteuerung*. Freiburg: Haufe-Lexware.

Klauck, K.-O., & Wünnemann, C. (2010). Wirkungsketten im Risikomanagment - Abbildung von Wechselwirkungen zwischen Risikofaktoren (Bank-Verlag, Ed.) *Risiko-Manager., 1*(4), 20–24.

Liermann, V., Li, S., & Schaudinus, N. (2019). Mathematical background of machine learning. In V. Liermann & C. Stegmann (Eds.), *The impact of digital transformation and fintech on the finance professional*. New York: Palgrave Macmillan.

Rappaport, A. (1986). *Creating shareholder value: The new standard for business performance*. New York: Free Press and Collier Macmillan.

Rieg, R. (2015). *Planung und Budgetierung*. Wiesbaden: Galber.

Schäfer, M. (2009). Moderne Planungsverfahren: Von der traditionellen Budgetierung zur kennzahlenorientierten Planung. In B. Jelinek & M. Hannich (Eds.), *Wege zur effizienten Finanzfunktion in Kreditinstituten* (pp. 453–468). Wiesbaden: Gabler.

Wild, J. (1982). *Grundlagen der Unternehmensplanung (WV-Studium, Bd. 26.4. Aufl.)*. Leverkusen-Opladen: Westdeutscher Verlag.

Zaich, R., Witzemann, T., & Schröckhaas, B. (2012). Forecasting in volatilen Zeiten - eine Herausforderung für Unternehmen. In U. Schäffer (Ed.), *Herausforderung Volatilität. Controlling & Management Review, 56* (pp. 28–33). Wiesbaden: Gabler.

8

Predictive Risk Management

Volker Liermann and Nikolas Viets

1 Introduction

Risk management practices, particularly with regard to financial risk management, have certainly improved in the aftermath of the most recent financial crisis. This is true both for financial and non-financial organizations and has been driven to a large degree by regulatory initiatives around the globe such as EMIR[1] (Dodd-Frank Act[2] Title VII in the US) or CRR[3]/CRD.[4]

Nevertheless, many organizations still have deficits in their approach to risk management, and this is especially the case for financial institutions. Either certain types of risk—although material with regard to the

---

[1]European Market Infrastructure Regulation.

[2]More precisely the Dodd–Frank Wall Street Reform and Consumer Protection Act was the US regulatory response to the 2008 global financial crisis.

[3]Capital requirements regulation.

[4]Capital requirements directive.

V. Liermann (✉)
ifb AG, Grünwald, Germany
e-mail: volker.liermann@ifb-group.com

N. Viets
ifb International AG, Zurich, Switzerland
e-mail: nikolas.viets@ifb-group.com

© The Author(s) 2019
V. Liermann and C. Stegmann (eds.), *The Impact of Digital Transformation and FinTech on the Finance Professional*, https://doi.org/10.1007/978-3-030-23719-6_8

institution's business model—are not being actively managed at all (real estate risk in mortgage institutions is probably the most prominent example). Or the risks are not managed appropriately in terms of methodology (e.g., only applying the concept of Value at Risk but not stress testing) and/or product coverage (e.g., ignoring credit risk in structured products). A general problem that can still be observed in most companies is that risk managers are fairly short-sighted, applying nothing more than a one-year horizon in their evaluation of the organization's risk situation.

Stress tests have been imposed by regulators in recent years that address some of these shortcomings. The main initiatives in this context are the European EBA[5] or ECB[6] stress test and American variants DFAST (Dodd-Frank Act Stress Test) performed by the FDIC[7] as well as CCAR (Comprehensive Capital Analysis and Review) and CLAR (Comprehensive Liquidity Assessment and Review) conducted by the Fed.[8] These stress test initiatives all have in common that they project the risk situation for one to three years into the future (with regulatory measurement concepts such as risk-weighted assets).

This shift toward a multi-period perspective can also be observed in the accounting landscape, with the CECL (Current Expected Credit Loss) framework introduced by the FASB,[9] the EV ("Erwarteter Verlust"— Expected loss) concept currently under development by Swiss FINMA[10] and with stage 2 of LECL (lifetime expected credit loss) within the IFRS 9 impairment regime.

Applying a multi-period view in stress testing requires inclusion of additional information (i.e., planning data for new business) to achieve meaningful statements. When looking at interest rate risk in the banking book and structural liquidity risk, planning figures have already become an important component, at least from a regulatory reporting point of view. Regulatory concepts are aimed at capturing key indicators (such as net interest income or the liquidity coverage ratio) at future points in time.

However, most risk domains still only incorporate existing business (e.g., models for portfolio credit risk, market risk in the trading book and short-term liquidity risk).

---

[5]European Banking Authority.

[6]European Central Bank.

[7]Federal Deposit Insurance Corporation.

[8]Federal Reserve.

[9]Financial Accounting Standards Board.

[10]Swiss Financial Markets Authority (Eidgenössische Finanzmarktaufsicht).

Fig. 1 Overview of the risk management pyramid—goals of risk management

The rest of this chapter is structured as follows: We begin Sect. 2 with strategic management considerations to show why we think a new approach to assessing risk is recommendable. Section 3 introduces the concepts of transversal risk and value driver design required to develop a risk projection framework that incorporates planning data, which is the focus of Sect. 4. We then provide a brief summary and conclude the chapter with perspectives on future developments in banks' risk management practices (Sect. 5).

2 Strategic Considerations: The Risk Management Pyramid

2.1 Predicting Profits Requires Predicting Risks

Figure 1 shows the three levels of modern risk management. The first level is aimed at assessing the risks faced today and preventing a bank from taking risks that instantly threaten its survival. The methods employed are Value at Risk and, to some extent, stress testing. These methods rely on data for existing business. Stress testing can be enhanced not only by altering the parameters, but also by identifying the drivers behind the parameter changes. An example for such a risk driver is the real estate market, which can be attached to probability of default (PD) and to loss given default (LGD) or, to be more precise, to the collateral value. Real estate risk in this environment is called a transversal[11] risk in conjunction with portfolio credit risk.

The second layer addresses the issue of whether risks conform to the overall strategy. The first challenge for many institutions is that they do not have a quantitative risk strategy. A quantitative risk strategy is a projection of risk exposure into the future. This projection can include various business (planning) scenarios as well as various market data and parameter scenarios. Defining the most probable scenario allows for an ex-post comparison of planned vs. actual risk exposure. Forward-looking alignment of the risk situation (i.e., the risks taken) facilitates testing of whether risks are developing according to plan. This approach enables the risk manager to discover deviations at an early stage with more options remaining to redirect and adjust than in traditional short-term risk management.

The third level in Fig. 1 represents an ex-post analysis to evaluate whether risks incurred are (at least) in balance with their respective profits. The main challenge here consists of attributing one unit of earnings to the associated unit of risk of a certain type. What might look like a trivial performance attribution exercise is actually an issue that many financial institutions cannot accurately respond to. And bear in mind that taking risk, managing risk and earning the risk premium is (or should be) the core business of financial institutions.

2.2 Scenario-Based Planning

Scenario-based (risk) planning integrates a multi-period perspective on risk management and value driver-oriented stress testing in a single concept. One of the two key components introduced is to take new business into account: financial planning data. This element allows for a multi-period projection of risk exposure. The other key component is designing value driver-based (stress) scenarios.

Value driver-based stress testing has two parts. The first step consists of identifying value drivers and their link to risk parameters or market data, respectively. Risk parameters in stress scenarios are then shifted, not arbitrarily but implicitly, by shifting comprehensible value drivers. This second step is often performed by way of expert judgment. At the end of the process, analysis is largely driven by a supply-and-demand calculus, which can

---

[11]Transversal risk refers to a risk with an impact across multiple risk types (e.g., credit risk or liquidity risk).

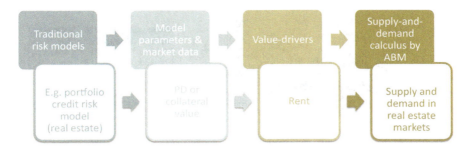

Fig. 2 Scenario-based planning including value driver modeling by ABM

be supported by agent-based models (ABM). The main advantage of agent-based models is that heterogeneous agent behavior can be defined at agent level. The impact of the behavior defined at micro-level is then analyzed at aggregate or macro-level.

Figure 2 illustrates the entire process as described. For example, supply and demand for real estate and the impact this has on rental prices can be simulated. Rental prices in turn affect both collateral values as well as the probability of default of property finance (if the loan is redeemed by the property's cash flows). Altered collateral values and the probability of default are processed by the portfolio credit risk model to calculate Credit Value at Risk. Value at Risk thus represents a projection of the risk situation given a certain supply and demand constellation.

3 Transversal Risks and Value Driver Design

The global financial crisis revealed that traditional risk management methods are not able to identify, let alone measure, all the financial risks that financial institutions are exposed to. Even, in 2018 the insight added by the regulatory stress test exercises is questioned in Europa.[12] We thus need to add a new perspective to the definition of risk. Transversal risks stand crosswise to conventional (and well-established) risk types and their identification helps in assessing the impact of certain events on an institution's risk situation. Value driver design aims to discover whether the movement of factors that affect risk and price can be linked to a set of background factors (the value

---

[12]Daniéle Nouy at a the conference in Frankfurt see also (Deters & Kröner, 2018).

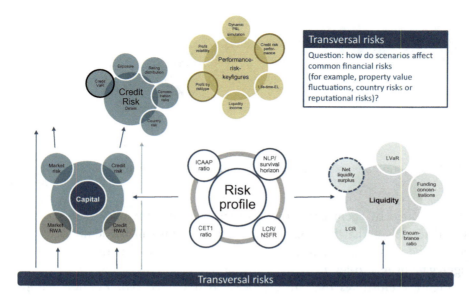

Fig. 3 Transversal risks

drivers). Combining these two trends provides a new tool set for identifying and analyzing previously undiscovered future threats.

3.1 Transversal Risks

We start by presenting a formal definition and then illustrate this based on two practical examples.

3.1.1 Definition

Etymologically, the word transversal comes from Latin transversus and means across or crosswise. A transversal risk is thus a risk that acts crosswise to conventional risk types by affecting more than one type of financial risk at once.

As shown in Fig. 3 the concept of transversal risks is intended to quantify the impact of a trend or an event on the organization's risk profile.[13] The risk profile is usually expressed in terms of measures such as exposure, capital

---

[13]We define risk profile as the aggregate and measurable condition of the institution in terms of risk exposure and other key risk indicators established in the organization.

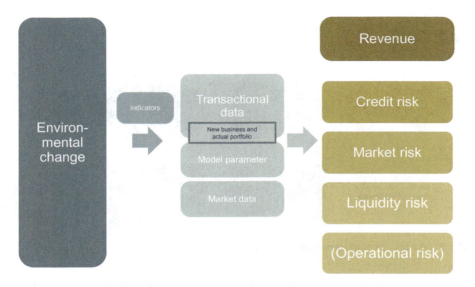

Fig. 4 General mechanics of transversal risks

ratios or risk budget utilization (when looking at risks to capital as in the ICAAP[14]) or in terms of ALM ratios such as LCR or NSFR (when looking at risks to liquidity as in the ILAAP[15]). This evaluation cannot and should not only be carried out at a high level, but should instead assess the impact of certain risks at a sufficiently detailed level.

In Fig. 4 the impact of an environmental change to revenue and financial risks develops by first affecting transaction data, model parameters and market data.

As explained earlier (see Sect. 4), when incorporating transaction data, it is highly advisable to not only include existing business, but also new business (as provided by financial planning).

To put this approach in a more process-oriented perspective, we specify the four main steps involved (see Fig. 5).

As in all scenario analyses or stress tests, the starting point should always be a "story" that is comprehensible for management.

The next step consists of translating this story into the impact on value drivers and risk. The translation can be achieved using expert judgment or

---

[14]ICAAP—Internal Capital Adequacy Assessment Process.
[15]ILAAP—Internal Liquidity Adequacy Assessment Process.

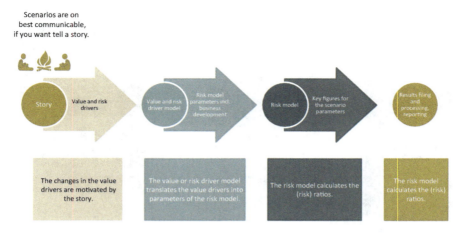

Fig. 5 Process of transversal risk calculation

even using statistical tools like machine learning.[16] This impact is then quantified and applied to the input factors of risk models (transactional data, model parameters and market data). The final step entails the recalculation of risk, which can then be reported or evaluated in terms of capital available for loss absorption.

3.1.2 Example 1: Climate Risk

The German Central Bank (Bundesbank) highlighted the importance of assumed climate change to the financial sector in several speeches during its annual conference in March 2018 (see Dombret, 2018). In their opinion, climate change is such a material event or trend that institutions should assess its impact (or the impact of climate regulation respectively) on their risk situation.[17] A natural approach could consist of looking at the bank's credit risk and allocating clients to three classes: green finance, brown finance and others (not primarily impacted by climate regulations). Green finance is investment in financial products and services with particular

---

[16]An example of using statistical tools can be found in Valjanow, Enzinger, and Dinges (2019), the mathematical foundation is provided in Li, Liermann, and Schaudinus (2019).

[17]Since the effect unfolds, not through climate change itself, but through regulations based on climate change, it is irrelevant whether or not climate change is a real threat.

consideration of environmental factors throughout the lending decision-making process. Brown finance is connected with "traditional" (some might say "dirty") energy-intensive industries like coal processing. Both can be affected negatively by changes in demand for their product or service resulting from climate legislation.

Another important aspect to be covered by this analysis is the impact on the insurance industry, which indicates the holistic nature of the approach.

"Green finance is often used interchangeably with green investment. However, in practice, green finance is a wider lens including more than investments as defined by Bloomberg New Energy Finance and others. Most important is that it includes operational costs of green investments not included under the definition of green investment. Most obviously, it would include costs such as project preparation and land acquisition costs, both of which are not just significant but can pose distinct financing challenges" (Zadek & Flynn, 2013).

"For the banking sector, green finance is defined as financial products and services, under the consideration of environmental factors throughout the lending decision making, ex-post monitoring and risk management processes, provided to promote environmentally responsible investments and stimulate low-carbon technologies, projects, industries and businesses" (PWC, 2013).

Figure 6 shows a possible process for estimating the impact of climate change regulation on an institution's risk profile.

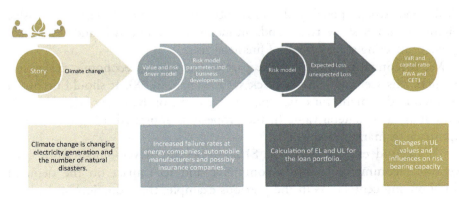

Fig. 6 Simulation of the impact of climate legislation on a company's risk profile

Fig. 7 The effect of the reduced demand for office space

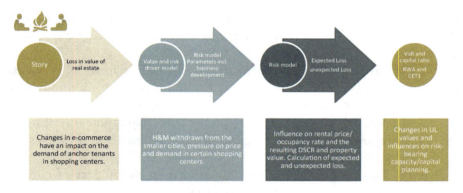

Fig. 8 The effect of increasing e-commerce market share

3.1.3 Example 2: Real Estate Risk

Real estate risk is possibly the most obvious example of transversal risks. Figures 7 and 8 show two trends inducing real estate risk and, in consequence, affecting several types of financial risk.

Macroeconomic downturns are part of the natural economic cycle and, as such, this scenario is *not* a black swan (Taleb, 2008). It should be noted that reduced demand for office space impacts the probability of default (PD) as well as the collateral value (if the property is appraised using the income approach or market values).

The second example (see Fig. 8) addresses the development from conventional commerce toward e-commerce and its impact on the demand for shopping centers. As in the previous example, the reduction in demand affects PD and collateral value.

3.2 Value Driver Design

We will now look at the general idea behind value driver design, which has certain similarities to value driver-based planning as introduced in (Valjanow et al. 2019).

A widespread approach taken in stress testing to generate scenarios consists of simple alteration or shifting of model parameters like PD or yield curves, etc. These mere parameter scenarios are certainly pragmatic, but lack intuitiveness and comprehensibility. What does an increase in the PD of a certain loan portfolio of 50% mean in terms of real-world developments? Is it an event that can be reasonably expected? What are the economic scenarios that would lead to such a scenario? The problem is that the magnitude of a change in model parameters (or market data) cannot be evaluated in terms of likelihood and thus plausibility. A CEO might therefore learn from their risk manager what the impact of a 50% increase of average PDs in their mortgage portfolio might be. But they will most likely have no idea how probable such a 50% increase actually is. Making any management decisions on such grounds would be like driving a car blindfolded. In other words, this stress test looks analytically sophisticated but in effect adds no value to managing the institution. It should be noted that even many of the regulatory stress tests conducted have the same underlying problem.

Instead, modern risk managers should dig deeper and look for value drivers or risk drivers that influence model parameters.

The key to adding value to both management and the affected business divisions is to find real-life value drivers that can be evaluated. Experts from business units are usually not nor want to be familiar with risk models and respective model parameters. They do, however, tend to have a pretty good understanding of the real-world drivers of their business and the inherent risks.

Again, real estate lending is a good example. Rent influences DSCR.[18] DSCR itself is a major factor for the project finance rating model, which estimates PD. PD in turn is an important parameter when evaluating the credit risk of a transaction. Thus, we can easily establish a link between PD as a model parameter and rent as the value or risk driver. By differentiating between location as well as the supply and demand for a property, we can develop meaningful, value driver-based, real estate risk management.

---

[18]The debt service coverage ratio (DSCR) is the ratio of cash available for interest and principal payments.

A common shortcut to modeling financial loss consists of simply applying LGD to expected exposure. This implies that expected loss is defined as

$$EL_1(t) = PD_1(t) \times EAD(t) \times LGD_1(t)$$

Equation 1: One-year expected loss

where $EL_1(t)$ is the one-year expected loss at time t, $PD_1(t)$ is the one-year PD at time t, $EAD_1(t)$ is the Exposure at default at time t for the following year and $LGD_1(t)$ is the one-year LDG at time t.

Taking a value driver-based perspective on credit loss (or change in value of the credit) means incorporating the collateral value into the equation. Assuming we have 100% LGD for the unsecured portion, expected loss is then given as

$$EL_1(t) = PD_1(t) \times \left(\overbrace{EAD(t) - CV_1(t)}^{unsecured\,portion} + CV_1(t) \times RR_1(t) \right)$$

Equation 2: One-year expected loss (collateral-value based)

where $CV_1(t)$ is the collateral value at time t for the following year and $RR_1(t)$ is the recovery rate of the collateral at time t for the next year. Including collateral value in the equation makes the influence of collateral value and recovery rate transparent. Collateral value serves as the perfect starting point for scenario analyses or stress tests.

3.2.1 Linking Model Parameters and Value Drivers

There are many ways in which model parameters[19] and value drivers can be linked. Analytical complexity ranges from simple (non-mathematical, non-data-based) expert judgment to highly sophisticated machine learning algorithms that predict a connection between the two based on big data.

The particular challenge in a mathematical and data-based approach is that relationships change in stress situations and relationships observed previously may no longer hold. Historical stress situations can be analyzed by restricting the time series data to these periods. Hypothetical stress tests must be developed by expert judgment or can use ABM to predict parameter fluctuations in the new scenario.

---

[19]The following remarks are not restricted to model parameters but also hold true for market data and transactional data.

The benefit of ABM is that behavior is formulated at a micro-level (by agent) and the impact on the entire system is then simulated by the model.

Besides conventional linear and non-linear regression models, deep learning algorithms like self-organizing maps (SOM), recurrent neural networks (RNN) or generative adversarial networks (GAN) can help create the link between a model parameter and its value driver.

3.2.2 Modeling Value Drivers (Supply-and-Demand Calculus)

Once we manage to estimate, in terms of sensitivity, a stable relationship between model parameters and value drivers, the subsequent step consists of looking at value drivers and how they respond to changes in fundamental background factors. In many cases, the movement of value drivers can be fed back into a supply-and-demand analysis. For example, real estate rental is highly influenced by the demand for housing space, supply of properties and planned construction. Again, ABM can help define basic micro-level dependencies and derive the impact on supply and demand and, thereby, on the value driver in a simulation.

3.3 The Risk Profile in Various Scenarios

When analyzing transversal risks, we look for external events that impact the institution's financial risk profile. The risk profile is then calculated using well-established and stable methods known from conventional financial risk management (like market risk, credit risk or, to some extent, liquidity risk). By assuming a value or risk driver we can causally link a certain stress situation and a risk model parameter.

One major advantage is that the selected scenarios can be communicated easily to management and to business units. Plausible communication means understanding and hence acceptance of the forecast risk situation.

4 Incorporating Planning Information in Risk Projections

In Sect. 2, we argued for a shift from a simplistic one-year horizon to a multi-year perspective in managing risks. The main benefit is that risks can be anticipated long before they impact the organization. As we have pointed

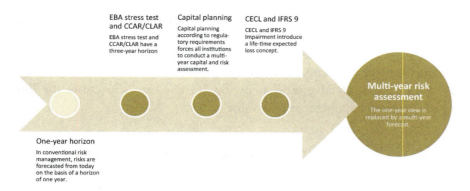

Fig. 9 Projection of the risk situation—motivation for change

out, this trend is also mirrored in several regulatory and accounting standard initiatives. Figure 9 summarizes these observations.

However, the benefits of the multi-period approach come with additional issues that must be dealt with. The most challenging one—owed to the long-term horizon—consists of integrating business planning in the risk exposure calculus.

Additional complexity arises from the fact that business planning and transaction scenarios for risk projections must be developed in alignment with one another. Model parameters and market data developments, on the one hand, as well as business developments, on the other hand, must be translated into transaction-level developments. We will address these two dimensions in the following section (Fig. 10).

As we will see in subsequent sections, projecting new and prolonged transaction scenarios is a significant ingredient of risk forecasting. As Nils Bohr, Nobel laureate in Physics, already knew, "prediction is very difficult, especially if it's about the future." Quality and reliability of long-term business forecasts fade with the length of the forecast period. Thus, we think the three-year horizon offers a good balance between quality and reliability and the chance to respond based on conclusions from risk projection. In practice, the three-year horizon corresponds to mid-term planning of a bank.

4.1 Model Parameter (and Market Data) Scenarios

The first components we alter are model parameters and market data for the calculation of the projected risk profile during the following years. A specific challenge consists of developing time-consistent market data and model

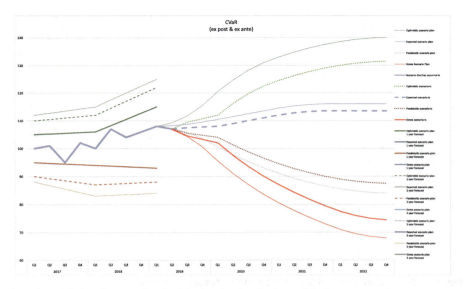

Fig. 10 High-level example—is risk developing in line with the strategy?

parameter scenarios. Consistent forward-rate curves are familiar examples. We encounter the same challenge when developing credit risk parameters (e.g., PDs derived from migration matrices).

Model parameter development should therefore be divided into two steps: (1) parameter transformation and (2) time transformation. The logic for parameter transformation is derived from the environment scenarios and could even be derived from transversal risks. The time transformation can be subject to vintage effects (e.g., retail portfolio PDs) or just the consistent evolution of model parameters over time (e.g., the forward rates or the PDs derived from the migration matrices). We will look at this in more detail in Sect. 4.3.

4.2 Transaction Scenarios

Transaction scenarios have a close link to the institution's planning and forecasting process. It could even be supplemented by ad hoc scenarios. It is important to remember that most market data and model parameter developments have a feedback effect on planning and forecasting (sometimes parameters are value drivers or closely linked to value drivers). Without incorporation of a transaction scenario, risk projection is not feasible.

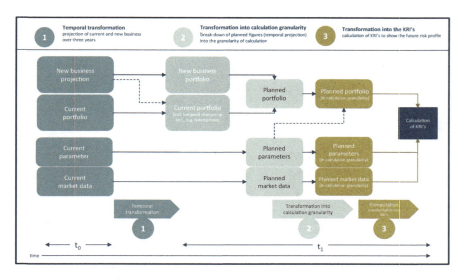

Fig. 11 Projection of the risk situation in the future—general

4.3 Transformations

In the previous section, we focused on the components to be considered in the framework. Now we will look at the methodology and the process of estimating the risk profile for different time horizons.

Figure 11 illustrates the three steps of the process:

1. The transformation in terms of time is the projection of market data and the model parameter subject to calculating a consistent set of input factors and the implications the vintage has for the transactions (e.g., redemptions).
2. Transformation of planning granularity to calculation granularity (focusing on transactions).
3. Calculation of KRIs (transformation into key figures). These risk figures then describe the projected risk profile.

Step 1 shifts the view from today (t_0) to tomorrow (t_1). The main parts of step 2 and 3 happen in t_1.

The time transformation must be observed from two angles. The first is time transformation of the parameters, guaranteeing the consistency of these parameters over time. It must also be taken into consideration that parameters (as well as market data) can be influenced further by value drivers in addition to a normal adjustment with the passage of time. The second angle is the transaction transformation. Actual transactions change over time due to redemptions, rights of cancellation, etc. Planned new transactions can be influenced by changes in model parameters, market data or even the underlying value drivers.

The final step consists of estimating the future risk profile, incorporating the transformed transactions portfolio (transformed current transactions and planned transactions potentially subject to change) as well as the adjusted model parameter and market data. The estimation methods applied in this context should be consistent with those used for the conventional one-year risk horizon.

4.4 Example: Credit Risk

Figure 12 shows a simplified credit risk prediction process. The point of departure is business planning that differentiates between corporate and retail clients. We refer to this level of differentiation as planning granularity. (A real-world process would differentiate more business units.) To deduce plan figures, the transactions of the current portfolio are transformed into the transaction profile at the future point in time. In addition, planned new business is linked with the transformed current transactions.

Furthermore, the credit risk parameter PD (by client group) is transformed according to the assumed migration matrices. LGDs, correlations

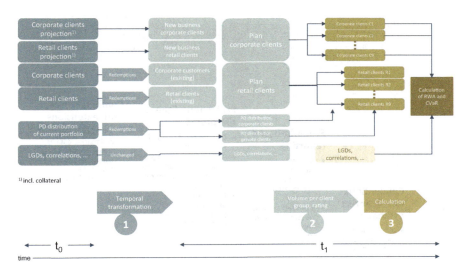

Fig. 12 Credit risk example (simplified)

and other parameters can remain unchanged. In more sophisticated implementations, even these parameters can be aligned with macroeconomic factors or other identified value drivers. Development of collateral values, which is strongly linked to the transversal real estate risk, is of special interest in the credit risk context.

5 Summary and Outlook

Having laid out the components in the preceding sections, we will now put them all together to illustrate the 'big picture'. In Fig. 13 we summarize the transition from conventional risk estimation to a framework of predictive risk analysis or 'risk intelligence'.

The first step consists of the transition from a distribution-based approach like Value at Risk (VaR) to a scenario-based approach. This transition has in fact already taken place in many institutions in the aftermath of the financial crisis, primarily by means of adopting internal stress testing. To some extent, these stress tests already entail mechanics like value driver analysis, albeit restricted to model parameters and market data.

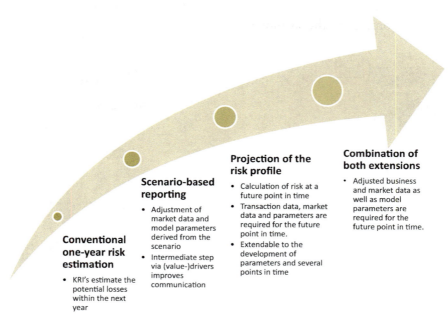

Fig. 13 Projection of the risk situation vs. scenario-oriented risk planning

The European and US regulatory stress test exercises (EBA stress test and CCAR/CLAR & DFAST) bridge the gap to stress test frameworks that do include planning information and can therefore be seen as a first step toward a projection of risk concept, as they calculate risk exposure at a future point in time. The question driving these approaches is: How severe is my potential loss after year two or three?

The model parameter and market data scenarios are carried forward self-consistently, ideally supported by value driver development.

The desired sophistication level of risk management is reached when the impact of stress scenarios—including both the effects of adjusted model parameters and market data as well as of new business—is combined with the projection of the risk profile.

The combination of value driver-based stress testing and the mechanics of risk projections reveal in-depth insight both into the current as well as probable future forms of an institution's risk. Being able to calculate and quantitatively predict the risk profile allows for better analysis and more qualified management of risks.

A stress scenario told as a real-world "story" and represented by a wealth of value driver changes is the precondition for successful risk communication with the business units and, more importantly, with top management. We are sometimes surprised by how far away from this objective many of the risk reports we see in institutions today still are. However, modeling value driver changes (especially with consistent development over time) is often a challenging task.

Modeling demand and supply with multiple factor interdependencies can be achieved using the agent-based modeling concept. The idea is to formulate certain mechanics at micro-level (i.e., defining a behavior by agent or agent type) and condense micro-level results into a general macro-level trend or general behavior.

Risk management has been undergoing fundamental change during the last 15 years. And there is still much more change to expect in the near future. Figure 14 shows this evolution of risk management.

The point of departure is traditional risk management with its short-term risk horizon of one year. This is the status quo in most risk controlling departments. It includes well-established and highly sophisticated models, which have been commoditized to a certain extent and have not changed radically in the last ten to twenty years.

The development stage many banks already find themselves in today can be described as risk management 2.0 and involves stress testing based on scenario analysis including new transactions and the projection of the risk

Fig. 14 Financial risk management—evolution in three steps

situation. Market data, model parameter scenarios and transactions scenarios are mainly derived by expert judgment and cover interactions in market data, model parameter scenarios and the transactions only on a small scale.

The logical next step focuses on modeling and quantifying these interactions to gain an independent and objective view of the scenarios underlying risk calculation.

References

Deters, J., & Kröner, A. (2018). *EZB-Chefaufseherin Danièle Nouy regt Änderungen beim EU-Bankencheck an. Der aktuelle Test liefere für die Finanzaufsicht zu wenige neue Erkenntnisse.*

Dombret, A. (2018). *Bankenaufsicht im Dialog 2018 - Schriftenreihe zum Bundesbank Symposium, Band 4.* Frankfurt: Deutsche Bundesbank.

Li, S., Liermann, V., & Schaudinus, N. (2019). Introduction in machine learning. In V. Liermann & C. Stegmann (Eds.), *The impact of digital transformation and fintech on the finance professional.* New York: Palgrave Macmillan.

PWC. (2013). *Exploring green finance incentives in China—Final report.* Shenzhen: PWC.

Taleb, N. N. (2008). *The black swan: The impact of the highly improbable.* New York: Random House.

Valjanow, S., Enzinger, P., & Dinges, F. (2019). Digital planning—Driver-based planning levaraged by predictive analytics. In V. Lierman & C. Stegmann (Eds.), *The impact of digital transformation and fintech on the finance professional*. New York: Palgrave Macmillan.

Zadek, S., & Flynn, C. (2013). *South-originating green finance: Exploring the potential*. Geneva: The Geneva International Finance.

9

Intraday Liquidity: Forecast Using Pattern Recognition

Volker Liermann, Sangmeng Li and Victoria Dobryashkina

1 Introduction

1.1 Intraday Liquidity Management

Management of a bank's intraday liquidity is a complex undertaking, mainly driven by expert knowledge to handle situations arising from other market participants acting, not acting or not acting as assumed. Due to the complex set of tools to react, this area is largely people-related and follows complex and changing patterns.

Intraday liquidity risk management is still a new and not settled[1] discipline within risk management. Before the regulatory requirements were

---

[1] Like, for example, the value at risk schemata.

V. Liermann (✉) · S. Li
ifb AG, Grünwald, Germany
e-mail: volker.liermann@ifb-group.com

S. Li
e-mail: sangmeng.li@ifb-group.com

V. Dobryashkina
ifb International AG branch office Austria, Vienna, Austria
e-mail: victoria.dobryashkina@ifb-group.com

© The Author(s) 2019
V. Liermann and C. Stegmann (eds.), *The Impact of Digital Transformation and FinTech on the Finance Professional*, https://doi.org/10.1007/978-3-030-23719-6_9

defined by the Basel Committee on Banking Supervision (BCBS) regarding intraday liquidity (see Basel Committee on Banking Supervision, 2013), intraday liquidity risk management was handled individually and pragmatically.

The approach taken by the BCBS is two-fold. First, the regulator requires a certain (not too complex) reporting on intraday flow. The key indicator here is the cumulative flow by day and the intraday throughput.[2] The second requirement is a stress test with four predefined stress scenarios. Reporting and most of the stress test calculations are ex-post, which means a forward-looking component is missing.

1.2 Machine Learning, but Not Only Machine Learning

Even though the regulators do not explicitly require a forward-looking view, the collected data (in particular the flows by customers and the cumulative flow by currency) is a good starting point for developing a forward-looking view on an intraday basis. The shapes of cumulative flow by customer can be used to cluster customer behavior and situations by day and by customer. The machine learning algorithms can extract a representative cumulative flow (and the single flows) for a cluster of customers in a specific situation. In the first place, these representative cumulative flows can be used to predict the customer flows for the actual day by customer and a forecast by currency can be executed by aggregating the customer flows.

To aggregate the clustered customer flows representing the assumed behavior and situation for the actual day, making the right decision based on purely statistical analysis is not an easy task to perform. Dashboarding and other visualization techniques can help assess a differentiated view of the analyzed historical data and to include own opinions on the situation and the deduced customer behavior.

The combined approach provides an optimal mix for forecasting the most probable development of intraday liquidity on the actual day and for determining what possible outcomes could occur in less comfortable situations. The less comfortable situations can be derived from events and patterns seen in the past (historical stress tests) as well as personal views developed by individuals, taking into account the actual situation, which cannot be expressed

---

[2]Cumulative flow by day and intraday throughput are defined in Sect. 2.2.

in the historical patterns (hypnotical stress tests, better known as black swans.[3])

1.3 Structure of the Chapter

Section 2 starts with some general remarks on liquidity risk management and details the requirements for intraday liquidity management. At the end of the section, the regulatory requirements of the BCBS are discussed. The third section provides an introduction to the methods of pattern recognition within the context of intraday liquidity management. How these results can be used to forecast the intraday liquidity solution is explained in Sect. 4. Section 5 shows an example dashboard implementation. The chapter is summarized in Sect. 6.

2 Liquidity Risk Management

In this section, we summarize the common approaches dealing with liquidity risk and, in particular, with intraday liquidity. The approaches vary from internal measures and processes through to the regulatory requirements of the BCBS and the EBA.

Besides a bank's capital adequacy, its liquidity adequacy is of the most challenging bank management tasks. A small amount of liquid assets held by the bank can cause bankruptcy on the short term, while an excessive amount is costly and can ruin a bank in the long term. The importance of this balance is documented in the EBA guidelines on the SREP (supervisory review and evaluation process, see European Banking Authority, 2018), in which ICAAP[4] and ILAAP[5] are given equal importance.

2.1 Liquidity Risk—The General Idea

The general idea of liquidity risk management is to have sufficient sources of liquidity in relation to the liquidity requirements. The liquidity requirements are considered over different time horizons.

---

[3]Introduction to black swans, see (Taleb, 2008).

[4]ICAAP—internal capital adequacy assessment process.

[5]ILAAP—internal liquidity adequacy assessment process.

Liquidity risk management can be divided into the three major areas of strategic liquidity risk, structural liquidity risk, and short-term liquidity risk (including intraday liquidity). The first area looks at instruments and a wider and long-term view of the banks' ability to generate liquidity from various sources. This area focuses on the available instruments and the agility to use them including recovery plans.

The second area looks at funding requirements and sources for generating liquidity in the period beyond one year. The major liquidity sources are capital markets or other long-term funding instruments. To a wider extent, the final area is the most important one.

In short-term liquidity risk management, liquidity is generated by selling assets or by pledging assets and gaining cash in return (REPO[6]). Short-term liquidity risk management consists of comparing the liquid assets (assets that can be used to generate liquidity) with the liquidity requirements. This exercise is carried out in a forward-looking way and performed for several time buckets. The main source of liquidity requirements is derived from the uncertainty of the banking products (e.g., NMD,[7] credit lines or the uncertainty of new business transactions). The other main source of this is the liquidity leverage, which arises when refinancing new asset-side transactions with a maturity mismatch. The LCR[8] is designed to use this calculation structure.

2.2 Intraday Liquidity Risk Management

In intraday liquidity risk management, the calculation idea is the same as in short-term liquidity risk management. The liquidity requirements are related to the ability to generate liquidity on an intraday basis. The sources for liquidity generation primarily consist of pledging assets and getting cash in return as well as opening credit lines with other financial institutions.

The liquidity requirements can be differentiated into the ones with a time-specific obligation and the others. The time-specific obligations are the payments to the central banks and to the clearing houses. The payments to other banks via LVPS[9] normally do not have a fixed payment time. The timing is bilaterally negotiated by the incorporated banks.

---

[6]REPO—repurchase agreement.
[7]NMD—non-maturing deposits.
[8]LCR—liquidity coverage ratio.
[9]LVPS—large-value payment system.

The two parts of an intraday liquidity stress test are described in Fig. 1. The standard rules are shown on the left. The first two are unexpected changes in an incoming payment (delay or reduction) and the third is a simulation of a reduction in the available liquidity buffer due to a loss in asset values.

Figure 2 shows a reporting example of two elements of an intraday liquidity stress test. In general, all graphs show the cumulative flow by day and currency, and the liquidity buffer. The size of the liquidity buffer

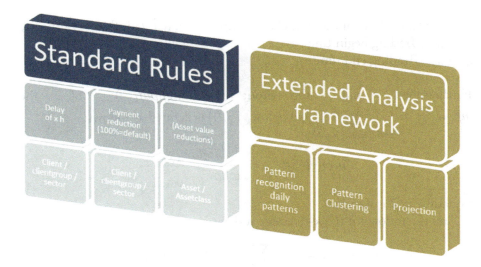

Fig. 1 Analysis framework

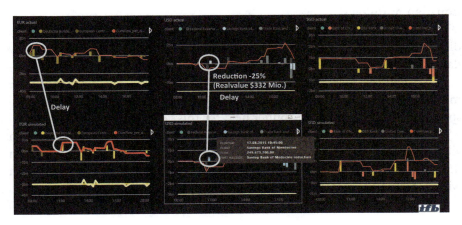

Fig. 2 Intraday liquidity—regulatory stress test (example)

is calculated as the sum of the asset's market value (dirty price) times one minus haircut.

The cumulative flow is calculated as the sum of flows from trading begin until time t.

$$flowC_{k,t,\hat{\imath}} = \sum_{t_i \in \left\{ t_{trandingmin}, t \right\}} flow_{k,t_i,\hat{\imath}}$$

Equation 1: Cumulative flow

$flow_{k,t,\hat{\imath}}$ Cash flows of the k-th client at time t in day $\hat{\imath}$: (+ inflow,—outflow),
$t_{tradingmin}$ Trading begin time,
$t_{tradingmax}$ Trading end time.

Furthermore, the throughput $(throughput_{k,t,\hat{\imath}})$ of the $inflow_{k,t,\hat{\imath}} = \sum_{t_i \in \left\{ t_{tranding,min}, t \right\}} max(flow_{k,t_i,\hat{\imath}}, 0)$ is defined as follows:

$$Throughput_{k,t,\hat{\imath}} = \frac{inflow_{k,t,\hat{\imath}}}{inflow_{k,t_{trading,max},\hat{\imath}}}$$

Equation 2: Throughput

And the inflow for the k-th client at day $\hat{\imath}$ is set as follows:

$$inflow_{k,t,\hat{\imath}} = \sum_{t_i \in \left\{ t_{tranding,min}, t \right\}} max(flow_{k,t_i,\hat{\imath}}, 0)$$

Equation 3: Inflows

The throughput is the portion of the total inflows up to a certain time divided by the total projected inflows for the day (by day and client or by day and currency).

A payment delay is shown on the left and a reduction of a payment in the middle. In both graphs, the cumulative flow by currency is defined in correspondence with the liquidity buffer held for this currency.

The right side of Fig. 1 shows an extended analysis framework, which allows the bank to project the further course of its intraday liquidity position during the day. The way such an extended framework can be set in action will be described in Sects. 3 and 4.

2.3 Regulatory Requirements

The regulatory requirements are primarily based on the demand of the BCBS (Basel Committee on Banking Supervision, 2013) as long as the EBA has not published any requirement beyond the known SREP guidelines (European Banking Authority, 2018).

2.3.1 Regular Reporting to Supervisors

Regular reporting to supervisors is a small set of monitoring tools. The first four are applicable to all banks, the next three to banks that provide correspondent banking services, and the last only applies to banks, which are direct participants:

A(i)   Daily maximum intraday liquidity usage
A(ii)   Available intraday liquidity at the start of the business day
A(iii) Total payments
A(iv)   Time-specific obligations
B(i)   Value of payments made on behalf of correspondent banking customers
B(ii)   Intraday credit lines extended to customers
C(i)   Intraday throughput.

The daily maximum intraday liquidity usage shown in figure A(i) will be calculated as the minimum cumulative flow during the day. The available intraday liquidity at the start of the business day in A(ii) is the (intraday) liquidity buffer available without any additional actions by the bank. The total payments in A(iii) are the sum of all outflows. The time-specific obligations in A(iv) are payments, which have a specific time attached when the payment (outflow) has to been made as the latest. The B figures cover the corresponding banks and the intraday throughput in C(i) monitors the participant's daily payment activities by calculating which pre-central portion of the total payments in A(iii) has been made by the participants up to a particular time.

2.3.2 Stress Tests

The BCBS requires the banks to perform stress tests in addition to the ex-post oriented regular reporting. The explicitly required scenarios are illustrated in Fig. 3.

Fig. 3 Stress test requirements overview

These stress tests have been widely implemented as ex-post analyses based on the data provided in regular reporting. Examples of the second scenario are the delay of outgoing payments by two or three hours for certain banks or banking groups. Then the impact of the delay on cumulative flows is estimated and compared with the liquidity buffer held by the bank in the related currency.

2.3.3 Critical Reflection on the Requirements

As already stated, regular reporting and the stress tests are ex-post oriented and can therefore only provide an answer to the question: "Would the bank have had liquidity issues yesterday, had bank X delayed its payments?". This is a good starting point, but provides no insight for operative management of the intraday position. It does not include a forecast of how the day is going to continue.

3 Pattern Recognition in Intraday Liquidity

3.1 Time Series Specific Clustering

Time series clustering is a common task used in signal processing, and since we are focusing on the intraday aspects, a detailed description of the algorithms and the corresponding mathematics is provided in Sect. 2 in Liermann, Li, and Schaudinnus (2019).

3.2 Numerical Example

The following result is implemented using the R-package *dtwcluster*.

3.2.1 Experiment Data

The data used for the numerical experiment is computed based on the traded cash flows (inflows or outflows) of 20 clients from 10 different countries, which is generated daily between 8 a.m. and 4 p.m. for a two-week interval. Cumulation by day and by client cash flows are time series, which are computed as Eq. 1. An example of cumulative cash flow is shown in the following figure, in which the first element is the cumulative cash flow at 8 a.m. (Fig. 4).

In the experiment presented in this section, the time series of cumulative cash flows are going to be used as objects for clustering. The total number of time series is 1240.

3.2.2 Clustering Analysis

We are going to cluster the time series introduced above. We expect that the time series with similar structures can be grouped into the same clusters. We are going to use two distance metrics: shape-based distance and global alignment kernel distance. Both of them are specific metrics for time series and introduced in Sect. 2. The number of clusters is going to be set from 5 to 9.

```
> series[[1]]
[1]  6952.205  7063.985  7209.141  7542.515  8702.530  3476.318  5820.787  6153.474 17530.890 28785.373
```

Fig. 4 Example of cumulative cash flows

	dakp_10	dakp_11	dakp_12	dakp_13	dakp_14	dtwSBDP_10	dtwSBDP_11	dtwSBDP_12	dtwSBDP_13	dtwSBDP_14
Sil	3.330259e-01	3.292729e-01	2.761239e-01	3.216063e-01	2.561468e-01	1.913509e-01	0.17805918	1.712606e-01	1.711497e-01	1.862735e-01
SF	4.957993e-01	4.949623e-01	4.929684e-01	4.881200e-01	4.700940e-01	2.026162e-01	0.18309690	1.693533e-01	1.507347e-01	1.446354e-01
CH	6.855372e+02	6.296863e+02	6.286274e+02	6.169300e+02	5.551871e+02	4.332829e+02	385.71209881	3.655262e+02	3.258136e+02	3.177324e+02
DB	1.687037e+00	1.464618e+00	1.464310e+00	1.294448e+00	1.745861e+00	1.475172e+00	1.43551032	1.398137e+00	1.278947e+00	1.303224e+00
DBstar	1.963031e+00	1.755718e+00	2.008268e+00	1.883592e+00	2.065068e+00	1.641542e+00	1.78234263	1.714932e+00	1.617295e+00	1.642056e+00
D	1.364578e-03	2.669132e-03	2.800516e-03	1.474483e-03	2.085454e-03	5.933144e-03	0.00924155	5.310243e-03	5.154252e-03	6.299165e-03
COP	1.251404e-01	1.141967e-01	1.164470e-01	9.524397e-02	1.034142e-01	2.096093e-01	0.20274154	1.955694e-01	1.930848e-01	1.844881e-01

Fig. 5 Evaluation of clustering result

Note that all the time series have to be z-normalized first (see Sect. 2) by setting the input argument *preproc* of function *tsclust()* into *zscore*.

The clustering results are collected and compared using the evaluation indices introduced in the paper (Liermann et al. 2019). As presented in the figure, each column represents evaluations of one clustering result and each row contains evaluations of one index. For example, the column with the name "dtwSBDP_10" stands for the clustering based on shape-based distance metrics and 10 clusters, and the row "Sil" contains all evaluations based on the Silhouette index (Fig. 5).

The best clustering result is "voted on" from all evaluation indexes as follows:

- For each index, we ordered all clustering results and assigned ranks to them.
- The clustering number with the highest averaged rank is taken as the best one.

In our example, clustering is suggested based on global alignment kernel distance and 13 clusters. The clustering result is presented in the following figure (Fig. 6).

3.2.3 Subclustering

Recall that all the time series were z-normalized, the mean was removed, and the variance was scaled to one. As an example, we pick the time series of cluster No. 3. The z-normalized time series are plotted in the left image of Fig. 7, while the original ones are on the right. Compared to the z-normalized ones, the original time series do not seem to have similar structures due to the influence of mean and variance. This motivates us to split this cluster again according to mean and variance. To understand this well, we point the mean and variance of all members of cluster No. 3 in Fig. 7. Subclustering aims at grouping the cluster members with closed mean and variance (Fig. 8).

9 Intraday Liquidity: Forecast Using Pattern Recognition 149

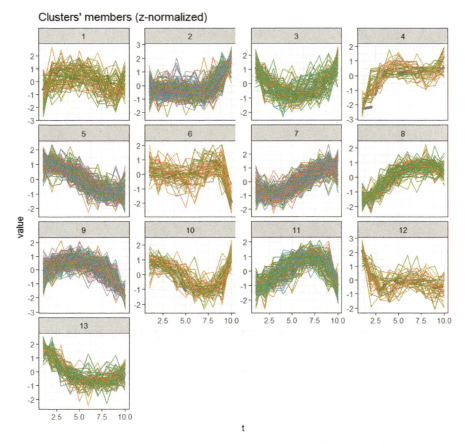

Fig. 6 Clustering result based on global alignment kernel distance and 13 clusters

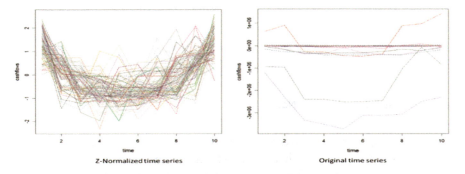

Fig. 7 Z-normalized vs. original time series of cluster No. 3

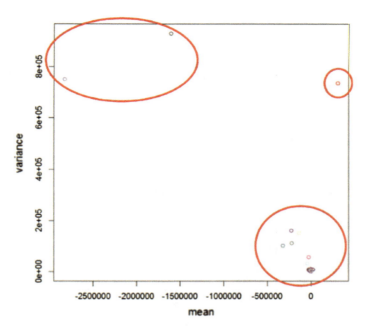

Fig. 8 Subclustering: grouping cluster members according to mean and variance

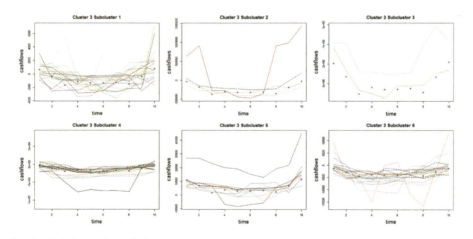

Fig. 9 Subclustering of cluster No. 3

As an example, we subdivide cluster No. 3 based on the two features mean and variance, in which the Euclidean distance is used. The result is presented in the following figure, in which 6 subclusters are formed (Fig. 9).

As a result, the members of each subcluster have not only similar shape (structure), but also close mean and variance.

4 Forecast for Intraday Liquidity

Suppose that, on a new trading day, the cumulative cash flow is given until a certain time such as 10 a.m. We aim at predicting the remaining part of this time series. We search for a cluster which "looks" the most similar or has the highest similarity (called nearest cluster) to the target time series. The members of the nearest cluster should have a structure similar to the target time series and can thus be used to "forecast" the remaining part of the target time series. We provide an example in Fig. 10. The target time series is shown until 10 a.m (bold curve). By using the center-based approach, which is going to be introduced in the next subsection, cluster No. 8 Subcluster No. 2 is found to be the nearest cluster. We therefore forecast the target time series using the members of cluster 8 subcluster 2.

4.1 The Nearest Cluster

As introduced above, the "nearest" cluster plays a key role in forecasting. In this subsection, we introduce two techniques that can be used to look for the "nearest" cluster. Suppose we have already proceeded with cluster analysis among a set of elements and arrived at the clustering result in Fig. 11, in which three clusters were formed. Given a new element (defined as A).

The first approach is defined based on the cluster centers. In this procedure, the cluster, whose center is closest to A, is considered to be the

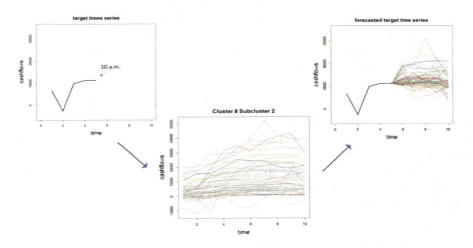

Fig. 10 Forecasting the target time series

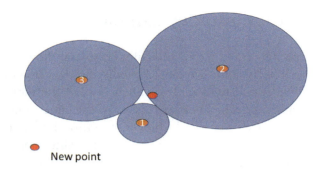

Fig. 11 Clustering result

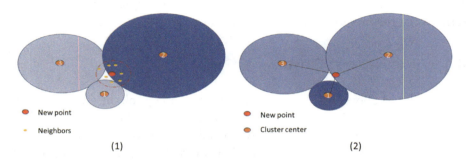

Fig. 12 (1) Nearest cluster based on nearest neighbors; (2) Nearest cluster based on cluster center

"nearest" cluster. As illustrated in Fig. 12 (1), cluster No. 1 will be chosen as the "nearest" cluster. The cluster center is a point that represents the whole cluster. There are various ways to define the center of a cluster. For example, mean-based center or median-based center, in which the cluster center is computed as mean/median among all cluster members (along each dimension).

The second approach is based on the neighbors around point A. This procedure has a single parameter $M \in N^+$. We pick M points that have the smallest distance to A. The cluster, to which the majority of neighbors are assigned, will be considered to be the "nearest" cluster.

As illustrated in Fig. 12 (2), cluster No. 2 will be considered as the "nearest" cluster according to the second approach, since it has 4 neighbors while the others have only 1. As opposed to the first approach, the information surrounding the target point will also contribute to searching for the "nearest" cluster when using the second approach. Therefore, this approach should provide a better cluster assignment. The choice of parameter M becomes challenging during the M-nearest neighbors approach. A small M might lead to the wrong assignment due to "incomplete" neighbors. In the case of a large M, "redundant and unnecessary" neighbors might result in choosing the wrong cluster.

5 Dashboard Example—R Shiny

In this section, we provide an example of an intraday dashboard, which visualizes the results introduced above. The dashboard is implemented using the R package *Shiny* and consists of the following four blocks.

5.1 Load Data

The time series are stored in a CSV file and loaded by clicking the "Load Data" button. The full path to the input file has to be entered here. After successful loading, the data has to be preprocessed, which includes normalizing the time series and computing the distance matrix (Figs. 13 and 14).

5.2 Clustering Analysis

The second block clusters the time series loaded in the first block. As illustrated in the following figure, after clicking the "clustering analysis" button, nine clusters are extracted. The right graph illustrates all the time series

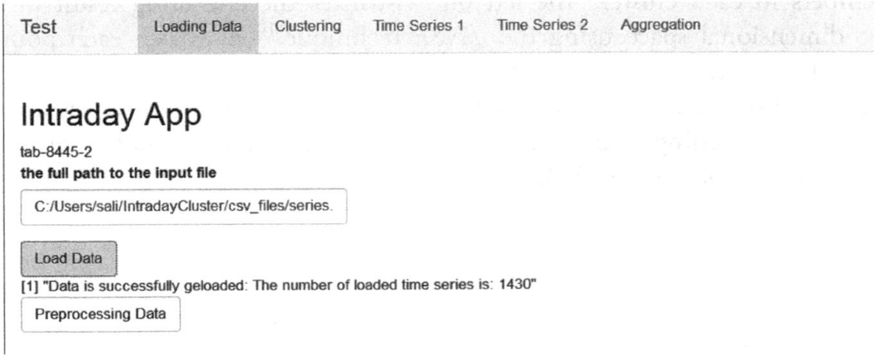

Fig. 13 R Shiny—loading data

154   V. Liermann et al.

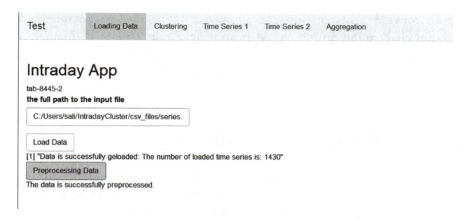

Fig. 14   R Shiny—preprocessing data

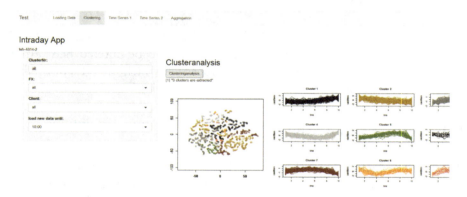

Fig. 15   R Shiny—extraction clusters

members in each cluster. The left one visualizes the clustering result in a two-dimensional space using the *TNSE* technique,[10] in which each point stands for one time series (Fig. 15).

In addition, the dashboard provides the possibility to filter the visualization result according to the FX, the client by using the selection box on the left of the dashboard (Fig. 16).

---

[10]van der Maaten, Accelerating t-SNE using tree-based algorithms (2014) and van der Maaten and Hinton, Visualizing High-Dimensional Data Using t-SNE (2008).

9 Intraday Liquidity: Forecast Using Pattern Recognition 155

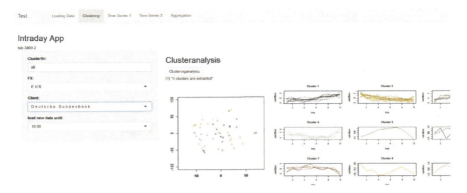

Fig. 16 R Shiny—clustering member filtering with FX=EUR and Client=Deutsche Bundesbank

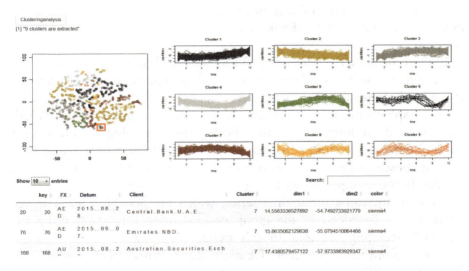

Fig. 17 R Shiny—brush the cluster members

Furthermore, the "brush" option in Shiny package enables the dashboard to show information on time series, which are selected in the graph by the user (Fig. 17).

5.3 Forecasting

The last block of the dashboard enables the user to forecast customer flows for the current day using the clustering result. Assume we have the following two customer flows:

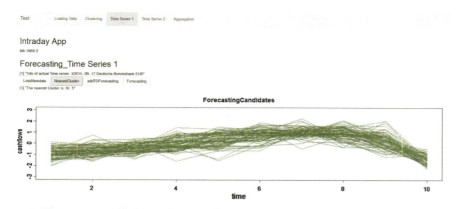

Fig. 18 R Shiny—load actual time series and search for the nearest cluster

No. 1: of Deutsche Bundesbank, in EUR;
No. 2: of European Central Bank, in EUR;

Both of them are available until 10 a.m. and need to be forecasted.

Customer flow No. 1: The information of the actual cash flow is provided at the head of the tab panel "Time series No. 1".

The graph in the middle collects the time series candidates, which will then be used for forecasting. After clicking the "searching for the nearest cluster" button, the cluster that looks the most similar to the actual time series is chosen and all its cluster members are illustrated in the graph in the middle. In the example of Fig. 18, cluster No. 5 is chosen.

Additionally, some other time series, which are possibly picked by an "Expert" can be added to the group of forecasting candidates using the "addTOForecasting" button. In this example, we added some historical time series from the same client "Deutsche Bundesbank" from cluster No. 4 (Figs. 19 and 20).

At the end, after clicking the "Forecasting" button, the actual time series is forecasted using the forecasting candidates (Fig. 21).

Actual customer flow No. 2: The second cash flow series is treated the same as the first one in the dashboard tab panel "Time series No. 2", in which cluster No. 2 is chosen as the nearest cluster and historical time series in EUR are added by "Expert" for forecasting (Figs. 22, 23 and 24).

5.4 Blockwise Aggregation

In the last tab panel, the forecasted time series are aggregated blockwise and the total cash flow for EUR is composed.

9 Intraday Liquidity: Forecast Using Pattern Recognition   157

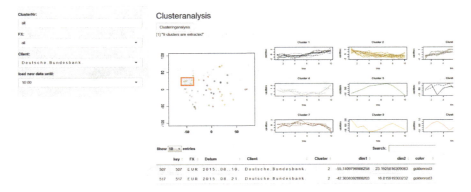

Fig. 19 R Shiny—select additional time series of "Deutsche Bundesbank" by "Expert"

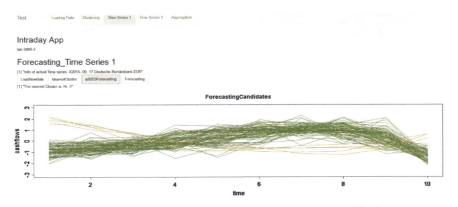

Fig. 20 R Shiny—add the selected time series into the group of forecasting candidates

As illustrated in the following figure, the two groups of the forecasted time series are sorted according to their maximum and split into N equally-sized blocks separately where the number of blocks N is determined by the user in the Shiny tool. The time series of the same block are then aggregated through all possible pair combinations (Fig. 25).

In the following, we provide two screenshots of aggregation results, in which the number of blocks is chosen to be 3 and 6 separately. Aggregated time series from different blocks are plotted (Figs. 26 and 27).

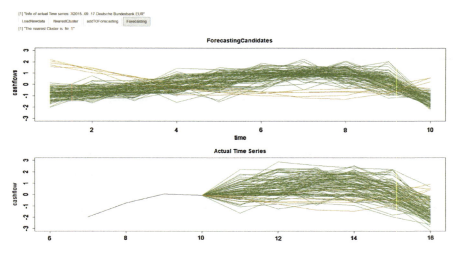

Fig. 21 R Shiny—forecasting the actual time series using the forecasting candidates

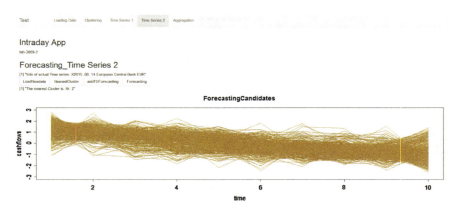

Fig. 22 R Shiny—load actual time series and search for the nearest cluster

6 Summary

The goal of this chapter is to develop a forward-looking forecast of a bank's liquidity situation by currency. This differs fundamentally from the approach taken by regulators (Basel Committee on Banking Supervision, 2013).

The procedure used in this chapter is representative for numerous use cases, in which machine learning approaches are applied. The approach

9 Intraday Liquidity: Forecast Using Pattern Recognition 159

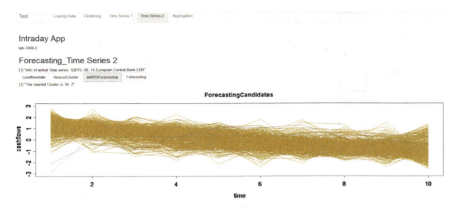

Fig. 23 R Shiny—add additional time series of the same currency "EUR" by "Expert"

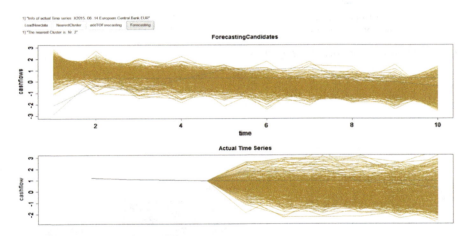

Fig. 24 R Shiny—forecasting the actual time series using the forecasting candidates

combines pattern and structural recognition with expert lead and to some extent manually driven decision-making.

In the first block, the provided data is analyzed to find structures that help cluster the liquidity situation (or, to be more precise, the payment pattern) by day and by client. The strengths of the statistical tools can be used here by analyzing an enormous volume of data. This task could only be approximately performed by experts with extensive experience with the data (or in data science). The analysis is instinct-driven and is not verifiable by an independent body. The ability to be verified by an independent body has always been in strong demand by regulators.

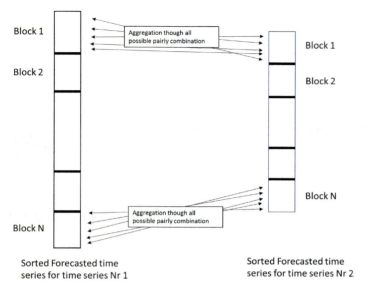

Fig. 25 R Shiny—blockwise aggregation

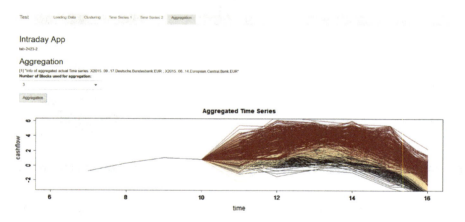

Fig. 26 R Shiny—aggregate the forecast time series with 3 blocks

In the second step, the identified clusters can be used to forecast the payment pattern of the clients on an actual day. Forecasting can be split into two strategies.

A. Automated
B. User driven (expert judgment).

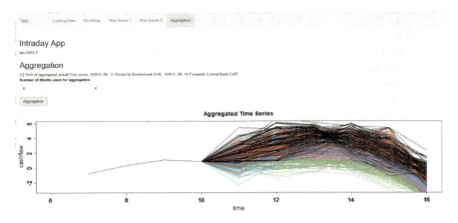

Fig. 27 R Shiny—aggregate the forecast time series with 6 blocks

The automated strategy generates a corridor of possible developments, purely relying on statistical tools. Whereas the statistical tools themselves rely exclusively on historical data and smart aggregation logic, this strategy is similar to autopilot and will have good applications in so-called "normal" time. Black swans are not covered in this forecast.

The user-driven strategy supplements the automated approach. It further allows for picking certain adverse patterns at client level and combining them into a possible aggregated forecast at currency level. By way of manual interception by experts (expert judgment), a much bigger scenario space can be observed and its impact can be analyzed and monitored.

The described approach combines the best parts of both strategies: expert judgment for exceptional situations incorporating the experts' long-term experience and the pattern recognition, which enables verification by an independent body.

Literature

Basel Committee on Banking Supervision. (2013). *Monitoring tools for intraday liquidity management (BCBS 248)*. Basel: BIS.
European Banking Authority. (2018). *Guidelines on the revised common procedures and methodologies for the supervisory review and evaluation process(SREP) and supervisory stress testing*. London: EBA.
Liermann, V., Li, S., & Schaudinnus, N. (2019). Mathematical background of machine learning. In V. Liermann & C. Stegmann (Eds.), *The impact of*

digital transformation and fintech on the finance professional. New York: Palgrave Macmillan.

Taleb, N. N. (2008). *The Black Swan: The impact of the highly improbable.* New York: Random House.

van der Maaten, L. (2014). Accelerating t-SNE using tree-based algorithms. *Journal of Machine, 15,* 3221–3245.

van der Maaten, L., & Hinton, G. (2008). Visualizing high-dimensional data using t-SNE. *Journal of Machine Learning Research, 9,* 2579–2605.

10

Internal Credit Risk Models with Machine Learning

Markus Thiele and Harro Dittmar

1 Introduction

1.1 Subject Intro

The basic concepts underlying machine learning are quite well understood and have been theoretically elaborated for quite some time (Mitchell, 1997). In certain business fields such as marketing, machine learning methods are already well established (TechEmergence, 2017). However, the most striking examples of its potential can probably be found in medical research due to the extremely demanding requirements with respect to the scope of the methods and quality of the results. It is possible, for example, to cure some of the most severe forms of epilepsy with the aid of artificial intelligence (Sowa et al., 2004). Sufficient predictive power is also highly significant for the estimation of credit risk parameters. Internal credit risk parameter models are strictly supervised by banking and insurance authorities, so that limitations of the predictive power have severe consequences for a bank or an insurance company.

Machine learning has just recently been used for banks' risk management, particularly for the estimation of credit risk parameters. There are two main

M. Thiele (✉) · H. Dittmar
ifb AG, Grünwald, Germany
e-mail: markus.thiele@ifb-group.com

H. Dittmar
e-mail: harro.dittmar@ifb-group.com

© The Author(s) 2019
V. Liermann and C. Stegmann (eds.), *The Impact of Digital Transformation and FinTech on the Finance Professional*, https://doi.org/10.1007/978-3-030-23719-6_10

reasons for this. First, the predictive power of previous models often turned out to be insufficient, as the available computing power at the time only allowed the use of very simple models (Goodfellow, Bengio, & Courville, 2016). However, emerging technologies like in-memory databases and distributed computing (e.g., Spark) are drastically augmenting technical performance and enabling the use of much more complex models with increased predictive power. Secondly, machine learning has been approached with caution, as the results were presumed to be hardly comprehensible (black box algorithms). Due to drastically enhanced predictive power of the algorithms and the relativization of non-comprehensibility, the psychological reservations toward machine learning have subsided in recent years. In summary, these developments make the application of machine learning to the estimation of credit risk parameters very attractive. In addition to high predictive power, adaptability is another positive aspect of machine learning that could change the mode of credit risk parameter modeling.

In this chapter, we focus on two different aspects related to credit risk parameter modeling. On the one hand, we examine the influence of machine learning on the mode of modeling and, on the other hand, we demonstrate its predictive power using a simple example.

1.2 Structure of the Chapter

The chapter is organized as follows: In Sect. 2.1 we explain some basic credit risk concepts required to understand the chapter. Details on the methodological aspects of machine learning can be found in another chapter of this book, so we only reference them here (Liermann, Li, & Schaudinnus, Deep learning—An introduction, 2019a). In Sect. 2.2 we address the implications of machine learning on the mode of credit risk parameter modeling. In Sect. 3 we present an exemplary calculation of a credit risk parameter with a neural network. The main results of this calculation are examined in Sect. 4. In Sect. 5 we briefly summarize our conclusions.

2 Model Outline

2.1 General Considerations

In this chapter, we focus on default risk, a very important component for the estimation of credit risk. Default risk is the risk of not receiving promised payments and outstanding investments due to the default of the business partner or the risk position, whereas credit risk is the encompassing risk of the portfolio value changing due to unexpected shifts in the credit qualities of business partners (McNeil, Frey, & Embrechts, 2005). Default risk can be measured both at the granular level (business partner, risk position) and at an aggregated level (portfolio). For default risk measurement at the granular level, there is a set of canonical parameters that reflects various aspects of default risk (McNeil et al., 2005)[1]:

- The probability of default (PD) reflects the likelihood of a business partner or a risk position defaulting within the time interval T as seen from the current point in time.
- The exposure at default (EAD) signifies the monetary amount of exposure and either refers to the exposure as a whole or portions thereof. It can include collaterized, uncollateralized, and non-guaranteed parts of the exposure.
- The loss given default (LGD) is the percentage of the EAD, which is to be considered lost in case of a default event. Depending on the model type, the LGD can correspond to the exposure or various portions of it.

As all three of these parameters refer to a default event by definition, the prediction of default events using the PD is key. Two primary conventional approaches are taken to determine PDs. According to the first approach, one has to define discrete rating categories, in which the PD is considered to be constant. Each of the rating categories is associated with a specific value for the PD, which depends on the number of measured defaults within the rating category. In the second approach (logistic regression), the PD is treated as a continuous variable which values are the direct result of an analytical function, the inputs of which are macroeconomic (and potentially also idiosyncratic) parameters such as the Gross Domestic Product. To help the reader easily comprehend and be able to reproduce our results, we consider a simplified version of the first model type here, for which data is publicly available (Eberly College of Sciences, 2019). This means we simply distinguish between defaulted and non-defaulted banking customers, which corresponds to a rating model with only two rating categories (binary classification into "good" and "bad" customers). The details of this model are explained further below. Since we here aim at the easy reproducibility of the

---

[1]More parameters such as expected and unexpected loss could be mentioned, but we focus on a simple example here.

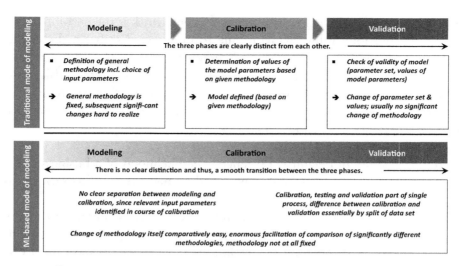

Fig. 1 Differences between the traditional mode and a machine learning based mode of modeling

results we refer to the academic literature for more comprehensive studies (Lessmann, Baesens, Seow, & Thomas, 2015). Before we explain our model in further detail, we first examine how the use of machine learning methods could change the mode of modeling in general (Fig. 1).

2.2 Mode of Modeling

The design of almost any credit risk model can be subdivided into three main tasks (irrespective of their regulatory relevance), in which each of the three tasks is clearly different and distinct from the two other tasks:

- **Modeling** starts with the development of the credit risk model. It comprises definition of the logic and assumptions with a set of (usually highly) parameterized rules and/or mathematical methods.
- **Calibration** is the second task in which the values of the tunable parameters that are used in the developed methodology are determined and optimized in order to reduce the uncertainty of predictions.
- **Validation** is the third task and aims at testing and proving the validity of both the methodology and the chosen values for the model parameters.

Once the methodology is defined in the development phase, it can essentially be considered fixed. Modifications of a model are triggered by the corresponding results of the validation phase and, in most cases, simply require recalibration of existing model parameters or adding new parameters that refine certain aspects without changing the general methodology. This process is repeated iteratively over the model lifetime. After each iteration, a new version of essentially the same model results (see image above). Revision of the credit risk parameter modeling mode is triggered using machine learning for at least three reasons:

I. **Automation**: The essence of machine learning consists of almost fully automated self-calibration of the model parameters. This means a distinction between model development and model calibration is no longer necessary. The time that would be spent on the calibration phase otherwise can be allocated to the pre-processing of the input data and the identification of relevant information from much larger and more diverse data pools. In cases where the availability (and coherence) of data and computational resources are no limiting factors, it can even be left to the model to distinguish irrelevant from indicative pieces of information. In this sense, machine learning algorithms challenge the "garbage in – garbage out" paradigm of conventional models: mathematically, the relevance of each input parameter is given by the values of the weighting factors of the machine learning model, but at the same time it is also the key result of the calibration of the model (see Sect. 1.1 in Liermann, Li, & Schaudinnus, Mathematical background of machine learning, 2019b).

II. **Availability**: Many different machine learning algorithms are freely available today, e.g., as part of open-source software in R or Python. In connection with the abstract nature (see next item), one can relatively easily switch between different types of models, e.g., between a random forest and a deep learning algorithm. This corresponds to modeling of a higher order, since one not only tries new input parameters while keeping the general methodology unchanged, but the methodology itself becomes a degree of freedom and can be changed fundamentally in the course of modeling.

III. **Abstraction**: Regarding its consequences, this last aspect may be the least obvious, but potentially has far-reaching implications. This is because machine learning methods are abstract in the sense that the same methodology and expertise can be applied to various situations. This can greatly support and facilitate an integrative view of risk parameter modeling. For example, one might suspect that there is a significant overlap between the risk factors for drawing a credit line (this refers to a credit conversion factor model), on the one hand, and the risk factors for drawing deposits on the other hand. However, the former is component of credit risk whereas the latter is an important part of liquidity risk. Nevertheless, both risk factors are candidates for methodological unification, as they can both be considered as achievements of a general drawing model. The abstract nature of ML algorithms is very useful, as one could consider using a larger set of input parameters, in which each of the parameters can be considered as a good candidate as input for a CCF model and/or a model for the drawing of deposits. The resulting sets of weighting factors for both cases could then be compared, as they contain quantitative information about case overlap and the degree of overlap among other things. This provides an integrative view of credit risk and liquidity risk.

In principle, one could argue that all three aspects hold true for traditional methodology as well. During conventional model development, for example, the methodology itself could also change significantly, even several times. But the decisive point here is that, due to the three aspects mentioned above, modeling is drastically facilitated. Please note that we have simplified things to a certain degree, as machine learning also has significant challenges, such as limitations of data quality and availability, the considerable effort to pre-process raw data to use as input parameters for a machine learning algorithm, and the risk of overfitting. We address some of these aspects in the following section.

3 Calculation Example

3.1 General Model Setup

In this simple example of implementing artificial neural networks (as a special kind of machine learning) with the use of open-source computational tools, three provisional models are used to predict the creditability of retail customers. This is an example of a binary classification as the simplest type of categorical target variables. Model performance is compared to general logistic regression as a benchmark.

The data used for our calculations contains credit ratings from a German bank and was downloaded from the Eberly College of Science website (Eberly College of Sciences, 2019). This data can be used to demonstrate the implementation of an artificial neural network that performs shadow rating. In other words, we try to teach artificial neural network to mimic the rules, after which a customer's creditability has been rated by the bank's scorecards.

The data file contains the anonymized information of 1000 customers from the 1990s, which is much less than the amount of contextual data in pictures and texts that is harvested by modern online platforms. It is sufficient to demonstrate and interpret basic trends, but one should keep in mind that the performance of artificial neural networks increases and becomes more competitive when more data is available to train them.

The simple models that are introduced here do not consider the individual financial consequences of true(T)/false(F), positive(P)/negative(N) predictions. These details would be necessary to bias the training steps and determine whether a small increase of the predictive power, as measured by the area under the ROC-curve (AUC), could have a significant effect on the profit of a bank. However, we will focus on those implementation parts that all models have in common.

A custom Python script was written to pre-process the data, build the artificial neural network and run experiments with different parameters. The script was written and tested in an Anaconda3 environment, which was downgraded to Python version 3.6.0 for compatibility with the TensorFlow library version 1.12.0, which was used to build the artificial neural networks. All these tools are available as open-source software. There are numerous coding examples on Github (GitHubGist, 2019) and tutorials available for the use of TensorFlow for image and text recognition on the developer's homepage (TensorFlowGuide, 2019). One can also find some instructive code samples for binary classification in similar contexts to credit rating (Russo, 2019). In our example, two important aspects are that (a) the model must handle combined input of categorical and continuous variables and (b) that it should include functions to calculate performance measures such as the accuracy and the AUC. Compared to image and text recognition, the amount of data per observation is much smaller and one does not have to worry about feeding functions, temporary storage and code parallelization. A full version of our script can be provided on request.

On viewing the data, the model would have to account for a maximum of 20 independent values that describe a customer, which will be referred to as features, to predict one binary target variable called creditability. It is easier for the artificial neural network to learn from concise and relevant information. This is particularly important in situations where the amount of data limits severely the complexity of the machine learning algorithm that can be trained with it effectively. In our data file, three of the features are continuous and not categorical, and some of the categories are sparse, so that some general pre-processing of the data is advisable independent of the model.

To identify important categories using exploratory data analysis (EDA), one investigates correlations between individual features and the target using contingency tables and scatter plots, for example. While it is trivial to assume that telephone numbers do not correlate with creditability, the optimal width of the bins that categorize income is not obvious. For the sake of comparability and simplicity, we apply the same scheme to aggregate categories as described on the Eberly College of Science website:

- Continuous variables are normalized across the entire dataset,
- Eight features are deemed irrelevant and the corresponding columns are not imported,
- Several sparse categories (e.g., "single" and "single/divorced") are combined.

Finally, the remaining categories are encoded using one-hot vectors (Mirjalili & Raschka, 2017), in which each category of each feature is assigned its own dimension. In this uniform representation, the customers' categorical features can be fed into the artificial neural network along with the continuous features.

Once the data has been cleaned and encoded, it is split into a training set and a test set. This enables calculation of basic performance measures that quantify how transferable the learned patterns are and how well they predict the creditability of new customers unknown to the model during the training process. In a real application, one must avoid the use of outdated training data, because customer behavior changes over time. The models presented here do not account for any such time-dependent trends and systemic long-term changes, which affect the predictive power and cause it to expire.

Generally, predictions should not only have a high level of sensitivity and selectivity (Altman & Bland, 1994), but also be transferable. It is therefore reasonable to look for performance measures that are independent of the split. A straight forward way to achieve this is to use validation methods that average over several alternative ways to split the data (see Liermann et al., Mathematical background of machine learning, 2019b). In this case, the split is performed by random subset selection, whereby the ratio of creditable to non-creditable individuals is not fixed. Ten independent runs are performed for each data point, individually starting with a reset memory. The standard deviations are shown as error bars in the corresponding figures. The analysis shown in the results section requires 100–1000 iterations of the entire training. If all individual runs are parallelized, the calculation finishes in under 10 Seconds, the duration of the longest training, and, if run sequentially on a single core of a Core i9-8950HK 2.9 GHz processor, in less than 15 minutes training.

3.2 Model Configuration

The initial model configuration was identical to the one used in the TensorFlow quick start guide (TensorFlow, 2019). This model uses 3 layers, in which the first layer consists of 10 neurons, the second of 20 neurons and the third of 10 neurons. As a rule of thumb, the number of nodes per layer is of the same order of magnitude as the number of independent features. The ideal setup and layer depth are basically determined by the unknown complexity of the patterns to be identified. The more complex these patterns and the more categories exist in a classification, the more data is needed to represent those patterns and to enable an artificial neural network to learn them. More complex models are hungrier for data, which results in more training steps.

TensorFlow provides a high-level API for deconvolutional neural networks (DNN) called DNNClassifier. The model has several customizable parameters. We have used a hyperbolic tangent activation function (tf.nn.tanh) and a stochastic gradient descent (SGD) optimizer to train artificial neural networks with three different hidden layer setups. The artificial neural network's complexity has been changed to explore the modification affects

a. its fit effectiveness (based on reproduction of creditability in the training set) and
b. its predictive power (based on inference of creditability in the test set).

The TensorFlow library is very flexible and allows for convenient modifications of the layers, the activation function and the optimizer by adjusting the parameters of the DNNClassifier. Table 1 summarizes configuration and

Table 1 Overview of different models that were used

Model name	Description	Nodes per hidden layer
DNN_2.2	2-layer deconvolutional network with hyperbolic tangent activation	[2, 2]
DNN_10.10	2-layer deconvolutional network with hyperbolic tangent activation	[10, 10]
DNN_10.20.10	3-layer deconvolutional network with hyperbolic tangent activation	[10, 20, 10]
LogReg	logistic regression (*sklearn.linear_model. LogisticRegression()*)	–

parametrization of the four compared models. Of course these exemplary changes are to be seen as a proof of concept rather than systematic adjustments that optimize the structure of the network. The available data may not be sufficient to train deep models with three or more layers.

3.3   Performance Measures

Two classical measures for the predictive power of a model are accuracy and the AUC (Hanley & McNeil, 1982). Although accuracy can be useful as a relative measure for comparing the predictive power in a series of similar models, it does not serve as an absolute measure of discriminatory ability, because it is influenced by the ratio of creditable to non-creditable customers in the training set. In our data file, for example, 70% of the customers are creditable, meaning that 0.7 sets the lower bar for the value of the accuracy. We expect a predictive model to perform better than a trivial prejudice like "all people are creditable". The lower bar for the AUC is always 0.5, thus corresponding to a model without discriminatory ability such as one that predicts all creditable customers correctly, but all non-creditable customers incorrectly. Since all reported trends were the same for both measures, only the AUC values are discussed in the following section.

4   Model Results Discussion

4.1   Dataset Partition

For a proposed number of relevant features, the more datasets are available, the better they populate the categories until the relation of every feature to creditability is represented in the best possible way. Only under this condition can transferable predictors be identified. To gain an indication of whether the data is representative of the rating rules in our case, we measured the influence of the size of the training set on the results after a fixed number of 1500 training steps. The AUC was measured for ten different sizes. Ten independent runs were performed for each size, in which the sets were generated with a function for random subset selection.[2] Figure 2 shows

---

[2]sklearn.model_selection.train_test_split().

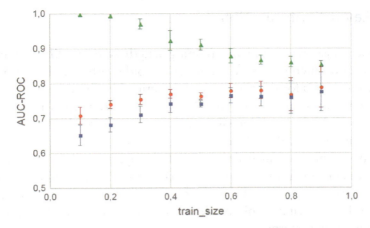

Fig. 2 The impact of splitting data into a training set and a test set on the performance of the resulting artificial neural network. The AUC after 1500 training steps for the test set of the DNN_10.20.10 model (boxes), the LogReg model (circles) and for the training set of the DNN_10.20.10 model (triangles)

how the AUC value changes for the DNN_10.20.10 (boxes) and LogReg (circles) when the size of the training set is increased from 10 to 90% of the available data. The AUC resulting from the training data is also shown as a measure of the fit effectiveness (triangles).

One can see that the AUC of both models increases until the split is even, where it levels out at about 0.76. This suggests the amount of data is sufficient and that more data will not further improve the performance of the predictions. The error, however, which is smallest for the even split, increases with the training size from 0.5 to 0.9. A possible explanation for this is that this error is dominated by overfitting—the process in which the artificial neural network starts to memorize the training set after it has learned general, transferable patterns. The error increases, because overfitting starts earlier when the network is fed larger batches of training data for a fixed number of training steps. Another clear trend is the decrease in fit effectiveness as indicated by the triangles: small training sets under 20% can be fitted perfectly in 1500 steps, but the larger they get, the longer it takes. We decided to use a ratio of 50:50 for the following experiments, mainly due to the smaller error of the AUC. According to these results, conventional logistic regression outperforms the artificial neural network quite consistently, which is explained in the following section.

4.2 Layer Configuration

The hidden layer setup and the training length were modified to explore possible improvements in performance and avoid overfitting. Figure 3 shows the resulting AUCs for the three models described in Table 1. Again, each of the data points was averaged over 10 independent runs (300 in total). The predictions of the logistic regression set a benchmark result of AUC=0.76, which was not exceeded by the other three models.

The upper line (second from top) with triangles represents the fit effectiveness (calculated from the training set) of the simplest model with two hidden layers, DNN_2.2. Even after 14,000 steps, the model has not reached a 100% match. This model is obviously not complex enough to learn the existing patterns.

The lower line (third from the top) with circles represents the predictive power (calculated from the test set). It reaches an AUC of about 0.76 only after 2000 steps, while the other two models require only half as many steps to reach a comparable AUC value. However, it has the advantage of not becoming overtrained as quickly simply because it is not capable of memorizing detailed datasets. The DNN_10.20.10 learned even faster, but also becomes overtrained earlier.

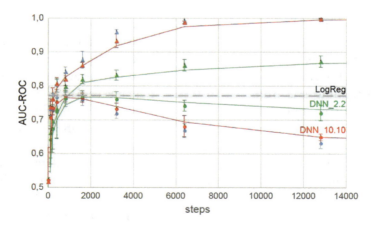

Fig. 3 Comparison of the performance of three different artificial neural networks: the AUCs for the test set (circles=predictive power) and for the training set (triangles=fit effectiveness) of the DNN_2.2 (inner lines), DNN_10.10 (outer lines), and DNN_10.20.10 (blue). The benchmark result of the logistic regression is shown as a gray line. The inner and outer curves simply serve as visual guides

4.3 Training Steps

Figure 2 shows that the complexity of the model and its ability to identify patterns in the data do not necessarily increase the number of steps required for optimal training. For the DNN_10.20.10, the AUC starts to diminish after about 500 steps, for DNN_10.10 after 1000 steps and for DNN_2.2 after 2000 steps. The training takes only a few seconds, mainly because of the small datasets compared to image recognition and other typical applications of artificial neural networks.

5   Summary

The use of machine learning algorithms has an impact on the mode of modeling through the aspects of automation, availability and abstraction. It can also help establish a much more integrative view of risk parameter modeling and thus of risk management.

Implementation of artificial neural networks to predict creditability in a shadow rating model could be demonstrated successfully. This implementation can be easily extended to different predictors and multi-categorical targets in other types of artificial neural networks using the flexible open-source library TensorFlow.

All the artificial neural networks and the logistic regression model reached comparable AUC values, which means that, considering the significantly higher computational cost, artificial neural networks offer no benefits in the studied case. The amount of data is probably the most important limitation regarding the precision of our performance measurements. Based on our limited results, one might speculate that feeding more data into the deep 3-layer model could eventually reveal more complex patterns that logistic regression would be inferior in detecting.

Since the scorecard, which defines the rules behind the rating is constant and independent of the real relation between creditability and its predictors, one would expect better fits from a shadow rating model than for a model that predicts actual probabilities of default. Nevertheless, information is still lost when several features are mapped onto one binary target variable by the rating. Due to this loss of information in the rating process, it may not be feasible to develop an artificial neural network that beats the predictions of the shadow rating of a simple logistic regression in this case.

Literature

Altman, D. G., & Bland, J. M. (1994). Diagnostic tests1: Sensitivity and specificity. *BMJ, 308*, 1552.

Eberly College of Sciences. (2019). *Analysis of German credit data*. Retrieved from https://newonlinecourses.science.psu.edu/stat508/resources/analysis/gcd/gcd.1;-file"german_credit.csv.

GitHubGist. (2019). Retrieved from https://gist.github.com/damienpontifex/1f03b966d36049b678efdddb54cef4eb.

Goodfellow, I., Bengio, Y., & Courville, A. (2016). *Deep learning*. The MIT Press.

Hanley, J. A., & McNeil, B. J. (1982). The meaning and use of the area under the receiver operating characteristic (ROC) curve. *Radiology, 143*(1), 29–36.

Lessmann, S., Baesens, B., Seow, H. V., & Thomas, L. C. (2015). Benchmarking state-of-the-art classification algorithms for credit scoring: An update of research. *European Journal of Operational Research, 247*(1), 124–136.

Liermann, V., Li, S., & Schaudinnus, N. (2019a). Deep learning—An introduction. In V. Liermann & C. Stegmann (Eds.), *The impact of digital transformation and fintech on the finance professional*. New York: Palgrave Macmillan.

Liermann, V., Li, S., & Schaudinnus, N. (2019b). Mathematical background of machine learning. In V. Liermann & C. Stegmann (Eds.), *The impact of digital transformation and fintech on the finance professional*. New York: Palgrave Macmillan.

McNeil, A., Frey, R., & Embrechts, P. (2005). Quantitative risk management. *Princeton Series in Finance*.

Mirjalili, V., & Raschka, S. (2017). Machine learning mit Python und scikit-learn und TensorFlow. *mitp Professional*.

Mitchell, T. M. (1997). *Machine learning*. McGraw-Hill Education Ltd.

Russo. (2019). Retrieved from https://vprusso.github.io/blog/2017/tensor-flow-categorical-data/.

Sowa, R. et al. (2004). Estimating synchronization in brain electrical activity from epilepsy patients with cellular neuronal networks. In M. G. T. Roska (Ed.), *Proceedings of the 8th IEEE International Workshop on Cellular Neural Networks and Applications (CNNA2004)*. Budapest, Ungarn: Amulett'98 Kft.

TechEmergence. (2017). *Machine learning marketing*.

TensorFlow. (2019). *Quick start guide*. Retrieved from https://www.tensorflow.org/guide/premade_estimators.

TensorFlowGuide. (2019). Retrieved from https://www.tensorflow.org/guide/.

11

Real Estate Risk: Appraisal Capture

Volker Liermann and Norbert Schaudinnus

1 Introduction

1.1 Market Situation

One of the most interesting investment tasks consists of setting up diversified and profitable asset allocation. Asset classes with different risk-return profiles are available to an investor. The primary conventional classes are cash, government and other bonds, property, equity and commodities, whereas the universe of alternative investments is even more diversified. Property and, in particular, real estate has become an interesting and challenging asset class.

Too much liquidity in combination with low-interest rates provided by the central banks since the financial crises of 2008 has led to a high demand for real estate. The demand of professional investors for stable and sufficient returns has triggered a rise in prices. Driven by inflation fears, private households have also generated massive demand. The increasing demand unfortunately has not been met by the supply in real estate to the same extent. This unbalanced demand–supply situation has led to higher prices and, in many cases, to a disconnect between (fundamental) value and price and created a thread of price bubbles.

V. Liermann (✉) · N. Schaudinnus
ifb AG, Grünwald, Germany
e-mail: Volker.Liermann@ifb-group.com

N. Schaudinnus
e-mail: Norbert.Schaudinnus@ifb-group.com

© The Author(s) 2019
V. Liermann and C. Stegmann (eds.), *The Impact of Digital Transformation and FinTech on the Finance Professional*, https://doi.org/10.1007/978-3-030-23719-6_11

Given the current market environment, profitable investment alternatives with a reasonable risk profile are lacking. As such, some investors do not see an alternative to real estate investment. As a widespread accepted investment (Markowitz, 1952) theory points out, reducing risk while maintaining the profit level is best achieved by diversification.

1.2   The Need for a Machine Learning Approach

In classical approaches to diversification in real estate, property location is the primary and, in some cases, only criterion. State of the art (value driver focused) modeling takes a deeper delve into property characteristics and the property users. The drawback of value driver focused modeling is the need for micro-based property characteristics and property users. In practical implementation and ongoing operation, having data in a structured model-ready form is the most challenging aspect if one is not willing to invest heavily in the required human workforce. The task of extracting property master data (once) and tenant or user data (dynamic data, continuously, maybe yearly) is rather unexciting although it can be quite complex. A classic business rule-based approach would therefore face difficulties due to the inherent range of appraisal structures. This would then also require human work to adjust the business rules.

An automated approach based on components from machine learning and, in some cases, deep learning is the best way to meet this challenge.

1.3   Structure of the Chapter

In Sect. 2 the key components of a value driver oriented real estate risk management are laid out and the primary components of micro-based real estate risk management are briefly introduced. The main part (Sect. 3) deals with the different aspects of natural language processing (NLP) and provides a framework for information extraction from contracts or export reports. The special challenges of real estate appraisals are highlighted in Sect. 4. The chapter ends with a summary in Sect. 5.

2   Real Estate Risk

Depending on the size and business model, banks face real estate risk in two ways: (A) property as a collateral and (B) property as an investment (often as an alternative to government bonds or other asset classes). In the second case, the real estate value is the key figure to include. In the first case (especially for operator-run properties), default-probability is driven by the users/tenant's economic abilities. These economic abilities are normally modeled by the DSCR.[1] See (Liermann, Viets, & Grossmann, www.risknet.de, 2018) for details. The net operating income in the DSCR is driven by the tenant.

In recent years, the focus for real estate risk has been on a single property or group of properties. The expertise of the responsible employees at property level is quite high incl. the micro environment and property specifics. At portfolio level, differentiation is established by location and asset type (e.g., office building, shopping mall, residential property, hotel, warehouse, etc.).

Value driver oriented real estate risk management looks deeper into the risk sources, by analyzing existing tenant or user structures. Furthermore, projection of tenant replacement based on the actual tenant composition in the property provides a future-oriented projection of property value development.

2.1 Introduction to Value Driver Oriented Real Estate Risk Management

The right side of Fig. 1 shows the four modules in the journey toward value driver oriented real estate risk management. The first step consists of gaining a summarized view based on property details. Property details (e.g., structural data like m^2, number of garages and dynamic data like tenants by unit and tenants grouped by clusters) allow for deeper analysis of the property's economic value. This is done by assigning the tenants and their ability to pay the rent to value drivers like macroeconomic factors. In the third step, value drivers can be altered or stressed to see the impact on the individual property value and the aggregated portfolio value. Based on the discovered portfolio sensitivities, the next and fourth step consists of developing a classic VaR model or a more sophisticated agent-based model (ABM) (see Enzinger & Grossmann, 2019).

The two key challenges of such an undertaking are allocating the value drivers and obtaining structured model-ready property data including the tenant composition.

---

[1]DSCR—debt service coverage ratio is the quotient of net operation income and debt service.

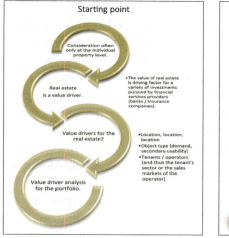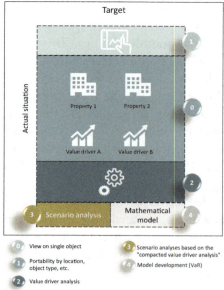

Fig. 1 Modularized approach

2.2 Necessity of Appraisals Capture

To be able to start any micro-based (i.e., scenario-oriented or model-oriented) analysis of a real estate portfolio, the property data needs to be available in a structured form. It should be pointed out that the information has to be available in the appraisals, and is used and known by the employee in charge. Harmonized data collection, however, which is essential for risk modeling (scenario-oriented or model-oriented), is normally not in place.

2.3 Key Elements to Capture

The key elements required to perform value driver-oriented real estate risk management are illustrated in Fig. 2. The left side shows the substance data, which is normally fixed over time, and the dynamic data, which changes over time. The occupancy rate is positioned in the middle of the figure, because the occupancy rate is driven by demand (and therefore by location and property type) and the price (normally expressed as monthly rent).

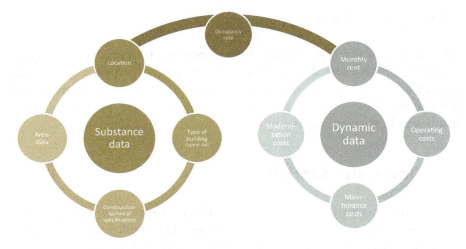

Fig. 2 Substance and dynamic data

2.3.1 Master Data (Substance Data)

The substance data is fixed over a long time period, normally of 30 years or more if no redevelopment is needed. This includes location information like the street address and postal code or even geodata, the surrounding area (differentiated between belonging to the property and the non-property surroundings), the type of building and usage, and the construction details (like square feet and number of floors, etc.).

2.3.2 Dynamic Data

The key dynamic data is the monthly rent and the occupation rate for the actual property state. Prediction of these two key figures is one of the most important challenges in real estate valuation and thus in real estate risk management. This is especially true when the property is financed by the bank and used as collateral. The impact is then not only measured through the real estate value (and thus the unsecured volume of the credit), but also through the default probability via the DSCR.

Operating and maintenance costs are to some extent fixed and projectable. Modernization costs are only important in the rare case of property redevelopment.

2.3.3 Appraisal Structure

The structure of the appraisal can differ depending on the appraiser/expert. Besides qualitative text descriptions of the property, the primary quantitative key figures are always included. These are most commonly summarized using tables. The structure is ambiguous and a purely rule-based approach is insufficient in terms of adaptability.

3 Tools and Models

In order to extract information from appraisals, a specific working process has to be conducted. This process can be roughly divided into two steps, which are explained in further detail in the following subsections.

The first step consists of retrieving raw text data. Depending on the structure of the source, raw text can either be mined from the encapsulated format or has to be retrieved from image content.

Secondly, the retrieved raw text data is scanned for relevant content. The methods used in this part stem from the field of NLP. In addition to statistical analysis and context search, machine learning algorithms are also utilized.

Finally, an application is suggested that interconnects the tools described to map the whole process of information retrieval.

3.1 Retrieval of Structured Text Data

As shown in Fig. 4, a typical sample appraisal does not necessarily contain relevant information in a structured form. On the contrary, required content is "wrapped" in a mixture of tables and continuous text. Moreover, retrieving the text content from a document is not straightforward. If the document is not a text file, two scenarios have to be distinguished.

3.1.1 Parsing PDF Files

In the best case, raw text is just encrypted in a text-based pdf file. Parsing tools can be used to extract text and even distinguish headers or identify table structures. There are many tools available, which offer APIs to high-level programming languages. An important feature of the intended tool consists of accurately extracting raw text and structured information without introducing artificial line breaks, for example. Especially pdf files with complex structures and mixed text blocks are difficult to scan. An appropriate parsing tool recognizes different text blocks and font sizes to preserve related information. As discussed below, analysis of text data requires intact sentences and table content organized in rows. One drawback of accurate tools often pertains to performance. In fact, more accurate parsing algorithms can be more than an order of magnitude slower than the fastest parsing tools.

PDFMiner is a convenient tool for Python environments. It is written in Python and, unlike other tools, focuses entirely on retrieving text data. It allows for identification of headers, fonts, sections and obtaining the exact location of text on a page. The latter is useful when it comes to generating previews to monitor the result of appraisal analysis. PDFMiner can scan text in building blocks using a layout analysis feature. Given a file handler, scanning the whole document works hierarchically. Each page is scanned for various text boxes, figures or tables. Each text box is then scanned for text content line by line or even character by character. Refined settings can be used to specify character encodings, word margins or line spacing, for example.

To obtain structured text data in our particular application, we use PDFMiner with the layout analysis function to obtain text block by block and conclusively concatenate results into a single string.

3.1.2 Optical Character Recognition

If text cannot be directly obtained, as is the case in scanned documents, the file has to be interpreted as an image. Optical character recognition (OCR) is the generic term used to describe the process of extracting text from images. The process of text recognition mostly involves machine learning techniques to recognize single isolated characters. Spellchecking algorithms are then utilized to derive words from arrays of characters. Most OCR tools have been developed and refined within the last decade. Further refinement also considers the structure of sentences or the context of the overall document.

One of the most well-known tools is Tesseract, which has been developed and sponsored by Google since 2006. It supports most platforms and APIs to high-level programming languages like R and Python. The Python-library Pytesseract enables scanning of images to text out-of-the box. The library Pyocr is an alternative wrapper for OCR tools including Tesseract and features additional functionality.

Image preprocessing is recommended for improving the OCR results of all tools. We include preprocessing that first converts the image to monochrome and smooths it using pixel interpolation. Postprocessing using spellchecking and removal of unknown characters is also recommended to improve the quality of the raw text data.

The output of image-to-text conversion using OCR results in a single string, as in the case of file-parsing mentioned in the last section. Common OCR tools generally don't provide information about fonts or text structure like headers and sections.

3.2 Natural Language Processing

Interpreting raw text and obtaining information is the central and most complex task. NLP is the term used to describe tools and methods that structure, analyze and interpret text. We introduce and briefly describe methods in order of their appearance in a workflow to gain predefined information from raw text data. A comprehensive tool that provides functionality in NLP is the natural language tool kit (nltk[2]), a Python-based library.

3.2.1 Tokenization and Stemmers

One of the basic steps used in NLP consists of subdividing text into functional pieces. The process of dividing continuous text into sentences and transforming sentences into lists of words is called tokenization. The tools that provide tokenized text work in a fairly straightforward way, recognizing whitespace and special characters as delimiters for words and periods for sentences. More advanced methods work in a language-specific way and, for example, recognize minimum sentence structures, possibly supported by a dictionary. Tokenized text is further processed by so-called stemmers, which are algorithms that reduce inflected words to their word stem or at least a word base. In this way, similar words are associated and can be easily recognized by algorithms for further processing. For example, *fished*, *fishing* and *fisher* would be mapped to the common stem *fish*. Basic stemming algorithms are rule-based. To account for the loss of information during stemming, more elaborate algorithms (also called lemmatizers) are applied, which

---

[2]NLTK—natural language toolkit is a platform for building Python programs to handle human language data see NLTK Project (2018).

provide a morphological analysis of words. Lemmatizing would attempt to distinguish *fishing* as a noun and a verb. It would also link the words *bad* and *worse*, for example. Lemmatization is drastically more expensive since it requires additional dictionary lookups. This increases for languages that contain much more morphology like German or Spanish.

3.2.2 Stop Words

Texts usually contain many common words, that appear most frequently in the respective language. These are called stop words. In English, the most common stop words are *I*, *me*, *my*, *we* etc. These words don't affect the information content of the text but increase the word count. Hence, stop words are usually removed before further processing.

Once raw text is transformed into lists of stemmed word lists and stop words are removed, the most basic functions for retrieving information can be applied. One basic function that provides information about the text content consists of counting the relative frequency of words within a document.

3.2.3 Term Frequency–Inverse Document Frequency (tf–idf)

The simplest way is to search for the most frequent word from a list of suggested words. To determine whether an appraisal contains a real value report or a traffic report, a word count applied to these two patterns would return the right type. The more elaborate method takes into account that specific relative frequencies of words in a document clearly characterize the document. Term frequency–inverse document frequency (tf–idf) is an algorithm that assigns a score to each word, which is proportional to its importance in the document. Most text-based recommender systems use tf–idf to classify text documents because the algorithm is fast and reliable.

Another basic function that can be directly applied to preprocessed text is a lookup algorithm that looks for specific patterns near buzzwords. For example, a numeric string should appear followed by a surface unit near (preferably after) the word *floorspace*. Dates or money amounts can be retrieved from the context in the same way. It is more cumbersome to extract locations or personal names, for instance. These have to be tagged beforehand to be precisely identified.

3.2.4 Named Entity Recognition

A common approach to identifying these so-called named entities is Named Entity Recognition (NER). NER is a subdomain of information extraction and is sometimes also called entity identification, entity chunking and entity extraction. NER attempts to locate and classify so-called named entities within a text. This classification maps the words or expressions to predefined categories (e.g., percentages, monetary values, time expressions, quantities, organizations, person names, locations). The method involves machine learning techniques and includes the most advanced tools utilized in the information retrieval approach. They are briefly described below. They are based on more simple approaches that facilitate recognizing similar words or finding search terms based on similar contexts.

NER can help enrich the text with more structured information that can then support the feature generation and pattern identification process. See Liermann, Li, and Schaudinnus, Deep learning—An introduction (2019) for a brief introduction.

3.2.5 Word2Vec Model

The so-called Word2Vec model is a well-known approach in NLP to produce word embeddings. The original paper on this was published in 2013 (see Mikolov, Sutskever, Chen, Corrado, & Dean, 2013). A couple of improvements have been made since then. See Sect. 3.3 in Liermann et al. (2019) for a brief introduction.

3.2.6 Mapping the Process in a Joint Application

Figure 3 illustrates the overall architecture of an application to retrieve information from appraisals. The upper left block summarizes the process of extracting text data from pdf files. Depending on the quality of the data source (scan or text-based pdf file), optical character recognition or simple pdf parsing must be performed to obtain the raw text.

The central block represents the main processing layer, which aims to extract the required information from the appraisal regarding the real estate property. This layer is assisted by two supporting layers—the database layer and the graphical user interface (GUI). The database layer holds the

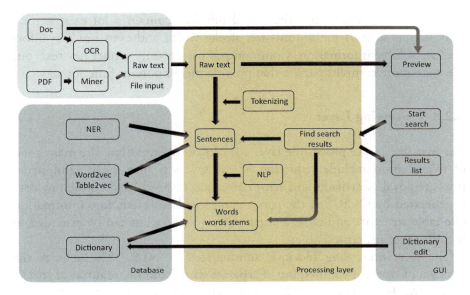

Fig. 3 Example scheme for an application built to extract information from appraisal documents

necessary information for performing NLP and the GUI provides the user a way to interact and improve the algorithm.

3.2.7 Input Layer

The input layer transforms the appraisal into raw text[3] for further processing. The raw text can include certain structural information such as headlines or chapter structures to improve pattern identification. Especially if the appraisal includes multiple properties or units within a property, the chapter structure helps group the relevant information.

Tables are often used in real estate appraisals to provide summarized information. This structural information is key for use in the processing layer.

There are generally two different types of input—scanned images of the original documents and text-based pdf files. Scanned images have to first be transformed into text. This task is quite common and many frameworks are

---

[3]Uncleaned, unprocessed character string.

available to accomplish it.[4] Text-based pdf files contain a lot of structural information such as fonts, font-size, stroke width and even heading information or table information. Common pdf parsers only extract raw text, but there are more complex parsers that provide this important functionality.

3.2.8 Processing Layer

The first step in the processing layer consists of tokenization. The main goals of tokenization include reduction of the raw text into meaningful structures, removal of artifacts and error correction (especially when the raw data is generated by OCR).[5] If the parser can provide sub-structure information like table structure and table content, then tokenization can be extended to include these structures.

The next processing block is summarized as NLP. This includes the removal of stop words, merging of separate words and the removal of special characters. These tasks are followed by stemming,[6] which reduces the number of features passed to the machine learning algorithms for training (like Word2Vec or Table 2Vec[7]).

NER and NLP are processing steps intended to reduce the complexity in the actual search or assignment task underpinning the actual extraction of information. The search algorithm then searches for predefined content or structures. Depending on the type of raw text and the performance of the machine learning algorithm, integration of lookup and methods supported by machine learning are needed to provide reasonable search results.

The process of training and applying is not a one-time task that can be applied without any further adjustment. The process of training and applying is an ongoing cycle. The learning ability aims to increase the precision of the algorithms automatically with the number of checked documents. This includes user-feedback for incomprehensible algorithm results. Individual adaptation should allow users to define individual boundary conditions to optimize the search.

---

[4]Only the table identification is not included in the simple packages.

[5]Some see tokenization as a part of the natural language processing.

[6]Stemming is the process of transforming words into unified (non-conjugated or declined) words relevant to content.

[7]For details on Table 2Vec, see Deng (2018).

3.2.9 Interaction with a Database

The database layer is needed to store the information required by NLP like NER, but also include problem-specific information like dictionaries to improve the learning process. The structural information from the trained Word2Vec (or Table 2Vec) also needs to be stored.

3.2.10 User Interface and Visualization

The user interface supports the user in monitoring and supervising the training process. While specific tasks like real estate appraisals are only covered to some extent by NER and NLP, continued learning has to be user-friendly. The user interface can be used to highlight the information assigned by the algorithm to a certain label and allow the user to monitor and adjust the label if required.

Figure 4 shows an example appraisal and connection to the key-figure database. During training the user can easily identify and review the source of the extracted information and then update and adjust the information if required. Even in the ongoing phase, it is important for users to be able to conveniently trace down the source of doubtful information.

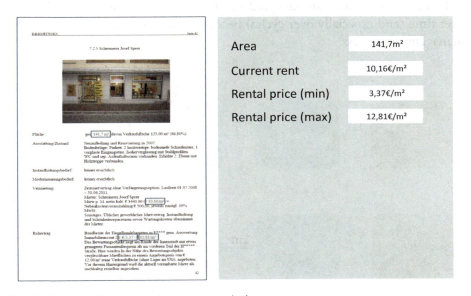

Fig. 4 Example German real estate appraisal

4 Application to Appraisals

As the structure described in the processing section is quite universal and can be used to extract information of various types (e.g., collateral contracts, loan agreements), we will mention some key aspects of real estate appraisals in the context of real estate risk in this section. As already laid out in Sect. 3, one of the key challenges in real estate risk management consists of obtaining detailed information on the real estate properties and the market situation in the region or local environment.

A quantitative description of the real estate property includes but is not restricted to the surface area in square meters/feet and other information like number of floors or number of garages assigned to the property. These numbers are important because they serve as the foundation for the different evaluation methods (see Fig. 2). Another important aspect is the structure of a property or a property collection.

Two possible alternative structures are shown in Fig. 5

Besides the hard facts of the property including the surface area in square meters/feet, soft facts like the arm's length principle (ALP) are normally included in the appraisal. These soft facts can vary between experts composing the appraisals, but the variation in the soft facts is important information when it comes to risk management for the properties. A huge variation in soft facts hints at a non-transparent and somewhat risky market situation.

Once the appraisals are analyzed on a longer-term basis, the variations over time (and especially over cycles) becomes a major ingredient in the risk management process.

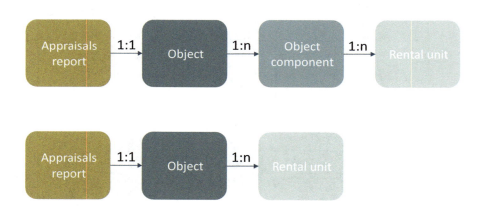

Fig. 5 Structure of extracted data

5 Summary

The extraction of information for contracts or appraisals can be extremely valuable, if not even a prerequisite, for risk management processes. The hard facts of real estate properties at property or rental unit level are fundamental for any micro-based portfolio evaluation or quantitative risk assessment. This information is available to financial institutions, but is usually not in a structured electronic form. Financial institutions can save massive manual effort in collecting data by using machine learning or deep learning algorithms to perform this task. The potential of this is clear, as it is a recurring task that usually has to be performed annually.

Besides the detailed aspect of real estate appraisals discussed in this article, there is much potential for other areas of application including collateral contacts or side agreements and cancelation classes in credit contracts.

Literature

Deng, L. (2018). *Table2Vec: Neural word and entity embeddings for table population and retrieval*. Stavanger: University of Stavanger.

Enzinger, P., & Grossmann, S. (2019). Managing internal and external network complexity. In V. Liermann & C. Stegmann (Eds.), *The impact of digital transformation and fintech on the finance professional*. New York: Palgrave Macmillan.

Liermann, V., Li, S., & Schaudinnus, N. (2019). Deep learning—An introduction. In V. Liermann & C. Stegmann (Eds.), *The impact of digital transformation and fintech on the finance professional*. New York: Palgrave Macmillan.

Liermann, V., Viets, N., & Grossmann, S. (2018, August). Retrieved September 19, 2018, from www.risknet.de https://www.risknet.de/themen/risknews/a-holistic-approach-to-real-estate-risk-management/5a179b5d33c31dd70fa3743aa-91f23a6/.

Markowitz, H. M. (1952). Portfolio selection. *Journal of Finance, 7,* 77–91.

Mikolov, T., Sutskever, I., Chen, K., Corrado, G., & Dean, J. (2013). *Distributed representations of words and phrases and their compositionality*. Mountain View: Google Inc.

NLTK Project. (2018, November 17). *Natural language toolkit—Home*. Retrieved from Natural Language Toolkit https://www.nltk.org/.

12

Managing Internal and External Network Complexity: How Digitalization and New Technology Influence the Modeling Approach

Stefan Grossmann and Philipp Enzinger

1 Introduction

Networks—in one form or another—have been an underlying theme in the financial industry since its beginning, when currencies or credit, combined with information, began trading across the globe, through various channels with various counterparties, intermediaries and financial products involved.

From a more modern standpoint, traditional banking has dealt for a long time with interbank clearing networks, payment system networks, the acquired client or customer base as closely linked entities, but also computer/mainframe/IT networks, employee management and collaboration networks and many other forms of networks within the financial industry. These have been evolving over time and coexist as the necessary backbone to doing business.

S. Grossmann (✉)
ifb Canada Management Consulting, Inc., Toronto, ON, Canada
e-mail: stefan.grossmann@ifb-group.com

P. Enzinger
ifb International AG, Zurich, Switzerland
e-mail: philipp.enzinger@ifb-group.com

© The Author(s) 2019
V. Liermann and C. Stegmann (eds.), *The Impact of Digital Transformation and FinTech on the Finance Professional*, https://doi.org/10.1007/978-3-030-23719-6_12

With the advent of disruptive technologies in the form of fintech, regtech, insurtech or just the digital (r)evolution in general, we are seeing some of these networks start to merge, evolve faster and become opaque or nontransparent due to the speed of this ongoing transformation. Consequently, they exhibit intrinsic risk and require a very different way of thinking and managing due to their deep-rooted complexity.

It is crucial to monitor these systems and measure and manage the network-intrinsic risk as well as possible. This is due to its key characteristic: If the given risk actually plays out in the internal or external network and if the potential for contagion is high, the network might collapse and recovery will be very costly.

In the case of external networks, this particular risk is usually referred to as systemic risk and defined as the risk of a financial system collapse due to contagion through the various interlinkages and interdependencies in the network. A combination of common underlying risk factors or drivers that are shared among the network's participants, aggravated by feedback effects that take effect through the network's channels or simply the failure of a big player can have a strong impact on many other participants in the network.

A recent review of network models of systemic risk (Caccioli, Barucca, & Kobayashi, 2018) singled out several different approaches and views in studying contagion effects on a more global scale (see Fig. 1).

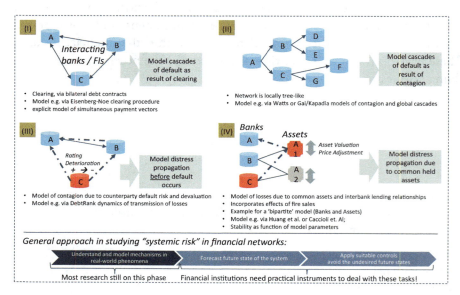

Fig. 1 Recent models of systemic risk

In summary, systemic risk has recently been studied with regard to the following aspects:

I. How is simultaneous clearing (e.g., OTC) explaining default behavior in interbank networks?
II. Are tree-like contagion models with contagion thresholds in a position to explain global contagion?
III. How can distress be modeled best even without necessarily assuming defaults, by observing propagation of down-rating induced effects on exposures and balance sheets?
IV. How is systemic stability affected by dependency on overlapping portfolios with commonly held assets?

While the quoted survey concluded that most academic research is still struggling with understanding and sufficiently modeling the real world, the practitioner and finance professional needs to have mechanisms *right now* to deal with these complex questions.

Fortunately, the toolset of the finance professional also evolves and provides many options for discovering this complexity and making monitoring and measurement more manageable, not all of which have been exploited to their full potential yet.

We propose taking a step back, acknowledging some structural properties of networks and then agreeing that they, and the complexity within, should be more offensively and proactively managed from a fresh perspective.

As a first step, we will attempt to provide an anatomy of networks relevant to the financial industry as a framework for looking at several dimensions relevant to future discussions (see Fig. 2).

1.1 Types

- Relevant questions: How concrete or abstract are networks? How relevant are they to the individual manager in a banking institution as compared to a regulatory supervisor?
- Notes: Fundamentally, networks have been grouped into those linking directly interacting agents (e.g., banks and their business partners) and those that only exist in an abstract sense, based on similarity or, in other words, based on information. An example of the latter can be observed in market price returns of different assets that have historically been shown to behave similarly.

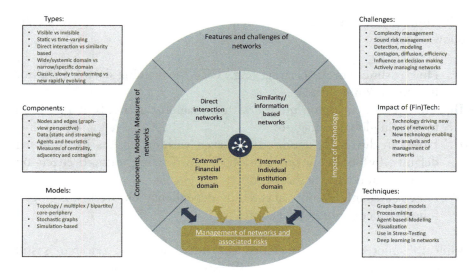

Fig. 2 Taxonomy of network complexity

A second broad type of network for our purposes will be internal networks (those that are essentially controlled by the individual organization) as compared to external networks that may span the whole financial industry. In literature, most emphasis has been put on systemic risk and contagion in the financial sector as a whole.

1.2 Components

- Relevant questions: How should we model the constituent parts of a network? What are the relevant entities? How can we measure the features of a given network and allow conclusions of a qualitative or quantitative nature?
- Notes: Powerful tools exist that allow us to draw conclusions about networks once these are represented in the form of graphs with nodes and edges that can be assigned properties, assuming some way of representing the topology of the network to be analyzed. On the other hand, in a framework that consists of numerous directly interacting participants (i.e., individuals or organizations), it is equally important to model these agents and their behavioral patterns.

1.3 Models

- Relevant questions: How can we represent the real-life network we are exposed to in an abstract way? How do we make it accessible?
- Notes: Once the network topology is largely determined, and linkage or interaction between "nodes" or "agents" established, we then need statistical/stochastic or other simulative tools to infer properties and manageable quantities, and gain insight. This will depend very much on the approach chosen to model the network and on the ability to make it computationally accessible.

1.4 Techniques

- Relevant question: How do we extract information from the model?
- Notes: We propose actively using the mathematical and computational tools that are available today and will review a select number of such techniques that prove promising for very different types of problems and use cases facing the finance professional.

1.5 Impact of Fintech

- Relevant question: How can fintech support or further influence the broader topic of networks in the financial industry?
- Notes: We certainly see a trade-off between new technology adding more tools to the arsenal of the financial professional, and more complexity introduced by constant change.

1.6 Challenges

The challenges presented by the different types and models of networks are as diverse as the networks themselves. Complexity management as an abstract term should be translated into very concrete risk and resource management. The natural first step should consist of determining and taking stock of all relevant networks in and around the organization. With the information propagating through the network, decision-making may be influenced in many ways—one of the goals of bank management consists of improving efficiency in dealing with networks in the organization after extracting insights from the respective network.

To summarize, oversight and management of all or parts of the financial industry, its sub-systems or the individual participating institutions requires profound knowledge and constant balancing of complexity and simplicity, prioritizing and scrutinizing some of the real-world types of prevalent networks. With the rapid advances of digitization and digitalization, far more emphasis should be placed on the management of networks as well as their associated risks.

2 The Digitalization Trade-off

Digitalization as well as the methods and tools used in fintech and regtech should be viewed as part of a trade-off.

With many obvious and often quoted benefits and value propositions dominating the discussions, there are also certain risks that have to be considered, reevaluated or even placed on the risk landscape for the first time.

2.1 Benefits of Digitalization/Fintech

- Easily available big data/big-compute power benefits models to make better predictions, deeper analyses and gain more real-time insight.
- Artificial intelligence (AI), a term often used synonymously or in combination with machine learning, allows for using self-learning patterns and setting up highly specialized expert systems that require hyperparameter-tuning but can otherwise be used in automation/robotics scenarios.
- Banks are—arguably to their benefit—forced to adopt, innovate and move fast as they otherwise face the risk of being pushed out off the market, as the modern app-based sharing economy has proven in other market segments.

2.2 Risks of Digitalization/Fintech

- Some of the new digitalization tools are just "black boxes" that are hard to explain, hard to defend and subject to bias.
- Dependency on a few large players and digital platform providers increases certain systemic risks and introduces new types of vendor risk.
- New levels of vulnerability, cyber risk and even reputation risk are evolving that overshadow many of the more traditional financial risk categories; this is directly related to how non-traditional (e.g., fintech-oriented) the company is right now or is willing to become.

- Some of the advanced models and algorithms are very hard to parametrize accurately; they depend on "hyperparameters" that are more art than science and difficult to tune without incurring bias.

As a prerequisite, dealing with digitalization certainly can be supported by

a. Having a good understanding of data being used or generated, models, data quality and the algorithms that are processing it.
b. Appropriate transformation risk management, which critically reviews and updates the risk drivers, with a stronger emphasis on including non-financial risk.

Historically, banks have been seen to move into new technologies and methodologies without appropriately considering the limitations and some of the risks involved (i.e., assuming normal distribution in market risk where fat tails and extremes are prevalent [methodology], dealing with CDO/CDS without knowing the true leverage and exposure [products], and originate-to-distribute sales models without considering sustainability [business strategy]).

In a world of digitalization, proceeding in this way could prove costly and should be avoided. Truly understanding the various networks an institution is involved in or exposed to should not be an abstract goal. The future will be radically different and therefore bank management must start to think in a radically different way.

3   Network Modeling and Management Approaches

To illustrate how to model and manage complex networks, we will look at several promising approaches that have been discussed recently and can leverage or benefit from modern technology.

3.1   External: Using Neural Networks to Monitor Systemic Risk

In this case study, we intend to highlight the power of machine learning and neural networks in particular. The case study uses machine learning methodology to model systemic risk via interbank linkages. For bank managers, it can be very valuable to know first whether the own institute is a high contributor to systemic risk and second which other players in the network are high systemic risk contributors. The former knowledge is valuable for several reasons. Shifting business models is a slow process. If a bank executive had the appropriate tools at hand in the financial crisis and drew the conclusion to move out of ABS markets, this takes time. Portfolios have to be sold; hedges need to be put in place; and alternative strategies need to be set up. Therefore, up-to-date information on systemic risk is key. Knowledge about the latter is valuable as systemic risk should play a role in pricing and, as we will see later, there are tools available to identify high systemic risk contributors in financial networks with public information.

More importantly, this case study should demonstrate the power of machine learning for use with complex problems. In 2017 Erik Liikaanen, former governor of the Bank of Finland, delivered a speech "On the digitalization of financial services—opportunities and risks" at the 2017 RiskLab/BoF/ESRB Conference on Systemic Risk Analytics (Liikanen, 2017). As he talks about contribution of digitalization to macroprudential analysis, he highlights the recent work on network algorithms as particularly relevant. In particular, he finds self-organizing maps (SOMs) to be one of the key contributions in this field.

In 2016 Kolari published an approach utilizing SOMs to measure the systematic risk contribution of the players in a financial network (Kolari & Sanz, 2016), which we will closely adhere to throughout this part as a use case. We think this approach is relevant for bank managers, as it allows identification of high systemic risk contributors with public information from financial statements or disclosure reports, for example. From a data perspective, it also features an easy-to-implement methodology for visualizing each player in the network and its current risk state, which is well suited for management reporting. This use case therefore shows quite well how machine learning can reduce complex problems to easy-to-comprehend visualizations that can be used for management.

3.1.1 Methodology

Neural networks are a form of machine learning. In this case study, we intend to focus on its application for clustering and dimensionality reduction. Neural networks are usually categorized into supervised or unsupervised machine learning. In supervised machine learning, the features that characterize a cluster are predefined. This means the modeler must define, e.g., which banks constitute high-risk or low-risk banks based on the characteristics provided in the training data set. In this use case, we will focus on unsupervised machine learning, in which the algorithm identifies clusters (i.e., risk categories) based on common features in the training data set. Definition of these features is the first step of calibrating a neural network. Features are characteristics that allow the algorithm to distinctly separate groups or clusters from each other. Kolari and Sanz use trait recognition for feature definition. For the neural network, the authors use a SOM, which uses the matrix of features for each bank as input to try to find features that are often exhibited by bad banks but seldom observed in good banks.

Trait Recognition

To be able to identify the features of good and bad banks, a data set first needs to be somehow divided into good and bad bank data. In general, banks are not inherently bad or good on the long term. Therefore, a more natural approach consists of identifying periods, in which many banks perform poorly. Furthermore, it makes sense to include the periods of systemic risk build-up, as the neural network should be a responsive tool that is able to give early warning signals for systemic risk. The data set used for feature identification consists of financial variables from the financial reporting of each bank in the network. The key is to not only use the distribution of each variable as a feature, but also their joint distributions to identify common risk patterns. To assess whether the observed value of a variable is high or low, the empirical distribution of all observations is divided into three areas. Therefore, each observation can be categorized into being a low (00) mid (01) or high (11) observation. For each time period in the data sets, a binary string can be created by concatenating the categorizations of each variable (cp. Fig. 3). This binary string then constitutes a feature.

Self-Organizing Maps (SOM)

Self-organizing maps belong to the class of neural network models. Neural networks are a form of machine learning specific to pattern recognition. Furthermore, SOMs are a form of unsupervised machine learning, which means that, as the name suggests, neurons organize themselves as clusters only based on the input data. For a more complete introduction to unsupervised machine learning, please refer to Liermann, Li, and Schaudinnus (2019).

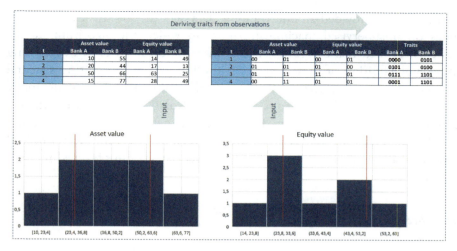

Fig. 3 Setting up trait matrices

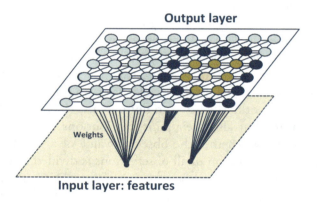

Fig. 4 Self-organizing map

A typical graphical representation of SOM is displayed in Fig. 4. In the example presented here, the SOM algorithm "converts non-linear relationships between high-dimensional input data into simple geometric connections between their image points on a low-dimensional display" (output layer) (Kolari & Sanz, 2016) while maintaining the most important topological characteristics and metrical relationships of the input data, as banks with similar features will be displayed close to one another on the output layer (Kohonen, 2001).

The output layer is a two-dimensional space, on which clusters are to be detected. The output layer also represents the management tool mentioned earlier, which allows monitoring of systemic risk, an institution's own but also its competitor's or counterparties' systemic risk contribution. The optimal size of the output layer in terms of neurons (a × b) can be determined by considering the quantification error[1] and the topological error.[2]

The input layer consists of the feature matrices of each bank. As explained before, a feature is a significant and economically reasonable combination of financial condition variables in the input data set.

In this example, a set of significant features is defined for all banks and a time series is created for the input layer that indicates whether a specific feature is exhibited by a particular institute at that point in time.

The two layers are connected by synaptic weights, which are the subject of optimization.

3.1.2 Implications for the Finance Professional

The authors show that employing trait recognition and SOMs allows them to map each institute from the data set to a CAMELS-like rating system[3] on a scale from 1 to 5 (1: low risk, 2–4: intermediate risk, 5: high risk) over time. The methodology allows for more clusters, but the optimal number of clusters just happened to be five in this case. Furthermore, they show that, beginning in 2003, big banks gradually started moving toward the high-risk cluster, resulting in 12 of 16 banks being in the high-risk cluster in 2009. It becomes clear that, if some bad features are persistent in different crises, the tool is very powerful in providing early warning signals that the industry is heading toward the next crisis. A key challenge for gaining valuable management insight consists of the training data used to identify and separate good from bad features. As the authors only use data from financial statements, there is already some robustness toward missing the indicators of the next crisis, because they do not use crisis-specific variables like real-estate indices or oil prices. On the whole, this example shows that neural networks allow bank managers to reduce complex problems with high-dimensional

---

[1]Quantification error (qe) is the average distance between each data vector and its best-matching unit (BMU), a measure of map resolution (Kolari & Sanz, 2016).

[2]Topological error (te) is the proportion of all data vectors, for which first and second BMUs are not adjacent units, thereby capturing topology preservation (Kolari & Sanz, 2016).

[3]The CELS or CAMELS rating was developed to classify a bank's overall condition. It is a supervisory rating system originally designed in the U.S., which evaluates (C)apital adequacy, (A)ssets, (M)anagement Capability, (E)arnings, (L)iquidity (also called asset liability management) and (S)ensitivity (sensitivity to market risk, especially interest rate risk).

data to low-dimensional ones that can be implemented in a way to provide an intuitive tool with results that can then easily be reported to top management.

3.2 External: Using Agent-Based Modeling to Assess Systemic Risk

In the first example, we highlighted why it is valuable, not only for regulators, but also for financial institutions to know the state of the financial sector as a whole in terms of systemic risk build-ups and their contribution to it. The methodology presented in this part will allow the user to evaluate the current state of the financial sector and enable them to incorporate knowledge about their own systemic risk contribution into its business decisions. The framework presented uses an advanced network modeling approach to map the channels through which banks can interact with one another. The agent-based modeling (ABM) approach introduces behavior for the banks via objectives and constraints. This allows for a multitude of different settings. For the scope of this part, we will closely follow the approach presented by Montagna and Kok (2016).

3.2.1 Methodology

Advanced Network Modeling Approaches

Network modeling is about finding a mathematical representation for the topology of a real-life network like interbank trading markets. The topology of a network can usually be described using nodes and edges. In finance, nodes usually represent companies but, as we will see later, they can also be viewed as organizational units, people or steps of a process. In the framework presented here, each node represents a bank with an individual balance sheet. The edges represent the dependencies between the banks and therefore their balance sheets. The first frameworks that utilized this methodology used interbank exposures for linkages as a natural starting point for network calibration (Allen & Gale, 2000). Interbank exposures are an example of a directed network as a net long exposure of Bank A to Bank B can be visualized by a directed node from A to B (cp. Fig. 5). Another example of linkage between banks that can be fitted to a network structure are similar securities exposures in different institutions. When one institution

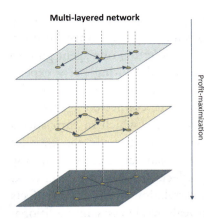

Fig. 5 Multi-layered network representation of interbank financial links

has to liquidate substantial parts of its portfolio under pressure, e.g., due to bankruptcy, other banks with similar exposures have to book the resulting mark-to-market losses due to market price decay. This is an example of an undirected network, as losses of Bank A and Bank B are correlated, but the losses of Bank A do not result from actions taken by Bank B and vice versa (cp. Fig. 5).

Montagna and Kok argue that there is a natural dependency between the liquidity/counterparty risk represented by interbank exposures and the market risk resulting from similar exposures. Even more so, they stress that earlier models drastically underestimated default correlations due to systemic stress by not taking into account the feedback loops in these "different" networks.

Therefore, they propose modeling these networks as several layers of a more global one, which allows for inter-layer correlations (cp. Fig. 5). This is called a *multi-layered network*.

Agent-Based Modeling (ABM)

For a more general introduction to ABM, refer to Sect. 3.4.2.

ABM enables the risk modeler to equip each bank, organizational resource, human resource, etc. with its own set of objectives while reducing their scope of actions by (mathematical) constraints.

In our example, each bank's objective consists of maximizing profits by optimizing its balance sheet.

Banks can interact with each other through the network structure by buying and selling assets while being constrained by regulatory liquidity and capital buffers. The system is set in motion by letting one agent go into default. Therefore, banks that are exposed to the defaulting party experience losses on their assets either due to direct credit exposure or due to the mark-to-market losses described above. As a result, connected agents have to withdraw deposits from other banks or sell assets, which in turn affects the liquidity needs of other banks in the network. Additionally, the fire sales from the defaulting agent affects all banks with similar exposures by way of fair-value hits. This can lead to spiraling effects for the entire network. The authors can conclude that the inter-risk correlation and feedback effects increase systemic risk significantly, which reveals weaknesses in traditional frameworks and shows the power of multi-layered network modeling.

3.2.2 Implications for the Finance Professional

The example presented above has two-fold implications for finance professionals. First, parameters like asset or default correlation are generally hard to estimate with stability and introduce the model risk into the risk modeling process. Risk managers can benefit from using network models as challenger models for these parameters. This is especially relevant, as risk model validation and model risk increasingly gain more regulatory attention. Furthermore, credit and market risk aggregation can benefit from the results of the model, as it provides a holistic and intrinsic approach to include inter-risk correlation in an overall framework. Additionally, the multi-layered networking approach can also be used to advance existing networking models. The same holds true for including ABM in existing models. As shown above, the dynamics that can be introduced into the model even without shocking the initial state can reduce many assumptions in more traditional risk models.

3.3 Internal: Using Process Mining to Analyze Business and IT Processes Developing Across Networks

3.3.1 Introduction

Process mining can be described as a natural extension to data mining, where the focus is to draw conclusions from the operational and business processes themselves that are fully or partially supported by information systems, and to discover, improve and manage process models.

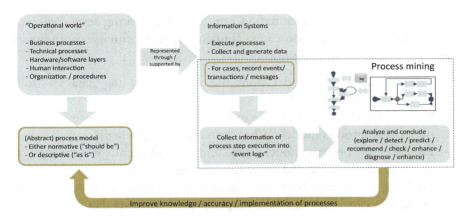

Fig. 6 Overview of process mining

As a recent discipline both in research and in practical application, process mining is still evolving and not all organizations have leveraged the potential it has to offer.

3.3.2 Methodology

Before we discuss the role process mining as a management tool can play, we will briefly recap some of the stylized facts and key characteristics (see also Fig. 6):

- Real-world processes are governed by organizations, individuals and systems that operate along certain encoded or otherwise established rules that are formalized into processes.
- As these processes are represented in or monitored by IT systems, they generate or have the potential to generate information on the individual steps or events that occur as a result of the execution of a process step (e.g., logging of execution times, delays, predecessors or successors).
- This information is usually not the "primary" concern generated through the process, but if this information is properly harvested into event logs, with as many attributes as feasible (e.g., on timing, roles involved, resources utilized, etc.) it can be subjected to further analysis; events could be as diverse as business workflow protocols, transaction logs or messages generated as part of execution in the IT system.

- The process and event information can be analyzed along several dimensions and for different use cases, constituting the primary components and features of process mining:

  - Discover a process model from the actual event log data set itself (What really happened?),
  - Check conformance of the discovered model vs. a normative (abstract/prescribed) process model (What should have happened?),
  - Enhance the process model itself, and therefore enhance the understanding of the real world or an abstract model itself,
  - Feed the conclusions back into the process modeling or process implementation capabilities of the enterprise/the decision-maker.

- However, the potential that process mining has to offer is even more comprehensive:

  - Predict and recommend actions and improvements on the real-world process,
  - Audit and compare current as-is and alternative to-be processes,
  - Diagnose and map the process landscape from various different viewpoints/levels of granularity.

Therefore, process mining is a discipline that is tightly connected to data science, big data, machine learning, visualization techniques, process model frameworks and enterprise architecture, and is overall a valuable tool that can explicitly support decision-making and overall process governance.

The minimum requirement is that an individual case (instantiation of a particular process) can be followed through a sequence of ordered activities, identifying particular "events". Information on these events is usually available in varied form (e.g., who executed the activity, when, how long it took, which resources were consumed in the process, what the target of the particular job was, etc.).

As with any real-world model, noise, over/underfitting and bias will also be factors to deal with in process model discovery, but many different algorithms are available, including heuristic, genetic or machine learning algorithms and can be applied simultaneously and analyzed for cost/benefit.

For an excellent introduction and overview of this topic, please refer to W. van der Aalst (2016).

Within the general context of networks, it is easy to realize that process mining offers multiple ways of supporting management of network complexity:

- Creating maps: discovering a process model from observable facts that are associated with a particular end-to-end process. In a complex network with many interacting systems and activities/roles, creating such a map alone may provide valuable insight that is otherwise not obtainable from conventional Business Process Modeling (BPM) or workflow modeling exercises.
- Abstraction: process mining techniques allow for representing the process flows on varying levels of granularity, focusing on both major links between top/"busy" nodes in the process chart as well as on the more exceptional less frequented "edges", depending on the particular question that needs to be answered. In a complex network, the most frequented pathways or whether there are sudden shifts in behavior that require more attention may not be intuitive or obvious.
- Analysis of weaknesses or shortcomings: if event logs can be enriched by some type of timestamp and/or resource consumption information, process mining becomes a valuable tool to detect bottlenecks.
- Prediction: once a process map has been discovered from historical data through any of the heuristics or more advanced approaches, it becomes possible to predict the performance of a particular process that is currently in progress by statistical analysis of past behavior vs. current situation/state of the process within the network.
- Recommendations: taking the analysis further, knowledge of the discovered process maps—enriched with statistical information that has been gathered from historical event logs—can also be utilized to detect shifts in overall behavior or available and less used channels or resources and thus create very concrete recommendations for redesign/updates/changes to the network design to respond to change.

3.3.3 Impact of Digitalization and Technological Advances

Digitalization also benefits the alignment of complex changing and not adequately mapped or enforced business processes as well as their realization and execution in IT environments:

- Event stream type information, which arises in financial contexts as diverse as e-commerce, fraud detection, product sentiment analysis and process controls, the inevitable big data aspects and constant flow of information can now be handled (see also the use cases in the next section).
- In-memory technology combined with data federation/less data replication paradigms including those of event log-type information allow for timely insights and updates including information on potential process bottlenecks.
- Various visualization techniques are available to represent the graphs and process networks and provide drill-down capability from cluster to individual process level.
- Open-source process mining technology, which is suitable for implementing rapid prototypes, for example, are available as well as off-the-shelf solutions, while some components are already integral parts or add-ons of larger enterprise resource planning packages and platforms; this should encourage active use of process mining methods.
- Advances in data science/machine learning/deep learning mean that the accuracy and "fit" of discovered process maps will continue to improve; automation in model selection/evaluation will make it easier to determine the best algorithm.

New technologies also present new challenges:

- In the "API economy" of manifold connected (micro-)services and applications, IT process networks will open up further, components may be exchanged and replaced more rapidly, unfortunately allowing more potential for non-conforming processes or over/under-utilization of certain nodes and edges within the network.
- Process mapping and process discovery become more involved and difficult and require constant updates.
- New types of networks, e.g., surrounding distributed ledgers, mobile consumer/product channels or 3rd party providers of financial services imply entirely new types of process flows and process organization, which are not as well-defined or documented as conventional setups.

3.3.4 Implications for the Finance Professional

Process mining and the presented approaches are predominantly relevant for intra-organizational networks, in which event log-type information is easily available and can be requested and stored. Transaction hashes should still allow some tracing across blind spots that are present when dealing with connected 3rd-party components outside the control of the organization. Some, but not all IT-processes may already be equipped with monitoring and logging capabilities, which could be enriched or specified further to allow cross-system tracking of cases (i.e., actual end-to-end processes).

Constant changes in the technology and the network at hand require ongoing updates of the processes that are designed to utilize this technology. It may not be feasible to comprehensively define prescriptive/normative process maps. Descriptive insight may also be restricted to certain parts of the network, e.g., through system monitoring tools that operate in an isolated capacity and don't provide an end-to-end view or sufficient non-technical insights for senior management.

Part of the data science/data mining/IT capabilities of the enterprise should be allocated to support the conventional business process management departments to define meaningful process layers that lend themselves to process mining activities and then to enable the harvesting of event logs.

As agile and dev-op type operations and implementation cycles become more prevalent, conventional static process maps rapidly become outdated and management should be very interested/invested in having a toolset at hand that can provide independent insight and recommendations on how to further improve business and IT processes.

Overall, drifts or adverse behavior in processes along networks are more likely to occur when the world, data, size and pace of human and technical interaction are changing more rapidly, so that early detection of those drifts is a natural priority of enterprise, financial and risk management.

The following scenarios represent some concrete use cases that have recently been discussed and implemented:

1. **Scenario**: event stream process mining and online real-time discovery (see Fig. 7)

   - *Problem statement*: update the process map continuously from streaming potentially large volume and high-frequency event data, while retaining only the required information; the entire log is never available and the process map has to be updated after every event (Leno, Armas-Cervantes, Dumas, Rosa, & Maggi, 2018).
   - *Aspects of process mining*: apply cache memory management techniques to delete or allow decay of non-recent or non-frequent event information from update processing; allow for online discovery of process maps for up-to-date in-memory representation.

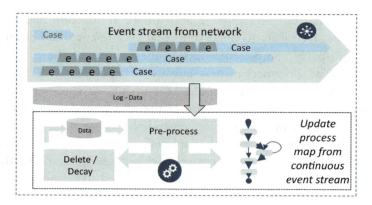

Fig. 7 Process mining use case—handling event stream data

2. **Scenario**: business process modeling and adaptation while optimizing allocation of cloud computing resources (see Fig. 8)

    - *Problem statement*: in large organizations, adapt processes to accommodate changed business process requirements in a constrained cloud computing IT infrastructure (SaaS, PaaS) with optimal allocation of available resources (Yongsiriwit, 2017).
    - *Aspects of process mining*: model heterogeneous business process models and cloud resources; utilize process mining techniques to assess generated/suggested (e.g., from genetic algorithm evolution cycles) process variants and optimize for resource/cost allocation.

3. **Scenario**: optimization of process flow in distributed application architectures (see Fig. 9)

    - *Problem statement*: with the trend toward API-based (micro-)services that are broadly distributed across the computing infrastructure, it becomes less clear how business and application layers are really connected, and how to detect bottlenecks and potential for performance improvements (Graeff, 2017).
    - *Aspects of process mining*: apply process mining techniques to discover relationship between business processes and their distributed application component counterparts; extend process mining to include performance characteristics of the infrastructure to optimize system and business performance; distributed tracing acts as an equivalent to event logging.

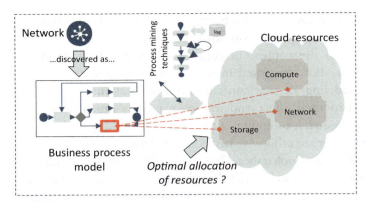

Fig. 8 Process mining use case—cloud resource allocation for business processes

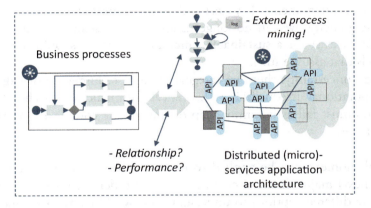

Fig. 9 Process mining use case—distributed application architectures

3.4 Internal/External: Using Agent-Based Modeling to Challenge Known Phenomena and Stress Test the Future

3.4.1 Introduction

Agent-based models have been playing a major role in the social and natural sciences to study the simulated behavior of individual autonomous entities that follow a strategy or rule set and that are exposed to an environment they interact with, with the goal of investigating any emergent behavior within the population. They have been used to a lesser extent in economics and finance, where market interactions have often been studied through methods such as Dynamic Stochastic General Equilibrium (DGSE) models, owing to economic general equilibrium theory.

However, in the context of complex networks, both internal or external, which are not structured in ways that lend themselves easily to mathematical modeling, or that contain (autonomous) entities that are not well understood in their effect and influence on the organization, ABM is an interesting approach to applying new lines of thinking and discovering network effects that are otherwise neglected or detected too late.

When Richard Bookstaber (2017) describes "the four horsemen of the econopalypse", he expresses the thought that, in today's extremely fast-paced world that is inevitably permeated with complex human interaction, even in real-world financial economics terms we are facing four broad phenomena:

1. Emergent phenomena: they exist and arise unexpectedly.
2. Non-ergodicity: we can no longer assume that baseline assumptions and equilibria exist for a sustainable time, and hence we should not rely on models that assume such.
3. Radical uncertainty: there are categorical limits to human knowledge.
4. Computational irreducibility: theoretical formulaic approaches to economics must fail as it cannot map or model true complexity on realistic timescales.

These phenomena can be applied to understanding systemic failure in the last (or next) major financial crisis, but they also demonstrate that we need to explore different options to understand real-world complexity, and ABM is such a device. It offers unique advantages, but certainly also challenges that are not particularly easy to overcome. Using modern technology, some of these limitations can be overcome or at least tackled efficiently.

3.4.2 Methodology

At its core, ABM is a computational simulation method that encourages you to model a typically large number of atomic autonomous entities (agents), equip them with a set of rules and resources, have them interact in and with an environment (simulated, or in the case of swarm-robotics, even real), and then study the emergent behavior by following the interaction of these agents over time.

The modeler/observer will define and equip an environment with features and resources, as well as an initial population of (various different types of) agents that are governed by a parametrized or fixed rule set, exhibiting certain behavior under certain conditions. Agents interact with each other as well as with the environment (see Fig. 10).

By repeating a typically large number of alternative trials or runs, each with given initial parameters and each consisting of performing the rules per agent over repeated discrete time intervals up to a certain termination condition, a range of (statistical) measures can be observed and evaluated.

Parts of the results are usually compared to certain observed real-world facts to assess the level of conformity of agent interaction with perceived reality. The parameters as well as the rule sets would be adjusted in a way to reach a desired level of real-world behavior, while other features will appear only as emergent behavior.

Agent-based models have recently been successfully applied to such diverse tasks as replicating the core-periphery structure of the interbank lending system (Lux, 2015), features of liquidity dynamics, models of liquidity and solvency interactions including funding shocks and fire sales of liquid assets (Hałaj, 2018).

More generally, ABMs also allow for a degree of freedom in using exploratory what-if scenarios and can be a valuable addition to any formal stress testing framework. As such, they are not restricted in their setup and in the definition of their desired inputs and outputs. They express greater descriptive richness and relate to complex (e.g., human) interaction and are thus well suited to complement other types of Monte-Carlo simulations. Their particular appeal lies in their extreme flexibility, which provides

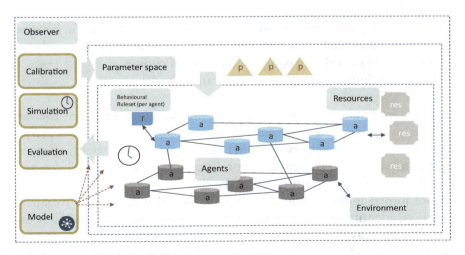

Fig. 10 Overview of agent-based modeling

an advantage over better known but over-simplifying analytically tractable mathematical/statistical models.

While ABMs are capable of reproducing stylized facts of real-world phenomena, it is not straightforward to parametrize them in such a way that they yield "realistic" results due to their dimensionality.

As with other models, validation and proper calibration of the parameter space are therefore very important tasks within ABMs. Generally, an indirect calibration approach has been suggested for ABMs (Windrum, Fagiolo, & Moneta, 2007) consisting of four steps:

1. Identify and describe the stylized facts that the observer/modeler seeks to explain.
2. Specify the model and timeline/step-by-step sequence of events and individual dynamics of the agent, possibly allowing for disturbances that are part of the setup and behavior of the environment.
3. After running the experiment/simulation for a sufficient number of iterations, including variations in the parameter space, conduct formal hypothesis testing to compare model results vs. known observations from real-world data sets.
4. Optional: subject the model to "policy changes" or policy analysis, by adjusting the implemented behavioral equations and studying the difference in outcome of the simulation.

3.4.3 Impact of Digitalization and Technological Advances

When reviewing the setup of an abstract agent-based model, it becomes apparent that this method is well suited to provide an approach to discuss and formalize many existing complex networks of choice.

Use cases include a wide range of application models:

- Simple, exploratory, toy-box model: stylize the components of the networks under investigation and set up exploratory what-if scenarios; answer questions such as "Is there an unexpected/inherent emergent behavior that has not yet been considered from a real-world financial impact, policy or risk/return perspective?"
- More formal model: while repeating the model with varying parameter settings, identify and collect the network's operations-critical behavioral "traits", such as observed patterns or repeated terminal conditions that could thus also be expected to be seen in the real-world network. Analyze and improve the real-world network with this insight.

- Stress test model: consider repeated evaluation of the ABM across a subset of the parameter space as an alternative form of stress test; this could be seen as "stress testing the future", as the ABM will not assume ergodicity, computational reducibility or certainty in any form and instead permit emergent behavior otherwise not present in conventional stress tests.
- "Think globally": employ an ABM to model the "global" financial and client/customer/business partner network of choice at a higher level, forcing yourself to clarify hidden assumptions and over-simplified perceptions of the world and its human/organizational entities as its agents. Based on simulation runs, would this view lead to predicted or unpredicted states of the world in the short/medium/long term? Would you revise your world view and reconsider strategies, policies and business practices?

A recurring problem of ABMs—very much the reason they have not been applied more often in financial risk management or financial economics in general—is that of calibration and adjustment or proper choice of the parameter space.

This is where digitalization and, in particular, recent data science/machine learning advances help bridge the gap. As suggested recently by Lamperti, Roventinib, and Sanic (2017), machine learning "surrogates" can be initially employed to sufficiently mimic the behavior of the ABM and then suggest a suitable parameter set or subspace that the actual ABM can be calibrated to as a result.

On the other hand, agents themselves can be subjected to operate as individual artificial neural networks, thus eliminating the need to specify the initial rule sets in too much detail and allow for self-learning. For these and other suggested connections between ABMs and deep learning approaches, see van der Hoog (2017).

Modern computing infrastructure, leveraging cloud infrastructure, Hadoop clusters and other distributed computing technology now support running agent-based simulations with thousands, even billions of interacting agents (Lyon & Harmon, 2018).

3.4.4 Implications for the Finance Professional

Agent-based modeling has been used in a variety of applications, including discussing systemic risk in the financial services industry from a central bank/regulatory perspective.

The implication for the risk professional therefore lies in analysis of suitable use cases and adopting ABM as a technique to solve them where applicable.

The following use case examples and scenarios provide some perspective:

1. **Scenario**: financial services industry (see Fig. 11)

   - *Model*: relationships between own institution, competitors and business partners dealing with financial instruments.
   - *Goal*: high-level understanding of dependencies between market participants with asymmetrical information, expected impact of central bank policies and propagation of shocks.
   - *Elements*: financial Intermediaries, households/clients, financial instruments/markets.

2. **Scenario**: new product launch (see Fig. 12)

   - *Model*: new product strategy relative to well-informed and connected clients that have choices in their consumer behavior.
   - *Goal*: formulation of effective marketing strategies, effects of information propagation (e.g., through social media) among clients, reaction of competitors.
   - *Elements*: target clients and immediate competitors, information propagation between clients, influencing factors governing customer behavior.

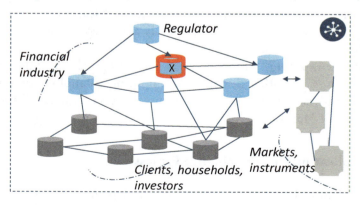

Fig. 11 Agent-based modeling use case—financial services industry

12 Managing Internal and External Network Complexity ... 219

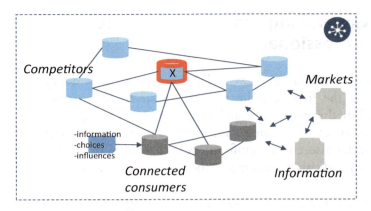

Fig. 12 Agent-based modeling use case—new product launch

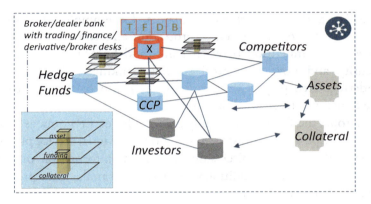

Fig. 13 Agent-based modeling use case—bond market participation

3. **Scenario**: corporate bond market (see Fig. 13)

- *Model*: interaction of the involved asset-dealing, funding and collateralization layers within the organization, external actors in the corporate bond markets representing active vs. passive elements with varying investment horizons.
- *Goal*: formulation of effective market strategies, impact analysis of shocks.
- *Elements*: disparate layers of the financial services framework involving hedge funds, cash and collateral providers, clearing partners, and corresponding financial instruments.

4 General Implications for Finance Professionals

Digitalization encourages new and more agile ways of doing business and reinventing the finance industry. The *digital transformation* is now being embraced by the entire value and process chain, starting from the customer/consumer up to the financial institution's management board. These new opportunities also entail significant new challenges in regulation, financial, operational and risk management, and affect a wide range of actors:

- The regulator strives to enable a level playing field for digital innovators and incumbents, while ensuring consumer protection and reducing any form of systemic risk.
  - The BIS and most national regulators, for example, are focused on aspects as diverse as consumer protection and consumer credit aggregates, the competition between banks and fintech companies, cybersecurity and how to control shadow banking and unregulated or underregulated players that tend to reach into or threaten to replace the domain of traditional banking.
  - In Europe, the PSD2 has recently gained a lot of attention, as it is opening up the payment infrastructure to non-traditional service providers.
  - Greater demands for disclosure of granular information on financial activities have led to additional requests of granular data provisioning by financial institutions.

- IT managers are concerned with transforming the enterprise in a way that enables new technologies. Digital innovations have to be included at a faster pace through agile organizational structures and versatile technology platforms often involving third-party components, while maintaining zero downtime and ensuring interoperability.
- The finance and risk manager, on the other hand, requires the training and adequate toolkit to produce true insights from an ever-growing wealth of information, while being confronted with a plethora of new or redefined risks and opportunities, involving new types of competitors, clients, vendors and exposure to public opinion:
  - As such, more access to and insight from internal and external data is required from an internal management perspective;
  - To identify value and risk drivers, and to judge the impact on KPIs and KRIs, new tools, methods and algorithms are available, but require the correct choices and assumptions to remain meaningful;

- The future is less predictable on a shorter time horizon, so that it is important to have appropriate ways of "stress testing the future" to identify critical constraints and dependencies within one's own business model and organization.

Generally, a new non-traditional way of thinking is required, and this extends to the way "networks" and "connectedness" of the various components of the enterprise and its business relations and use of technology are to be defined.

All these elements imply that the finance professional is challenged with rapidly changing, heterogeneous sets of business partners, technologies and problem statements that express themselves in a set of complex overlapping internal and external networks.

5 Conclusion

Considering digitalization and digital transformation, we encourage the finance professional to rethink and reimagine the concept of "networks" within the domain of their own organization.

With constant and rapid change now being the new normal, this change extends to all architectural layers of the enterprise, from business roles, processes and capabilities to policies and procedures, data and information as well as technology and application layers.

The meta-process setup required to efficiently deal with increasing network complexity can be summarized in these six steps (see Fig. 14).

Digitalization and fintech/regtech innovations can support overall bank management aspects with big data, predictive analytics, modern on-demand cloud infrastructures and open IT architectures with internal and external service providers.

As the traditional boundaries between domains blur, traditional management approaches become less suitable.

"Redrawing the map" in terms of redefining and reconsidering the various interacting internal and external networks an organization is exposed to, and then applying some less traditional methodologies such as neural network analysis, process mining and ABM, offers a chance to gain a different and better understanding of features, challenges, constraints and ways to positively influence and manage complexity.

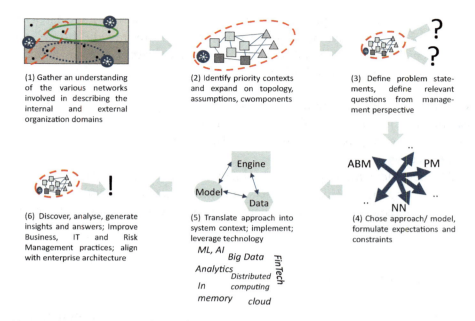

Fig. 14 Meta-process coping with network complexity

Literature

Allen, F., & Gale, D. (2000). Financial contagion. *Journal of Political Economy, 108,* 1–33.
Bookstaber, R. (2017). *The end of theory*. Princeton, NJ: Princeton University Press.
Caccioli, F., Barucca, P., & Kobayashi, T. (2018). Network models of financial systemic risk: A review. *Journal of Computational Social Science, 1,* 81–114.
Graeff, J. (2017). *Enhancing business process mining with distributed tracing data in a microservice architecture*. https://wwwmatthes.in.tum.de/pages/3etmvww9w3i6/Master-Thesis-Jochen-Graeff.
Hałaj, G. (2018). *Agent-based model of system-wide implications of funding risk*. ECB Working Paper Series. https://doi.org/10.2866/182473.
Kohonen, T. (2001). *Self-organizing maps*. Berlin and Heidelberg: Springer-Verlag.
Kolari, J., & Sanz, I. (2016). Systemic risk measurement in banking using self-organizing maps. *Journal of Banking Regulation*. https://doi.org/10.1057/s41261-016-0002-3.
Lamperti, F., Roventinib, A., & Sanic, A. (2017). *Agent-based model calibration using machine learning surrogates*. https://doi.org/10.1016/j.jedc.2018.03.011.
Leno, V., Armas-Cervantes, A., Dumas, M., Rosa, M. L., & Maggi, F. M. (2018). *Discovering process maps from event streams*. arXiv:1804.02704v1 [cs.LG].

Liermann, V., Li, S., & Schaudinnus, N. (2019). Mathematical background of machine learning. In V. Liermann & C. Stegmann (Eds.), *The impact of digital transformation and fintech on the finance professional*. New York: Palgrave Macmillan.

Liikanen, E. (2017). *On the digitalization of financial services—Opportunities and risks*. BIS Central Bankers' Speeches.

Lux, T. (2015). Emergence of a core-periphery structure in a simple dynamic model of the interbank market. *Journal of Economic Dynamics and Control, 52,* A11–A23.

Lyon, J., & Harmon, R. (2018). *Computational simulation—The next frontier for better decision-making*. Retrieved from https://www.researchgate.net/publication/317433805_Computational_Simulation_-_The_next_frontier_for_better_decision-making. Accessed 15 July 2019.

Montagna, M., & Kok, C. (2016). *Multi-layered interbank model for assessing systemic risk* (ECB Working Paper No. 1944).

van der Aalst, W. (2016). *Process mining*. Heidelberg: Springer.

van der Hoog, S. (2017). *Deep learning in (and of) agent-based models: A prospectus*. arXiv:1706.06302v1 [q-fin.EC]. Accessed 15 July 2019.

Windrum, P., Fagiolo, G., & Moneta, A. (2007). Empirical validation of agent-based models: Alternatives and prospects. *Journal of Artificial Societies and Social Simulation, 10,* 1–8.

Yongsiriwit, K. (2017). *Modélisation et fouille de variants de procédés d'entreprise dans les environnements cloud* [Modeling and mining business process variants in cloud environments]. Modeling and simulation.

13

Big Data and the CRO of the Future

Richard L. Harmon

1 Introduction

This is an exciting time to be a Chief Risk Officer (CRO) at a financial services firm. Over the past decade, the role of CRO has become significantly more vital to an institution's success on several fronts—from meeting evolving regulatory compliance requirements to driving a digital risk transformation program. Going forward both of these efforts will be leveraging some of the latest advances in machine learning, AI and cloud computing.

Since the financial crisis a decade ago, much work has been done by enterprise risk groups, partially driven by enhanced regulatory oversight, to strengthen their data management processes, improve data quality controls, adopt machine learning and AI approaches for risk modeling, streamline regulatory and internal stress testing capabilities, enable intraday risk monitoring and begin to leverage bursting cloud computing capabilities. Much of this has been executed through the adoption of a big data and analytics platform based upon the open source Apache Hadoop project led by Cloudera. These improvements are generally still a work in progress for most financial services firms and will continue to drive innovation and automation for the foreseeable future.

R. L. Harmon (✉)
Cloudera, London, UK
e-mail: rharmon@cloudera.com

© The Author(s) 2019
V. Liermann and C. Stegmann (eds.), *The Impact of Digital Transformation and FinTech on the Finance Professional*, https://doi.org/10.1007/978-3-030-23719-6_13

With the above mentioned changes underway and well documented in the literature, I want to focus on a few specific trends facing CROs going forward.

1. Technology
2. Cloud computing
3. Digital risk transformation
4. Adoption of machine learning and AI
5. Risk 3.0 and the future of stress testing

2 Technology

Data, analytics, and IT architecture are the key enablers for modernizing the enterprise risk function. Highly fragmented IT and data architectures cannot provide an efficient or effective framework for digital risk. A clear institutional commitment led by the CRO is thus required to define a comprehensive data vision, upgrade risk data systems, and establish robust data governance, data quality and metadata structures that are the foundation toward building the right data architecture.

2.1 The Big Data Revolution

One of the most impactful technological changes relevant to enterprise risk groups is the open source big data revolution that began over a decade ago with the Apache Hadoop project. This continues today and is rapidly driving the transition from the traditional data warehouse to what we call the modern data warehouse. The modern data warehouse enables real-time data streaming, company-wide access to diverse data sources and massively scalable computational capabilities. For instance, the big data revolution is enabling new capabilities such as the automation of real-time streaming and processing of data to enable real-time alerts based on-demand repricing of portfolios to support quicker risk analysis and decision-making.

2.2 Traditional Data Warehouse

The traditional data warehouse has been the workhorse for enterprise risk groups for decades. The advent of new types of data, the explosive growth in the volume of data and the need for real-time data streaming coupled with

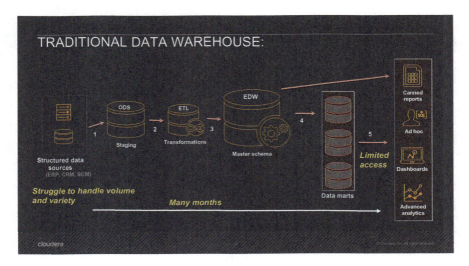

Fig. 1 Traditional data warehouse

compute-intensive workloads are being driven by such things as the need for on-demand risk aggregation, intraday risk monitoring and the adoption of data-intensive machine learning techniques. These new requirements have exposed the severe limitations of the traditional data warehouse to cost-effectively address these new risk requirements.

The traditional data warehouse architecture, as seen in Fig. 1, requires significant movement of data that is typically optimized for structured data. Wide data access is typically provided via rigid data marts that can require many months for IT groups to deliver data enhancements to their business partners. This environment can become very costly to scale for big data or compute-intensive workloads.

2.3   Modern Data Warehouse

As outlined in the introduction, enterprise risk groups are rapidly replacing or reducing the role of their legacy enterprise data warehouses using the modern data warehouse. Fig. 2 illustrates this new simplified architecture which supports the agile environment required by enterprise risk groups going forward.

The modern data warehouse, based on the open source Apache Hadoop project, allows for all data in its raw form (structured and unstructured) to be ingested into the platform, where teams can generate curated data subsets

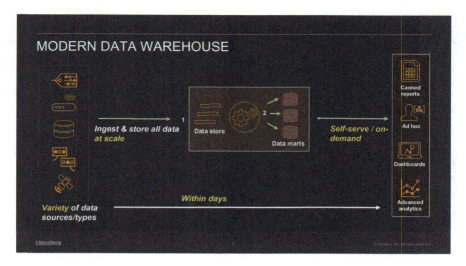

Fig. 2 Modern data warehouse

on-demand. There is very little data movement and customers can have an experimental data mart built within days of deployment—not months. As all data can be stored, there is no limitation as to what data can be made available.

The options provided by query engines and the ability to serve the data to different skill level audiences will also expedite a self-serve organization and fuel collaboration across organizational borders.

The modern data warehouse supports the future enterprise risk platform by providing an agile, scalable, secure, cost-effective technology environment that is also cloud enabled. The CRO's role is critical in this process in that she/he ensures the technology changes being implemented across the organization result in real improvements in measuring, monitoring and managing risk exposures. In the future, CROs will work more closely with their IT colleagues to ensure timely and relevant adoption of the latest advances in technology that supports a rapidly changing data, analytics and regulatory environment.

One critical driver for enterprise risk technology innovation across the financial services industry has been the tsunami of regulatory changes since the financial crisis that began in 2008. This has impacted much of the risk landscape both from a technology and a methodology perspective. Regulatory authorities have come to realize that prevention is critically important for successfully confronting future crises. This new concentrated focus on monitoring risk exposures ensures that the regulatory landscape will continuously be enhanced, thus forcing CROs to continuously modernize their enterprise risk platforms. One area where this change will be most profound will be in the adoption of cloud computing capabilities.

3 Cloud Computing

At Cloudera, cloud computing is transforming the big data architecture into what we now call the enterprise data cloud. The enterprise data cloud supports both hybrid (on-premise and cloud) as well as multi-cloud deployments, providing enterprises with the flexibility to manage all their analytics and data workloads in a safe, secure and governed manner regardless of platform. Cloudera ensures that this is fully open source, open storage, open compute and open for integration with any application provider.

The benefits of the enterprise data cloud to the CRO and enterprise risk groups include a simplified architecture that provides a more efficient, agile and secure environment to support new regulatory requirements as well as leverage new data sources and analytic tools, while avoiding being locked into a single cloud provider.

This environment also provides linearly scalable, high-performance computing (HPC) capabilities that enable intraday recalculation of risk exposures and cater to other on-demand analytic needs. The enterprise data cloud infrastructure provides bursting compute capabilities that allow firms to limit the growth of their legacy on-premise footprint yet be able to access compute grids for short-term requirements. We have customers that have this agile, hybrid configuration in place with the ability to shift workloads to the cloud whenever circumstances require.[1]

Ultimately, the enterprise data cloud architecture is all about supporting the CRO and the enterprise risk group in managing all of their analytic and data needs in a safe, secure and governed manner, regardless of where they chose to do so.

4 Digital Risk Transformation

As with other digital transformation programs in other areas of a financial services firm, the focus of the CRO will be toward implementing automation where possible, enabling intraday risk monitoring and deploying agile

---

[1]Harmon (2018).

risk systems with embedded analytics that can adopt to rapidly changing regulatory and business requirements.

Digital transformations in risk create real business value by improving risk effectiveness and efficiency, especially with projects that enable process automation, decision automation and digitalized monitoring and early warning systems. This is achieved through recent innovations in such areas as workflow automation, optical-character recognition, advanced analytics (including machine learning and artificial intelligence) and new data sources, as well as the application of robotics to processes and interfaces. Essentially, digital risk transformation implies a concerted adjustment of processes, data, analytics and IT. It will also require significant changes in the overall organizational setup, including talent and culture.[2]

A key benefit of a digitalized risk function is to provide better monitoring and control, resulting in a more agile and effective regulatory compliance function. CROs have been wary of the test-and-learn approaches characteristic of digital transformation projects carried out in other parts of the organization, as the cost of errors in the risk environment can be unacceptably high. As a result, progress in digitalizing risk processes has been slow.[3]

A recent McKinsey study has tried to quantify the potential benefits of greater efficiency and productivity, and estimated possible cost reductions of 25 percent or more in end-to-end credit processes and operational risk. Much of these gains are achieved by way of deeper automation and the use of advanced analytics. They also identify improvements in risk effectiveness gained through better management and regulatory reporting and greater model accuracy due to better data quality.[4]

5   Adoption of Machine Learning and AI

Going forward, machine learning and AI will impact nearly all areas of enterprise risk management. The primary benefits will include support in driving operational and cost efficiencies, as well as improved insight into the hidden risks that existing approaches might not fully capture. While these benefits are substantial, there are many limitations impacting the speed and

---

[2]Härle, Havas, Samandari, Kremer, and Rona (2016).
[3]Härle et al. (2016).
[4]Portilla et al. (2017).

breadth of adoption of the most sophisticated ML algorithms across the risk management landscape.

The limitations typically cited in CRO surveys and independent studies include the limited availability of the right quality and quantity of data, an insufficient understanding of the inherent risks in the application of machine learning and AI techniques, a firm's culture, and finally the regulatory hurdles for wider acceptance of these tools. When taken as a whole, these limitations create strong barriers, whether real or perceived, to widespread adoption of machine learning and AI across all aspects of risk.[5]

The black-box nature of many of these algorithms makes understanding and explaining the behavior of machine learning based models a top priority for banks and their regulators. In particular, regulators are worried about banks ceding control to black-box algorithms. As a result, significant effort is under way to develop rigorous model-governance frameworks specifically for models based on machine learning.

Despite these limitations, machine learning and AI applications are of great interest, as they can analyze vast quantities of data to identify patterns and make decisions based on them. Additionally, these applications can be programmed to learn from the data they are supplied with, either as a one-off at the time of their design, or on a continuous basis, allowing the algorithms to refine the way decisions are made over time. This means the quality of any decision made by a machine learning and AI-based solution significantly depends on the quality and quantity of the data used. An absence of large sets of high-quality data is, in general, one of the major obstacles to the application of machine learning and AI solutions. For many financial services firms, this is exacerbated by the prevalence of legacy systems and organizational silos, which can prevent the seamless flow of data and impact its quality.

The obscurity of some machine learning and AI techniques similarly poses practical challenges with regard to certain regulations, such as the new General Data Protection Regulation (GDPR) in the EU, which requires firms to be able to explain to customers how their personal data is used and give them a meaningful explanation of the assumptions and drivers behind a fully automated decision that can impact the customer. Regulations such as the GDPR are key drivers of the changes surrounding transparency and data ownership.

---

[5]Grasshoff et al. (2018).

A further challenge facing the CRO will be the need for risk staff's expertise to become more technologically focused as well expand the staff skill sets to include data management experts, IT architects, ML & AI specialists that complement the traditional risk experts, who have deep risk, market and product knowledge. The blending of these diverse skill sets into a well-coordinated team will typically require some adjustments in corporate culture and organizational structure. As mentioned above, digital risk transformation programs will push the frontiers of automation, requiring the CRO to support specialized company-wide Center of Excellence (CoE) units, where innovative approaches can be tested while leveraging capabilities across the organization. These entities provide the opportunity to accelerate innovation and adoption across the various risk functions.

To highlight how these changes might impact the CRO function, we will now focus in further depth on stress testing and the shift toward what many scholars and risk practitioners are calling Risk 3.0.

6   Risk 3.0 and the Future of Stress Testing

One clear outcome of the financial crisis a decade ago was the realization that regulators, risk managers and market participants did not have a full view of institutional or market-wide risk exposures. A result of this has been a global effort to develop a wide range of stress testing scenarios that are used to evaluate a bank's capital adequacy and avoid future systemic risk events.

Despite these efforts, the current stress testing environment has several well-known shortcomings. For example, the Basel Committee on Banking Supervision argued in a 2015 report that stress tests conducted by bank supervisors continue to lack a genuine macroprudential component. The report identifies several shortcomings, including the inability to measure "endogenous reactions and feedback effects to initial stress."[6]

Similarly, Vítor Constâncio, Vice-President of the ECB, at the ESRB Annual Conference in September 2017 stated:

We know from experience that the impact of a stress test event hitting a financial institution is often amplified via its interactions with the rest of the financial

---

[6]Supervision (2015).

system. Therefore, failing to account for such interactions may risk overestimating the resilience of single institutions and the system as a whole.[7]

A more strategic view on stress testing is outlined by Richard Bookstaber and others, who have identified three distinct levels of sophistication.[8,9]

6.1 Risk 1.0—Value at Risk

This refers to the standard Basel risk measure called value at risk (VaR) and its derivative forms. These depend entirely on historical experience and only focus on changes in market value—with each bank in isolation. VaR-based approaches work well as long as the future is drawn from the same distribution as the past.

6.2 Risk 2.0—Static Stress Testing

After 2008, regulators and risk managers started to depend more noticeably on so-called static stress testing, which is used to define common macro-level stress scenarios that determine bank-level losses. This provides insight on common and correlated losses across different banks, which is relevant for financial stability analysis. These types of tests have been implemented in many countries to varying degrees of complexity and frequency.

As outlined above, the major shortcomings of the current static stress testing regime include[10]:

- The correlation of losses only arises from common shocks and no explicit "endogenous" contagion mechanism is considered.
- The tests are limited to a semi-aggregate view of a bank's portfolio with derivative impacts largely treated via linear approximation.
- Bank portfolios are assumed to remain static throughout the stress test horizon, which can be limited to one year. In the real world, financial institutions respond quickly when faced with stress. This is particularly true when they are constrained by capital, liquidity, leverage ratios, as

---

[7]Constâncio (2017).

[8]Bookstaber, The end of theory—Financial crises, the failure of economics, and the sweep of human interaction (2017).

[9]Cont and Gordy (2017).

[10]Cont and Gordy (2017)

they may sell assets, thus impacting their market value and leading to such things as a fire sale contagion.

6.3 Risk 3.0—Dynamic Stress Testing

This stage recognizes that a static stress testing approach will miss important dynamics that lead to feedback, contagion and cascade impacts. The dynamic stress testing approach has the potential to offer a more robust quantitative, forward-looking assessment of the resilience of individual banks and of the financial system as a whole to destructive shocks.

A recent IMF study asserts that dynamic stress testing models "need to capture the behavioral responses of banks, such as changes in business strategies and portfolio compositions directed at coping with external shocks. The ability to improve the modeling of bank responses should ultimately allow us to have a more realistic view of the potential impact of shocks on solvency, liquidity and profitability."[11]

One innovative approach that is gaining traction among regulators and financial institutions is the use of computational simulation methods for analyzing a wide variety of models of real-world systems. Only through detailed simulations are we able to incorporate the dynamics, feedback and related complexities that are required to accurately represent real-world events.

Prescriptive analytics use optimization and simulation algorithms to generate a wide range of possible future outcomes that are not dependent on historical experience. They can quantify the effect of future business decisions or actions to advise on possible future outcomes before the decisions are actually made.

Agent-based modeling (ABM) is a computational simulation technique that supports prescriptive analytics, thus enabling risk managers to evaluate many possible future outcomes to consider both adaptive and reactive effects in the marketplace. It is ideally suited to the development of high fidelity models, such as a model of bank risk exposures and their interconnected impact on the wider financial system.

As outlined in Fig. 3, ABMs are also well-suited to stress testing and the exploration of balance sheet risks guiding the appropriate interventions that risk managers must undertake to mitigate those risks.

---

[11]Anderson et al. (2015).

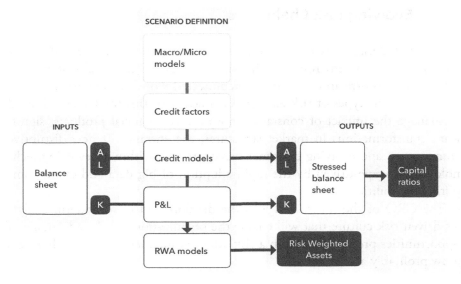

Fig. 3 Agent-based model—Example

An agent-based counterparty risk model, as outlined above, is a tool that can be used to computationally generate thousands of risk scenarios, which allows the risk manager to consider not only first-order counterparty credit risk, but also credit risk presented by second, third and higher order connections. Within this context, ABMs provide a natural framework for recreating credit-based network contagion processes for a more robust stress testing environment.

One well known example of this approach is a study conducted with the US Treasury Office of Financial Research by Bookstaber, Foley, and Tivnan (2015),[12] which develops an ABM model to analyze the dynamic interactions of a network of financial agents who borrow, lend and invest; and trace the path of a variety of shocks deriving from the agents in the system. They simulate fire sales and follow the propagation of the initial shock among the actors, given that they have different constraints and behavioral assumptions. The model shows that the extent of losses in the system relies more on the reactions to the initial shock rather than in the shock itself.

---

[12]Bookstaber, Foley, and Tivnan, Toward an understanding of market resilience: Market liquidity and heterogeneity in the investor decision cycle (2015).

6.4 Evolving Risk Challenges

As the last decade has demonstrated, the CRO of the future will face a complex, dynamic environment, in which the global financial system continues to transform into a more interconnected world, where existing risks evolve and new types of risk emerge. Coupled with this the CRO will need to manage the impact of constant innovation in financial products, significant transformations in market structures, the entrance of new disruptive competitors, and evolving customer behaviors—all within an evolving technology landscape driven by the rapid adoption of big data and cloud computing capabilities.

The CRO of the future will lead the development of a modern, analytics-driven risk culture that will enable the organization to take advantage of opportunities proactively and in a risk-adjusted manner to help the business grow profitably and safely.

Literature

Anderson, R., Danielsson, J., Baba, C., Das, U. S., Kang, H., & Basurto, M. A. (2015). *Macroprudential stress tests and policies: Searching for robust and implementable frameworks.* Washington, DC: IMF.

Bookstaber, R. (2017). *The end of theory—Financial crises, the failure of economics, and the sweep of human interaction.* Princeton: Princeton University Press.

Bookstaber, R., Foley, M. D., & Tivnan, B. F. (2015). Toward an understanding of market resilience: Market liquidity and heterogeneity in the investor decision cycle. *Journal of Economic Interaction and Coordination, 11,* 205. Berlin/Heidelberg: Springer. https://doi.org/10.1007/s11403-015-0162-8.

Constâncio, V. (2017). *Macroprudential stress-tests and tools for the non-bank sector.* Prepared remarks by Vítor Constâncio, Vice-President of the ECB, at the ESRB Annual Conference, Frankfurt am Main, 22 September 2017. https://www.ecb.europa.eu/press/key/date/2017/html/ecb.sp170922_3.en.html.

Cont, R., & Grody, M. (2017). Special Issue: Monitoring Systemic Risk: Data, Models and Metrics. *Statistics & Risk Modeling, 34*(3–4), 89. Berlin/Boston: Walter de Gruyter GmbH.

Grasshoff, G., Pfuhler, T., Coppola, M., Mogul, Z., Villafranca, V., Gittfried, N., … Wiegand, C. (2018). *Global risk 2018: Future-proofing the bank risk agenda.* Boston Consulting Group. https://www.bcg.com/publications/2018/global-risk-2018-future-proofing-bank-agenda.aspx.

Härle, P., Havas, A., Kremer, A., Rona, D., & Samandari, H. (2016). *The future of bank risk management,* McKinsey Working Papers on Risk.

Harmon, R. L. (2018). *Cloud concentration risk: Will this be our next systemic risk event?* Cloudera White Paper, June 2018. https://www.cloudera.com/content/dam/www/marketing/resources/whitepapers/cloudera-white-paper-systemic-risk.pdf.landing.html.

Portilla, A., Vazquez, J., Harreis, H., Pancaldi, L., Rowshankish, K., Samandari, H., … Staples, M. (2017). *The future of risk management in the digital era*, Institute of International Finance and McKinsey & Company, Inc.

Supervision, B. C. (2015). *Making supervisory stress tests more macroprudential: Considering liquidity and solvency interactions and systemic risk* (BIS Working Paper, Vol. 29).

Part III

Regulatory Aspects

In this part we will address regulatory aspects sometimes referred to as RegTech. There is no proper definition of the term RegTech at this time. The FCA defines it as applying "to new technologies developed to help overcome regulatory challenges in financial services." (Financial Conduct Authority, 2019).

We see two areas of technology as supporting financial services companies in meeting regulatory requirements:

1. RegTech in a narrow sense: anything that supports financial institutions in regulatory reporting and passing any kind of data to regulators. These primarily reflect the pillar II requirements of Basel III.[1]

2. RegTech in a wider sense: this includes pillar II and pillar III requirements, but also all other demands made by regulators.

Especially the new technologies associated with digitalization (i.e., ML, DL, big data in general and distributed ledger technology) can make a difference in meeting regulatory requirements.

Digital technologies, however, can themselves result in new regulatory requirements. Blockchain or distributed ledger technology currently has no official legal basis. Some countries are working on such a law aiming to provided legal certainty [e.g., Liechtenstein, see (Ministerium für Präsidiales und Finanzen, 2018)].

Chapter 14 "How Technology (Or Algorithms like Deep Learning and Machine Learning) Can Help to Comply with Regulatory Requirements"

---

[1]in the banking context and solvency II in the insurance context.

defines a wide scope for discussing the aspects of RegTech (Plenk, Levant, & Bellon, 2019). Besides discussing the application of common digitalization tools like AI and blockchain, the authors describe the case of AuRep, an individual Austrian approach to regulatory reporting intended to lower the effort and costs associated with regulatory reporting.

Chapter 15 "New Office of the Comptroller of the Currency Fintech Regulation: Ensuring a Successful Special Purpose National Bank Charter Application" provides information on how fintech companies can meet the American regulators' (OCCCurrency[2]) complex requirements (Philo, 2019).

Literature

Financial Conduct Authority. (2019). RegTech. *Financial Conduct Authority.* [Online] [Cited: January 17, 2019.] https://www.fca.org.uk/firms/regtech.

Ministerium für Präsidiales und Finanzen. (2018). *Vernehmlassungsbericht—die schaffung eines gesetzes über auf vertrauenswürdigen technologien (vt) beruhende vertrauenswürdigen technologien (vt) beruhende transaktionssysteme (blockchain-gesetz; vt-gesetz; vtg).* Lichtenstein: s.n.

Philo, A. (2019). New office of the comptroller of the currency FinTech regulation. In V. Liermann & C. Stegmann (Eds.), *The impact of digital transformation and fintech on the finance professional.* New York: Palgrave Macmillan.

Plenk, M., Levant, L., & Bellon, N. (2019). How technology (or algorithms like deep learning and machine learning) can help to comply with regulatory requirements. In V. Liermann & C. Stegmann (Eds.), *The impact of digital transformation and fintech on the finance professional.* New York: Palgrave Macmillan.

---

[2]OCC—Office of the Comptroller of the Currency.

14

How Technology (or Distributed Ledger Technology and Algorithms Like Deep Learning and Machine Learning) Can Help to Comply with Regulatory Requirements

Moritz Plenk, Iosif Levant and Noah Bellon

1 Introduction

Regulatory reporting of financial transactions is one of the key tasks involved in post trade processing for financial institutions. The fulfillment of the increasing regulatory burden is challenging and causes costs for banks.[1] The most recent implementations of new regulatory requirements further increase the complexity and effort required to cope with banking regulation. Regulatory rulebooks like AnaCredit, EMIR II and MIFID II indicate that banking supervision is heading into the direction of more granular data. Besides the high level of effort, industry participants are faced with challenges regarding a sufficient data quality, timely delivery of required data and the remaining necessity to manually process some parts of regulatory reporting.

---

[1]English and Hammond, Cost of compliance 2018 (2018).

M. Plenk (✉) · N. Bellon
BearingPoint, Stuttgart, Germany
e-mail: Moritz.plenk@bearingpoint.com

N. Bellon
e-mail: Noah.bellon@bearingpoint.com

I. Levant
BearingPoint, Frankfurt am Main, Germany
e-mail: iosif.levant@bearingpoint.com

© The Author(s) 2019
V. Liermann and C. Stegmann (eds.), *The Impact of Digital Transformation and FinTech on the Finance Professional*, https://doi.org/10.1007/978-3-030-23719-6_14

With the rise of the digital era and the most recent innovative technological developments, the ability to overcome these difficulties could finally be within reach. Three innovations, in particular, bear capabilities to face the challenges in different dimensions: Artificial intelligence (AI), big data and distributed ledger technology (DLT), which is often referred to as blockchain.

This chapter investigates the impact these technologies could have on the regulatory value chain and seeks to shed light on possible approaches as well as challenges and benefits that arise with their utilization. It is structured as follows: Section 2 shows how an input-driven approach can increase the effectiveness of regulatory reporting. Section 3 shows how adoption of DLT could influence the regulatory reporting environment. Section 4 looks at the implications of AI and big data, and provides three specific regulatory requirements, for which they could be adopted. Section 5 provides a conclusion.

2 From Template-Driven to Input-Driven Regulatory Reporting

The current landscape of regulatory reporting is shaped by a form-based approach. Financial institutions are required to report numerous data points that must be filled into different templates. Despite the growing amount of required data that must be reported to regulators, the approach in most jurisdictions still relies on this template-driven approach, in which each bank has to submit reporting relevant data individually. A concrete example of this is the requirement of the AnaCredit regulation. The issuance of a credit by a foreign subsidiary must be reported both in the country of the parent company and the country of the subsidiary. In the worst case, these two countries have different reporting obligations. In case both trading counterparties are subsidiaries of different financial institutions in different countries, the single transaction requires a four-fold reporting.

This leads to a multiplication of data sets for the same trade and widens the scope of possible discrepancies and errors in the databases of regulating entities. Moreover, the approach is far from real-time availability of reporting relevant data, even though reporting times have already been squeezed from months to weeks or even days.[2]

---

[2]BearingPoint Institute (2015).

One of the first solutions to getting closer to real-time availability of data relevant to reporting as well as an elimination of the described double reporting of identical data sets was adopted in Austria in 2014. A consortium of the major Austrian banks collaborated with the Austrian supervisory authority to shift regulatory reporting from a template-driven to an input-driven approach. In this case, each regulated entity prepares its data in a standard format as required by the regulator. The granular input data is stored in so-called data cubes that guarantee data protection for the reporting institutions regarding day-to-day business with respect to other financial institutions and regarding non-reporting relevant data with respect to supervisors.

The data collection required for these data cubes is executed by the Austrian reporting company (AuRep), which is owned by the participating banks, thus avoiding possible governance issues in advance. It is a buffer company between supervisors and banks, which transforms the input cubes into a series of cubes that are enriched with further information and formatted according to the regulator's data requirements. This input-driven approach enables data queries without the need for completing multiple templates. Instead, data can be gathered from the uploaded input data cubes, which are transformed into the required data set for the regulator by AuRep.

The enabling methodology behind this is a consensus about the data model between the banks of the consortium, which represents over 80% of the Austrian market. Unification of the data model makes this input-driven approach possible, which serves to eliminate error-prone multiple data reporting and standardize data collection. What is more, the unified data model and the processing through AuRep, which is co-owned by the consortium members, allows for sharing of compliance costs.

The input-driven approach based on cube-based data collection on a granular data level shifts regulatory reporting closer to real-time, as compared to the output-based, template-driven approach.

Since implementation of the AuRep case, a new technology has started to rise that could take the benefits arising from this way of proceeding to the next level. This is DLT.

3 Distributed Ledger Technology in Regulatory Reporting

3.1 Capabilities of Distributed Ledger Technology

Understanding why DLT has the potential to transform current regulatory reporting requires that it is broken down into its six main characteristics.

3.1.1 Decentralization

In contrast to a centralized database, the information is not processed through particular servers acting as central data collectors and data distributors, but is distributed among network participants.[3]

3.1.2 Immutability

Once data is stored on a distributed ledger, it becomes immutable. After reporting relevant data has become part of a distributed ledger, it can therefore no longer be manipulated.[4]

3.1.3 Single Point of Truth

Immutability of data results in a single point of truth.[5] There are no divergent data sets on a distributed ledger. Using a consensus mechanism for transaction verification guarantees the validity and uniqueness of each transaction. Following validation, the same data is available to every permitted node.[6] At the same time, this data is always up to date.

3.1.4 Transparency

Data that is stored on a distributed ledger is transparent. Depending on the network design, this transparency is defined in different ways. In a

---

[3]Bauerle, What is the difference blockchain and database (2018b)

[4]Brown, Carlyle, Grigg, and Hearn (2016).

[5]World Economic Forum (2016).

[6]Brown et al. (2016).

permissionless system like the bitcoin protocol, every network participant has a copy of the entire blockchain.[7] Therefore, every network participant has the same information available. Other designs rely on a permissioned network structure, in which the transparency of transaction data only holds for parties that need to know this particular information.[8] Nevertheless, the transparency of shared facts is guaranteed for involved parties and the network as a whole includes completely decentralized storage of the ledger data. From a bank's perspective, it is ensured that trading banks have relevant information, but transaction data is not shared with third parties, which would be undesirable for banks.

3.1.5 Programmability

It is possible to execute code on a distributed ledger. These so-called smart contracts allow for mapping of legal rights and obligations.[9] This programmability allows complex business logic to be encoded in a distributed ledger. This characteristic makes DLT very flexible in its possibilities of utilization. Among other things, it allows for implementation of regulatory compliance as smart contract rules.

3.1.6 Cryptography

To enable business interactions with DLT, network participants must be identifiable. This requirement is met using cryptographic keys. A combination of a public and a private key makes a network node identifiable for other nodes.[10] The combination of cryptographic technologies and the consensus mechanism is what makes DLT tamper-proof.[11] This ensures the reporting counterparties are identifiable and that no fraudulent parties can pretend to be another party.

Each characteristic individually would not be enough to make the technology this innovative, but the combination of all the properties results in disruptive potential and a variety of possible use cases spanning multiple

---

[7]Nakamoto (2008).

[8]Brown et al. (2016).

[9]Brown et al. (2016).

[10]Bauerle, What can a blockchain do (2018a).

[11]Hong Kong Applied Science and Technology Research Institute (2016).

industries. One use case that is particularly suitable and which is investigated in this chapter is the utilization of DLT in regulatory reporting.

3.2 A Distributed Ledger as a Landing Zone for Reporting Relevant Data

The AuRep case has shown how a unified data model with a common landing zone for regulatory reporting data can simplify regulatory reporting. A permissioned distributed ledger environment would fulfill the same purpose and require the same preconditions. Network participants inside the permitted network must agree on a common data model, as the regulatory reporting network cannot fulfill its purpose otherwise.

Participants store their data relevant to reporting on the distributed ledger. As with AuRep, this is not aggregated data but granular input data. In contrast to the AuRep model, instead of actively uploading the required input data, DLT makes it possible to bind banks' pre-systems to the distributed ledger. It then serves as a landing zone for the financial institutions' data relevant to reporting. In a more extreme scenario, even the banks' pre-systems wouldn't be necessary anymore, because all data could be stored in a DLT network from the start. Using the input-based approach, as in case of AuRep, data is available on a granular basis and can be utilized for multiple purposes. Moreover, the characteristics of DLT only allow authorized participants to access specific data, thus preserving privacy. The data on the distributed ledger can therefore be utilized by regulators as network participants with special reading rights.

As such, a regulatory reporting network based on DLT takes the Austrian approach with regard to a common landing zone for reporting relevant data. It takes the benefits of the input-driven approach to the next level. It also enables global availability of regulatory reporting data as opposed to specified input data cubes. Therefore, it further reduces the required effort by doing away with the need to actively upload data. Moreover, the on-ledger data is available in real-time.

3.3 Automation of Regulatory Reporting with Smart Contracts

Smart contracts can be used to address one of the cost drivers of regulatory reporting, namely the data reconciliation effort. Data validation is currently achieved after entering input data. Therefore, it is possible to submit data that does not match regulatory reporting requirements and corrections must be implemented afterward. Data reconciliation incurs effort and requires manual interference.

Using smart contracts, validation rules of regulatory content as well as data consistency rules can be programmed as a precondition for transaction execution. This shifts the time of data validation to the beginning of the process and thus makes it impossible to submit non-compliant data with regard to regulatory requirements. A transaction containing data that does not meet regulatory requirements is not executed and only correct data is reported to the supervisory authorities.

Furthermore, utilization of smart contracts can automate transaction execution. The smart contract can be designed so that, once two counterparties agree on a transaction report by signing it with their respective digital signatures, it is submitted to the network and both (bank internal) ledgers are updated with the same data. Hence, double reporting can no longer take place. This prevents errors and possible inconsistencies in the reports submitted by banks in advance, which would otherwise lead to the previously mentioned data reconciliation effort, thereby decreasing costs and increasing quality of regulatory data and efficiency of regulatory reporting.

3.4   An EMIR II Proof of Concept

In a specific use case, a proof of concept (PoC) has been conducted to check whether implementation of regulatory compliance by smart contracts in a DLT environment is technically feasible, which is the first premise to enable a shift toward a new technology. This PoC proved feasibility of the process of reporting a plain vanilla interest rate swap that meets the requirements of the European Market Infrastructure Regulation (EMIR II) utilizing the DLT Corda.

For this purpose, the regulatory requirements of EMIR II were programmed as rules of a smart contract. The smart contract uses these rules as preconditions for executing a transaction report. Besides the validation rules that are directly derived from the regulation, consistency rules are implemented as execution pre-checks. Thus, it is not possible to report data that is not compliant with regulatory requirements and inconsistencies between data sets cannot arise per design. What is more, counterparties don't send their reports using individual templates. Instead, counterparties verify the truth of the transaction data with their respective digital signatures.

This event triggers automated forwarding of the report to a notary node, which verifies the validity of the signatures, i.e., it guarantees that the respective signatures truly belong to the counterparties. Once this is validated, the transaction report is executed and the ledgers of both parties are updated with the same data. The regulator is also defined as a node in this network. This node is designed to have a special role, that is, to be able to look into the ledgers of all counterparties. Therefore, the regulator has access to every validated transaction data point on the DLT network. As a result, the previously required active double reporting of a single transaction becomes obsolete, while it is guaranteed that the regulating entity still has all required data available for each counterparty.

3.5   Implications for Banks and Regulatory Authorities

As the findings show, the capabilities of DLT can have many implications for banks and regulators. This chapter focuses on implications for the execution of tasks for and of regulators.

First, application of DLT in regulatory reporting has the potential to help address the challenges associated with the extensive effort required to comply with regulations. It can reduce processing times and the use of smart contracts with the associated preponement and automation of data validation and consistency checks results in less required manual interference. Furthermore, it provides a single point of truth, allowing for the expectation of less data reconciliation effort as diverging data points on the same issue are not possible. Hence, using DLT for regulatory compliance could help financial institutions overcome the ongoing problem of resource scarcity for regulatory compliance.

Second, according to Thomson Reuters reports on the costs of compliance, both in 2017 and 2018, the main challenges facing financial institutions with regard to compliance are changing and increasing regulations.[12]

The PoC shows that regulatory reporting of a derivative using DLT is feasible and valuable. As the structure of other transaction-based regulatory requirements is similar, the PoC indicates that DLT is a valuable technology for transaction-based reporting in general. Therefore, it might also be helpful

---

[12]English and Hammond, Cost of Compliance 2017 (2017); and English and Hammond, Cost of Compliance 2018 (2018).

in addressing the challenge of increasing regulation for banks and can very likely be used for other regulations as well.

Third, adoption of DLT for regulatory purposes raises the issue of governance of a DLT-based system. Who defines the principles of governance and who ensures their adherence must be clarified. The initiative to define a proper approach to govern a DLT system could come from the regulator. On the one hand, this would be an opportunity for supervisors to lead the DLT system by defining rules for participation and consequences for misbehavior. Having the regulator be the system's governing body could solve the risk of discrepancies regarding the governing entity of the system, because the regulator is the most neutral body within this permissioned network. On the other hand, it shifts effort toward regulating entities, which might not be desirable from the supervisor's point of view.

At the same time, the use of DLT provides regulators with a key benefit of real-time data availability at the most granular level without inconsistencies.

This implies three things in particular. First, the data quality that regulators base their decisions on increases strongly, as there are no data inconsistencies between reported data.

Second, real-time data availability enables supervisory authorities to act on time. This could result in an increase in its ability to protect the stability of the financial system.

Third, availability of data at the most granular level makes data analysis more reliable while at the same time opening up new possibilities of data analysis for the regulating entities. It allows for a strong increase in flexibility regarding analyses of regulatory data and could therefore enable supervisors to recognize systemic risks earlier and verify them in a more reliable way. This implication arises due to the possibility of using the granular data itself to check for other possible explanations without being forced to wait for the banks to submit additional data.

To make optimal use of the emerging opportunities, other technologies can supplement DLT and add new dimensions of possibilities. These include AI and big data.

4 AI and Big Data

4.1 Artificial Intelligence—A Matter of Trust

The financial industry currently generates tremendous amounts of unstructured and structured data that has to be stored and processed. Outdated methods for achieving this are failing or yielding inadequate results and the effort is usually not proportional to a financial institution's profits. Since 2008, we have been experiencing a tsunami-like wave of new regulatory requirements aimed at strengthening markets and customers and the end is nowhere in sight. In Europe alone, MiFID II, AnaCredit and GDPR all had to be implemented last year. As requirements are becoming more complex and granular, while often also including unrecognized overlaps, the cost of regulatory compliance is exploding.

History is often the best teacher and the year 1968 provides a good lesson in this regard.

By 1968, daily trading volume had hit 12 million shares per day. The sheer mass of stock certificates and other paperwork overwhelmed many Wall Street back offices as the groups working behind the scenes to settle and clear trades.

What would become known as the "Paperwork Crunch" forced the New York Stock Exchange to restrict trading to four days a week. The exchange closed every Wednesday for months and sometimes had to close early on other days to give firms additional time to process their huge backlogs.[13]

AI with machine learning and data science promise long-awaited support, which should lower costs, increase quality and open new horizons in compliance with regulatory requirements.

Many financial institutions have recognized this, as seen in the following examples[14]:

- PayPal developed an in-house fraud detection engine
- Deutsche Bank recently deployed AI to sift through volumes of recordings
- Danske Bank has used an AI Framework to increase its fraud detection rate by 60%
- Citigroup uses an AI-based system to pass the US federal government's stress test

What inspired these changes? One reason is the massive increase in computational power, especially through the use of GPUs along with improved algorithms. The second decisive influence is big data, as the amount of data that can be collected and evaluated has grown exponentially in recent years.

---

[13]https://www.finra.org/investors/when-paper-paralyzed-wall-street-remembering-1960s-paperwork-crisis.
[14]CMR (2018).

New tools like Hadoop Ecosystem have been developed to handle these immense data volumes. The speed of the networks has also been adapted to these data sets, so that distributed data systems can effectively exchange the data.

The data also provides the critical context for the machine learning algorithms to quickly and effectively recognize the new patterns in the dynamic environment to make the decisions. Evaluation could start with structured regulatory texts by using natural language processing (NLP) to find decisive articles that affect one's own business and plan the implementation processes. In the next step, it is often necessary to filter the data for the required aspects, during which the audio recordings would need to be converted into text form with the recurrent neural network (RNN) providing great help in speech recognition. The possibilities of machine learning in the classification of content, whether supervised or unsupervised, opens up new ways of detecting anomalies such as fraud detection. In the case of financial transactions, simple monitoring is often not enough, as it is necessary to understand what the context is and to what extent there is a connection, especially in the case of Know Your Customer (KYC) and Anti-Money Laundering (AML), in which the regulatory requirements for Personally Identifiable Information (e.g., GDPR) are to be observed. These issues present us with such a complexity of factors and dynamics that, without application of AI, the tasks could not be solved within an acceptable time frame.

The big fear is that the use of AI-based systems will result in a "black box", in which it is no longer possible to trace how the decision was made. This is comparable to the fear of flying. When applying AI techniques, we are dealing with clear mathematical models, whose functionality can be proven and the problems quickly recognized. Stable convergence in Generative Adversarial Networks (GAN) is an example of this. With sufficient knowledge it is always possible to retrace the decision and to name the determining factors.

In machine learning, we often have to work with probabilities that determine the output. However, we are confronted with the same situation with almost all models that are currently used by financial institutions involving decisions on lending, trading models, risk management, fraud detection and much more. We can never rule out extreme events, for which our models are not prepared, but our main goal is for computers to be able to make decisions faster, more accurately, and more predictably than they currently can. With AI-based systems, it is possible to analyze the larger contexts to determine the relationships between individual factors more efficiently, to recognize patterns and to subject existing processes to dynamic stress tests that adapt to the market situation.

From the regulatory reporting perspective, introduction has decisive advantages, which can take many burdens off the shoulders of financial institutions in times of rapid changes in the financial markets, while drastically reducing the costs of regulatory compliance.

The developed solutions can be better scaled, the number of false alarms can be reduced, and decisions can be made faster and more accurately, which can also increase customer satisfaction. The decisive factor is always the context and scope of the information available, as most algorithms need a basis for training, especially in the field of machine learning. Information is the new currency. The following examples make this particularly clear.

4.2 Stress Testing

The stress test scenarios became more complex and sophisticated in the wake of the 2007–2008 crisis and this applies equally to the approaches of all regulators including the FED, the EBA, the ECB and the SEC. The main concept consists of predicting how stable the situation of a financial institution will be with respect to changes in the market situation, which poses new challenges for the financial institution in terms of data infrastructure and process automation.

The stress tests are a double-edged sword. On the one hand, they incur costs and effort. On the other hand, they can open new horizons, such as interaction and synergy effects with regard to IFRS 9. The financial institutions are anxious to run the tests faster with higher data quality and create better process automation.

AI techniques and machine learning approaches can play an important role in passing stress tests. It is of utmost importance that the data required for scenarios can be quickly made available, can withstand an audit, and reports can be generated automatically to notify the appropriate employees on time. Through continuous testing of requirements coupled with machine learning approaches, outliers can be intercepted and rapid action taken to ensure the tests are passed later. At the same time, backtracking methods help identify the factors that could have the greatest impact to reveal human error, wrong model behavior or changing market conditions.

It is possible to develop your own stress tests based on reinforcement learning in a new direction that was not covered previously to reveal the weaknesses of the existing models.

One of the important aspects is how the adjustments we make during the stress tests are correlated and how internal models can prove their robustness. The machine learning algorithms allow us to learn better from the unstructured data and map the specifications to the existing portfolios using GAN in combination with the RNNs as one of the possible solutions.

4.3 Anti-money Laundering/Know Your Customer

Customers are the livelihoods of financial institutions. They value transactions that are executed without delay and a minimum of additional requests from the financial institution to verify the information they provide.

Today, regulators want to ensure that sufficiently strong controls in Customer Due Diligence (CDD) are in place and there is no hesitation in penalizing a financial institution for failing to meet its obligations.

According to Boston Consulting Group, banks worldwide have paid $321 billion since 2008 for violations resulting from money laundering, market manipulation and terrorist financing.[15]

Deutsche Bank alone was fined $204 million by British regulator FCA for serious AML control failings.[16]

It should be noted that, in most cases, financial institutions would not be accused of any intent. Especially the big players on the financial market have to comply with different, often incomparable laws regarding AML, sanctions screening and KYC such as FATCA, MAS, OFAC, 4AMLD, which leads to rising legal costs.

A cost driver is the amount of manual work involved in evaluating alarm signals, as most processes follow a rule-based approach, with the amount of false positive signals expected to be extremely large. For issues such as sanctions, the rules are rather vague, as often only the projects or areas against which the limits have been imposed are indicated.

An AI approach can be very helpful here, as it can be used to achieve much greater automation and efficiency.

Customer onboarding is one area, in which the advantages of AI can be used, as the main profile is already to be created here and later maintained. It is also important to ensure identification documents are genuine using

---

[15]Grasshoff et al. (2017).
[16]CNBC (2018).

many sources that provide unstructured data including social networks or news, which bring techniques like NLP or CNN into play.

Link analysis provides crucial support in understanding the extent to which individual parties are connected and the money flows between them.

This plays a critical role in MIFID and compliance with sanctions, as the source and the end user often determine whether the transaction can be executed.

As mentioned above, it is often the case that the sanctions list is not deterministic and the affected group should be determined first, using techniques such as DBSCAN or embeddings, in which missing data from the additional sources could be delivered with additional semantic analysis using NLP on the audio, video and text sources.

In the controls of the transactions in relation to AML, one sees that criminal techniques constantly improve and adapt. This necessitates recognition of new patterns and ongoing system adaptation, which is associated with a high level of manual effort. Machine learning can help detect and classify anomalies much faster than humans due to the number and complexity of the factors involved. The time it takes to respond to dynamic input data is also decisive, which requires constant adjustment of specifications and an ongoing search for explicit formulations, which are not always readily available.

Despite all the advantages of AI techniques, it is important to be clear about the protection of customer data and which data sources may be evaluated. With new legal requirements like the GDPR in the EU, legislators are increasingly focusing on the purposes for which personally identifiable information is used and whether the person concerned has provided their consent. Article 22 of the GDRP does not allow an entity to make a fully automated decision, except in certain exceptional circumstances. The definition of this can be interpreted in different ways at this point.

4.4 Unstructured Data and MiFID II: Better Customer Protection

The European Directive 2014/65/EU (MiFID II) officially entered into force throughout the European Union on 3 January 2018 and replaced the former MiFID Directive.

The ultimate objective of MiFID II is to eliminate the information asymmetries that have caused many problems in the past and to raise the quality standards of financial players to ensure financial markets provide more transparency and protection to investors.

The main problem with MiFID II is its complexity and scope, which regulates almost all aspects of relationships between clients and financial institutions, in which regulation of pre-trading and post-trading processes plays an important role

The MiFID II legislation is described by well-structured documents, which provides a good opportunity to approach it using AI tools and break down the draft legislation into individual basic concepts, e.g., Article 27(5):

..... < object > The order execution policy < #object > shall < action > include < #action >, in respect of each < type > class of financial instruments < #type >, information on the different < attribute > venues < #attribute > where the < object > investment firm < #object > executes....

A decision graph can be generated to help identify articles affecting the financial institution, classify players and define deadlines. In view of the abundance of regulatory requirements, it is often very difficult to see the overlap in legislation to intercept unnecessary duplication of implementation, such as between MiFID II and PRIIP or MiFID II, Article 16(6), and GDPR, Article 32(1)(a).

One of the main issues here is that all kinds of communication, e.g., emails, calls and faxes to customers concerning possible financial transactions should be recorded and stored for 5 years (Article 16).

Huge amounts of data therefore have to be evaluated and this can be accomplished in two ways: hiring more personnel or automating evaluation of the recordings.

All audio sequences first have to be converted quickly and accurately into text form, so that we can make them searchable in the data lake, whereby NLP algorithms (e.g., RNNs) provide a tremendous help in this regard.

All communication must not only be recorded, but also actively monitored so that mis-selling or other bad practices can be identified. Here, too, the benefits of AI cannot be overlooked, whereby different strategies could be pursued depending on the approach. Consider two possible approaches: a trigger system can be created where an alarm is triggered when predefined words or phrases are used. Semantic analysis of the conversations, which provides additional information such as context, would be much more effective. NLP based on machine learning algorithms could be used for this. The second approach can be followed up with reinforcement learning and supervised learning. Article 24(10) of MiFID II, which is intended to ensure customers get the best financial instrument based on their requirements, can be used as a good example. The required information can be extracted from the communication using CNN or RNN, for example, and can then be brought into a standard form, which corresponds to the data model and can be used for training a neural network.

In regulatory reporting, financial institutions must deal with a flood of data points every day, as has become clear in the examples shown, whereby AI can provide significant support if the new techniques are not considered to be a magic wand. Investments have to be made, but they will pay off at a later stage, and experts in this field are needed for the transformation to be successful.

5   Conclusion

There is little doubt that DLT, big data and AI will have an impact on the regulatory value chain, because they can lower costs, increase quality of regulatory reporting processes and data quality, and possibly open up new ways of compliance.

The various, already existing use cases and PoCs show that technical feasibility does not seem to be the main remaining challenge to widespread adoption in Regtech. On the contrary, they show that there is a lot of potential for utilizing these technologies in the regulatory sphere. First and foremost, the potential is this great because banking regulation in Europe is based on written rules and data. This allows for using the smart contract functionalities of DLT as well as machine learning, NLP and further functionalities of AI, which can be seen in the examples of EMIR II, Stress Testing, AML and MIFID II.

With regard to DLT, this would be simplified by consensus about a common data model, as in the AuRep case, and therefore requires a collaborative approach between banks and regulators to overcome important adoption hurdles such as governance issues.

It is important to overcome the fear of AI as a black box that makes it impossible to comprehend how decisions are made. As the threat seems unsubstantiated, this concern must be reduced by clarifying how backtracking of decisions can be handled. A more important challenge is the quality of initial data used to implement AI solutions. AI initially requires context to improve decisions. If the information provided to AI is incorrect, it will hamper the creation of high-quality results.

This is where DLT and AI can complement each other. A DLT network, serving as a consistent data pool between participants and guaranteeing adherence to regulatory rules, would certainly provide input data for AI algorithms with high quality. AI can build on this existing data and involve more contextual information, leading to the possibility of an improved evaluation of context. This, in turn, results in more explicit high-quality decisions.

In a rather extreme scenario, a DLT network could span the financial sector that serves as a consistent data pool, which is enriched by the vast amount of data points that can be processed because of big data analytics and improves itself through the capabilities of AI and self-learning algorithms, thus further adding to the database. This could result in a self-improving financial cycle.

References

Bauerle, N. (2018a). *What can a blockchain do*. Abgerufen am 28 September 2018 von Coindesk https://www.coindesk.com/information/what-can-a-blockchain-do/.

Bauerle, N. (2018b, September 29). *What is the difference blockchain and database*. Retrieved from Coindesk https://www.coindesk.com/information/what-is-the-difference-blockchain-and-database/.

BearingPoint Institute. (2015). *Reforming regulatory reporting: Are we headed toward real-time?* Bearingpoint.

Brown, R. G., Carlyle, J., Grigg, I., & Hearn, M. (2016). *Corda: An introduction*.

CMR. (2018). *15 Global use cases of AI in BFSI*. Von CyberMedia Research http://cmrindia.com/15-global-use-cases-of-ai/. abgerufen.

CNBC. (2018, November 16). *Deutsche Bank fined $204 million by British regulator FCA for serious anti-money laundering control failings*. Abgerufen am 16 November 2018 von CNBC https://www.cnbc.com/2017/01/31/deutsche-bank-fined-204-million-by-british-regulator-for-serious-anti-money-laundering-control-failings.html.

English, S., & Hammond, S. (2017). *Cost of compliance 2017*. Thomson Reuters.

English, S., & Hammond, S. (2018). *Cost of compliance 2018*. Thomson Reuters.

Grasshoff, G., Mogul, Z., Pfuhler, T., Gittfried, N., Wiegand, C., Bohn, A., & Vonhoff, V. (2017). *Global risk 2017: Staying the course in banking*. Von BCG www.bcg.com/de-de/publications/2017/financial-institutions-growth-global-risk-2017-staying-course-banking.aspx. abgerufen.

Hong Kong Applied Science and Technology Research Institute. (2016). *Whitepaper on distributed ledger technology*. Hong Kong Monetary Authority.

Nakamoto, S. (2008). *Bitcoin—A peer-to-peer electronic cash system*. https://s3.amazonaws.com/academia.edu.documents/54517945/Bitcoin_paper_Original_2.pdf?response-content-disposition=inline%3B%20filename%3DBitcoin_A_Peer-to-Peer_Electronic_Cash_S.pdf&X-Amz-Al-

gorithm=AWS4-HMAC-SHA256&X-Amz-Credential=AKIAIWOWYYG-Z2Y53UL3A%2F20190722%2Fus-east-1%2Fs3%2Faws4_request&X-Amz-Date=20190722T154942Z&X-Amz-Expires=3600&X-Amz-SignedHeaders=host&X-Amz-Signature=db9d8b5bb71f25dd01f6698b2a7484a054042f803bb-8bc9807bf9ee0ff42fc64.

World Economic Forum. (2016, August). *The future of financial infrastructure—An ambitious look at how blockchain can reshape financial services.* Retrieved September 28, 2018, from https://www.weforum.org/reports/the-future-of-financial-infrastructure-an-ambitious-look-at-how-blockchain-can-reshape-financial-services.

15

New Office of the Comptroller of the Currency Fintech Regulation: Ensuring a Successful Special Purpose National Bank Charter Application

Alexa Philo

1 Introduction

Financial technology (fintech) companies evaluating whether to apply for an Office of the Comptroller of the Currency (OCC) Special Purpose National Bank[1] (SPNB) charter must consider a variety of factors. Among them are: the regulatory and compliance requirements they will need to adhere to; the work involved in applying for the charter and transitioning to full conformance; the challenges (and opportunities) associated with competing against traditional banks; and the strategic and operational changes that may be required down the road to align with the OCC's expectations on an ongoing basis.

---

[1]The OCC defines a Special Purpose National Bank as a national bank that engages in a limited range of banking or fiduciary activities, targets a limited customer base, incorporates nontraditional elements, or has a narrowly targeted business plan. Banking activities include one or more of the core banking functions of taking deposits, paying checks or lending money. However, the SPNB Supplement targeted specifically to fintech companies does not extend to deposit taking of any kind, whether insured by the Federal Deposit Insurance Corp., non-insured, or fiduciary in nature.

A. Philo (✉)
Brooklyn, NY, USA

© The Author(s) 2019
V. Liermann and C. Stegmann (eds.), *The Impact of Digital Transformation and FinTech on the Finance Professional*, https://doi.org/10.1007/978-3-030-23719-6_15

2 Application Requirements

In its July 2018 policy statement, the OCC emphasized that requirements and standards in its accompanying fintech Charter Application Supplement[2] will be tailored to the company's business model, delivery channels, products and services. Indeed, as part of its mandate, the OCC tailors its supervision of individual banking organizations to their size, complexity and overall risk profile. However, the OCC may be under pressure to apply its supervisory framework consistently to fintech companies and traditional banks and to promote a level playing field between the two sectors.

Thus, even fintech companies with the most limited business models should not discount the OCC's fundamental standards and expectations elaborated below. Further, fintech companies' status as new nontraditional entrants facing a unique set of risks as well as legal challenges underway from other regulators will place certain processes and controls (e.g., those to conform with Governance, Risk Management, Financial Inclusion/ Consumer Compliance and Contingency Planning requirements) under even higher scrutiny than has heretofore been applied to the OCC's chartered banks.

The application has informal and formal components and is likely to involve multiple iterations to demonstrate that the applicant:

- Has the processes and controls in place to adhere to safety and soundness standards and relevant regulations;
- Will provide fair access to its products and services and promote healthy competition; and
- Thus has a reasonable chance of gaining OCC approval for the SPNB charter.

The entire application process, including the pre and post-filing phases and a decision phase, could require at least 12–24 months, and potentially longer, depending on the complexity of the business model and other factors addressed below. The decision phase will include a preliminary approval stage accompanied by conditions and requirements, an organization phase during which the company raises capital and prepares for opening as a bank,

---

[2]Officer of Comptroller of the Currency Policy Statement on Financial Technology Companies' Eligibility to Apply for National Bank Charters, July 31, 2018, including companion Licensing Manual Supplement, Considering Applications from Financial Technology Companies, July 2018.

and the final approval stage, once all associated requirements and conditions have been met. During these phases, applicants will also need to ensure that they have a full understanding of, and preparedness for, requirements associated with other regulators, including the Federal Reserve, the Bureau of Consumer Financial Protection, and potentially other regulatory bodies, as relevant. The OCC will coordinate as relevant with other regulators to facilitate consideration of any applications or approvals that will be required by those other regulators.

Fintech companies that can demonstrate their readiness (i.e., a strong command of the requirements, the requisite skills and experience on their Board of Directors and management teams as well as key processes and controls in place) from the outset and have already undertaken considerable steps to prepare, will save a lot of time and have a better shot at being granted the charter. Even firms heading into the process with robust governance, risk management and compliance frameworks will be well served to engage independent experts on the subject with in-depth experience in bank regulation and traditional banking operations. This will ensure that the Board of Directors and key management staff have a full picture of the expectations, the work that will be required to apply for the charter, and what it takes to remain well managed and financially resilient in the eyes of the OCC on an ongoing basis.

3 Competitive Considerations

A fintech company's competitiveness in key banking segments—including nationwide access to core banking activities of paying checks, facilitating payments electronically and lending money—has the potential to increase with the SPNB charter. This is primarily due to Federal Preemption laws that enable an OCC chartered SPNB to largely avoid state-by-state licensing and supervision, while offering products to a national customer base. However, the OCC's fintech-oriented Licensing Supplement does not extend to bank deposit taking. Fintech companies interested in taking insured deposits would be required to obtain FDIC insurance and would need to apply for a full-service national bank charter.

Within this context, many fintech companies are positioned to leverage advanced digital technologies, infrastructure and systems overall in a manner that requires less time to conform to a given requirement, and at a lower cost. This is particularly the case for new or changing supervisory standards, rules and regulations, including post-financial crisis standards for risk, finance and capital/liquidity, data collection and reporting, as well as intensive data and reporting requirements.

A key assumption is that the core competitive edges of fintech companies in the digital technology space can be brought to bear on regulation and supervision, particularly pertaining to data collection and reporting, and more readily adapted to emerging regtech developments. Additionally, fintech companies, with their shorter legal histories, do not have the burden of legacy infrastructures and systems associated with the multitude of M&A deals that resulted in operational inefficiencies for many traditional banks over the years. Thus, fintech companies' generally more advanced and streamlined infrastructures, technology and systems, as well as simpler legal entity structures, may enable the OCC to tailor its supervisory strategy, and potentially result in a less expensive and time-intensive regulatory compliance program that has less negative impact on the bottom line (Brear, 2015).

From a business model and strategy perspective, however, any given fintech company may have reason to pause prior to signing up for participation in certain heavily regulated markets, in which the potential for penalties or reputational risk is high (e.g., due to violations of consumer protection or anti-financial crime laws). Many traditional banks have the advantage of years of experience and built-up expertise to conform to financial inclusion, consumer privacy, bank secrecy, anti-money laundering and other significant compliance requirements of this kind (Brear, 2015; Lang, 2018).

4 Supervisory Expectations

In addition to the conventional components of a robust business plan, the OCC will be looking for information on the firm's board and senior management oversight, risk assessment, risk management framework, capital, liquidity and funding, contingency planning, compliance and financial inclusion aspects elaborated below.

- **Board and Senior Management Oversight**: The OCC will expect the governance structure to be commensurate with the risk and complexity of the fintech company's products, services and activities. The Board of Directors should set clear direction regarding the company's strategy and risk appetite based on comprehensive and reliable information, hold senior management accountable, support the independence and stature of risk management and internal audit, and maintain a capable board composition and governance structure. The Board of Directors will need to prove that it is actively overseeing management, providing credible challenge and exercising independent judgment. The OCC will look for evidence of the financial and business expertise of management in highly regulated industries, with experience and skills relevant to the business plan, strategy and risk appetite (e.g., sufficient technology experience will be just as important as banking and financial experience) (Office of the Comptroller of the Currency, 2018).

- **Risk Assessment**: Fintech companies preparing to file should refer to the OCC's Risk Assessment System (RAS), a risk-based examination framework that can also be used by the company directly to ensure that it is adequately identifying, measuring, monitoring and controlling key risks as it prepares for its SPNB application. The RAS is used to assess policies, processes, personnel and control systems, and the extent to which they provide a consistent means of managing the quantity, quality and aggregate level of these risks, and the direction of each key category of risk—including credit, interest rate, liquidity, price, operational, compliance, anti-financial crime (Bank Secrecy Act/Anti-Money Laundering) and reputational risk. The latter addresses the risk to earnings, capital or franchise value resulting from negative public opinion. Reputational risk may arise from data breaches, privacy concerns, frequent changes in senior staff and non-compliance with consumer protection laws, to name a few drivers. The RAS also takes into account the effectiveness of internal controls and internal audit. The RAS and related processes and controls must be used comprehensively in the identification, measuring and monitoring of key risks, candidly and self-critically to be effective.
- **Enterprise Risk Management**: The OCC will expect the firm to have an enterprise risk management (ERM) framework in place that addresses the identification, measurement, monitoring and controlling of key risks to the company. An effective ERM framework must be embraced at the most senior levels of the organization. Key components include having the relevant committees and policies and procedures in place, with clearly defined accountabilities, roles, and responsibilities for overseeing the key risks to the firm. The ERM framework should also provide for oversight and risk management of third-party contractor relationships. As the OCC notes in its ERM guidance, firms will benefit from periodic review of the ERM process by an independent party.
- **Capital Planning/Funding**: SPNBs will be subject to the OCC's risk-based and leverage capital ratios, including 10% total risk-based capital (RBC), 8% tier 1 RBC, 6.5% common equity tier 1 RBC and a 5% leverage ratio that apply to all banks. These ratios define minimum

thresholds for determining that the company is well capitalized relative to its assets and off-balance sheet exposures. However, these levels may not be sufficient for firms with limited balance sheet assets or nontraditional strategies, such as a high volume of off-balance sheet activity conducted, and other risks associated with the business plan. Demonstrating adherence to relevant capital thresholds will require subject matter expertise in risk-weighted asset calculation and other elements of bank regulatory capital, as well as strong capital planning capabilities in general. The OCC will expect companies' capital plans to be dynamic, forward-looking and incorporate changes in the SPNBs' business focus, risk tolerance levels, business plans, operating environment and other factors that reflect capital adequacy (Office of the Comptroller of the Currency, 2018).

- **Liquidity/Funds Management**: The application will also need to address liquidity and funds management and especially the capacity for a fintech company to readily meet its cash and collateral obligations taking into account planned and unplanned balance sheet changes, under varying interest rate scenarios and market conditions. Since SPNBs may rely on well-functioning securitization markets, the business plan for such companies will need to describe how adequate funding levels will be maintained in volatile environments and include contingency plans to address significant stress that could threaten the viability of the bank in stress scenarios, to which the firm is most vulnerable (Office of the Comptroller of the Currency, 2018).

- **Stress Scenarios**: On the operational side, stress scenarios that would prompt activation of the contingency funding plan are likely to include data/privacy breaches, system failures or the detection of systemic fraud or money laundering with the potential to trigger financial and reputational concerns. Fintech companies with a reliance on the originate-to-distribute business model must necessarily consider scenarios, in which the securitization market closes in the face of existing pipelines of loans held for sale.

- **Contingency Planning:** Contingency plans must include strategies for restoring the SPNB's financial strength and reputation, as well as options for selling, merging or liquidating the bank in a situation, in which the recovery strategies prove ineffective. Consideration must also be given to any concentrations such as a customer base concentrated regionally or according to a particular segment (e.g., preponderance of low-income customers with fewer banking alternatives), which would drive the need to consider not just the firm-specific, but also the external impacts of a given stress scenario (LendingClub Corporation, 2017; Office of the Comptroller of the Currency, 2018).

- **Financial Inclusion:** The OCC expects a fintech company applicant to demonstrate a commitment to financial inclusion that includes providing or supporting fair access to financial services and fair treatment of customers.
- Ongoing OCC supervision.

The supervisory process has become more dynamic and interactive than the traditional notion of just being subject to one examination annually or every eighteen months. The OCC has also become increasingly encouraging of communication throughout the supervisory cycle including requests and reviews between onsite examinations. This includes quarterly offsite reviews, in which the OCC examiners take stock of any observed changes in the SPNBs' financial condition. Newly chartered SPNBs should expect more frequent and intensive supervision in their initial years of operation, including frequent contact with the board of directors and management (Office of the Comptroller of the Currency, 2018).

Composite ratings evaluate the SPNBs' conformance with requirements and standards for managerial, operational, financial, risk management and compliance performance. Generally, SPNBs will require a satisfactory or strong supervisory rating to pursue their growth strategies.

5   Preparing to Engage with the OCC

There are a number of principles concerning engagement with all bank regulators that should be factored into the applicants' preparation. While by no means exhaustive, two examples are worth noting here:

One of the foremost rules of thumb is that there should be no surprises. Transparency is key to an effective relationship with regulators. A company that starts its relationship with the OCC recognizing that a culture of no surprises and full transparency will ultimately be required should find that adherence to these principles shortens the application time frame and increases the prospect of successful OCC approval of the charter application.

This is a high demand, particularly when firms are often working hard to communicate effectively with the Board of Directors and other internal stakeholders when material risks or issues arise. When a concern of relevance to bank supervisors surfaces, one of the first things that should come to mind is being prepared to apprise the supervisor on a very timely basis. When examiners start probing the issue at hand, their line of questioning will seek to determine when the issue was discovered and what actions were taken by management to escalate, etc.

If there is a significant lag in communication to the regulator on a risk or issue of any magnitude, examiners will want to know why that was the case. When communication is not transparent, examiners will be compelled to dig deeper and ask more probing questions. In contrast, taking immediate steps to communicate thoroughly with the fintech company's Board of Directors and supervisors alike promotes confidence and enables the examiners to take more of what they are hearing at face value. Above all else, an applicant or chartered SPNB will want to ensure that its regulator learns of any issues or vulnerabilities from the appropriate management personnel inside the company, and not inadvertently from another department or, in the worst case, from an outside party such as the media or equity analysts.

Another key ingredient to building a culture of transparency is documentation. This includes committee charters, terms of reference and minutes associated with key meetings; robust policies and procedures; and detailed written descriptions of the technologies, systems and models used to deliver products and services, measure risk and carry out other complex processes and controls. The following should be observed with regard to documentation:

- Supervisors expect to see minutes for Board and key management committee meetings that record the information presented to these committees, the discussion that ensues and key decisions and outcomes that arise from these meetings.
- Examiners will expect policies and procedures to cover all aspects of adherence to the aforementioned requirements. While the policies should be principles-based, the policy framework and related procedure documents should not just repeat the regulatory requirements and state the company's commitment. They should instead detail the processes and controls in place to ensure that such requirements are met.
- Post-crisis requirements for model governance put the onus on model developers, users and validators to document their methodology, governance and other elements, focusing on the reliability and relevance of underlying data, assumptions, etc.

A second key principle worth noting, in this case grounded in law, is that companies should under no circumstances share supervisory information with any party, even another regulator, without explicit approval from the relevant agency. For example, one might think it appropriate to include reference to a Consumer Financial Protection Bureau finding in the OCC application (e.g., under discussion of how Consumer Compliance controls have been enhanced). This may make sense as long as the relevant agency has authorized such disclosure in writing. Similarly, if the OCC provides feedback to an applicant on potential gaps in its filing, and the company engages a consulting firm to assist with remediation, it is prohibited to share the OCC's feedback with even the most trusted outside adviser without the explicit written approval of the OCC.

Applicants are strongly encouraged to seek out the advice of relevant experts on the subject to understand the full array of principles, prohibitions and potential pitfalls. This will further ensure a successful, issue-free application process.

6 Next Steps to Ensuring a Successful Application

Exercises that can help fintech companies prepare for the application process and the initial OCC examination can range from coaching key employees on effective communication with banking regulators to full-blown mock exams that enable the companies to identify any gaps or vulnerabilities in advance, which may present a challenge to obtaining a satisfactory or strong rating in the initial exam cycle under OCC supervision.

- **Coaching on Effective Communications:** Dos and don'ts associated with responding to examiners' inquiries. This includes ways to ensure key personnel understand the questions that examiners are asking and what the OCC expects from management's responses; and how to be honest and transparent, while not providing unnecessary information beyond what is being asked. The latter can inadvertently prompt examiners to go beyond the scope of their initial questions in a manner that could have been avoided if the responders had understood the precise questions being asked.
- **Mock Examinations:** This entails a more elaborate simulation of an annual or eighteen-month examination. It addresses what to expect from an OCC exam and preparations in advance to anticipate and mitigate operational and financial gaps, vulnerabilities or challenges that may impact the company's supervisory ratings.

Some components of preparation for the charter application are common sense. Others require a deep understanding of the rules and requirements, as well as the precedents that have been set by traditional banks within the realms of Governance, Risk Management, Compliance and other aspects of maintaining and demonstrating to regulators a safe and sound, financially and operationally resilient banking organization.

Stay tuned for additional perspective on other key requirements for successful applications and initial examinations, including those associated with Consumer Compliance, Inter-company Transactions, Oversight of Third Party Contractors and Model Governance, as well as standards for an Independent Internal Audit function.

Literature

Brear, D. (2015, July 20). *What differentiates banking and fintech*. Retrieved November 28, 2018, from The Financial Brand https://thefinancialbrand.com/53102/banks-fintech-start-up-comparison/.

Lang, H. (2018, August 17). *Fintechs have more work to do to prevent discrimination: Congressman*. Retrieved November 28, 2018, from American Banker https://asreport.americanbanker.com/news/fintechs-have-more-work-to-do-to-prevent-discrimination-congressman?tag=00000159-ad66-d644-af5f-eff61aca0000.

LendingClub Corporation. (2017, December 31). *SEC 10-K filing*. Retrieved November 28, 2018, from Securities and Exchange Commission https://ir.lendingclub.com/Cache/392292654.pdf?IID=4213397&FID=392292654&O=3&OSID=9.

Office of the Comptroller of the Currency. (2018, July). *Considering charter applications from financial technology companies*. Retrieved November 28, 2018, from https://www.occ.treas.gov/publications/publications-by-type/licensing-manuals/file-pub-lm-considering-charter-applications-fintech.pdf.

Part IV

Methods, Technology and Architecture

To a certain extent, the part "Methods, Technology and Architecture" serves as an annex to the business-driven chapters in this book.

The valuable methods of machine learning and deep learning are discussed in Chapter 16 "Machine learning—an introduction" (Liermann, Li, & Schaudinnus, 2019b) and Chapter 17 "Deep learning—an introduction" (Liermann, Li, & Schaudinnus, 2019a). Many publications already exist on these two subjects. It would extend far beyond the scope of this book to provide a comprehensive summary of machine learning and deep learning methods. (Liermann et al., 2019b) provides a categorization and overview of the most common machine learning algorithms. Selected algorithms are discussed in further detail, driven by the other chapters in this book related to machine learning. The same applies to the chapter on deep learning. Following a brief introduction and an overview of the most common neural network patterns, only the approaches relevant to the subjects addressed in this book are described in more depth. Although the two chapters are predominantly overviews, they both show how multifaceted and complex these classes of algorithms are.

As data and especially readily accessible mass data is the fuel for these models, the next three chapters deal with modern approaches to storing data. Chapter 18 "Hadoop: A Standard Framework for Computer Cluster" introduces the main motivations and concepts behind data lakes as well as the Hadoop and Spark frameworks (Akhgarnush, Broeckers, & Jakoby, 2019). Many of the applications driven by digitalization would not be realizable without fast and scalable mass data storage. Not surprisingly, Google

(Hadoop) and Facebook (Spark) are the initial contributors to these open source frameworks. Chapter 19 "In-memory databases and their impact on our (future) organizations" introduces and provides insight into the concept of in-memory databases and the impact on transactional and analytical systems (Kopic, Teschome, Schneider, Steurer, & Florin, 2019). In addition to providing an introduction to SAP's in-memory framework Hana, the chapter presents a fast cash flow generator use case. The final chapter in this part is "MongoDB: The Journey from a Relational to a Document-Based Database for FIS Balance Sheet Management", which provides insight into document-based databases and their potential in a rapidly changing environment (Bialek, 2019). MongoDB provides an example of the opportunities within the context of the analytical application of balance sheet management. Documents-based databases change the optics from the relational view back to a content-driven approach versus a shredded one and the case of a deeply relational subject as banking risk gives a good introduction to those changes.

Literature

Akhgarnush, E., Broeckers, L., & Jakoby, T. (2019). Hadoop—A standard framework for computer clusters. In V. Liermann & C. Stegmann (Eds.), *The impact of digital transformation and fintech on the finance professional*. New York: Palgrave Macmillan.

Bialek, B. (2019). MongoDB—The journey from a relational to a document-based database for FIS balance sheet management. In V. Liermann & C. Stegmann (Eds.), *The impact of digital transformation and fintech on the finance professional*. New York: Palgrave Macmillan.

Kopic, E., Teschome, B., Schneider, T., Steurer, R., & Florin, S. (2019). In-memory databases and their impact on our (future) organizations. In V. Liermann & C. Stegmann (Eds.), *The impact of digital transformation and fintech on the finance professional*. New York: Palgrave Macmillan.

Liermann, V., Li, S., & Schaudinnus, N. (2019a). Deep learning—An introduction. In V. Liermann & C. Stegmann (Eds.), *The impact of digital transformation and fintech on the finance professional*. New York: Palgrave Macmillan.

Liermann, V., Li, S., & Schaudinnus, N. (2019b). Mathematical background of machine learning. In V. Liermann & C. Stegmann (Eds.), *The impact of digital transformation and fintech on the finance professional*. New York: Palgrave Macmillan.

16

Mathematical Background of Machine Learning

Volker Liermann, Sangmeng Li and Victoria Dobryashkina

1 Overview

Machine learning (ML) techniques are concerned with general pattern recognition or the construction of universal approximators of relations in the data in situations where no obvious a priori analytical solution exists. As a new trend of ML, deep learning (DL) showed up at the end of last century and became one of the most efficient learning algorithms. As the name "deep" suggests, DL subtracts features and represents data by means of multiple hierarchical levels. The most well-known example of DL techniques are neural networks, which will be introduced in the coming chapters. In this chapter, we provide fundamental mathematical background on some common ML.

V. Liermann (✉) · S. Li
ifb AG, Grünwald, Germany
e-mail: volker.liermann@ifb-group.com

S. Li
e-mail: sangmeng.li@ifb-group.com

V. Dobryashkina
ifb International AG branch office Austria, Vienna, Austria
e-mail: victoria.dobryashkina@ifb-group.com

© The Author(s) 2019
V. Liermann and C. Stegmann (eds.), *The Impact of Digital Transformation and FinTech on the Finance Professional*, https://doi.org/10.1007/978-3-030-23719-6_16

Due to their importance, the DL techniques are addressed in detail in a separate chapter (see Liermann et al., Deep learning—An introduction, 2019b).

1.1 Domains of Machine Learning

Figure 1 provides an overview of the domains addressed in this book.

Artificial Intelligence (AI) is intelligence demonstrated by machines, whereas natural intelligence is demonstrated by animals or humans. In terms of computer science, AI research is mainly defined as the study of intelligent agents [see e.g., Chapter 2 (Russell & Norvig, 2003)]. Artificial intelligence was first mentioned in a research application submitted to the Rockefeller Foundation (McCarthy, Minsky, Rochester, & Shannon, 1955). In the proposal, AI was defined as "every aspect of learning or any other feature of intelligence can be so precisely described that a machine can be made to simulate it". Since then the Dartmouth Conference has been seen as the founding event of artificial intelligence as an academic discipline.

ML can be defined as a group of extensions to the classic statistical tools like estimation and classification. In Fig. 2, item (D) is the main part that differentiates ML from conventional statistical methods.

The following formal definition is derived from Sect. 2.3 of the Bank of England's working paper (Chakraborty & Joseph, 2017). A ML problem is

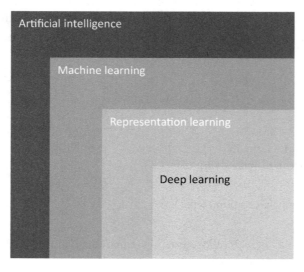

Fig. 1 Domains of machine learning

Fig. 2 Components of a machine learning system

formulated as an optimization problem, the solution of which determines a set of model parameters $\vec{\beta}$.

$$F\left(X, Y, \vec{\beta}, \vec{\lambda}\right) \xrightarrow{\text{optimisation algorithm}} \beta$$

Equation 1: ML definition—problems.

$F(\cdot, \beta)$ is an objective function in terms of prediction quality. $\vec{\lambda}$ is a vector of hyper parameters which can differ from the model class. The input data X and target variable Y are of dimensions $m \times n$ and $m \times 1$, respectively. m is the number of observations and n is the number of features included in the model.

$$X = \begin{pmatrix} x_{1,1} & \cdots & x_{1,n} \\ \vdots & \ddots & \vdots \\ x_{m,1} & \cdots & x_{m,n} \end{pmatrix}$$

Equation 2: Features.

$$Y = \begin{pmatrix} y_1 \\ \vdots \\ y_m \end{pmatrix}$$

Equation 3: Labels.

The features X are sometimes referred as independent or right-hand-side (RHS) variables and the labels are referred as dependent or left-hand-side (LHS) variables.

Representation learning, which is sometimes also referenced as feature learning, is a set of techniques that addresses the automated discovery for representations needed for feature determination and raw data classification. These techniques can replace manual feature engineering. Representation learning can be seen as a subdomain of automated machine learning (AutoML). AutoML automates a broader range of components of a ML problem, such as data preparation, model selection and hyperparameter optimization. Examples are H2O AutoML, H2O Driverless AI, Google AutoML and Auto Keras. The final two software packages focus on deep neural network architecture search.

DL also known as deep structured learning or hierarchical learning is a class of optimization methods for artificial neural networks. These interesting methods are discussed in a separate chapter (see Liermann et al., Deep learning—An introduction, 2019b).

1.2 Supervised and Unsupervised Learning

The following two sections establish an important classification of the algorithms: supervised and unsupervised learning. In the first class, the labels are applied in advance of optimization. In the second class, no labels are applied to the algorithms, but the algorithms provide for label-free clustering of the data. Labels can then be assigned to the clustering-results of unsupervised learning. This is not the same as semi-supervised learning.[1]

Other ML categories to be mentioned are active learning and reinforcement learning. As in semi-supervised learning, in active learning the labels are not assigned for all data columns. The distinction between this and semi-supervised learning is that a user is provided a proposal for the label to approve (see e.g., Schaudinnus & Liermann, 2019). More details are provided in Sect. 1.3.

1.2.1 Supervised Learning

A classic problem for data scientists is classification, which primarily aims at building a predictive model to assign objects into different groups based on a set of features important for extraction based on observations. One example is illustrated in the Figs. 3 and 4.

The task is to assign observations to two different classes with the labels "cats" and "dogs". Therefore, the two features domestication and size are considered. We denote the features by $x_{i,j}$, in which i stands for observation and j for features. Each set of features $(x_{i,1} x_{i,2})$ maps to a label y_i. The characteristic of these approaches is that the observations are all labeled. ML techniques which predict labels are called supervised learning.

The model aims to correctly predict the label by applying a function $h(x_{i,1} x_{i,2}; \beta)$, where β is corresponding parameters. In the

---

[1] Typically, in semi-supervised learning, a small amount of labeled data with a large amount of unlabeled data.

16 Mathematical Background of Machine Learning

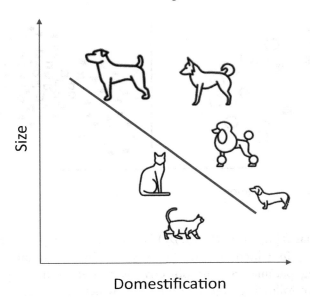

Fig. 3 Classification graph

	Domestication	Size		Label
Observation 1	$x_{1,1}$	$x_{1,2}$		y_1
Observation 2	$x_{2,1}$	$x_{2,2}$		y_2
Observation 3	$x_{3,1}$	$x_{3,2}$		y_3
$\vdots$	$\vdots$	$\vdots$	$h(x_{i,1}, x_{i,2}; \beta)$	$\vdots$
Observation i	$x_{i,1}$	$x_{i,2}$	$\longrightarrow$	y_i
$\vdots$	$\vdots$	$\vdots$		$\vdots$
Observation n	$x_{n,1}$	$x_{n,1}$		y_n

Fig. 4 Linear classification

example illustrated in the figure, h is a function with the three parameters β_1, β_2 and β_3.

$$h(x_{i,1}, x_{i,2}; \beta_1, \beta_2, \beta_3) = \begin{cases} "dog", & if\ \beta_{1,} * x_{i,1} + \beta_2 * x_{i,2} + \beta_3 > 0 \\ "cat", & if\ \beta_{1,} * x_{i,1} + \beta_2 * x_{i,2} + \beta_3 <= 0 \end{cases}$$

Equation 4: Linear classification.

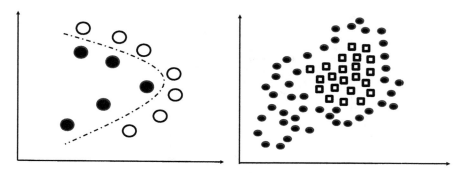

Fig. 5 Nonlinear classification

Assume that $h(x_{i,1}, x_{i,2}; \beta_1, \beta_2, \beta_3)$ is a hypothesis representing the predictive model, in which features $(x_{i,1} x_{i,2})$ are input variables and β_i the corresponding parameters. The objective is to determine mapping h that minimizes the following objective function, which measures the prediction quality by using the quadratic sum:

$$F(X, Y, \beta) = \sum_{i=1}^{n} \left| h(x_{i,1}, x_{i,2}; \beta_1, \beta_2, \beta_3) - y_i \right|^2$$

Equation 5: Objective function.

Since this specific classification problem is based on a linear combination of features, it is referred to as linear classification. More general classification problems are nonlinear, as illustrated in the Fig. 5.

Simple nonlinear classification tasks are solved either using extensions of the linear model or transformations in the space of feature variables. Particularly, support-vector machines use the latter approach by applying the so-called kernel trick.

Other methods work quite differently. For example, decision trees and random forests solve classification problems by applying decisions for each feature, one after another. These models make binary decisions and improve their accuracy by optimizing selectivity for each decision. Both methods are discussed below in further detail.

Modern ML methods facilitate mapping features to labels by means of a network structure. The most prominent representatives of these methods are neural networks and Bayesian networks. These methods are introduced in more detail below.

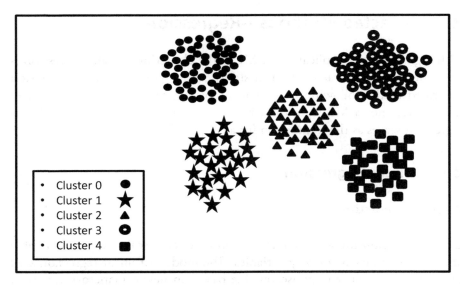

Fig. 6 Clustering

1.2.2 Unsupervised Learning

Contrary to supervised learning, in Unsupervised learning labels of observations are not provided. Consequently, the error function introduced above cannot be applied to adjust model parameters. However, the model is able to determine/group the data structure using various approaches. One of the standard examples of unsupervised learning is clustering, which aims at grouping similar objects into a set referred to as a cluster. Objects in one cluster are likely to differ from objects of another cluster. One example can be seen here. We will provide a deeper introduction to clustering in Fig. 6.

1.3 Reinforcement Learning

The third mentionable ML paradigm is reinforcement learning. Reinforcement learning defines an incentive system to optimize its performance. The main advantage of reinforcement learning is that the algorithm can optimize itself without further user input. This functions in a way similar to labels in the supervised learning case.

In reinforcement learning, data (in the form of rewards and consequences) are given as feedback to the program's actions in a dynamic environment. This technique enabled the breakthrough in the game Go (see AlphaGo by Google DeepMind (Google, 2019)).

2 Selected Methods—Regression

Although the main application of ML is the clustering of data, regression is an important historical method in statistical analysis. The linear regression described in the following chapter is, according to the definition provided in Sect. 1.1, not a ML algorithm, but deserves mention, because the linear regression serves as the foundation for a couple of ML algorithms.

2.1 Linear Regression

2.1.1 Introduction

Linear regression models the relationship between a scalar response variable and one or more explanatory variables. The models of linear regression seek to estimate the scalar response variable based on new explanatory variables. If the response variable has more than one dimension (is no longer scalar), then the models are referred to as multivariate linear regression.

2.1.2 Definition

The problem can be described using the following formula:

$$y = \beta_0 + \beta_1 x_1 + \cdots + \beta_n x_n + \epsilon$$

Equation 6: Linear regression.

Where y is the scalar response variable, $\vec{x} = \begin{pmatrix} x_1 \\ \vdots \\ x_n \end{pmatrix}$ the vector of n explanatory variables and ϵ is the error term or noise.

For multivariate linear regression, the problem can be formulated as follows in a matrix.

$$\vec{y} = X\vec{\beta} + \vec{\epsilon}$$

Equation 7: Multivariate linear regression.

$\vec{y} = \begin{pmatrix} y_1 \\ \vdots \\ y_n \end{pmatrix}$ is the vector of n response variables, $\vec{\beta} = \begin{pmatrix} \beta_0 \\ \beta_1 \\ \vdots \\ \beta_p \end{pmatrix}$ is the $p+1$-dimensional parameter vector and $\vec{\epsilon} = \begin{pmatrix} \epsilon_1 \\ \vdots \\ \epsilon_n \end{pmatrix}$ the n-dimensional error-term vector.

The matrix $X = \begin{pmatrix} 1 & x_{11} & \cdots & x_{1p} \\ \vdots & \vdots & \ddots & \vdots \\ 1 & x_{n1} & \cdots & x_{np} \end{pmatrix}$ is the set of explanatory variables and the first column is used to incorporate a fixed intercept term β_0 into the model.

Estimation methods for solving Eq. 6 are mostly based on least-squares estimation.

2.1.3 Generalized Linear Models

The generalized linear models (GLM) are linear models, which restrict the response variables to be bounded or discrete. The boundaries arise from the application context (e.g., positive values for populations or prices, or categorical data). The GLM are to some extent closer to the clustering models discussed in the following Sect. 3.

2.2 Nonlinear Regression

Nonlinear regression is a kind of regression analysis where the response variable is modeled by a function, which is a nonlinear combination of the model parameters. As any regression, nonlinear regression depends on one or more explanatory variables (independent variables). In a most general formulation, the model can be described by the following formula:

$$\vec{y} = f(X, \vec{\beta})$$

Equation 8: Multivariate nonlinear regression.

As in the previous section $\vec{y}$ is the vector of observed dependent variables, $\vec{\beta}$ the set of parameter variables and X is the matrix of explanatory variables. The function f establishes a nonlinear relation between $\vec{y}$ and X.

In the case of a scalar response variable, the formula can be simplified as follows

$$y = f(\vec{x}, \vec{\beta})$$

Equation 9: Nonlinear regression—scalar response variable.

With y being the scalar response variable, $\vec{x}$ the vector of explanatory variables and $\vec{\beta}$ the vector of parameter variables.

In the multivariate case, an approximation of the function f can be delivered by the first-order Taylor series of f.

$$f\left(\vec{x}_i, \vec{\beta}\right) \approx f\left(\overrightarrow{x_i}, \vec{0}\right) + \sum_{j}^{p} J_{ij}\beta_j$$

Equation 10: First-order Taylor series approximation.

With $J_{ij} = \dfrac{\partial f\left(\overrightarrow{x_i}, \vec{\beta}\right)}{\partial \beta_j}$ being the derivation of f by β_j for the explanatory variable vector $\overrightarrow{x_i}$.

Another method for handling nonlinear dependencies involves support-vector machines (SVM) see Chapter 17 Sect 3.15. Support-vector network (SVN) in Liermann et al., Deep learning—An introduction, 2019b. In addition, the DL networks proved to be good models for handling nonlinear relations [see (Liermann et al., Deep learning—An introduction, 2019b)].

3 Selected Machine Learning Methods—Clustering

In ML the two concepts of retrieval and clustering go side-by-side. While the former concerns itself with discovering the best match as a result, the latter is aimed at dividing those potential results into disjointed sets of objects possessing the most common properties in each set, meanwhile having the most dissimilar properties to the other ones. For now, we will concentrate on the latter, as it is often considered to be the aid of retrieval, therefore being of principal interest to the developers.

Clustering is a statistical tool widely used to analyze sample structures by subdividing data into groups (clusters) based on member similarities. Since first introduced in the early part of the last century, various techniques that deal with data according to the original goals of analysis have been invented. However, the general principle has remained the same for all of them: the most alike are to be assigned to one cluster, while being as dissimilar as possible to the others. How resemblance is determined has to be decided in advance. The following has to be considered for the algorithm: definition of a cluster within a specific analysis, a similarity measure such as distance, density, etc., and an efficient procedure. Additionally, one can differentiate between hard and fuzzy clustering. In the former, each point of a set is either a member of a cluster or not, whereas, in the latter, it can belong to each to a certain degree.

The following algorithms are commonly used for the static data, which includes time independent or single point observations: connectivity-based, centroid-based, distribution-based and density-based, or mixtures of these.

3.1 Connectivity-Based Models

The connectivity-based model with the hierarchical clustering algorithm to be mostly known uses distance between the points in the sample for decision-making. The type of distance, however, is also a subject of specification. In such a model, the linkage criterion (single-linkage clustering with minimum object distances, complete-linkage with maximum, or average-linkage[2] clustering) plays a big role, as it defines how, and between which points the distances are to be calculated in relation to the other ones. The shape of the final clusters will depend on this. After all, if we allow all the points that lie on the x maximum distance from n neighbors as the only requirement to be in one cluster, then the forms of such clusters can be less geometrically definable. There are also two approaches with this model: agglomerative (bottom-up, starting with one point and expanding) and divisive (top-down, dividing the original sample into smaller groups).

3.2 Centroid-Based Models

The centroid-based (with k-means as a representative) model clusters have a more recognizable ellipsoid form. This is explained by the main methodological difference, which is the division of the data into clusters according to the nearest mean or central vector, which does not have to be a part of a sample. In case of the k-means algorithm, the number of clusters k has to be manually specified. However, various optimization techniques for finding the best number and further process automation, such as based on the minimal sum of squared distances, might be applied. The original tendency of the model is to output clusters of the same size, which might produce a biased analysis, if not taking this into consideration. Another weakness of this type of cluster modeling is that it does not handle cases when the clusters cannot be plane-separated. It does work well, however, for those with a hyperspherical shape.

---

[2]Unweighted pair group method with arithmetic mean or UPGMA.

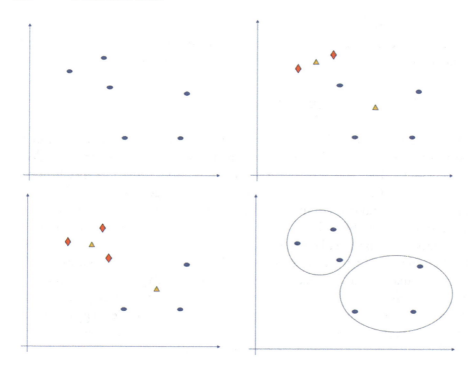

Fig. 7 Steps in centroid-based models

Nevertheless, this *k*-means clustering algorithm is commonly used and, contrary to the hierarchical one, can manage big data. The procedure consists of five steps, which are illustrated in Fig. 7. First, the number *k* is chosen. In the second step, sample points are randomly assigned to different *k* clusters. Next, the centroids of those randomly-composed clusters are calculated. Further, provided the newly calculated central points, the sample points are reassigned depending on their distance to the centroid, such that each point now belongs to the cluster in which the distance between its center and the point is minimized. In the fifth and final step, the centroids are recalculated and the process stops when no better assignment can be made. Otherwise, the last two steps are repeated. To control this algorithm for precision, there is a handful of cluster validity indices, based on which the thresholds for further optimization can be set.

3.3 Distribution-Based Model

The more statistical approach is used in the distribution-based model. The distribution of data points is taken for the principal property, upon which the clusters are formed. In such model dependence, structure and correlation are considered. However, in frames of real data, it might be difficult to tailor the data clusters to a clearly defined distribution, e.g., Gaussian might have assumptions that are too strong.

3.4 Density-Based Models

Shapes of the density-based model can sometimes echo those of the single-linkage connectivity model. This is due to the fact that single-linkage and the density have at least one common property: the smaller the distances between notches, the higher the density and vice versa, given an equal number of points. Depending on the need to set the ε, the value of range parameter, different methods can be used: OPTICS,[3] which reduces the problem to a hierarchical solution approach applied to linkage clustering, DBSCAN,[4] which is a special case of the former having to define the density criterion, or DeLi-Clu,[5] applying R-tree[6] to make the ε completely obsolete.

Since each of the classic aforementioned models has either the outlier/border points problems or becomes biased or inefficient on the large multidimensional data sets, more recent models attempt to address those flaws. Among those are subspace and correlation clustering.

3.5 Time Series Specific Clustering

Despite the common belief that clustering can only be performed on static data, cluster analysis is also used for time series. Moreover, clustering strategies for time series are, in principal, the same as the initial ones for time-independent data, but with specific distance measure used to assess dissimilarity or calculate prototypes. In this section, we introduce some time series specific distance metrics.

---

[3]Ordering points to identify the clustering structure (see Ankerst, Breunig, Kriegel, & Sander, 1999).

[4]Density-based spacial clustering of applications with noise (see Ester, Kriegel, Sander, & Xu, 1996).

[5]Density-link clustering (see Achtert, Böhm, & Kröger, 2006).

[6]Access method for multi-dimensional data, made to structure indexed records (see Guttman, 1984).

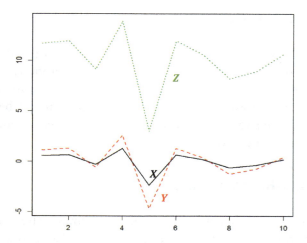

Fig. 8 Normalization

3.5.1 Normalization of Time Series

There are two important features of times series: mean and standard variation. The first one measures the averaged value the time series takes and the second one indicates how strong the time series varies around its mean. The mathematical definitions of both features are as follows:

Given a positive integer T, suppose that $(X_t)_{t=1,2,...T}$ is a R-valued time series. The mean and standard variation of X are defined as

$$m(X) = \frac{1}{T}\sum_{t=1}^{T} X_t$$

Equation 11: Mean.
and

$$sd(X) = \sqrt{\frac{1}{T-1}\sum_{t=1}^{T}(X_t - m(X))^2}$$

Equation 12: Standard deviation.
respectively.

Three time series are illustrated in Figs. 8 and 9. Computing this is not difficult:

$$m(X) = 0, \quad m(Y) = 0, \quad m(Z) = 10$$
$$sd(X) = 1, \quad sd(Y) = 2, \quad sd(Z) = 3$$

16 Mathematical Background of Machine Learning 285

X: 0.5632992 0.6459451 −0.2883303 1.3117987 −2.3338339 0.6553178 0.1923299 −0.6090922 −0.3584139 0.2209797

Y: 1.1265984 1.2918903 −0.5766607 2.6235973 −4.6676678 1.3106355 0.3846599 −1.2181844 −0.7168279 0.4419594

Z: 11.689898 11.937835 9.135009 13.935396 2.998498 11.965953 10.576990 8.172723 8.924758 10.662939

Fig. 9 Example of three time series X, Y and Z

Z-normalization is a common fundamental preprocessing technique used to work with and analyze time series. Given a time series $(X_t)_{t=1,2,...T}$, the z-normalized time series $(\bar{X}_t)_{t=1,2,...T}$ is defined by

$$\bar{X}_t = \frac{X_t - m(X)}{sd(X)}, \text{ for } t = 1, 2 \ldots .T$$

Equation 13: Z-normalization.
where $m(X)$, $sd(X)$ are mean and standard variation of X, respectively.

The mean is subtracted from the original time series and the standard variation of the Z-normalized time series is equal to one. This type of normalization technique is usually referred to as "normalization to zero mean and unit of energy". The normalized time series are illustrated in Fig. 8. In contrast to the original ones, the normalized ones look more similar to each other. Further removing the influence of mean and standard variation, the time series becomes more comparable and thus more efficient cluster analysis can be provided.

3.5.2 Times Series Specified Distance Metric

There are different metrics for measuring the similarity between two time series. In the following, we will briefly introduce the three mostly commonly used distance measures.

3.5.3 Dynamic Time Wrapping Distance[7]

Dynamic time wrapping distance (DTW) is a common measure, which is calculated using a technique that compares two time series using optimal alignment. One example is provided in Fig. 10.

---

[7]DTW (algorithm) see Sakoe and Chiba (1978), Berndt and Clifford (1994).

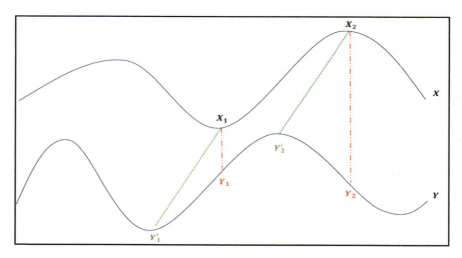

Fig. 10 Dynamic time wrapping

Both times series look similar. The Euclidean metric will deliver a large "distance" between them, as X_1 and X_2 are aligned to the points Y_1 and Y_2, respectively. DTW provides the possibility to optimally align both time series. In our example, X_1 and X_2 will be aligned to Y'_1 and Y'_2, respectively. Therefore, the DTW distance represents the similarity between the time series more precisely. In comparison to the Euclidean distance, DTW is developed based on a selected alignment path. Given $X = (X_1, X_2, \ldots X_n)$ and $Y = (Y_1, Y_2, \ldots Y_m)$ of length n and m with $n, m \in N^+$. We call π an alignment between X and Y, if it is a sequence of pairs $(\pi_1(1), \pi_2(1)), (\pi_1(2), \pi_2(2)) \ldots \ldots (\pi_1(p), \pi_2(p))$ with $1 \leq p \leq m + n - 1$ where

- $(\pi_1(1), \pi_2(1)) = (1, 1), (\pi_1(p), \pi_2(p)) = (n, m)$ and
- $\begin{pmatrix} \pi_1(i) - \pi_1(i-1) \\ \pi_2(i), -\pi_2(i-2) \end{pmatrix} \in \{ \begin{bmatrix} 0 \\ 1 \end{bmatrix}, \begin{bmatrix} 1 \\ 0 \end{bmatrix}, \begin{bmatrix} 1 \\ 1 \end{bmatrix} \}$ for any $i = 2, 3 \ldots \ldots p$.

As illustrated in Fig. 11(1), the alignment is a monotonic increasing (not necessary to be strictly monotonic) path starting from (1,1) and ending at (n, m).

In case $m = n$, the diagonal line is the alignment path (Fig. 11(2)) applied in Euclidean distance.

The DTW aims to define the optimal alignment path, such that the distance between two time series is minimized. The mathematical definition of DTW is defined as

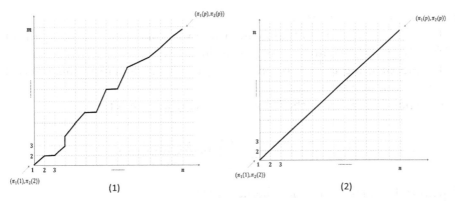

Fig. 11 Alignment path

$$DTW(X,Y) = \min_{\pi} D_{X,Y}(\pi)$$

Equation 14: Dynamic time wrapping.

where $D_{X,Y}(\pi) = \sum_{i=1}^{|\pi|} |X_{\pi_1(i)} - Y_{\pi_2(i)}|$ and $|\pi|$ is the length of π. The squared Euclidean metric can be also used in $D_{X,Y}$ and we get,

$$D_{X,Y}(\pi) = \sqrt{\sum_{i=1}^{|\pi|} |X_{\pi_1(i)} - Y_{\pi_2(i)}|^2}.$$

Equation 15: Dynamic time wrapping distance.

3.5.4 Global Alignment Kernel Distance[8]

In contrast to DTW, which aims at searching for optimal minimal alignment, the global alignment kernel (GAK) is defined as the exponential soft-minimum of all possible alignment distances.

Given the same times series X, Y as above, and $D_{X,Y}(\pi)$ is the Euclidean distance between wrapped time series according to alignment π, the GAK distance is defined as:

$$GAK(X,Y) = \sum_{\pi} e^{-D_{X,Y}(\pi)} = \sum_{\pi} \prod_{i=1}^{|\pi|} e^{-|X_{\pi_1(i)} - Y_{\pi_2(i)}|}.$$

---

[8] See Cuturi (2011).

Equation 16: Global alignment kernel.

It provides richer information for the given time series in comparison with only getting the minimal alignment in DTW.

Instead of using $e^{-|x-y|}$ by measuring the local similarity, some kernel functions can be also applied.

One possible variant is the Gaussian kernel where we get,

$$GAK(X, Y) = \sum_{\pi} \prod_{i=1}^{|\pi|} \kappa_\sigma(X_{\pi_1(i)}, Y_{\pi_2(i)})$$

Equation 17: Global alignment kernel distance.

where $\kappa_\sigma(x, y) = e^{-\frac{1}{2\sigma^2}|x-y|^2 - \log(1 - e^{\frac{|x-y|^2}{2\sigma^2}})}$ with parameter $\sigma > 0$.

Another alternative variant is to combine the Gaussian kernel with a triangular kernel, which provides the possibility to measure the similarity of point positions:

$$TGAK(X, Y) = \sum_{\pi} \prod_{i=1}^{|\pi|} \kappa_{\sigma,T}(X_{\pi_1(i)}, Y_{\pi_2(i)})$$

Equation 18: Gaussian kernel.

where $\kappa_{\sigma,T}(X_l, Y_k) = \frac{\omega(l,k)\kappa_\sigma(X_l,Y_k)}{2 - \omega(l,k)\kappa_\sigma(X_l,Y_k)}$ and $\omega(l, k) = \left(1 - \frac{l-k}{T}\right)^+$ with parameter $\sigma > 0, T \in N^+$.

3.5.5 Shaped-Based Distance[9]

This algorithm is known as a faster alternative to DTW since a distance metric for every pair of time series has to be computed in DTW and this requires a lot of memory. This algorithm is based on cross-correlation with coefficient normalization (NCC) and given as,

$$SBD(X, Y) = 1 - \frac{\max(NCC(X, Y))}{||X||_2||Y||_2}$$

Equation 19: Shaped-based distance.

where $||\cdot||_2$ is the L^2- norm of time series and NCC is the cross-correlation sequence, which is defined as follows:

---

[9]See Paparrizos and Gravano (2015).

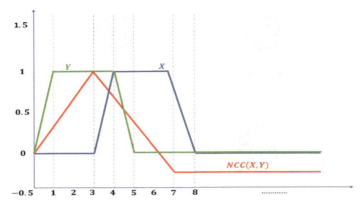

Fig. 12 Example of cross-correlation

Given two time series $X = (X_1, X_2, \ldots X_n)$ and $Y = (Y_1, Y_2, \ldots Y_n)$ of length n with $n \in N^+$, the cross-correlation NCC at delay $d \in N^+$ is given as

$$NCC(d) = \frac{\sum_{i=d+1}^{n} (X_i - m(X))(Y_{i-d} - m(Y))}{\sqrt{\sum_{i=1}^{n} (X_i - m(X))^2} \cdot \sqrt{\sum_{i=1}^{n} (Y_i - m(Y))^2}}$$

Equation 20: Normalized cross-correlation.

It measures the degree of two time series correlation, given one is shifted at d. In comparison to DTW, this can be also understood as an alignment with a shift at d. The larger the correlation, the higher the similarity between time series. A correlation being equal to one indicates that the given two time series are positively linearly correlated. One example is given in Fig. 12 where the maximum correlation is found at a delay of 3.

3.6 Bayesian Network

Bayesian networks are a kind of directed and acyclic probabilistic graphical models, which are famous for modeling and specifying the (multivariate) joint distribution over a number of random variables, which have complicated relationships/dependencies among them. In Bayesian networks, each node stands for a random variable, while each directed edge (arrow) connecting two nodes indicates the conditional dependency between two random variables. The nodes not connected with each other are always

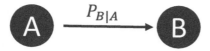

Fig. 13 Example Bayesian network

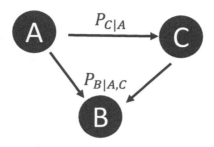

Fig. 14 Example Bayesian network

conditionally independent. We will explain the definition of conditional independence later in this subsection. Let's start with a simple example of a Bayesian network given in Fig. 13.

There are two random variable A and B, which are associated with initial probability distribution P_A and P_B, respectively. Both probability distributions could be discrete or continuous. The arrow between A and B indicates that the knowledge of whether A occurs provides information on occurrence of B. The conditional distribution of B given A is given as $P_{B|A}$, which is assigned to the arrow in addition. Given P_A, P_B and $P_{B|A}$, the joint distribution of A and B is easily computed by

$$P_{A,B} = P_{B|A} \cdot P_A,$$

Equation 21: Conditional probability.
that is, for any values a, b from domains of random variable A and B, we get

$$P(A = a, B = b) = P(B = b|A = a) \cdot P(A = a).$$

Equation 22: Conditional probability.

In this example, A is called the parent of B and B is the child of A.

A three-node Bayesian network is shown in Fig. 14, where B has two parents and the knowledge of A also has an influence on C. $P_{B|A,C}$ is the probability distribution of B given its parents A and C.

In this case, the joint distribution of A, B and C is computed as,

$$P_{A,B,C} = P_{B|A,C} \cdot P_{C|A} \cdot P_A$$

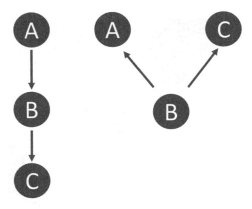

Fig. 15 Examples of conditional independence

Equation 23: Joint probability distribution.

Another important concept in the Bayesian network is conditional independence. In probability theory, two random variables X and Y are conditionally independent given a third random variable Z if the occurrence of X and Y has no influence on each other when Z is given. In both Bayesian networks illustrated in Fig. 15, the random variables A and C are conditionally independent given B.

As mentioned above, unconnected nodes are always conditionally independent in Bayesian networks.

We end this subsection by presenting a practical example of a Bayesian network, in which it is used to analyze the problem of creditworthiness.

Reading from the structure in Fig. 16, we have

- given the event "Reliability", the "Payment History" and "Work History" are conditionally independent.
- all three parents "Ratio of Debits to Income", "Reliability" and "Age" have an influence on "Creditworthiness".

3.6.1 Training the Bayesian Network

Training the Bayesian network consists of structure learning and parameter learning. The first one learns the structure of the network, set edges and direction of edges between nodes. The second one fits the initial probability distribution of each nodes and the conditional probability distribution between nodes.

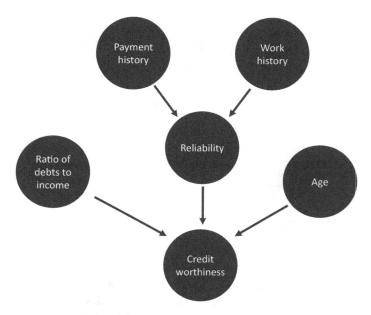

Fig. 16 Example Bayesian network—creditworthiness

- Structure learning: Several approaches were developed in the last ten years. Most of them benefit from the Markov blanket discovery algorithms.[10] The Markov blanket of a random variable X is the minimal set of random variables conditioned on which all other random variables are independent of X. In other words, it is enough to determine X by indicating the knowledge of the members in Markov blanket. An example is illustrated in Fig. 17, where the Markov blanket of node "X-ray" are the nodes "Lung Cancer" and "Smoking". Two famous algorithms for discovering the Markov blanket are known as grow-shrink (GS) algorithms and incremental association Markov blanket (IAMB) algorithms. Both of them consist of one forward phase and one backward phase. In the forward phase, all the Markov blanket candidates are searched and collected according to their strength of association with the target random variable. The backward phase moves some false positive candidates away by applying some conditional tests of independence. Markov blanket contributes strongly to discovery of the local structure around each node during the construction of the Bayesian network.

---

[10]Tsamardinos, Aliferis, and Statnikov (2003), Yaramakala and Margaritis (2005).

16 Mathematical Background of Machine Learning

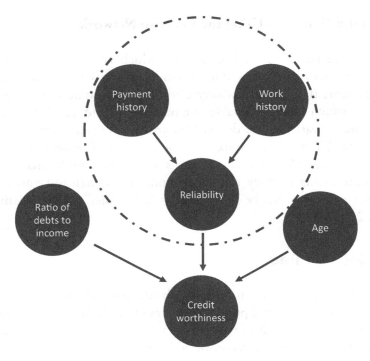

Fig. 17 Markov blanket

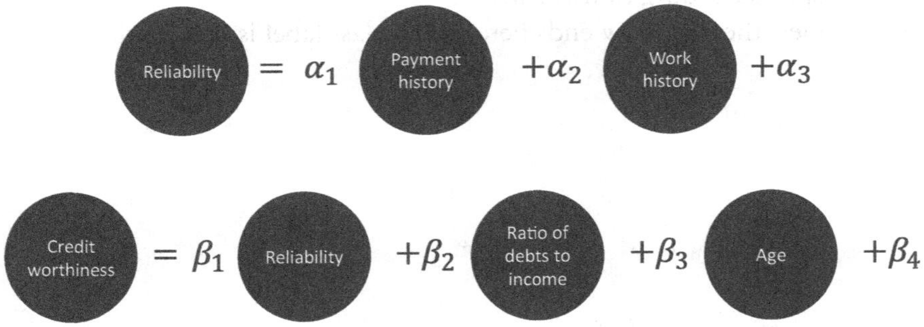

Fig. 18 Bayesian network parameter learning

- Parameter learning: The key concept in parameter learning consists of rewriting the Bayesian network into a hierarchical linear regression (as shown in Fig. 18). The regression parameters are then estimated using the maximum likelihood or Bayesian parameter method.

3.6.2 Fraud Detection Using the Bayesian Network

Anomalies can be understood as outliers, which are significantly different from the others, or the events which are unlikely to occur. The Bayesian network represents the joint probability distribution of random variables using a graph, in which random variables are nodes and conditional dependencies among random variables are directed by arrows. We can compute the conditional probability of occurrence of an observation of nodes based on joint probability distribution. The observations with lower conditional probability are some events unlikely to happen under the currently favored theory of domain and these can be recognized as "anomalies" (see also Babbar & Chawla, 2006).

3.7 Decision Tree

Decision tree is a predictive model, which uses a set of binary or multiway rules to solve a classification problem. One example is illustrated in Fig. 19.

This decision tree predicts whether a customer will buy a given kind of computer. It consists of two classes of nodes as follows:

- Decision nodes: a splitting rule is denoted on one feature and the data flow is split according to this rule.
- Leaf nodes: the data flow ends here, and a class label is delivered.

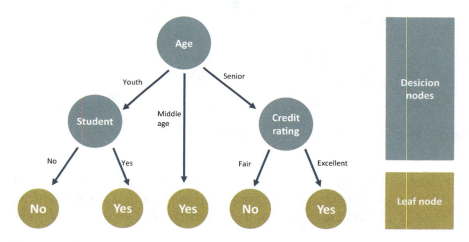

Fig. 19 Decision tree

The nodes form a tree structure. Data flows from top to bottom along the nodes where the decision rules are followed. At the end, the class label is produced.

Decision tree training is a recursive process, which constructs nodes from top to bottom. The node is determined by choosing the best splitting rules, such that the split data subsets have the most similar classification labels (also called homogeneous). Normally, the information homogeneous is measured based on entropy. All possible candidates of splitting rules are analyzed for each node and the one with the highest level of information homogeneous is chosen to construct the node.

3.7.1 Random Forest

Decision trees sometimes cause problems. On one hand, a small tree is not able to precisely represent/extract the data structure. On the other hand, it has higher possibility of suffering from overfitting if the tree is too deep. Ensemble modeling is a common statistical technique, which aims at processing more than two models and synthesizing the results into a single score, while a single model might have high variability or outright inaccuracies. One example of ensemble modeling is called random forest. This includes simultaneously training a number of decision trees based on a randomly sampled subset of data. The subset of data could be sampled with or without replacement, which are also called bagging and pasting. Prediction of the random forests is formed by voting among all decision trees to determine, for example, an average of predicted results of all decision trees. A random forest has the following three main parameters:

- N: number of decision trees in forest.
- n: number of randomly selected data samples used for training the decision tree.
- m: number of features, based on which the nodes of the decision tree are constructed.

As illustrated in Fig. 20, the random forest algorithm is proceeded as follows:

- n data samples are sampled from training data randomly using the "sample with replacement" method.
- m features are sampled randomly from the set of features.

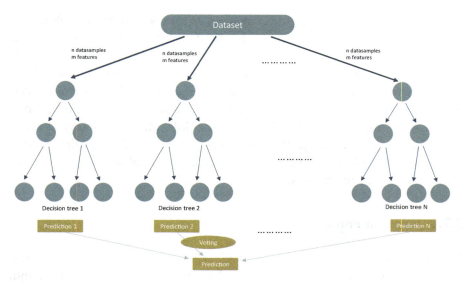

Fig. 20 Random forest

- A decision tree is constructed/trained on the sampled n data samples where the nodes (splitting rules) are only constructed based on the selected m features.
- The three steps above are repeated N times, such that N decision trees are trained.
- The predicted result of random forest is voted on by all decision trees.

Random forest performs better than decision tree, as it combines the predicted results of several decision trees. In addition, each tree in a forest is smaller since it is trained on a subset of the data set. This leads to lower possibility to overfitting.

4   Model Validation

Model validation is an important subtask in model development. The standard pattern applied in model development consists of fitting the model to a given data set. The drawback here is that model fitting might be too specific to the used data and cannot be used for new or other data. One of the issues that comes with a pure fitting on one data set is the problem of overfitting. An example of overfitting is discussed in "COMMON MISTEAKS MISTAKES IN USING STATISTICS—Overfitting" (Smith, 2019).

An approach to addressing this problem consists of partitioning the given data into a training data set and a testing data set. If selection of models or a variation on meta-parameters is not part of the model development process, then validation is performed only on two data sets.

The following two data sets are necessary to create a model:

- Training set: used for fitting the model,
- Testing set: used for providing the unbiased evaluation of the fitted model.

It is always possible to change splitting of the data set into the training set and testing set. One common approach to achieving this is known as cross-validation. The model is trained and validated iteratively on different data sets where $\alpha\%$ of the data set are sampled randomly as the training set and the rest $(1-\alpha)$ % as the testing set with a fixed parameter α.

In general, cross-validation methods are differentiated into exhaustive and non-exhaustive cross-validation. Exhaustive cross-validation methods aim to cover all possible combinations in splitting the original data into training and testing data sets. The approach is comprehensive but costly due to the huge amount of combinations. The number of combinations is calculated using the binominal coefficient $\binom{N}{p}$ with N being the size of the whole data set and p being the size of the testing data set.

Non-exhaustive cross-validation benefits from random data set splitting, such that the performance estimate is less sensitive to partitioning of the data. K-fold cross-validation is the most popular example of cross-validation.

4.1   Model Validation: K-Fold Cross-Validation

K-folds cross-validation is a common statistic evaluation method used to measure the stability and effectiveness of a model and show how good the model can be fit to the training data and how accurately it can be used in prediction.

Given a positive integer $K \in N^+$, we split the data set into K groups. For each group of data, we proceed through the following steps:

1. Taking this group of data as the *testing set* and the rest of the data as the *training set*.
2. Fitting the model on the training set.
3. Testing the model on the testing set and computing the evaluation score. As an example, precision could be used, which is a percent number and indicates how much testing data is correctly predicted using the trained model.

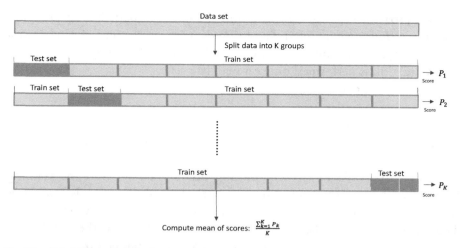

Fig. 21 K-fold cross-validation procedure

The mean of all evaluation scores is always delivered as the result of K-fold cross-validation. In k-fold cross-validation, each observation is used for training K-1 times and for testing 1 time (Fig. 21).

If the model development process includes a model selection or a variation in meta-parameters, then a three-fold approach can help solve the problem.

The given data set is divided into three data sets. The first data set is called the training data set and is used to fit the model. The validation data set is the second data set and provides an evaluation of a model fit for fine-tuning the model meta-parameters (e.g., the number of layers or neurons). The performance of the different models is compared and serves as the main criteria for model selection. The third testing data set is then used to validate how good the final selected/completely trained model is. The train-validation-test split ratio is specific to use cases.

The cross-validation concepts described above can be applied including the validation data set and testing data set in analogy.

4.2 Cluster Evaluation

There are numerous methods to choose from to perform cluster analysis and the same now applies to cluster evaluation. As with the choice of algorithm, one needs to understand the specifics of the data, to which it is applied, and the objectives to be able to use the parameters of evaluation correctly to determine which cluster analysis is more appropriate for the case. There is usually not a single or universal measure, but rather a bundle of them.

The general requirements of evaluation include determining the performance of the applied algorithm and deciding on the number size, shape, etc. of clusters or sometimes even sub-clusters. Cluster validity indices (CVI) can be used to assess the issue.

There are the two types of CVIs: internal and external. External CVIs can be used only when the true number of clusters is known (hence the name) since it then compares the result of a procedure partition to it. Internal CVIs are to be applied to all other cases. The other distinction is their method applicability, which can either be a crisp (hard) or a fuzzy (soft) clustering.[11] However, the former might be converted into the latter if needed.

Of over half a hundred different indices, we describe some of those we had an option to choose from[12] when evaluating the clusters created throughout this chapter.

The following external CVIs were selected in our cluster evaluation process:

Crisp partitions:
- Rand index (to be maximized).
- Adjusted rand index (to be maximized).
- Jaccard index (to be maximized).
- Folkes–Mallows (to be maximized).
- Variation of information (to be minimized).

Fuzzy partitions:
- Soft rand index (to be maximized).
- Soft adjusted rand index (to be maximized).
- Soft variation of information (to be minimized).
- Soft normalized mutual information based on max entropy (to be maximized).

Since the external cluster validity indices gauge the propriety of data distribution into the simulated clusters in accordance with the distribution in the true ones, one needs to deal with a confusion matrix, which is based on the

---

[11]Hard or crisp clustering involves strict and excluding placement of a data point in relation to a particular cluster, meaning that an observation cannot belong to two or more clusters at the same time. This would be possible under using fuzzy or soft partitioning and one point would belong to clusters to differing extents.

[12]The list of CVIs is taken from Sarda-Espinosa (2019).

affiliation of data with the two partitions, the simulated P_1 and the true P_2 partition, with such possible entries:

1. yy: the two points belong to the same cluster, according to both P_1 and P_2
2. yn: the two points belong to the same cluster according to P_1 but not to P_2
3. ny: the two points belong to the same cluster according to P_2 but not to P_1
4. nn: the two points do not belong to the same cluster, according to both P_1 and P_2

We also need to define several other values.

N_T the total number of pairs of data points such as:

$$N_T = \frac{N(N-1)}{2} = yy + yn + ny + nn$$

Equation 24: Total number of pairs.

P The precision coefficient, the proportion of points rightly grouped together in P_2:

$$P = \frac{yy}{yy + ny}$$

Equation 25: Precision coefficient.

R The recall coefficient, the proportion of points grouped together in P_1 which are also grouped together in partition P_2:

$$R = \frac{yy}{yy + yn}$$

Equation 26: Recall coefficient.

F The harmonic mean of the precision and recall coefficients:

$$F = \frac{2}{\frac{1}{P} + \frac{1}{R}} = \frac{2P \times R}{P + R} = \frac{2yy}{2yy + ny + ny}$$

Equation 27: Harmonic mean of the precision and recall coefficients.

Having introduced the principal theory, we will describe in further detail several of the indices mentioned above:

The Rand index is defined as following: $C = \frac{yy + nn}{N_T}$,[13] the value of which should approach 1, in which case the proportion of cases assigned to different partitions is minimized, meaning the two have minimal contradiction.

---

[13] C stands for criterion.

The adjusted Rand index is the modification of the original definition through enabling of negative values in case it is marked other than expected and yields a smaller value.

The Folkes–Mallows index has the following notation: $C = \frac{yy}{\sqrt{(yy+ny)\times(yy+yn)}} = \sqrt{PR}$, which is again maximized when the contradictions, yn and ny, are minimized.

The Jaccard Index can be calculated as follows: $= \frac{yy}{yy+yn+ny}$, with the same idea as in the two previous equations.

For the internal indices, one would need to study more comprehensive theory to be able to mathematically describe them.[14] However, intuition can be presented for some nevertheless:

The Silhouette index describes the quality of alignment of an object to its own cluster. It ranges from -1 to 1, where 1 means that the object fits the cluster best, while having the worst match with the neighboring clusters.

The Dunn index can be written in the following form: $C = \frac{d_{\min}}{d_{\max}}$, where $d_{\min}$ is the smallest possible distance between the two points from different clusters, while $d_{\max}$ is the largest possible distance between the two points within a cluster. Using this index, one can see the spread of a cluster proportional to its size.

The Davies–Bouldin index is calculated using the following formula:

$$C = \frac{1}{k} \sum_{k=1}^{K} M_k = \frac{1}{K} \sum_{k=1}^{K} \max_{k' \neq k} \left(\frac{\left(\delta_k + \delta'_k\right)}{\Delta'_{kk}} \right)$$

Equation 28: Davies–Bouldin index.

where δ_k is a centroid of cluster k and Δ'_{kk} is a distance between the two barycenters of the k and k' clusters. This is a variation of an above index, having the same meaning.

The Calinski-Harabasz index can be written as:

$$C = \frac{\frac{BGSS}{K-1}}{\frac{WGSS}{N-K}} = \frac{(N-K)BGSS}{(K-1)WGSS}$$

---

[14]In case of interest, one can refer to Desgraupes (2019).

Equation 29: Calinski-Harabasz index.

where *BGSS* and *WGSS* are the between-group dispersion and the pooled within-cluster sum of squares, respectively. K is the number of clusters and N is the sample size. Again, the larger the ration, the better defined and separated clusters are obtained.

5 Summary

The field of ML is extremely broad and has the potential to continue improving quite dynamically in the coming years. The chapter provides a general definition of ML (see Sect. 1.1) and a restricted overview of some of the most important models. Although we touched on time series analysis in Sect. 3.5, we left out classic time series analysis using ARIMA models [as further reading, we recommend Brockwell and Davis (2002) or Montgomery, Jennings, and Kulahci (2008)]. A compact introduction was provided to the two popular classification models Bayesian networks and random forest. The interesting DL model class has also been excluded from this chapter, as this model class is addressed in a separate chapter in this book (see Liermann et al., Deep learning—An introduction, 2019b).

Besides the general importance of the mentioned models, selection was driven by the use cases discussed in the book. Linear regression (including Glm) have applications in scenario analysis and integrated planning (see Liermann & Viets, Integrated scenario analysis and integrated planning, 2019; Valjanow, Enzinger, and Dinges, 2019). The time series specific clustering was used to forecast intraday liquidity (see Liermann, Li, & Dobryashkina, Intraday liquidity—Forecast using pattern recognition, 2019). Bayesian networks and random forests are used within the context of pattern recognition in batch processes (see Liermann, Li, & Schaudinnus, Batch processing—Pattern recognition, 2019a).

Given the digital transformation taking place in all industries, but especially in the financial industry, these models and methods[15] will become common knowledge and tools which are naturally used on the journey toward a complete digital vision.

---

[15]The importance of the deep learning models described in Liermann et al., Deep learning—An introduction (2019b) could possible increase more dynamically.

Literature

Achtert, E., Böhm, C., & Kröger, P. (2006). DeLi-Clu: Boosting robustness, completeness, usability, and efficiency of hierarchical clustering by a closest pair ranking. In W.-K. Ng, M. Kitsuregawa, & J. L. Chang (Eds.), *Advances in knowledge discovery and data mining* (pp. 119–128). Singapore: Springer.

Ankerst, M., Breunig, M. M., Kriegel, H.-P., & Sander, J. (1999). *OPTICS: Ordering points to identify the clustering structure.* Munich: Institute for Computer Science, University of Munich.

Babbar, S., & Chawla, S. (2006). *On Bayesian network and outlier detection.* Sydney: School of Information Technologies, University of Sydney.

Berndt, D., & Clifford, J. (1994). Using dynamic time warping to find patterns in time series. In *Proceedings of the 3rd International Conference on Knowledge Discovery and Data Mining* (pp. 359–370). Palo Alto, CA: AAAI Press.

Brockwell, P. J., & Davis, R. A. (2002). *Introduction to time series and forecasting.* New York: Springer.

Chakraborty, C., & Joseph, A. (2017). *Staff working paper no. 674—Machine learning at central banks.* London: Bank of England.

Cuturi, M. (2011). Fast global alignment kernels. In L. Getoor & T. Scheffer (Eds.), *Proceedings of the 28th International Conference on International Conference on Machine Learning* (pp. 929–936). Bellevue, Washington, USA: Omnipress.

Desgraupes, B. (2019, January). *Clustering indices.* Retrieved from The Comprehensive R Archive Network https://cran.r-project.org/web/packages/clusterCrit/vignettes/clusterCrit.pdf.

Ester, M., Kriegel, H.-P., Sander, J., & Xu, X. (1996). A density-based algorithm for discovering clusters in large spatial databases with noise. In E. Simoudis, J. Han, & U. M. Fayyad (Eds.), *Proceedings of the Second International Conference on Knowledge Discovery and Data Mining* (pp. 226–231). Menlo Park, CA: The AAAI Press.

Google. (2019). *Home.* Retrieved from AlphaGo https://deepmind.com/research/alphago/.

Guttman, A. (1984). *R-trees: A dynamic index structure for spatial searching.* Berkeley: University of California.

Liermann, V., Li, S., & Dobryashkina, V. (2019). Intraday liquidity—Forecast using pattern recognition. In V. Liermann & C. Stegmann (Eds.), *The impact of digital transformation and fintech on the finance professional.* New York: Palgrave Macmillan.

Liermann, V., Li, S., & Schaudinnus, N. (2019a). Batch processing—Pattern recognition. In V. Liermann & C. Stegmann (Eds.), *The impact of digital transformation and fintech on the finance professional.* New York: Palgrave Macmillan.

Liermann, V., Li, S., & Schaudinnus, N. (2019b). Deep learning—An introduction. In V. Liermann & C. Stegmann (Eds.), *The impact of digital transformation and fintech on the finance professional.* New York: Palgrave Macmillan.

Liermann, V., & Viets, N. (2019). Integrated scenario analysis and integrated planning. In V. Liermann & C. Stegmann (Eds.), *The impact of digital transformation and fintech on the finance professional*. New York: Palgrave Macmillan.

McCarthy, J., Minsky, M., Rochester, N., & Shannon, C. (1955). *A proposal for the Dartmouth summer research project on artificial intelligence*. Retrieved from http://www-formal.stanford.edu/jmc/history/dartmouth/dartmouth.html.

Montgomery, D. C., Jennings, C. L., & Kulahci, M. (2008). *Introduction to time series analysis and forecasting*. Hoboken, NJ: Wiley.

Paparrizos, J., & Gravano, L. (2015). k-Shape: Efficient and accurate clustering of time series. In T. Sellis, S. B. Davidson, & Z. Ives (Eds.), *Proceedings of the 2015 ACM SIGMOD International Conference on Management of Data* (pp. 69–76). New York: ACM.

Russell, S. J., & Norvig, P. (2003). *Artificial intelligence: A modern approach*. Upper Saddle River, NJ: Prentice Hall.

Sakoe, H., & Chiba, S. (1978, February). Dynamic programming algorithm optimization for spoken word recognition. *IEEE Transactions on Acoustics, Speech, and Signal Processing, 26*, 43–49.

Sarda-Espinosa, A. (2019, January 29). *Package 'dtwclust'*. Retrieved from The Comprehensive R Archive Network https://cran.r-project.org/web/packages/dtwclust/dtwclust.pdf.

Schaudinnus, N., & Liermann, V. (2019). Real estate risk—Appraisals capture. In V. Liermann & C. Stegmann (Eds.), *The impact of digital transformation and fintech on the finance professional*. New York: Palgrave Macmillan.

Smith, M. K. (2019, February 2). The University of Texas at Austin—Department of Mathematics. Retrieved from COMMON MISTEAKS MISTAKES IN USING STATISTICS—Overfitting https://web.ma.utexas.edu/users/mks/statmistakes/ovefitting.html.

Tsamardinos, I., Aliferis, C. F., & Statnikov, A. (2003, May 12). Algorithms for large scale Markov Blanket discovery. In I. Russell & S. Haller (Eds.), *Proceedings of the Sixteenth International Florida Artificial Intelligence Research Society Conference* (pp. 376–381). Menlo Park, CA: AAAI Press.

Valjanow, S., Enzinger, P., & Dinges, F. (2019). Digital planning—Driver-based planning leveraged by predictive analytics. In V. Liermann & C. Stegmann (Eds.), *The impact of digital transformation and fintech on the finance professional*. New York: Palgrave Macmillan.

Yaramakala, S., & Margaritis, D. (2005). Speculative Markov Blanket discovery for optimal feature selection. In *Proceedings of the Fifth IEEE International Conference on Data Mining (ICDM)* (pp. 809–812). Washington, DC: IEEE Computer Society.

17

Deep Learning: An Introduction

Volker Liermann, Sangmeng Li and Norbert Schaudinnus

1 Introduction

1.1 Overview

In the past few years, deep learning has become both popular and successful for certain applications. Even the most technically knowledgeable personalities like Google's chief of development Sergey Brin have underestimated this development.[1] Figure 1 shows where deep learning is positioned in relation to representation learning, machine learning and artificial intelligence.

---

[1]Sergey Brin admitted, "I didn't see AI coming" at the World Economic Forum in Davos 2018. "I didn't pay attention to it at all, to be perfectly honest. Having been trained as a computer scientist in the 90s, everybody knew that AI didn't work. People tried it, they tried neural nets and none of it worked."

V. Liermann (✉) · S. Li · N. Schaudinnus
ifb AG, Grünwald, Germany
e-mail: volker.liermann@ifb-group.com

S. Li
e-mail: sangmeng.li@ifb-group.com

N. Schaudinnus
e-mail: norbert.schaudinnus@ifb-group.com

© The Author(s) 2019
V. Liermann and C. Stegmann (eds.), *The Impact of Digital Transformation and FinTech on the Finance Professional*, https://doi.org/10.1007/978-3-030-23719-6_17

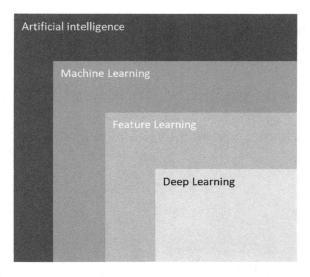

Fig. 1 Deep learning in the artificial intelligence context

As the subdivision of artificial intelligence has already been laid out in Liermann, Li, and Schaudinnus (2019), we provide an overview of different structures of neural network models in the next sections.[2]

1.2 Structure of the Chapter

In Sect. 2 we describe the general setup and structural contents of neural networks. Section 3 provides an overview of the most common neural network patterns. The neural network architecture applied in the use case described in some other chapters of this book are discussed in Sect. 4. Section 5 sums up the different frameworks available and includes a benchmark comparison. Finally, Sect. 6 provides a summary and outlook.

---

[2]Sometimes feature learning is also referenced as representation learning (see Goodfellow, Bengio, & Courville, 2016).

2 General Aspects

2.1 Basic Components and Structures

This section introduces some important basic concepts within the context of deep learning. Neural networks are a class of deep learning models inspired by biological neural networks, which received much attention and have been widely used in the last twenty years. We will begin by describing two simple networks or network components, the perceptron and the feedforward neural network. These basic networks are shown in Fig. 2 with the perceptron on the left and the feedforward network on the right.

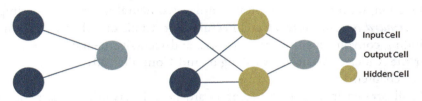

Fig. 2 Perceptron and feedforward network

In the above picture and in the following sections, nodes represent artificial neural network cells. In each cell, the signal is processed by a so-called activation function.

2.1.1 Perceptron

The initial ideas for copying systems in a neural network were discussed in the middle of the last century. The general idea is simple. (Input-)signals x_1 and x_2 are linearly combined with the edge weights w_1 and w_2 $v_1 = w_1 \times x_1 + w_2 \times x_2$. The result is then transformed via an activation function $act()$. Various types of activation functions have a different impact on signal propagation in neural networks. Some activation functions are applied on specific positions of the neural network like the softmax activation which is located at the output layer for classification networks. Figure 3 illustrates the interaction of inputs and outputs. Written using vector notation:

$$y = act(u_j) = act(\vec{w}^T \vec{x}) = act(\sum_{i=1}^{N} w_i x_i)$$

Equation 1: Perceptron network.

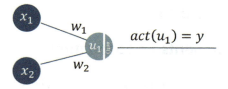

Fig. 3 Perceptron—weights and activation functions

2.1.2 Feedforward Neural Network

The perceptron, which was introduced in the subsection above, is the most basic form of neural network and has only one layer and one neuron. In this section, we introduce a typical multilayered neural network—the simple *feedforward neural network* architecture. For details on other architectures including convolutional neural networks and recursive neural networks, we refer the reader to Goodfellow, Bengio, and Courville (2016) or Sect. 2.1.4 of this chapter.

As illustrated in Fig. 4, the feedforward neural network[3] consists of one input layer, two hidden layers and one output layer. The input layer is where the training data is entered into the network, while the output layer is where the data flow ends and output is produced. The hidden layers in between are concealed from the "outside" and propagate information forward toward the output layer.

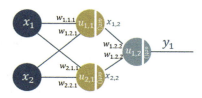

Fig. 4 Simple feedforward neural network (FF or FFNN)

Each layer is made up of several neurons. Neurons from successive layers are connected by weighted inputs, which are the weighted average of the output flow from the previous layer delivered as input flow to the next layer. Each neuron includes an activation function, which represents the activation level of the neuron and maps the input flow into output flow.

---

[3]If FFNNs consists of only few or only one hidden layer they are also called shallow models.

Using the notation form Figs. 3 and 4, the calculation in the feedforward neural network can be notated as follows:

$$x_{i,2} = act(u_{i,1}) = act\left(\overrightarrow{w_{i,1}}^T \overrightarrow{x_1}\right) = act\left(\sum_{j=1}^{N} w_{i,j,1} x_{j,i}\right) \vee i \in \{1,2\}$$

Equation 2: Signal hidden layer.

$\overrightarrow{w_{j,k}} = \begin{pmatrix} w_{1,j,k} \\ w_{2,j,k} \end{pmatrix}$ the vector of the weighted inputs for the j-th (source-)node in the k-th layer.[4]

$\overrightarrow{u_1} = \begin{pmatrix} u_{1,1} \\ u_{2,1} \end{pmatrix}$ the weighting (result) of the (first) hidden layer before activation function.

$\overrightarrow{x_2} = \begin{pmatrix} x_{1,2} \\ x_{2,2} \end{pmatrix}$ the signal (result) of the (first) hidden layer (second layer in the network).

$\overrightarrow{x} = \overrightarrow{x_1} = \begin{pmatrix} x_{1,1} \\ x_{2,1} \end{pmatrix}$ input the signal (first layer in the network).

$$x_{1,3} = act(u_{1,2}) = act\left(\overrightarrow{w_{1,2}}^T \overrightarrow{x_2}\right) = act\left(\sum_{i=1}^{N} w_{i,1,2} x_{i,2}\right) = y_1$$

Equation 3: Signal output layer.

Having described a simple feedforward neural network, we will now look at a more complex example.

By using the similar notation form Figs. 4 and 5, the calculation in the feedforward neural network can be notated as follows.

$$x_{i,2} = act(u_{i,1}) = act\left(\overrightarrow{w_{i,1}}^T \overrightarrow{x_1}\right) = act\left(\sum_{j=1}^{2} w_{i,j,1} x_{j,1}\right), for\, i = \{1,2,3\}$$

$$x_{i,3} = act(u_{i,2}) = act\left(\overrightarrow{w_{j,2}}^T \overrightarrow{x_2}\right) = act\left(\sum_{j=1}^{3} w_{i,j,2} x_{j,2}\right), for\, i = \{1,2\}$$

---

[4]Although a conventional feedforward network has only one layer, deep feedforward networks can have more hidden layers. Figure 5 shows a more complex network.

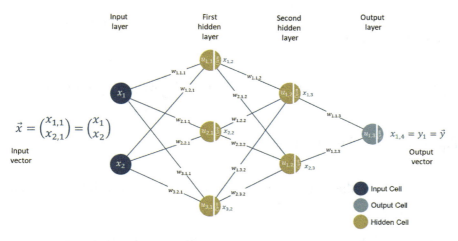

Fig. 5 Feedforward neural network (FF or FFNN)—architecture

$$x_{i,4} = act(u_{i,3}) = act\left(\overrightarrow{w_{i,3}}^T \overrightarrow{x_3}\right) = act\left(\sum_{j=1}^{2} w_{i,j,3} x_{j,3}\right), for\, i = 1$$

Equation 4: Feedforward neural network.

$\overrightarrow{w_{j,k}} = \begin{pmatrix} w_{1,j,k} \\ w_{2,j,k} \\ \vdots \end{pmatrix}$ the vector of the weighted inputs for the j-th (source-) node in the k-th layer.

$\overrightarrow{u_k} = \begin{pmatrix} u_{1,k} \\ u_{2,k} \\ \vdots \end{pmatrix}$ the weightings (result) of the k-th layer before activation function.

$\overrightarrow{x_k} = \begin{pmatrix} x_{1,k} \\ x_{2,k} \\ \vdots \end{pmatrix}$ the signals (result) of the k-th layer (after activation function).

$\vec{x} = \overrightarrow{x_1} = \begin{pmatrix} x_{1,1} \\ x_{2,1} \end{pmatrix}$ input the signal (first layer in the network).

2.1.3 Activation Functions

There are several activation functions, which are proved to have a positive impact on model performance. In this section, we only list the most common ones.

The simplest activation function is a linear function. With this activation function, a neural network is nothing more than a linear regression problem and can be solved using the well-established methods from this area. We will therefore look at some nonlinear activation functions, which provide a network for producing nonlinear classification.

In the classical setup, the activation function is logistic. Radial Basis Function Neural Networks (RBF), on the other hand, have a radial basis function as an activation function. The network structure of an RBF is the same as a classical FF.

As derivation of the activation function is used in network training, we include this information in our list.

$$\text{act}_{\text{sigmoid}}(x) = \frac{1}{1 + e^{-x}}$$

$$\frac{d\text{act}_{\text{sigmoid}}(x)}{dx} = \frac{-e^{-x}}{(1 + e^{-x})} = \text{act}_{\text{sigmoid}}(x)\left(1 - \text{act}_{\text{sigmoid}}(x)\right)$$

Equation 5: Activation function—sigmoid.

The sigmoid is sometimes referred to as a logistic function.

$$\text{act}_{\text{softplus}}(x) = \log(1 + e^{x})$$

$$\frac{d\text{act}_{\textit{softplus}}(x)}{dx} = \frac{e^{x}}{1 + e^{x}} = \frac{1}{1 + e^{-x}} = \text{act}_{\text{sigmoid}}(x)$$

Equation 6: Activation function—softplus.

$$\text{act}_{Relu}(x) = \begin{cases} 0, x < 0 \\ x, x \geq 0 \end{cases}$$

$$\frac{d\text{act}_{Relu}(x)}{dx} = \begin{cases} 0, x < 0 \\ 1, x \geq 0 \end{cases}$$

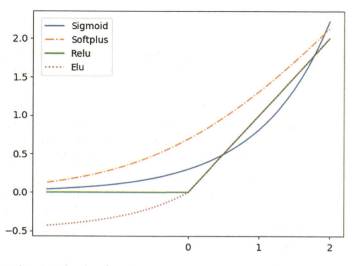

Fig. 6 Overview—activation functions

Equation 7: Activation function—rectified linear unit (ReLU).

$$\text{act}_{Elu}(x) = \begin{cases} x & x > 0 \\ \alpha(e^x - 1) & x \leq 0 \end{cases}$$

$$\frac{d\text{act}_{Elu}(x)}{dx} = \begin{cases} 1 & x > 0 \\ \alpha(e^x) & x \leq 0 \end{cases}$$

Equation 8: Activation function—exponential linear unit (Elu).

Figure 6 shows an overview of the activation functions.

We will first describe a couple of well-known neural networks and continue with a more in-depth description of the networks used within the context of this book.

2.1.4 Training the Feedforward Neural Network

The neural network trains itself by updating all the weights iteratively until the neural network's performance is maximized. Performance is usually measured using a loss function, which calculates the gap between the target output (to be predicted) and the predicted output (output flow of the trained network). The learning process aims at seeking the optimal choice of weights to minimize the loss function. The most popular and standard technique for solving such optimization problems consists of using Gradient Descent Algorithms (GDA). Given a function $f(x_1, x_2, \ldots, x_n)$, the gradient of the function is a vector-valued function and always points in the direction of greatest change in the function.

As illustrated in Fig. 7, the GDA starts with an initial parameter set a_0 and incrementally updates the parameter against the direction of the gradient until the objective function is minimized.

In the case of feedforward neural networks, the parameters are the weights between nodes and the objective function is the loss function. The GDA functions in the following way: given a set of initial weights (estimated values), the predicted output is computed. The error (i.e., loss/gap between the target output and the predicted output) is back propagated from the right layer to the left layer against the direction in which the data flow is delivered (Fig. 8). The weights are adjusted according to the back-propagated error signal. The process described above proceeds iteratively until the loss function reaches a user-defined preference boundary.

The classical gradient decent algorithm is simple to implement, but sometimes does not perform as well as expected. Some variations of the classical gradient algorithm such as Momentum and Adadelta, which have significantly better convergence rates compared to the minimum, are being developed and currently used around the world in most neural network training processes. For further details, we refer the reader to A. Botev, Lever, and Barber (2017) and Zeiler (2012).

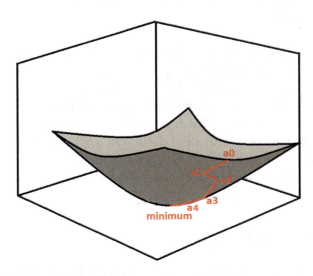

Fig. 7 Gradient descent algorithms

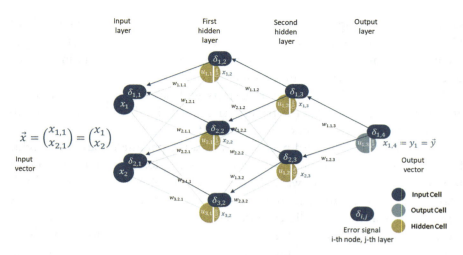

Fig. 8 Back propagation

2.2 Model Validation

Model validation is an important part of model design. There are a couple of well-established model validation methods. An overview is provided in section 4 in Liermann et al. (2019).

3 The Main Model Classes of Neural Networks

In the following sections, we will highlight the differentiating factors of neural networks and briefly discuss the application focus of these networks. The appearance and icons are inspired by the work of von Veen (2019). As you can see in the bibliography, the overview does not include all articles published in the last three years, but it is a solid collection of publications on common neural networks. Not all of them have applications in the financial sector yet. The goal is to demonstrate some of the complexity and variational diversity of the neural networks and how deep learning has been developed thus far.

3.1 Deep Feedforward

The first class of neural network we will look at is deep feedforward (DFF), which is a simple extension of the feedforward neural network. When

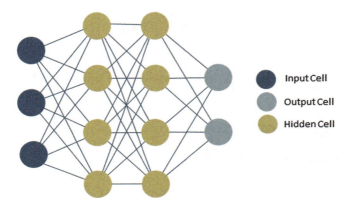

Fig. 9 Deep feedforward network (DFF)

implementing more than one hidden layer, the network is referred to as DFF. Figure 9 shows an example of this class.

The hidden layers of the deep feedforward network do not have connections between the nodes inside a layer. Although the deep feedforward networks were invented in the early 1990s, it took more than a decade to find algorithms to train these more complex (in comparison to FFNN) networks. The applications are like those of FFNN, but the results are better.

3.2 Recurrent Networks

The main difference between the deep feedforward networks and the recurrent neural networks (RNN) is that the latter allows connections between the nodes of the hidden layer and connection with the nodes itself. The other difference to the DFF is that the hidden cells become more complex in RNN. They become recurrent cells. Recurrent cells are network cells that relate to themselves and can thus develop a kind of memory (Fig. 10).

RNN are used when the context of information processed is important. One of the main applications for this is speech recognition, as the same word can have multiple meanings depending on the sentence (or context) it is used in.

At first glance, it is difficult to imagine how such a cell would work. Figure 11 shows how a recurrent cell can be transformed into a simpler or at least more intuitive form.

The left side of the graph shows that the state of a cell in t is influenced by the state of cell in $t-1$. The RNN can handle long-term dependencies, but

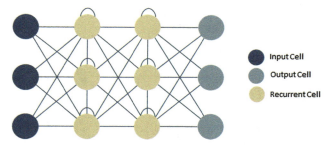

Fig. 10 Recurrent neural network (RNN)

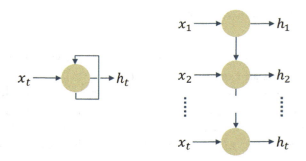

Fig. 11 Translation of a recurrent cell

RNN are not easy to fit (see Bengio, Simard, & Frasconi, 1994; Hochreiter, 1991). The memory cells of a long-/short-term memory (LSTM) network are designed more complexly to solve this problem.

Figure 12 shows the simplest structure of a recurring cell. Figure 13 shows the far more complex structure of a memory cell. Please note that x_t is the signal from the preceding cell (input layer or output of a memory cell in the network), h_{t-1} the result of the previous period of the memory cell h_t the result of the memory cell, C_{t-1} the "state" of the cell in the previous period and C_t the actual state of the cell. Memory cells have an even larger number of different designs.

The structure of an LSTM network as shown in Fig. 14 is like an RNN, but has special cells in the hidden layers. These are the memory cells.

Memory cells consist of a couple of elements and can even be seen as mini networks in themselves.

Gated recurrent units (GRU) have a similar structure but act more dynamically using a different memory cell design (see Cho et al., 2014). There is no longer a state, but a different relation in which the components interact (Fig. 15).

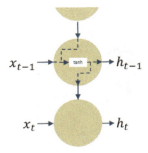

Fig. 12 Simple recurring cell

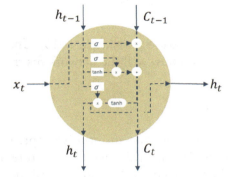

Fig. 13 Memory cell in detail

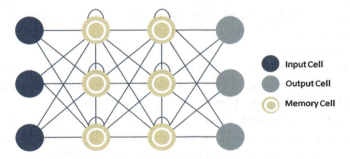

Fig. 14 Structure of long-/short-term memory (LSTM) and gated recurrent unit (GRU)

The difference in applying the various network types is a hot topic in the scientific community. Some think there is not a big difference in terms of performance (see Greff, Srivastava, Koutnik, Steunebrink, & Schmidhuber, 2017). Others see differences in performance depending on the problem at

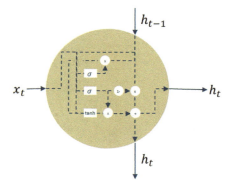

Fig. 15 Gated recurrent unit—memory cell

hand (see Jozefowicz, Zaremba, & Sutskever, 2015). The benefit will always evolve from the use case and how well the network fits the use case.

3.3 Autoencoder

Autoencoder (AE) networks provide an intuitive approach to detect anomalies. The left side of Fig. 16 shows the general structure of an AE. The idea is similar to principal component analysis in classical machine learning. The goal is to find a low-dimensional representation of the dataset. Inside the network structure, the input information is reduced toward a central coding layer. The intention is to reduce the input to the minimal information (in the reduced hidden layer) and then nonetheless be able to generate output almost equal to the input.

Figure 16 shows a simple AE, while Fig. 17 shows the opposite concept of a spare autoencoder (SAE). SAEs have more cells than the input and output layers. These networks can, in certain circumstances, provide better results by finding hidden grouping patterns in the input data.

Variational autoencoders (VAE) attempt to extract probabilities rather than features or, more precisely, feature structures. To achieve this, the VAE replaces the hidden cells with probabilistic cells. Figure 18 shows this type of network. The probabilistic cells can add some noise to the input signal. This is not carried out on the input signal itself, but on the latent variable of the structuring AE.

Another AE network structure is the denoising autoencoder (DA). In this case the noise is added on the input layer level, so the underlying AE is

17 Deep Learning: An Introduction 319

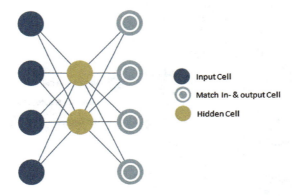

Fig. 16 Autoencoder (AE)

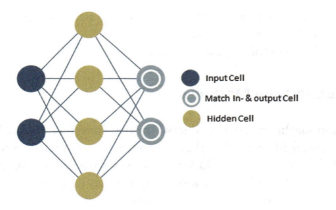

Fig. 17 Spare autoencoder (SAE)

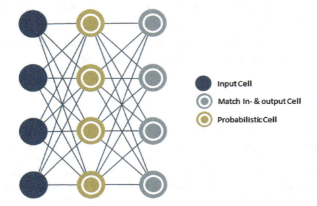

Fig. 18 Variational autoencoder

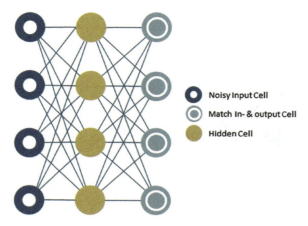

Fig. 19 Denoising autoencoder

forced to reconstruct the matching output on a bit noisy input, which supports selection of more common robust features.

Figure 19 shows this type of network.

3.4 Boltzmann Machines

Boltzmann machines are neural networks that have their source in the structure of a Hopfield network.[5] They are sometimes also referred to as stochastic Hopfield networks with hidden units. As shown in Fig. 20, the input and output is established by the backfed input cells, while the hidden cells are probabilistic cells adding noise on the hidden layer.

Restricted Boltzmann machines (RBM) as illustrated in Fig. 21 are derived from the Boltzmann machines, cutting out the vertexes between all backfed input cells and all probabilistic hidden cells so the complete graph[6] is transformed into a bipartite graph.[7]

RBMs have been used for dimensionality reduction, classification, collaborative filtering, feature learning and topic modeling.

---

[5]For a definition of a Hopfield network, see Hopfield (1982).

[6]In the graph theory field of mathematics, a complete graph is a simple undirected graph, in which every pair of distinct vertices is connected by a unique edge (Complete Graph, 2018).

[7]In the graph theory field of mathematics, a bipartite graph (or bigraph) is a graph, the vertices of which can be divided into two disjoint and independent sets U and V such that every edge connects a vertex in U to one in V. Equivalently, a bipartite graph is a graph that does not contain any odd-length cycles (Bipartite graph, 2018).

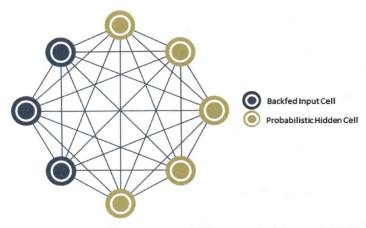

Fig. 20 Boltzmann machines

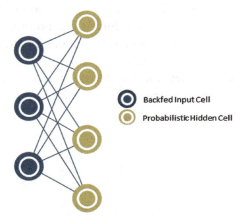

Fig. 21 Restricted Boltzmann machines

3.5 Deep Belief Networks

Deep belief networks (DBN) are an accumulation of layers of RBMs surrounded by VAEs. DBNs can be combined so one network can train the other. They can therefore be used to generate data by already learned patterns. DBN are learned one layer at a time (Fig. 22).

DBN are used for generating and recognizing images and video sequences.

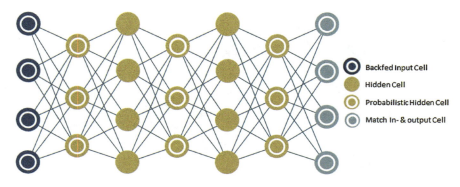

Fig. 22 Deep belief networks (DBN)

3.6 Deep Convolutional Network (DCN)

Deep convolutional networks (DCN) are a combination of kernel cells and pool cells to simplify the features (mainly using nonlinear functions, e.g., max.) and reduce unnecessary information. Figure 23 shows convolutional cells forming a funnel (used to compress and reduce features). The result of reduction is the input for a classical deep feedforward neural network (DFF).

Image pattern recognition is one of the main applications.

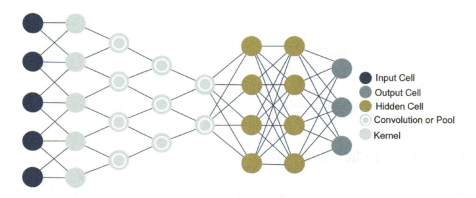

Fig. 23 Deep convolutional network (DCN)

3.7 Deconvolutional Network (DN)

Deconvolutional networks (DN) have a structure quite similar to DCN, but reversed (Fig. 24).

17 Deep Learning: An Introduction 323

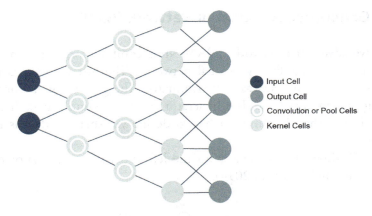

Fig. 24 Deconvolutional network (DN)

3.8 Deep Convolutional Inverse Graphics Network (DCIGN)

Deep convolutional inverse graphics networks (DCIGN) have a structure similar to that of AE, but the way the reduction and decomposition are accomplished varies from that of a conventional AE.

Figure 25 shows an example network. DCIGNs are used in image processing with a focus on processing images the network hasn't been trained with. The classic example of this is the transformation of a horse picture into a picture of a zebra.

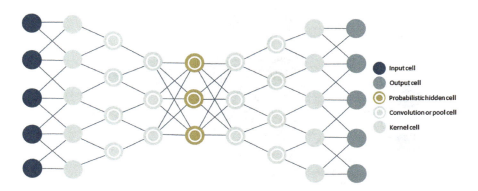

Fig. 25 Deep convolutional inverse graphics network (DCIGN)

3.9 Generative Adversarial Network (GAN)

Generative adversarial networks (GAN) are a combination of two networks and represent a huge family of dual networks. The first network is a generator and the second acts as a discriminator. The goal is for the networks to engage in an interplay. The generator proposes sample data (real and generated) and the discriminator has to decide whether the data is real or generated.

Figure 26 shows the generator on the left and the discriminator on the right (see Goodfellow et al., 2014).

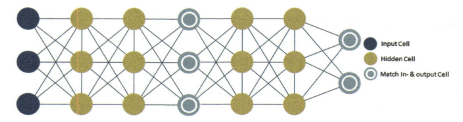

Fig. 26 Generative adversarial network (GAN)

3.10 Extreme Learning Machine (ELM)

Extreme learning machines (ELM) are neural networks that work like deep feedforward networks (DFN), but with reduced vertexes in the network (Fig. 27).

ELM are an attempt to reduce network complexity by randomly generating sparse hidden layers with reduced connections (vertexes).

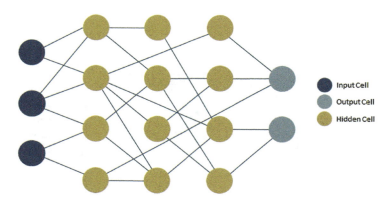

Fig. 27 Extreme learning machine (ELM)

3.11 Liquid State Machine (LSM)

Liquid state machines (LSM) are randomly generated in the same way as ELM, but they use special cells called spiking hidden cells for the spare hidden layers. The idea behind spiking hidden cells is adopted from biological neurons, which use short and sudden increases in voltage to send information. The signals are called action potentials, spikes or pulses. This is implemented by replacing the activation functions dynamically adapting threshold levels (Fig. 28).

Applications include computer vision and speech recognition systems.

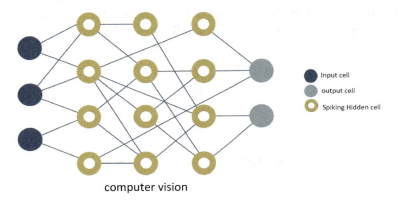

Fig. 28 Liquid state machine (LSM)

3.12 Echo State Machine (ESM)

Echo state machines (ESM) use recurrent cells in the hidden layers and a special estimate based on the recurrent features of the recurrent cells. As

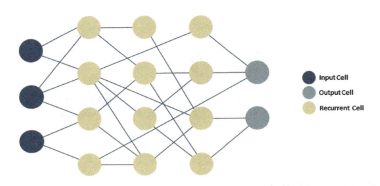

Fig. 29 Echo state machine (ESM)

such, ESM are a subtype of RRN with reduced vertexes in the network structure (Fig. 29).

ESM are sometimes used for theoretical benchmarks, but haven't yet found their domain of expertise.

3.13 Deep Residual Network (DRN)

Deep residual networks (DRN) add connections between the hidden layers of a conventional deep feedforward network (DFN). As shown in Fig. 30, the information is passed from the first hidden layer directly to the third hidden layer.

To some extent, these networks are like RNN without an explicit delay.

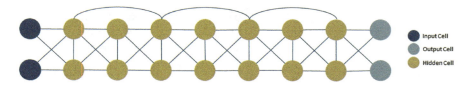

Fig. 30 Deep residual network (DRN)

3.14 Kohonen Machine (KM)

Kohonen machines (KM) were first introduced by Teuvo Kohonen (see Kohonen, Self-organized formation of topologically correct feature maps, 1982; Kohonen & Honkela, Kohonen network, 2007) and belong to the class of self-organizing maps (Fig. 31).

KM can be used for classification problems.

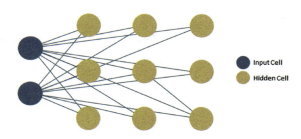

Fig. 31 Kohonen machine (KM)

3.15 Support-Vector Machine (SVM)

Support-vector machines (SVM) are networks with just one cell in the output layer (see Cortes & Vapnik, 1995). Although SVMs can be written as neural networks (see Eq. 9), they are intended to solve linear optimization problems and not to design networks. Therefore, SVMs are not always considered to be neural networks (Fig. 32).

Equation 9: Linear optimization problem for SVM.

$$W^T x + b = b + \sum_{i=1}^{n} \alpha_i x^T x^{(i)}$$

SVM are used for binary classification.

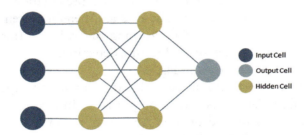

Fig. 32 Support-vector machine (SVM)

3.16 Neural Turing Machine (NTM)

Neural Turing machines (NTM) address one main criticism of neural networks in general, namely that they can be a kind of black box. As shown in Fig. 33, NTM look like a feedforward network with extractable

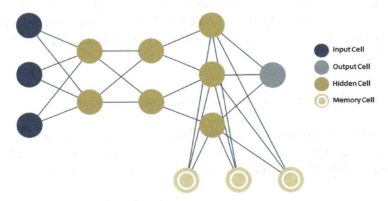

Fig. 33 Neural turing machine (NTM)

(transparent) memory cells. As NTM have memory cells, they are classified as RNN.

A theoretical background can be found in Graves, Wayne, and Danihelka (2014). The article (Collier & Beel, 2018) focuses on the implementation of NTM.

4   Selected Deep Learning Methods in Detail

4.1   Autoencoders

AEs are artificial neural networks—usually deep networks—which are capable of performing unsupervised learning tasks, i.e., learning from unlabeled data. They do so by learning an efficient representation of the input data within the network structure. The AEs are therefore often categorized among the so-called representation learning algorithms. Their strengths include dimensionality reduction and feature detection.

The layout of an AE is shown in Fig. 34.

Like an ordinary deep neural network, AEs contain an input layer followed by several hidden layers and an output layer. In fact, this architecture is often referred to as stacked or deep AE, since it contains several hidden layers. The crucial difference between this and ordinary neural networks is the objective to reconstruct the input data in the output layer. For this reason, the network layers can be grouped into two parts. First, an encoder reduces the dimensionality of the input data for internal representation—the coding layer. Then a decoder attempts to reconstruct the original data starting from the coding layer.

The structure of a stacked AE is typically symmetrical regarding the coding layer. During encoding, the number of neurons per layer is reduced, which lowers the dimension of internal representation. In that sense, AEs reduce dimensionality. Optimized AEs use the minimal dimension of internal representation that is still sufficient to reconstruct the input data when decoding.

4.1.1 Fraud Detection Using Autoencoders

AEs provide the possibility to detect fraud by way of statistical deviations. The reconstruction of an input data set will be less accurate for samples with low probability. The so-called reconstruction error is used to measure the

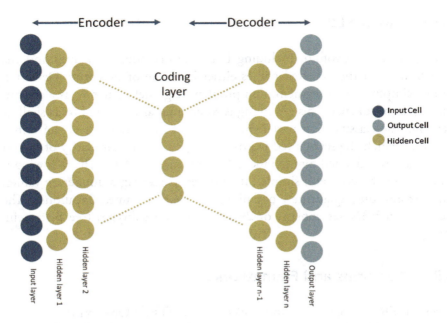

Fig. 34 Autoencoder

difference between input and output data. The network structure further helps AEs trace back statistical deviations to the input layer through weights of the individual neurons. Thus, AEs can not only classify anomalies but also compute error probabilities for the underlying data.

4.2 NER

Named-entity recognition (NER) is a subdomain of information extraction. NER attempts to identify and classify named entities—one or many words or phrases (expressions)—in a text. Classification can map to predefined categories (e.g., percentages, monetary values, time expressions, quantities, organizations, person names, locations) or aim to map to rigid designators.[8]

---

[8]A term is a rigid designator or absolute substantial term if it refers to the same thing in all possible contexts, in which that thing can be viewed (see Blackburn, 2008).

4.2.1 Steps in NER

The approach is twofold, including both the detection of names and the classification of the detected names either by name or by entity. Detection can be simplified as a segmentation problem (e.g., define names as a continuous span of tokens). This chunking is sometimes also referred to as shallow parsing. The classification part requires a set of categories (ideally an ontology[9]), to which the segmented words are mapped. The granularity of the set of categories is defined by the task to be performed in NLP. The following is an example of a common simple category set (percentages, monetary values, time expressions, quantities, organizations, person names, locations). The well-known BBN set consists of 29 types and 64 subtypes (see Brunstein, 2002).

4.3 Platforms and Frameworks

Several NER platforms or frameworks exist. GATE,[10] OpenNLP,[11] SpaCy[12] and Stanford NER[13] are some notable NER platforms. GATE offers NER predefined language support for many languages and domains. It includes a graphical user interface and a Java API. OpenNLP has statistical and rule-based components for NER. SpaCy is an open-source framework for NER, which features a named-entity visualizer and fast statistical NER.

Stanford NER is part of the CoreNLP toolkit and is also known as CRFClassifier. It is an implementation of linear chain Conditional Random Field (CRF)[14] sequence models.

---

[9]An ontology includes a representation and definition of the categories or relations between the concepts and entities (see Wikipedia, 2019).

[10]GATE—General Architecture for Text Engineering is a framework for NLP written in Java by the University of Sheffield (The University of Sheffield, 2019).

[11]Apache OpenNLP is an NLP toolkit develop b the Apache Software Foundation (The Apache Software Foundation, 2019).

[12]SpaCY is a software library for NLP primarily written in Python (Explosion AI, 2019).

[13]Stanford NER is an implementation of a Named Entity Recognizer in Java (Stanford NLP Group, 2019).

[14]Conditional random fields (CRFs) are a class of statistical modeling method often applied in pattern recognition and machine learning and used for structured prediction.

4.4 Word2Vec

The Word2Vec[15] model is an implementation of a word embedding model.[16] The goal of word embedding models consists of mapping (or embedding) words or phrases into a vector space, which means transforming the words or phrases into vectors or real numbers. The model aims to transform highly dimensional word space[17] into a lower dimensional continuous space by preserving contextual relations.

This word space can then be used for further analysis, e.g., using nearest neighbor's classification algorithms to identify similar words or phrases or word-vector-operations like work analogies.

Figure 35 provides an example of the distributed representation that can be used to apply grouping using classification algorithms or identify words not likely to be in this context.

Figure 36 illustrates the simple math of the vector representation. The following question can therefore be answered: If the words man and woman have a certain relation, what would be a similar relation to the word king? Answer: queen! Or denoted in vector writing:

$$\overrightarrow{king} - \overrightarrow{man} + \overrightarrow{woman} = \overrightarrow{queen}$$

Equation 10: Vector notation of word analogies.

Or with the explicit numeric:

$$\overrightarrow{king} - \overrightarrow{man} + \overrightarrow{woman} = \begin{pmatrix} 0.3 \\ 0.7 \end{pmatrix} - \begin{pmatrix} 0.2 \\ 0.2 \end{pmatrix} + \begin{pmatrix} 0.6 \\ 0.3 \end{pmatrix} = \begin{pmatrix} 0.7 \\ 0.8 \end{pmatrix} = \overrightarrow{queen}$$

Equation 11: Vector notation of word analogies—with numerics.

The Word2Vec framework supports two model architectures to generate distributed representation of words: (A) continuous bag-of-words (CBOW) or (B) continuous skip-gram (SG). Both model architectures are discussed in the following sections.

The CBOW does not take the word sequence into account, as this is the general idea behind a bag-of-words. In contrast to this, the continuous SG

---

[15]The original paper for Word2Vec was published in 2013 (see Mikolov, Sutskever, Chen, Corrado, & Dean, 2013).

[16]Another popular framework for this task is GloVe, which was developed at Stanford University (see Pennington, Socher, & Manning, 2014).

[17]One dimension by word of the corpus.

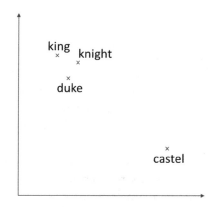

Fig. 35 Distributed representations

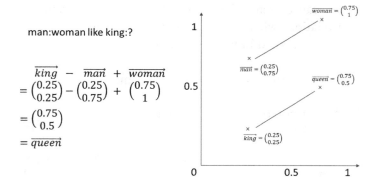

Fig. 36 Word analogies

model starts with a word and tries to predict the surrounding words. The two model architectures differ in application. While CBOW is faster, the SG model architecture is slower but does a better job with infrequent words (see Google, 2019).

The CBOW model is designed to only take into account the surrounding words, unbiased by the distance to the word (not differentiating whether the word is one, two or three words away). But let us start with a simplified CBOW model with one word in the context.

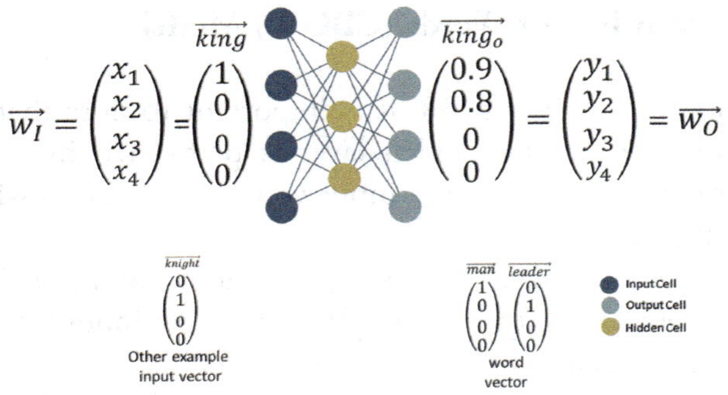

$$\overrightarrow{w_I} = \begin{pmatrix} x_1 \\ x_2 \\ x_3 \\ x_4 \end{pmatrix} = \begin{pmatrix} 1 \\ 0 \\ 0 \\ 0 \end{pmatrix} \qquad \begin{pmatrix} 0.9 \\ 0.8 \\ 0 \\ 0 \end{pmatrix} = \begin{pmatrix} y_1 \\ y_2 \\ y_3 \\ y_4 \end{pmatrix} = \overrightarrow{w_O}$$

$\overrightarrow{king}$ $\qquad$ $\overrightarrow{king_o}$

knight
$$\begin{pmatrix} 0 \\ 1 \\ 0 \\ 0 \end{pmatrix}$$
Other example
input vector

man *leader*
$$\begin{pmatrix} 1 \\ 0 \\ 0 \\ 0 \end{pmatrix} \begin{pmatrix} 0 \\ 1 \\ 0 \\ 0 \end{pmatrix}$$
word
vector

● Input Cell
● Output Cell
● Hidden Cell

Fig. 37 A simple CBOW model with one word in the context

4.4.1 Bigram Model

As in the main CBOW model, the input words are mapped to a one-hot vector[18] and the output context words are mapped accordingly. Figure 37 shows one-hot vector for king, knight (input) and output vector $king_O$ for the word king in a simplified representation of the neural network. The output vector $king_O$ can be interpreted in such a way that the word king matches the expression man and leader.

The network will mainly be defined by the two weight matrices (one from the input layer to the hidden layer $W_{4\times3}$ and one from the hidden layer to the output layer $W'_{3\times4}$). The activation function from the input layer to the hidden layer is linear (simply passing the weighted sum) and softmax is the activation function form the hidden layer to the output layer. The output for a single node of the output layer can be interpreted as a conditional probability $p(y_i|w_I)$ for the context (or word) y_i given the input word w_I. The vector $\overrightarrow{w_O}$ can be used to identify similarities and word analogies, as described in Sect. 4.3.[19]

The idea is to map words in a context (word), which works well. In practical applications, one is more interested in mapping a multi-word context to a single word (or expression) representing the context of this (unsorted) group of words.

---

[18]A one-hot vector is a vector, that has a 1 in one dimension and 0 in all other dimensions.

[19]If the dimension of the output layer is chosen lower than the input layer, word embedding with dimension reduction is established. Our figure shows the same dimension in the input and the output layer.

4.4.2 Continuous Bag-of-Words (CBOW) Model

This approach is shown in Fig. 38. It is important to note that calculation from the input layer to the hidden layer is performed by averaging the results of the metrics multiplication input vectors three times with the same weight matrix $W_{4\times 3}$.

The output vector can again be interpreted as a conditional probability $p(y_i|w_I)$ for the output $\overrightarrow{\text{context (or word)}}$ y_i given the input word w_I (which consists of the three vectors $\overrightarrow{king}$, $\overrightarrow{knight}$ and $\overrightarrow{duke}$).

Further details on the model architecture are described in Rong (2016).

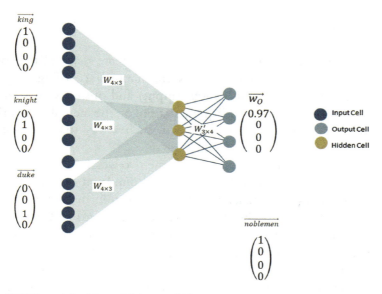

Fig. 38 CBOW model with multiple words for one context

4.4.3 Skip-Gram (SG) Model

The SG model architecture works similarly, but the size of the input layers and output layers are switched. The input is one word of the corpus and the model tries to predict the other words (output) which could be the phrase the input word is used in. Figure 39 illustrates an example of this using the sentence "A man will go." As in CBOW the weight metrics used from the hidden layer to the output layer is three times the $W'_{3\times 4}$ metrics, but the activation functions for input layer to the hidden layer and from the hidden

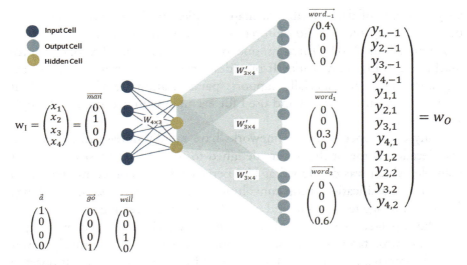

Fig. 39 Skip-gram (SG) model

layer to the output layer differ from the one used in the CBOW model architecture.

Interpretation of the output is of similar structure to that of the CBOW model architecture. The output is the conditional probability for the word before the input word and the two words behind the input word or any other defined structure.

5 Machine Learning Frameworks

Although concepts and algorithms had already been developed by the 1970s, machine learning and AI experienced a renaissance in the early 2000s based on reliable computational performance. The development and successful application of algorithms and especially neural networks for specific tasks in various fields like information filtering, image recognition or natural language processing revealed a huge demand. Libraries and frameworks have been developed, thus making methods accessible to a larger variety of users.

Modern machine learning relies on adequate preparation of input data or so-called feature engineering. Typical tasks in machine learning are addressed best by an interplay of both conventional statistical algorithms like logistic regression, clustering algorithms, decision trees or random forests and modern approaches like deep neural networks. A suitable framework therefore has to provide a large variety of modules. It also has to be scalable to tackle large amounts of data, flexible to map complex machine learning architectures and integrable to build on top of software environments.

Launched in 2002, Torch is one of the oldest complex open-source machine learning frameworks. It provides most of the common deep learning algorithms and especially supports parallelization via GPUs. Torch is strongly community-driven and used for example within Facebook, Google and Twitter.

Many other open-source frameworks have rapidly developed in the past two decades. Some of them were designed to solve specific tasks. Caffe, for example, which was developed at UC Berkeley, focuses on computer vision and image classification using convolutional neural networks. Apache Singa focuses on image recognition and natural language processing.

Other open-source frameworks have been actively developed by companies. The most famous of these is TensorFlow, which was originally developed for internal use and then finally released in November 2015. It boasts a rapidly growing user community and has quickly become the most popular open-source tool. Some of TensorFlow's highlights include the fact that it can run on any device including iOS and Android. It also features several APIs for high-level programming platforms like Python and R. High-level APIs built on top of TensorFlow like Keras provide a simple way to construct network architectures out of the box. In 2016, Google announced the tensor processing unit (TPU), a chip specifically designed to speed up neural network machine learning performed by TensorFlow. In 2018, Google indicated it would make TPUs available to other companies via its cloud computing services, the Google Cloud Platform.

Opening up software to a large community has helped improve quality and resolve issues much more quickly. It also serves to stimulate innovation and further development. Open-source tools for machine learning are currently the market leaders. One of the most recognizable start-ups that built on this hype is H2O.ai. In 2011, the company started developing an open-source software platform that features interfaces to most of the other existing open-source frameworks and develops individual algorithms, which can be applied out of the box. H2O.ai has interfaces for high-level languages like R an Python and also provides solutions for GPU parallelization as well as analysis of data in cloud computing environments and distributed file systems, supporting integration for Hadoop and Spark. The H2O.ai platform's functionality is accessible through a graphical user interface for the most common browsers.

According to the Gartner Magic Quadrant for data science and machine learning platforms 2017/2018, H2O.ai was in the lead in this area, thus surpassing well-established companies like IBM and Microsoft (KDnuggets, 2019).

As illustrated in the graph, many commercial software platforms fell by the wayside when it came to the integration of machine learning capabilities into their frameworks. SAS is still in a leading position among commercial software solutions. Within its cloud computing platform Azure, Microsoft also provides a wide range of machine learning algorithms, which can easily be embedded in existing Microsoft solutions.

Mathworks and SAP are not yet at the same level. Both companies just recently launched their machine learning platforms. SAP built its Predictive Analytics Library around the in-memory database HANA and thus far provides the most common machine learning and a limited number of deep learning algorithms. However, interfaces to open-source platforms and algorithms provide the possibility to integrate their capabilities. So it is not surprising, that RapidMiner and KNIME have developed 2019 to the top leaders (rapidminer, 2019).

6 Summary

The field of algorithms based on deep learning is wide and has grown significantly in the last decade. Section 3 provides a selection of the common neural networks and an idea of the complex reach driven by the various use cases, of which the smallest number originated in the financial services sector. Only a few deep learning algorithms are discussed in more detail in Sect. 4, as they are implemented in the use cases described in this book.

Section 5 provides an overview of the tools, frameworks and software packages that are already available today. While some frameworks are propriety and owned by software vendors, most software packages are distributed under one of the open-source licenses[20] (see Open Source Initiative, 2019). This shows the speed of innovation driven by the open-source community in combination with contributions from universities and firms like Google. Especially the low barriers provided by the open-source availability of most algorithms widens the community and will help drive deep learning toward common use in the financial sector, but also in all other business sectors.

---

[20]Open-source licenses in the deep learning space include the Apache License 2.0, the GNU General Public License (GPL) and the MIT license.

Some neural networks pattern like Word2vec and NER can be used across industries due to the similarity of the tasks at hand, e.g., NLP. It is likely, however, that some of the neural network patterns mentioned in Sect. 3 will be adopted to the needs and applications in the financial industry (as has already happened with AEs). Furthermore, it is expected that certain neural networks patterns will be developed for special tasks in the financial sector like the convolutional neural networks for image recognition.

As we have not covered all aspects of deep learning (like hardware, social aspects or AI in general) we recommend (Lauterbach & Bonime-Blanc, 2018) for further reading.

Naturally, not all challenges in financial management and risk management can and will be solved by deep learning algorithms, but especially when nonlinear structures are considered they can offer a decent toolset to work with. The other challenge facing deep learning and, to some extent, machine learning, is the memory—both database-driven and primary computer memory—and computer performance required. Both of these requirements could be met using cloud computing. As shown in Thiele and Dittmar (2019), the computational and memory resource demand is higher in the training phase, whereas the resource requirement when applying the models is quite similar to that of the conventional statistical algorithms used in the past decades.

Literature

Bengio, Y., Simard, P., & Frasconi, P. (1994, March). Learning long-term dependencies with gradient decent is difficult. *Transactions on Neural Networks, 5,* 157–166.

Bipartite Graph. (2018). Retrieved from wikipedia https://en.wikipedia.org/wiki/Bipartite_graph.

Blackburn, S. (2008). Definition rigid designator. In *Oxford dictionary of philosophy* (revised 2nd ed., p. 318). Oxford: Oxford University Press.

Botev, A., Lever, G., & Barber, D. (2017). Nesterov's accelerated gradient and momentum as approximations to regularised update descent. In *2017 International Joint Conference on Neural Networks (IJCNN)* (pp. 1899–1903). http://discovery.ucl.ac.uk/10062712/1/07966082.pdf.

Brunstein, A. (2002, August 3). *LDC catalog.* Retrieved from Annotation Guidelines for Answer Types https://catalog.ldc.upenn.edu/docs/LDC2005T33/BBN-Types-Subtypes.html.

Cho, K., van Merrienboer, B., Gulcehre, C., Bougares, F., Schwenk, H., Bahdanau, D., & Bengio, Y. (2014). *Learning phrase representations using RNN encoder–decoder.*

Collier, M., & Beel, J. (2018). Implementing neural turing machines. In V. Kůrková, Y. Manolopoulos, B. Hammer, L. Iliadis, & I. Maglogiannis (Eds.), *Artificial Neural Networks and Machine Learning—ICANN 2018*. LNCS, 11141. Cham: Springer.

Complete Graph. (2018). Retrieved from wikipedia https://en.wikipedia.org/wiki/Complete_graph.

Cortes, C., & Vapnik, V. (1995). Support-vector networks. *Machine Learning, 20,* 273–297.

Explosion AI. (2019, January 14). *Industrial-strength natural language processing.* Retrieved from Spacy https://spacy.io/.

Goodfellow, I., Bengio, Y., & Courville, A. (2016). *Deep learning.* MIT Press. Retrieved from http://www.deeplearningbook.org.

Goodfellow, I., Pouget-Abadie, J., Mirza, M., Xu, B., Warde-Farley, D., Ozair, S., … & Bengio, Y. (2014). Generative adversarial nets. In *Advances in neural information processing systems* (pp. 2672–2680). Tahoe: Curran.

Google. (2019, January 8). *Word2vec—Goggle code archive.* Retrieved from Goggle Code https://code.google.com/archive/p/word2vec/.

Graves, A., Wayne, G., & Danihelka, I. (2014). *Neural turing machines.* London: Google DeepMind.

Greff, K., Srivastava, R. K., Koutnik, J., Steunebrink, B. R., & Schmidhuber, J. (2017, October). LSTM: A search space odyssey. In *IEEE transactions on neural networks and learning systems, 28*(10), 2222–2232. https://doi.org/10.1109/TNNLS.2016.2582924.

Hochreiter, J. (1991). *Untersuchungen zu dynamischen neuronalen Netzen.* München: Technische Universität München.

Hopfield, J. J. (1982, April). Neural networks and physical systems with emergent collective computational. *Proceedings of the National Academy of Sciences of the USA, 79,* 2554–2558.

Jozefowicz, R., Zaremba, W., & Sutskever, I. (2015). *An empirical exploration of recurrent network architectures.*

KDnuggets. (2019, Februray). *Gainers and losers in Gartner 2018 magic quadrant for data science and machine learning platforms.* Retrieved from KDnuggets https://www.kdnuggets.com/2018/02/gartner-2018-mq-data-science-machine-learning-changes.html.

Kohonen, T. (1982). Self-organized formation of topologically correct feature maps. *Biological Cybernetics, 43,* 59–69.

Kohonen, T., & Honkela, T. (2007). *Kohonen network.*

Lauterbach, A., & Bonime-Blanc, A. (2018). *The artificial intelligence imperative: A practical roadmap for business.* Santa Barbara, CA: Praeger Frederick.

Liermann, V., Li, S., & Schaudinnus, N. (2019). Mathematical background of machine learning. In V. Liermann & C. Stegmann (Eds.), *The impact of digital transformation and fintech on the finance professional.* New York: Palgrave Macmillan.

Mikolov, T., Sutskever, I., Chen, K., Corrado, G., & Dean, J. (2013). *Distributed representations of words and phrases and their compositionality.* Mountain View: Google Inc.

Open Source Initiative. (2019, January 14). *Open source initiative—Home page.* Retrieved from Open Source Initiative https://opensource.org/.

Pennington, J., Socher, R., & Manning, C. D. (2014). *GloVe: Global vectors for word representation.* Stanford.

rapidminer. (2019, February). *2019 Gartner magic quadrant for data science and machine learning platforms.* Retrieved from rapidminer https://rapidminer.com/resource/gartner-magic-quadrant-data-science-platforms/.

Rong, X. (2016). *Word2vec parameter learning explained.*

Stanford NLP Group. (2019, January 14). *Stanford named entity recognizer (NER).* Retrieved from The Stanford NLP Group https://nlp.stanford.edu/software/CRF-NER.shtml.

The Apache Software Foundation. (2019, January 14). *Welcome to Apache OpenNLP.* Retrieved from Apache OpenNLP http://opennlp.apache.org/index.html.

The University of Sheffield. (2019, January 14). *GATE—Home page.* Retrieved from GATE https://gate.ac.uk/.

Thiele, M., & Dittmar, H. (2019). Credit risk models and deep learning. In V. Liermann & C. Stegmann (Eds.), *The impact of digital transformation and fintech on the finance professional.* New York: Palgrave Macmillan.

von Veen, F. (2019, January 19). *The Asimov Institute.* Retrieved from The Neural Network Zoo http://www.asimovinstitute.org/neural-network-zoo/.

Wikipedia. (2019, January 14). *Wikipedia.* Retrieved from Ontology (information science) https://en.wikipedia.org/wiki/Ontology_(information_science).

Zeiler, D. (2012). ADADELTA: An adaptive learning rate method. *CoRR*, abs/1212.5701.

18

Hadoop: A Standard Framework for Computer Cluster

Eljar Akhgarnush, Lars Broeckers and Thorsten Jakoby

1 Hadoop—A Standard Framework for Computer Cluster

1.1 How Big Is "Big Data" Actually?

In this section about data lakes and how to utilize it, we want to discuss the open source Software Hadoop and some components which grew around it. Since the first publication of Hadoop in 2006 (Archive.org, 2018), a lot of components were developed, which build their foundation on Hadoop, like Hive and Spark or others like HBase, Pig, Chukwan, ZooKeeper, Flink, Ignite, Sqoop and many more.

Hadoop was initiated by Doug Cutting and Mike Cafarella in 2001. It was originally developed to help the Lucene subproject Nutch, which

---

E. Akhgarnush (✉) · L. Broeckers · T. Jakoby
ifb AG, Grünwald, Germany
e-mail: eljar.akhgarnush@ifb-group.com

L. Broeckers
e-mail: lars.broeckers@ifb-group.com

T. Jakoby
e-mail: thorsten.jakoby@ifb-group.com

© The Author(s) 2019
V. Liermann and C. Stegmann (eds.), *The Impact of Digital Transformation and FinTech on the Finance Professional*, https://doi.org/10.1007/978-3-030-23719-6_18

Table 1 Price development of hard disk storage

Year	1956	1964	1975	1987	1991	1997	2000	2006	2009	2018
EUR per GB	12Mio	8Mio	70,000	12,000	9000	1000	250	15	2.5	0.019

is a web crawler and is named after the yellow toy elephant his son called "Hadoop" (Bappalige, 2014). The availability of cheap storage was dramatically rising over the years as shown in Table 1 and led to the accumulation of bigger and bigger data piles. These amounts of data need to be managed and analyzed, therefore the need for tools which can keep up was intense. A highly scalable, fault tolerant as well as easily maintainable distributed file system was needed. Here is where Hadoop steps in. Additionally, Hadoop implements "MapReduce", a programming model which was presented by Google and published in a paper in 2004 (Dean & Ghemawat, 2008). MapReduce is capable of large-scale computations on a distributed file system. Google, for example, used this programming model to run a Petasort in 2007—a standardized task of sorting pieces of 100-byte records, with the first 10 bytes being the key, adding up to 1 peta byte (Dvorský, 2016). The task took around 12 hours to complete. In 2012 Google already sorted 50 PB in merely 23 hours using the same technique.

In order to access the calculated data in a user-friendly way, Hive was created. It leverages the Hadoop distributed file system as a data warehouse for providing OLAP. To do so, Hive comes in with a query language called "Hive Query Language" (HQL), which is based on SQL. HQL doesn't have the full range of SQL statements, but extends SQL by adding the functionality of MapReduce in its queries. Hive was developed by Facebook and subsequently handed over to the open source community in 2008.

Spark was developed at the AMPLab of the University of California in Berkeley and is available as an open source project since 2010. Spark generalizes the MapReduce feature of Hadoop by modeling the calculation steps as a Directed Acyclic Graph (DAG). This approach is 100–1000 times faster than MapReduce, depending on the size and task given. Spark code can be written in several languages including Scala, Java, SQL, Python and R.

1.2 What Hadoop Is Not

There are many misunderstandings about Hadoop and the related tools. First, the data lake Hadoop distributed file system has a high latency when used on its own. This means that fast responding queries and tasks are no such things that this software can handle well. In order to decrease the latency, tools like HBase and Phoenix were developed, which utilize in-memory techniques. Furthermore, Hadoop isn't a database at all. In the earlier versions and even now it's not possible by default to update and delete table entries in Hadoop/Hive when certain versions are used. There are options to enable the update and delete features in Hive but they might restrict Spark from accessing these tables due to version incompatibilities.

2 A Brief Introduction to Hadoop/HDFS

The great success of Hadoop is based on its scalability and open source character. It can be scaled up by using highly available, common and cheap hardware. There is no need of highly specialized and expensive hardware. This characteristic gives enterprises the ability to buy or rent hardware on demand, without having the trouble of complex integration processes within the existing data management strategy.

Hadoop is organized in a cluster composed out of single nodes. Files, which will be stored on one node, will be duplicated such that there are several copies of this file distributed in the cluster. Adding new nodes to the cluster will make them part of this replication process without additional managing effort. Hadoop is offering its own file system and isn't restricted by the underlying operation system. To be more precise, the navigation in the file system reminds the user of the UNIX file system with the root directory "/" contrary to the Windows-based systems, which normally operate on the "C:\" drive. The file system of Hadoop is composed of a 128 MB block, where everything is stored. This means that every file will be put in these blocks. For larger files this means that they will be split up into several blocks. By doing so, Hadoop is using a decades-old technique, which is also used by the current operation system. Ever wonder while checking the properties of a file what the difference is of the "Size" and the "Size on disk"? The size is the "actual" size of the file in bytes. In the picture on the right side this would be 113 bytes. This means that when this file should be transferred over the network, these 113 bytes need to be transported (ignoring all the protocol overhead). The same holds true for writing the same file on a USB stick. The difference here is, that a second copy of the same file can't be placed directly next to the first file. The first copy is reserving 4096 bytes of the USB stick, but practically using only 113 bytes of this reservation. Hadoop is doing basically the same thing, just a little smarter; it isn't actually blocking the 128 MB of disc space of the underlying operation system (deRoos, 2013). The choice of 128 MB is due to the metadata which needs to be managed. There's a server in the cluster which keeps track of the metadata of each block. Would these blocks be too small, then the server managing the metadata would be overwhelmed by the amount of metadata.

The cluster is organized in a master-slave manner, whereby the master is the NameNode and the slaves are the DataNodes (Kumar, 2017). This makes the NameNode the single point of failure, which means, whenever the NameNode isn't available or down, the cluster isn't accessible by any user. The NameNode takes care of the above-mentioned metadata, manages the system tree for all files and does not store the actual files in the HDFS system. To manage all the DataNodes, the NameNode tracks the blocks stored, the size of the files, permissions, duplications and more. The NameNode is doing so, by working with two files—the "FsImage" and "EditLogs". The FsImage is a snapshot of the system and needs not necessarily to be up to date. To get the current system state, the second file EditLogs is needed. This file contains all the changes (deltas), meaning each file uploaded, every renaming of a file or any other operation on the file system. Because of this apparent importance of the NameNode the service should be run on a highly available server architecture.

In an unfortunate case of a server failure while running the NameNode, the server needs to be restarted (if possible), which will take more time than when the NameNode was run earlier. In the startup process all changes must be merged into the last snapshot file "FsImage". Depending on the usage of the network this is an unacceptable situation. In order to avoid this situation, it is possible to set up a backup NameNode which is capable of replacing the primary NameNode. This would take less time than a full recovery (Fig. 1).

The idea is to have a second NameNode (called Checkpoint node) which is fetching the EditLogs from the primary NameNode in a given interval (default of one hour). Initially, the backup NameNode will also get the FsImage, on which the received deltas will be included. By having a newer FsImage file, the number of delta values to be computed in a case of failure is reduced, which leads to a faster recovery of the system. This updated FsImage file can now be copied back to the main NameNode. This update of the FsImage file helps the primary NameNode in case there isn't a fatal error and the system can be restarted. The second component of the cluster, the DataNode, is responsible for actually storing the date.

MapReduce

Another advantage of Hadoop is the MapReduce computing schema. It is designed to make computations on distributed files possible. When

18 Hadoop: A Standard Framework for Computer Cluster

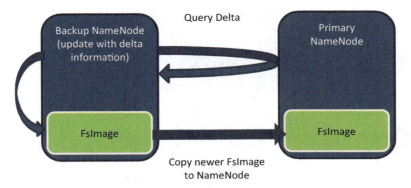

Fig. 1 FsImage

operating with workloads of higher magnitude, you don't want to transport that data over the network to your computation cluster and move the output data back to the data lake. Here is an example to get a feeling what kind of magnitude we are talking about. In September 2017, the internet exchange point DE-CIX in Frankfurt, Germany published a new world record and was capable of streaming 5.88 Terabits (735 Gigabyte) per second. According to the provider the exchange point can handle up to 48 Terabits (6 Terabyte) per second. Assuming that most enterprises don't have this capacity, it is easier to bring the code to be executed to the data and not the other way around. MapReduce works on a two-staged key-value principle. The first task is the mapping process. In this stage bigger parts of data are split up into smaller parts and the cluster creates a task according to the amount of smaller data pieces (Gerecke & Poschke, 2010). Each task calculates a key-value-based result. These intermediate results are sorted by the key component; this is called the sort and shuffle process, which completes the mapping process. Thereafter starts the reduce process, which takes the intermediate results and computes an answer set. In order to fill this abstract concept with life, let's assume we want to invite our friends and bake pizzas for everyone. Since our friends are really hungry we need a lot of pizzas and buy the ingredients beforehand. One of our friends organized what we need to buy, but unfortunately this friend just wrote down which pizzas should be baked and not what to buy in the store. Therefore, we ask our friend kindly if he can help us with this task. In the first step (mapping), we identify which pizzas are ordered and we split up the amount of pizzas, so we both have to take a look at half of the pizzas. In the next step each one of us writes down (independently) which ingredients are needed for which pizza (determining key-value pairs). After this, each one makes a tally list and

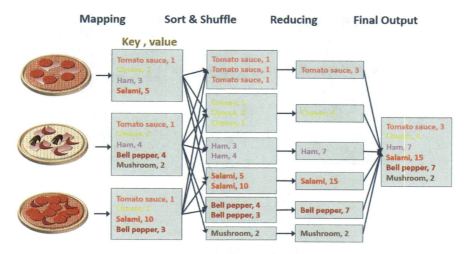

Fig. 2 MapReduce

writes down which ingredient is used how often. After each of us has finished we put our ingredients list together and sort them by ingredients (sort and shuffle). Now we can split up the work again and each one of us sums up how often each ingredient is needed and we receive our shopping list. Figure 2 depicts this process pictured with 3 pizzas and two friends helping.

3   What's the Hive About?

Big data sets stored in the Hadoop environment need to be queried, analyzed, summarized or transported in some cases. Therefore, a data warehouse infrastructure is required which introduces tables. For Hadoop, Apache Hive was introduced as a data warehouse infrastructure by Facebook and transferred to the open-source universe of Hadoop in 2008.

Since many data warehouses already used a Structured Query Language (SQL) dialect and its performance, an adaptation of SQL was the result of the data access. With the introduction of the Hive Query Language (HQL or Hive-QL) it was possible to open the new Hadoop platform to the great number of existing SQL engineers. Hive also opened the door to transfer existing relational databases based on SQL to the Hadoop world. However, HiveQL does not match completely with the ANSI SQL standard, like other SQL dialects from the SQL family, provided by Oracle, MySQL and Microsoft SQL Server, which also differ from each other (Capriolo, Wampler, & Rutherglen, 2012).

18 Hadoop: A Standard Framework for Computer Cluster 347

The data warehouse can store data in different formats, starting from uncompressed csv files to the highly compressed ORC format. Therefore, Hive can use different file types and some common formats will be explained. To begin with, it does not make sense to use any non-splittable file format with Hadoop. The Extensible Markup Language (XML) type is a common mistake, because an XML file needs a beginning and a closing tag at the end of the file. Hence an overview of the most practicable file formats, Avro, RC,[1] ORC[2] and Parquet, will be given in the following (Haas, 2017).

Avro files are quickly becoming one of the best multipurpose storage formats within Hadoop. Avro files store metadata with the data but also allow specification of an independent schema for reading the file. This makes Avro the epitome of schema evolution support since you can rename, add, delete and change the data types of fields by defining a new independent schema. Additionally, Avro files are splittable, support block compression and enjoy broad, relatively mature tool support within the Hadoop ecosystem. Avro is a row-based format, which makes it slow in the case of large table joins within the cluster, but fast for streaming applications.

The first columnar file format adopted in Hadoop were Record Columnar Files, also known as RC files. Like columnar databases, the RC file enjoys significant compression and query performance benefits. However, the current SerDes for RC files in Hive and other tools do not support schema evolution. In order to add a column to your data you must rewrite every preexisting RC file. Although RC files are good for query, writing an RC file requires more memory and computation than non-columnar file formats. They are generally slower to write.

RC Files are slowing down the performance of Hive. Therefore, ORC Files or Optimized RC Files were invented to optimize performance. The ORC file format is primarily backed by HortonWorks. Compared to RC Files, ORC files feature the benefits and limitations, but fit better for Hadoop. This means, the compression of ORC files is better than RC files and the querying is faster. However, the schema evolution is still not supported. Some benchmarks indicate that ORC files compress to be the smallest of all file formats in Hadoop.

From Hadoop creator Doug Cutting's Trevni project, the Parquet Files are yet another columnar file format that was evolved. With Parquet it

---

[1]RC—record columnar files.
[2]ORC—optimized RC files.

should make the advantages of compressed, efficient columnar data representation available to any project in the Hadoop ecosystem. Like RC and ORC, Parquet enjoys compression and query performances and is slower to write than non-columnar file formats in general. However, unlike RC and ORC files Parquet supports limited schema evolution. In Parquet, new columns can be added at the end of the structure. Native Parquet support is rapidly being added for the rest of the Hadoop environment. When working with Parquet, it is very important that the column names are lowercase. If your Parquet file contains mixed-case column names, Hive will not be able to read the column and will return queries on the column with NULL values and not log any errors (The Apache Software Foundation, 2018).

By this advantage of Hive, an option for the data access to the stored information was given.

4   Let Spark fly

Transferred into the ownership of the Apache Software Foundation in 2013 and renamed as "Apache Spark", this standalone Hadoop extension seeks without avail its equals in the proprietary software environment (Aunkofer, 2016)—and that despite its open source project status or rather exactly because of it. The reason for being widely seen as an extension stems from the seamless connection to the HDFS. Nevertheless, due to the APIs of Spark, the data of other systems can be extracted as well, e.g., from S3, Cassandra or MongoDB.

As a "Top Level Project" the presented Data Processing Engine for extremely fast queries on large terabytes of data has experienced quick adoption across a vast variety of companies (Meerasahib, 2018). Like Hadoop, Spark is top-performing due to parallelization and is being extensively equipped with libraries (e.g., machine learning) and interfaces (e.g., HDFS). It can process data from different data repositories (e.g., HDFS, Apache Hive, NoSQL, etc.) (Laskowski, 2018). Spark boosts the performance of big data analytics applications by supporting in-memory processing. At the same time, it is also capable of performing conventional disk-based processing, whenever data sets are too extensive to match the available system memory. All in all, Spark can handle more than the batch processing applications that MapReduce is limited to running giving Spark a time boost of the factor 100–1000 compared to MapReduce.

4.1 Spark Architecture

4.1.1 Spark Core

The architecture of Spark consists of partially interdependent components with "Spark Core" representing the foundation of the project. It provides basic infrastructural functionalities like distributed tasks, scheduling, I/O and many more, put out via an application programming interface (for Scala, R, Python, Java, etc.) using the resilient distributed data (RDD) set. The latter is a read-only (partial) stock of data formed according to logical criteria, which can be distributed over several computers and is maintained in a fault-tolerant way. After aggregating data and distributing it over a cluster of machines, here the data can be then computed and either run through an analytical model or moved to various data stores.

RDDs can contain all types of Scala, Java or Python objects and can be generated from external sources (e.g., SQL, file,…) or as a result of using several transformation functions (map, reduce, filter, join, group,…). Furthermore, most of the computational complexity is supposed to be hidden from users by the design of the RDD (Burns, 2015). The various definitions of the location of sent files or of the used computational resource to store or retrieve files are omitted.

Lastly, apart from programming in the area of RDD-functionalities, Spark enables two restricted ways of shared variables. First, the broadcast variables reference read-only data, which needs to be available on all nodes. Secondly, accumulators being able to be used to program reductions imperatively.

4.1.2 SparkContext and DAGs

As part of the Spark Core framework, SparkContext represents rather a subcategory within the architecture. It embodies an entry gate to all Spark functionalities and is created by driver programs as a result of running Spark applications. SparkContext enables the driver programs to access the cluster with the help of a resource manager (Shreya, 2017). Spark Standalone, Apache Mesos or YARN can be the resource manager (Fig. 3).

Strongly linked to SparkContext—since embedded in the job execution procedure of Spark—comes the sophisticated DAG engine, supporting acyclic data flow. DAG (Directed Acyclic Graph) is a programming style for distributed systems as conventional programs would not work here due to the data being split across nodes (Baskaran, 2014). Each job in execution

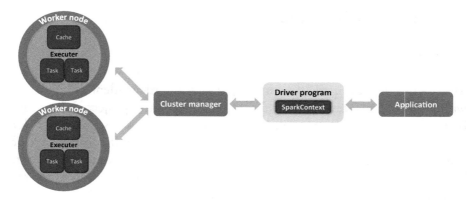

Fig. 3 SparkContext within the Apache Spark Framework

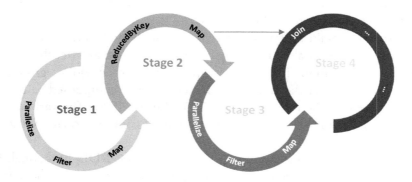

Fig. 4 DAG Visualization

procedures initiates a DAG of task stages to be launched via a cluster manager. Unlike MapReduce, which has only two predefined stages (map and reduce), DAGs created by Spark can create various stages (e.g., in the shape of a tree structure). Deductively, DAG operations can yield better global optimizations than other systems like MapReduce (DataFlair Team, 2017). Simple jobs are completed after solely one stage, while more complex tasks need a single run of many stages rather than the necessity of being split into multiple jobs. For e.g., in the scope of executing a SQL query DAG is more flexible with more functions like parallelize, filter, map, etc. (Fig. 4).

4.1.3 Spark Libraries

Next in the architecture of Spark, the four different built-in libraries, which are components on top of Spark Core, are introduced: Spark SQL, MLlib (Machine Learning library)/SparkML, Spark Streaming and GraphX. These

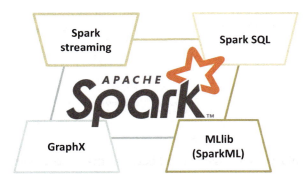

Fig. 5 Overview of built-in libraries in Apache Spark

libraries of code are used in data analytics applications and come along with the Spark API environment, as which the Spark Core engine partly functions. These libraries integrate algorithms and programming capabilities and are designed to streamline and accelerate data preparation, exploration, and analysis. The libraries enable users to automate certain tasks and save some of the coding work that is usually required (Fig. 5).

The most commonly used one of those four libraries, Spark SQL, is a module in the Spark framework that handles relational processing with the functional orientation of Spark (Rouse & Burns, 2017). The basic data structure of Spark SQL are data frames that are equivalent to tables with column labels. Spark contains the main advantage of providing a consistent way to query a variety of structured data types in addition to the Hive tables, including Parquet and JSON files.

One of Spark's peculiar strength, released in 2013 and second in usage frequency, is machine learning enabled through the components MLlib/SparkML or SparkR (using R libraries directly under Spark). In contrast to Hadoop's MapReduce algorithm, which involves a batch process, Spark can smoothly handle iterative loops that are useful for machine learning algorithms, such as, for example, the K-Nearest Neighbor Algorithm (Meng & Bradley, 2016).

Next in line, Spark Streaming, added to Spark in 2013, is an extension of the core Spark API that allows data engineers and data scientists to process near real-time data from various sources like Kafka, Flume and Amazon Kinesis. Its key abstraction is a DStream (Discretized Stream), which represents a stream of data divided into small batches. DStreams are built on RDDs, Spark's core data abstraction. This allows Spark Streaming to seamlessly integrate with any other Spark components like MLlib/SparkML and Spark SQL (Das, 2015) (Fig. 6).

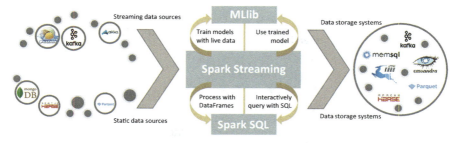

Fig. 6 Relationship and processing in and between the Apache Spark libraries (Das, 2015)

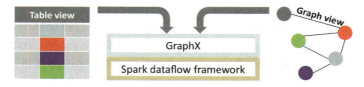

Fig. 7 Overview over graph analytics pipeline in GraphX

Lastly, GraphX is Spark's graphs compilation library. It contains graph algorithms that allow users to structure, search and view data in graphs, depending on the relationships between different objects. In short, GraphX supports huge-scale graph processing and provides a mighty API for implementing learning algorithms that can basically be viewed as large graph problems (Fig. 7).

4.1.4 Spark Languages

At last, within the scope of its architecture and apart from the libraries and APIs, the programming languages used in Spark are introduced. With Java, Python, R and Scala the most common languages in data science are deployed. Thus, short setup times and high degree of flexibility justify the broad use of Spark in countless projects. Since it's possible to work with multiple programming languages in Spark (polyglot), the difficulty of building a data science team with the same programming languages is at least partially circumvented.

4.2 Application Areas

In addition to the architecture, it is also useful as a final step to list application areas or rather examples (Das, 2015; Litzel, 2016) of Apache Spark:

ETL/Data Integration: Spark with HDFS are excellent at filtering, cleaning up and merging data from various systems.

Interactive Analysis: Thanks to its query system Spark is ideal for interactive analysis of large amounts of data. Typically, inquiries arise from Business Analytics (e.g., production capacities, available monthly figures for sales areas).

Real-time Analysis of Data Streams: While Data Stream Processing was barely possible for Hadoop, Spark is a common application for that task. High-speed merging and analysis of data generated simultaneously by multiple systems is possible with Spark (e.g., analysis of near real-time financial transactions for recognition of potential credit card misuse).

Machine Learning: The performance of machine learning can be improved with more data being fed into machine learning algorithms. With the ability to perform iterations on in-memory data, parallelized in a cluster, Spark is able to play out its strength in machine learning areas to the fullest (e.g., online recommendation systems).

5 Connection to SAP

As Hadoop could quickly spread as a data warehouse system it was obvious to become a part in the enterprise business field. Next to Hive, there are plenty of other applications to bring forth the best out of Hadoop. Some common examples are: For the use of transferring data between relational databases and Hadoop, the Apache foundation introduced Sqoop as a command-line interface. In addition, Apache Oozie is the only workflow engine with built-in Hadoop actions as well as handling callbacks from MapReduce jobs. It becomes the obvious choice for scheduling works and managing jobs in the Hadoop environment.

Furthermore, some companies, which are already in the market of Big Data, used the Hadoop environment to develop some additional software like SAP HANA Vora. SAP HANA Vora builds structured data hierarchies for Hadoop data and integrates them with data from HANA to enable in-memory Online Analytical Processing (OLAP)-style analytics via an interface using Apache Spark SQL (Abyson, 2018; Shankar, 2017; Schuler, 2017).

6 Summary and Outlook

In total, Hadoop and its vastly complex environment is perfectly suited to store large amounts of data and run long running analysis/computations on it. Due to its open source nature, it is very easy to receive support from the community, and security issues will be found as well as fixed and not as in proprietary software, where mostly security issues will be only found. The high demand of big data solutions is caught up and lets companies emerge which focus solely on providing support for this environment.

The haystack of big data will only pile up. Right now, sensor data, market data, social data and many more are creating an impressing amount of data, while on the doorstep IoT devices, self-driving cars, social credit data and personal assistance devices are waiting to pile up the haystack even more. Hadoop can be easily extended over time and is capable of combining old and new hardware in a cluster without the necessity to throw away/replace old infrastructure. This feature makes it possible for the infrastructure to grow over a long time without the need of redesigning it. Furthermore, they empower Hadoop to head into a bright future.

Literature

Abyson, J. (2018, July 18). *sap.com* (SAP). Retrieved December 23, 2018, from sap. com https://blogs.sap.com/2017/07/18/understanding-the-basics-of-big-data-hadoop-and-sap-vora/.

Archive.org. (2018). *archive.org* (Firma). Retrieved December 22, 2018, from archive.org http://archive.apache.org/dist/hadoop/core/.

Aunkofer, B. (2016, August 3). *data-science-blog.com*. Retrieved December 23, 2018, from data-science-blog.com https://data-science-blog.com/blog/2016/08/03/was-ist-eigentlich-apache-spark/.

Bappalige, S. P. (2014, August 26). *opensource.com*. Retrieved December 22, 2018, from An introduction to Apache Hadoop for big data https://opensource.com/life/14/8/intro-apache-hadoop-big-data.

Baskaran, A. (2014, October 9). *quora.com*. Retrieved December 23, 2018, from quora.com https://www.quora.com/What-are-the-Apache-Spark-concepts-around-its-DAG-Directed-Acyclic-Graph-execution-engine-and-its-overall-architecture.

Burns, E. (2015, 9). *searchenterprisesoftware.de*. Retrieved December 23, 2018, from searchenterprisesoftware.de.

Capriolo, E., Wampler, D., & Rutherglen, J. (2012). *Programming Hive: Data warehouse and query language for Hadoop.* Sebastopol: O'Reilly Media, Inc.

Das, T. (2015, November 30). *datanami.com.* Retrieved December 23, 2018, from datanami.com https://www.datanami.com/2015/11/30/spark-streaming-what-is-it-and-whos-using-it/.

DataFlair Team. (2017, April 8). *data-flair.training* (Data Flair). Retrieved December 23, 2018, from data-flair.training https://data-flair.training/blogs/dag-in-apache-spark/.

Dean, J., & Ghemawat, S. (2008). MapReduce: Simplified data processing on large clusters. *Communications of the ACM, 51*(1), 107–113.

deRoos, D. (2013, April). *dummies.com.* Retrieved December 23, 2018, from dummies.com https://www.dummies.com/programming/big-data/hadoop/data-blocks-in-the-hadoop-distributed-file-system-hdfs/.

Dvorský, M. (2016, February 18). *History of massive-scale sorting experiments at Google* (Google). Retrieved December 22, 2018, from cloud.google.com https://cloud.google.com/blog/products/gcp/history-of-massive-scale-sorting-experiments-at-google.

Gerecke, K., & Poschke, K. (2010). *IBM system storage-Kompendium.* Ehningen, Germany: IBM.

Haas, K. (2017, November 7). *hitachivantara.com.* Retrieved December 23, 2018, from hitachivantara.com https://community.hitachivantara.com/community/products-and-solutions/pentaho/blog/2017/11/07/hadoop-file-formats-its-not-just-csv-anymore.

Kumar, A. (2017, September 14). *quora.com.* Retrieved December 23, 2018, from quora.com https://www.quora.com/What-is-NameNode-in-Hadoop.

Laskowski, J. (2018, December 4). *jaceklaskowski.gitbooks.io.* Retrieved December 23, 2018, from jaceklaskowski.gitbooks.io.

Litzel, N. (2016, September 1). *bigdata-insider.de.* Retrieved December 23, 2018, from bigdata-insider.de https://www.bigdata-insider.de/was-ist-spark-a-572706/.

Meerasahib, A. (2018, June 22). *tdwi.org.* Retrieved December 23, 2018, from tdwi.org https://tdwi.org/articles/2018/06/22/ta-all-apache-spark-and-big-data-whats-ahead.aspx.

Meng, X., & Bradley, J. (2016). MLlib: Machine learning in Apache Spark. *Journal of Machine Learning Research, 1,* 1235–1241.

Rouse, M., & Burns, E. (2017, June). *techtarget.com.* Retrieved December 23, 2018, from techtarget.com https://searchdatamanagement.techtarget.com/definition/Apache-Spark.

Schuler, F. (2017, November 28). *sap.com* (SAP). Retrieved December 23, 2018, from sap.com https://blogs.sap.com/2017/11/28/connect-your-sap-data-hub-to-sap-vora-and-hadoop/.

Shankar, N. (2017, April 5). *sap.com* (SAP). Retrieved December 23, 2018, from sap.com https://blogs.sap.com/2017/04/05/sap-meets-big-data-sap-hana-and-hadoop-ecosystem/.

Shreya. (2017, November 14). *quora.com*. Retrieved December 23, 2018, from quora.com https://www.quora.com/What-is-the-use-of-SparkContext-in-Apache-Spark.

The Apache Software Foundation. (2018). *apache.org*. Retrieved from apache.org https://parquet.apache.org/documentation/latest/.

19

In-Memory Databases and Their Impact on Our (Future) Organizations

Eva Kopic, Bezu Teschome, Thomas Schneider, Ralph Steurer and Sascha Florin

1 Introduction to In-Memory Databases

1.1 Subject Intro: Real-Time Analysis and Prediction—Science or Fiction?

Washington, DC in the year 2054. A crime is about to happen. Someone is about to stab his wife with a pair of scissors for cheating on him. Detective John Anderton needs to act fast. He does not know the murderer's name nor the site of the crime yet. All he has is the visions of the Precogs. All three of them predict the same scene. Anderton stands in front of a glass panel wearing a pair of remote-control gloves and swiping the Precogs' images from left to right across the screen, rewinding and fast forwarding as if trying to find the single best scene in his favorite movie. He must find a hint as to where the murder is going to happen. He extracts an image of

---

E. Kopic (✉)
ifb AG, Grünwald, Germany
e-mail: eva.kopic@ifb-group.com

B. Teschome
ifb AG, Grünwald, Germany
e-mail: bezu.teschome@ifb-group.com

T. Schneider
ifb AG, Grünwald, Germany
e-mail: thomas.schneider@ifb-group.com

© The Author(s) 2019
V. Liermann and C. Stegmann (eds.), *The Impact of Digital Transformation and FinTech on the Finance Professional*, https://doi.org/10.1007/978-3-030-23719-6_19

the offender and instructs his partner to consult facial recognition patterns. Within seconds the results are displayed on the glass screen. Six potential suspects share the same facial patterns as the offender in the vision. He compares them one by one, swiping away the first and second one, but pauses at the third. That's him! Howard Marks, who lives in Georgetown. Anderton is still focusing on the screen. He knows the suburb now, but where exactly is it going to happen? The vision shows a typical suburban house made of brown bricks. There are too many houses like this in Georgetown. There are only six minutes left until the murder. He is running out of time. He needs a hint—something, anything! His eyes catch a glimpse of a child in front of the murderer's house. Something doesn't quite fit. The child is moving, but how? It is not walking or jumping. It is more like floating from left to right and back again. Anderton stares at the image. And then he gets it. The child is not moving like this itself. It is sitting on an old merry-go-round! There is a merry-go-round in front of the house! He shouts the information to his partner, while getting ready to go. His partner searches the database for roundabouts in the area, and within a few seconds they get the result: there is only one left in Georgetown. They have it! Wasting no time, they immediately fly to the designated location and arrest Howard Marks just in time to prevent him from killing his wife.

This is a scene from Stephen Spielberg's movie Minority Report from 2002. Back then it was a true science fiction movie, but how about now? Is it still fiction or is part of it already reality? We want to have instant access to all the available information. We can ask Siri about the weather conditions or tell Alexa to play our favorite music without a single touch of a button, but just by saying a few words. We can search the internet for anything seemingly interesting while standing a hundred feet underground waiting for the next subway.

How does this tendency of hastening and availability affect today's enterprises and their data storage concepts? Just as Anderton needed every possible bit of information on Howard Marks in a split second to help save a

---

R. Steurer
ifb International AG, Zürich, Switzerland
e-mail: ralph.steurer@gmx.ch

S. Florin
ifb AG, Grünwald, Germany
e-mail: sascha.florin@ifb-group.com

woman's life, today's enterprises want to track their key figures in real-time to adapt their controlling strategies accordingly.

But as rapid access to information gets increasingly important, how can modern databases deliver their data in a faster, more agile, and more precise way than ever before?

In-memory databases are a possible solution to these challenges. The concept sounds simple: Since hard drive access is slow and time-consuming, let's just put the whole database in RAM. After all, replacing the transfer of mass data from the application layer to the database layer with the mere transfer of the code of computationally intensive operations to the database can serve to increase performance tremendously (see Fig. 1).

Conventional system environments can be extensively thinned out by omitting analysis and aggregation layers. This can serve to reduce data redundancy, save memory volume and reduce administration effort (illustrated in Fig. 2).

1.2 Structure of the Chapter

In this chapter, we will describe the pros and cons as well as a use case of in-memory technology and provide insight on what to consider when contemplating whether to implement this technology in your enterprise. First, we will provide an overview of the in-memory database concept and today's main suppliers of in-memory technology. After that, we will dive deeper into the technological details and assess the advantages and disadvantages.

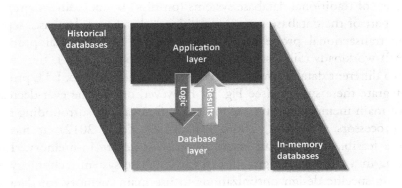

Fig. 1 Big data or computationally intensive operations relocated to in-memory computing

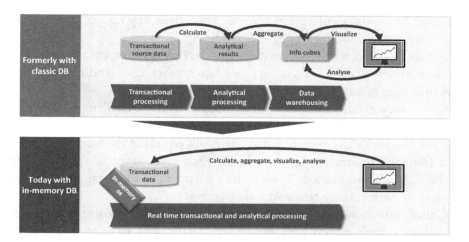

Fig. 2 Adapted system environment

Finally, we will present a concrete use case to demonstrate how in-memory technology can be put to good use in practice.

2 In-Memory Databases

2.1 History of In-Memory Databases and Vendors

The in-memory database system concept has been around since the 1980s (DeWitt et al., 1984; Garcia-Molina & Salem, 1992). In the early eighties, most research and development work primarily focused on improving performance of traditional database systems (on-disk) by including main memory as part of the database system. Traditional disc-based databases separate online transactional processing (OLTP) and online analytical processing (OLAP) workloads (Silberschatz, Korth, & Sudarshan, 2011), thus requiring two different database management systems and complex ETL processes to integrate these systems (see Fig. 3). However, due to the ever-decreasing cost of main memory and the technological innovations surrounding multi-core processors (Patterson, 2006; Plattner & Zeier, 2012), it has now become feasible to build an entire database structure in-memory. This is resulting in a major paradigm shift in the database system technology, thus requiring specific design optimizations to use main memory for data storage. High-performance data access cannot be achieved solely by storing all data in the memory and therefore this requires data structure redesign, query

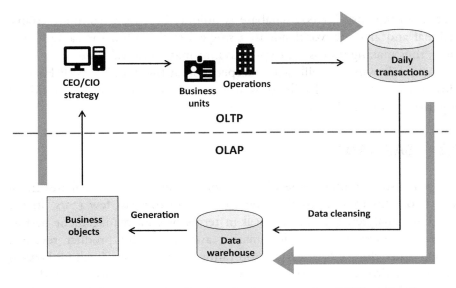

Fig. 3 Traditionally separated online transaction processing (OLTP) and online analytical processing (OLAP)

execution rules and advanced algorithms (Lehman & Carey, 1987; Whang & Krishnamurthy, 1990). Hence, several vendors now offer a variety of in-memory database solutions with a wide range of features.

Most vendors integrate in-memory technology with their existing database system. Oracle, for example, offers a dual-format architecture, i.e., column-oriented and row-oriented data storage, to combine the existing Oracle-database with in-memory technology (Oracle, 2019). This requires the storage of data both in row and column formats. The row format is most suitable for transactional queries, whereas column-oriented format provides better performance for analytic queries. Oracle therefore developed SQL Optimizer to differentiate between transactional and analytical queries and to route them either to the column or the row format tables, thus assuring high-performance data access. Similarly, Microsoft offers two separate tools—in-memory OLTP and in-memory Columnstore—that can be fully integrated with the existing SQL-server (Microsoft, 2019). In-memory OLTP is mainly optimized for OLTP workloads, whereas in-memory Columnstore serves to increase performance for analytic queries. IBM integrates an in-memory Columnstore feature with IBM DB2 for analytics applications (Raman et al., 2013). These three vendors provide an option to include features of in-memory applications in the database system to optimize in-memory processing at table level. SAP, on the other hand, claims that its in-memory HANA database is unique, because it combines transactional and analytic workloads in a single system within the same logical table, thus making it possible to process information in real time.

In the following we will take a deeper look at the world of SAP HANA. However, most of the details, pros and contras provided here are valid for any in-memory database on the market.

2.2 SAP HANA

SAP was listed among the leading vendors for in-memory databases in all reports on this topic from Forrester Research in the past few years. In the respective analyses, SAP scored well in terms of data management performance, transaction capabilities, market awareness, and product revenue, among other things. SAP earned top ratings, for example, in the following criteria: architecture, analytical queries, implementation support, and data security (Yuhanna, Gualtieri, Leganza, & Lee, 2017; Yuhanna, Leganza, Warrier, & Miller, 2017).

But what is it that makes SAP's in-memory database HANA so remarkable? Why are more than 18,000 customers placing their trust and money in this technology (SAP, SAP cloud platform—Data & storage services, 2018)? Is it just the above-mentioned ability to combine analytical and transactional workloads in the same database?

2.2.1 The Evolution of SAP HANA

In the beginning SAP HANA, which stands for High Performance Analytic Appliance, was designed for just that purpose, to represent a very fast analytic application architecture. In 2008, teams from SAP SE, the Hasso Plattner Institute and Stanford University introduced their design, which they had been working on for two years. The first customer release of HANA followed in November 2010. It was considered to be in its infancy at that time, however, even though it seemed to be made for the new challenges businesses were facing in the era of big data and the like. Nevertheless, HANA became the fastest growing product in SAP's history and in 2012 the first HANA-optimized product was announced: SAP BW powered by SAP HANA (Fig. 4).

Based on the idea of implementing conventional algorithms and applications right in the database, HANA developed into a platform. As a result an increasing number of applications were transferred to HANA. SAP HANA

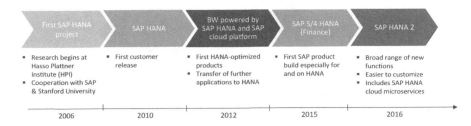

Fig. 4 SAP HANA time line

has since enjoyed growing popularity for its broad range of built-in features and its possibility to learn new capabilities quite quickly. It represents an open platform, which can also run very specific and special applications for specific business needs. As the first SAP product that was not transferred and improved by HANA, but rather built especially for and on HANA, the SAP Business Suite 4 SAP HANA, which is abbreviated to SAP S/4HANA was released in 2015 (SAP, SAP HANA timeline, 2018; SAP, Was ist eigentlich SAP HANA?, 2018).

The SAP Cloud Platform, which was launched in 2012 and includes SAP HANA, makes it possible to broaden the range of applications used. The SAP Cloud Platform is a platform as a service (PaaS) and was developed to give customers the opportunity to easily create new applications or extend existing applications (Marson, 2018). The SAP HANA platform enables online transaction and analytical processing with a single data copy on a single platform. Data is stored in high-speed memory organized in columns, and is partitioned and distributed across multiple servers. This enables fast queries that aggregate data more efficiently, while avoiding intensive full-table scans (SAP, Rethink the possible with the SAP HANA® platform, 2017) (Fig. 5).

In 2016 SAP announced the release of SAP HANA 2 as the next generation. It includes new features for the database and data management including a new active/active read-enabled option, which allows secondary systems to offload read-intensive workloads for additional load balancing and improved hardware utilization (SAP, SAP HANA Roadmap, 2018). SAP HANA 2 was also built to make it even easier for customers to build new applications on it with increased capabilities for application development and more machine learning embedded directly in the platform itself. In addition, SAP HANA cloud microservices, accessible through SAP hybris as a service, are meant to increase innovation of insight-driven applications.

In terms of analytical intelligence, HANA 2 engines for analysis of text, geodata, graphic data, and streaming data can be embedded in applications

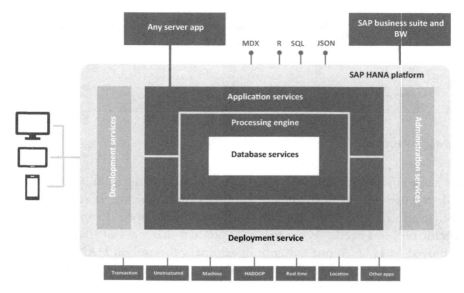

Fig. 5 SAP HANA platform overview

to support them with broad information. The Predictive Analysis Library was complemented with further algorithms to help data scientists detect patterns, and enables customers to include machine learning in their own applications. SQLScript can be used to build and run customized logic, algorithms, and procedures in a HANA database (O'Donnell, 2018; SAP, Rethink the possible with the SAP HANA® platform, 2017; SAP, SAP HANA Roadmap, 2018).

2.2.2 The Advantages and Disadvantages of SAP HANA Technology

There are several advantages that customers experience when using SAP HANA in general. The unique feature of it is that it can manage both transactional and analytical data at the same time. No temporary copy of the data in the main storage is needed to process it and all data originates from a single source. This enables real-time processing capabilities. For example, transactions can be included in analysis directly after being conducted (SAP, Was ist eigentlich SAP HANA?, 2018).

Data in the main memory can be processed 100,000 times faster than data on a hard disk. In-memory is therefore generally able to achieve much higher performance and processing rates than standard database systems (Berg & Silvia, 2013). On the other hand, RAM hardware is much pricier than hard disk storage and even SSD flash drives cannot compete with hard disks in this regard.

The main question that arises on encountering in-memory technology is often: What happens to my data in case of system failure or power outage?

The ACID principle, which was established in the 1980s, provides an answer to this question. The ACID principle describes the general requirements of database transactions. Atomicity (A) means each transaction succeeds or fails completely and, in the case of failure, the database remains unchanged. Database consistency (C) also has to be ensured. Only valid transactions can and should lift the database to a new consistent state. Concurrent transactions have to run isolated (I) from each other to prevent interference and transactions should be durable (D), which means they never get lost once they have been committed! To meet this final requirement, in-memory databases have to be backed up on persistent storage (hard disk or non-volatile RAM). In addition, the SAP HANA database's two-phase commit protocol protects atomicity, logs changes and can restore the database condition using restore points written in commit-log entries in case of failure. As SAP HANA can be run on multiple, isolated, tenant databases, backup and recovery is supported at both tenant and system level. Several third-party backup and recovery tools are also certified for working with SAP HANA (Berg & Silvia, 2013; SAP, Rethink the possible with the SAP HANA® Platform, 2017).

SAP HANA uses recent encryption technology to keep communication, data storage, and application services secure. It applies strategies such as single sign-on and the Security Assertion Markup Language (SAML). The SAP HANA Cockpit includes a security dashboard, which allows users to monitor security performance indicators (SAP, Rethink the Possible with the SAP HANA® platform, 2017).

Although in-memory data space is expensive, it can be minimized using other concepts like data tiering, which involves dividing data into hot, warm, and cold parts based on how frequently the respective information is accessed. Only the currently required data is placed in the hot or warm areas, while cold data can be stored in cheap conventional memory. The SAP HANA dynamic tiering software allows tables to span across disk and memory and supports data aging using time selection by range, hash-range, and range-range partitioning (SAP, Rethink the possible with the SAP HANA® platform, 2017).

By pursuing all options, the cost intensive acquisition and implementation of an in-memory database can quickly reduce operating costs.

2.2.3 FSDP—An SAP Innovation Made Possible by and on HANA

As a result of the financial crisis 2007/08, increased requirements were specified for the financial sector and a whole array of new and intensive reporting standards were defined by international and national authorities. Among other things, these require higher levels of granularity and traceability than ever before.

The increased amount of data and the need for real-time queries require the data platforms to perform better. SAP developed its Financial Services Data Platform (FSDP) as a new HANA-based data platform for the financial sector to meet this need.

The underlying management (FSDM) was first released in December 2017. SAP used its many years of experience with SAP Bank Analyzer to create a suitable, unified data model, representing the "single point of truth" in the application. A conceptual data model as well as a derived physical data model are provided and the standard model can be extended to reflect a customer's specific interests (SAP, Administrator's guide for SAP financial services data management—Getting started, 2018).

FSDP runs in an XSA development environment and therefore relies on HANA as the underlying database. Source system data is integrated via SDI/SDA (Smart Data Integration/Access) and individual data can be accessed using views to create various reports, for example. An interface generator currently provides read, erase, and write procedures for the part of the bitemporal versioning that SAP HANA does not yet support (SAP, Administrator's guide for SAP financial services data management—Getting started, 2018).

Data is managed using the SAP tool WebIDE via SQL commands.

The December 2018 release makes it possible to connect with the third-party application Hadoop for sourcing out cold data.

2.3 Use Case: Cash Flow Generator on HANA

About 2 years ago, SAP introduced a new lightweight application server called SAP HANA XSA (extended application services, advanced module) based on Cloud Foundry. It offers a microservices architecture that completely decouples UI, application logic and database. The communication between these modules is facilitated through Representational State Transfer (REST) APIs. In other words, data is transferred using HTTP and all calls are independent of each other. It also promotes the "bring your own programming language" paradigm. Instead of ABAP, the application logic can now be written in JavaScript, Java, C++, and other languages with ABAP in planning as well. In XSA, modules can be created in different programming languages, but deployed as a single application (called MTAR, multi-target archive).

Based on this new architecture, ifb has developed a performance optimized Cash Flow Generator (CFG) based on the SAP HANA 2.0 database. Complex calculation logic is pushed down to the database while a state-of-the-art UI5 GUI provides user-friendly configuration and process monitoring. The CFG makes it possible to generate cash flows for products such as loans, bonds, and deposits. Cash flows can be generated by specifying repayment types (annuities, fixed principal, interest only, etc.), reference rates as well as interest rate shock scenarios (BCBS). The CFG provides so-called cash flow scenarios to model different cash flow generations for shock and other ALM relevant scenarios (as illustrated in Fig. 6). The goal of the CFG is therefore to provide the data foundation for all kinds of ALM reports.

The CFG includes out-of-the-box delta logic that ensures a minimal data footprint to reduce HANA licensing costs. In addition to this, the standard data compression mechanism in HANA (dictionary compression and columnar storage) usually offers a data storage reduction by a factor of 2 compared to traditional RDBS. When storing huge amounts of data, write performance becomes crucial. As mentioned above, ifb's CFG only stores

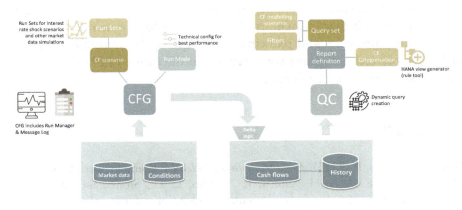

Fig. 6 Cash Flow Generator (CFG) and Query Creator (QC)

the actual data required based on its delta logic. As HANA is an in-memory database, writes are generally much faster than on traditional DBs, in which data is written to memory and to disk. Only the transaction log is persisted on the disk and later asynchronously replayed to guarantee persistent storage.

Besides a CFG, ifb's Modern ALM provides a very flexible reporting framework for dynamically creating queries on the generated cash flows (as shown in Fig. 6). ALM reports can be created within minutes without additional performance tuning. It also provides a Calculation Rule Editor with predefined calculation logic for complex topics such as Delta EVE. The reporting framework provides simulation options on top of the persisted cash flows, such as due date scenarios and haircuts. On-the-fly generated cash flows can also be discounted using the reporting framework. This allows businesses to quickly gain insight into the development and stability of their product portfolio.

3   Summary

In-memory databases provide significant advantages over traditional databases when it comes to storing and processing data. This technology guarantees real-time high-performance data access, making it particularly essential for companies that are dealing with big data.

While stressing some major pros and cons is relatively easy, the decision to introduce an in-memory database and how to design the systems around it is quite a bit harder to make. Many specific aspects have to be considered, which can't be illustrated in a single article without knowing the current landscape, the overall data volume and especially the required business capabilities. The fact is that in-memory databases have high potential for boosting company processes and reducing redundancies. The possible profitably of in-memory technology for your business in the future can be determined by way of a simple proof-of-concept study.

Literature

Berg, B., & Silvia, P. (2013). *Einführung in SAP HANA*. Bonn: Galileo Press.
DeWitt, D. J., Katz, R. H., Olken, F., Shapiro, L. D., Stonebraker, M. R., & Wood, D. A. (1984, June). Implementation techniques for main memory database systems. In *SIGMOD Rec.* (pp. 1–8).

Garcia-Molina, H., & Salem, K. (1992, December). Main memory database systems: An overview. *IEEE Transactions on Knowledge and Data Engineering, 4,* 509–516.

Lehman, T. J., & Carey, M. J. (1987, December). A recovery algorithm for a high-performance memory-resident database system. In *SIGMOD Rec.* (pp. 104–117).

Marson, L. (2018, November 29). *What can the SAP HANA cloud platform do for you?* (SAP SE). Retrieved November 29, 2018, from techtarget https://searchsap.techtarget.com/tip/What-can-the-SAP-HANA-Cloud-Platform-do-for-you.

Microsoft. (2019, February 10). *SQL server 2016.* Retrieved February 10, 2019, from microsoft https://www.microsoft.com/en-us/sql-server/sql-server-2016.

O'Donnell, J. (2018, November 29). *SAP HANA 2 features cloud microservices, geospatial analytics* (SAP SE). Retrieved November 29, 2018, from techtarget https://searchsap.techtarget.com/news/450402670/SAP-HANA-2-features-cloud-microservices-geospatial-analytics.

Oracle. (2019, February 10). *In-memory column store architecture* (oracle). Retrieved February 10, 2019, from Oracle help center https://docs.oracle.com/en/database/oracle/oracle-database/12.2/inmem/in-memory-column-store-architecture.html#GUID-2D072622-139C-4617-88ED-F07D530B8E1E.

Patterson, J. L. (2006). *Computer architecture, fourth edition: A quantitative approach.* San Francisco, CA: Morgan Kaufmann Publishers.

Plattner, H., & Zeier, A. (2012). *In-memory data management.* Berlin and Heidelberg: Springer Berlin Heidelberg.

Raman, V., Attaluri, G., Barber, R., Chainani, N., Kalmuk, D., KulandaiSamy, V., … Zhang, L. (2013, August). DB2 with BLU acceleration: So much more than just a column store. In *Proceedings of the VLDB Endowment* (pp. 1080–1091).

SAP. (2017). *Rethink the possible with the SAP HANA® platform.* Walldorf, Germany: SAP SE. Retrieved from Rethink the possible with the SAP HANA® platform.

SAP. (2018). *Administrator's guide for SAP financial services data management—Getting started* (SAP). Retrieved December 4, 2018, from SAP Help Portal https://help.sap.com/viewer/74e201edd88a4cfcb682c1ae2296b53c/1.3/en-US.

SAP. (2018). *SAP cloud platform—Data & storage services.* Retrieved November 28, 2018, from SAP https://d.dam.sap.com/m/bcpr7Lj/SAP%20Cloud%20Plaform%20-%20Data%20%26%20Storage%20-%20Overview%20-%20June%202018.pdf.

SAP. (2018, November 29). *SAP HANA roadmap* (SAP). Retrieved November 29, 2018, from Roadmap https://www.sap.com/products/roadmaps.html.

SAP. (2018, November 29). *SAP HANA timeline* (SAP SE). Retrieved November 29, 2018, from SAP slideshare https://www.slideshare.net/SAPTechnology/sap-hana-timeline.

SAP. (2018, November 29). *Was ist eigentlich SAP HANA?* (SAP SE). Retrieved November 29, 2018, from SAP News Center https://news.sap.com/germany/2015/09/ist-eigentlich-sap-hana/.

Silberschatz, A., Korth, H. F., & Sudarshan, S. (2011). *Database system concepts.* New York: McGraw-Hill.

Whang, K.-Y., & Krishnamurthy, R. (1990, March). Query optimization in a memory-resident domain relational calculus database system. *ACM Transactions on Database Systems,* 67–95. https://doi.org/10.1145/77643.77646.

Yuhanna, N., Gualtieri, M., Leganza, G., & Lee, J. (2017). *The Forrester Wave™: Translytical data platforms.* Forrester Research.

Yuhanna, N., Leganza, G., Warrier, S., & Miller, E. (2017). *The Forrester Wave™: In-memory databases.* Forrester Research.

20

MongoDB: The Journey from a Relational to a Document-Based Database for FIS Balance Sheet Management

Boris Bialek

1 Introduction

The FIS risk application family has been providing Balance Sheet Management (BSM) solutions for over 25 years. Originally emerging as stand-alone components with individual infrastructures and data management for each component, a strategy was implemented in 2014 to move toward an integrated BSM platform. FIS BSM is now used by almost 1000 banks around the world, ranging from large D-SIBs to small private banks with less than $1B in assets under management.

The FIS BSM components have been utilizing Microsoft SQL Server as their RDBMS of choice since the early 2000s. The database sizes were initially under 50 GB total volume and have not changed much over the first few years. Then clients grew and the largest systems had a total data volume of around 200 GB. Since 2010, the impact of increasingly granular regulations and the fact that clients can now achieve more with the FIS BSM solution stack have been driving exponential database growth. In 2014, the introduction of dynamic balance sheet simulations provided a broad set of forward-looking simulations, which changed the landscape from a backward-looking model to a scenario-based forward-looking model that banks often employ with 20–50 different scenarios. Banks have databases of up to 25 TB for a single production setup and the concept of relational

---

B. Bialek (✉)
FIS, Zürich, Switzerland
e-mail: Boris.Bialek@fisglobal.com

© The Author(s) 2019
V. Liermann and C. Stegmann (eds.), *The Impact of Digital Transformation and FinTech on the Finance Professional*, https://doi.org/10.1007/978-3-030-23719-6_20

data management is hitting its limits in usability. Starting in 2014, the FIS team started evaluating various options and focused on document-based databases as best matching the needs of BSM positions, result sets and other banking risk-related data. Release of the 2017 product generation completed the transition. FIS Data Hub is a MongoDB-based data platform used to provide the common BSM data platform across all previously diverse components. It introduces concepts like end-to-end data stewardship, which provides business analysts direct control over their data at all times. In the old day of relational databases, analysts had to work with an IT team to perform data operations. This transition also allows for features like data versioning, change tracking, and end-to-end data lineage, the capability to backtrack any result field in a report or analysis to the actual input data even if data has been aggregated and compressed along the processing stream. What is really the secret sauce here? What are document-based databases and MongoDB in particular all about?

2   A Brief Excursion into History

The relational database concept originated in the 1960s starting with IBM's System R and the introduction of the Standard Query Language (SQL). This database technology focused on improving relational storage and several major industry players emerged right when medium-sized computers were becoming database machines. With the emergence of ERP, SCM and other solutions, SQL databases became the de facto standard for relational databases and the question of deployment only involved selecting vendor, not whether a relational database was needed. For a long time, research focused on improving SQL, optimizing queries, and storing data at increasing densities on media. During the dot-com boom at the end of the 1990s, universities again started examining fundamental database concepts that were clearly needed due to the explosion of data needs across the internet.

Object-oriented databases came first, reflecting the drive for OO technology. Then came several XML-based systems, the most familiar of which were XPATH, XQUERY, and XSTORE as "industry standards" for those systems. However, the use of these systems was also quite cumbersome and they proved to be everything other than an improvement over SQL and relational databases. With the second wave of internet and smart applications and digitalization, database concepts were suddenly front and center in the development community.

Several camps have since emerged, which are competing for the title of best database concept and claiming they have found the holy grail of IT. The Apache Hadoop camp promotes the "any data, any time" approach using a non-structured data approach. Redundancy and easy replication of data allow for larger data sets and all the actual logic is put into higher application layers and tool chains, e.g., Apache ATLAS for MDM and Apache Spark for data aggregation and interpretation. This market has shrunk over the past few years as people have realized that unlimited flexibility comes with the burden of complexity and support. This has resulted in a merger of the leading software vendors Hortonworks and Cloudera into a new entity.

The second group emerged with very specific databases for narrowly defined functions and feature sets. A good example of this is InfluxDB, a time series database that is often used for performance monitoring and system infrastructure.

The last group is the one that is attempting to bridge both the limitations of the classic Relational Database Management Systems (RDBMS) and the rather complex structures and feature sets of Hadoop. This category of databases is made up of so-called NoSQL databases. It ranges from smaller systems including the IBM Cloudant database, Couchbase, and MemDB to large ones like MongoDB and Cassandra. The latter ones have proven themselves over the course of many years as viable databases that merge the best of the classic database world—compliance with the ACID test (transaction safe concepts) being the most obvious—with the advantages of Hadoop including replication, scale-out, and usage of low cost hardware for enterprise-level DBMS.

3 Introducing Document-Based Databases

Relational databases split data into its sub-components to optimize storage based on the fact that storage was expensive at one time. For example, when storing a financial position consisting of asset information (e.g., stock name, CUSIP, etc.) and the actual trade information (e.g., volume, price, etc.), you would store the data separately so the asset information would only have to be stored once to avoid repeating it. This concept requires merging data from different tables for data alignment. Each data field also has to be well defined using data types and can only store data that is perfectly fitted to it. This need implies extensive data cleansing and alignments between different systems and leads to the greatly appreciated art of Extract-Transform-Load (ETL) to describe the interaction between various data streams. It goes without saying that this all requires a lot of time and resources.

A document database functions more like a folder on a desk. The document has a label and "pages" as content. Each page can have any kind of data in the folder and each folder can have different structures. The need for strict versioning, which is also commonly referred to as strict schema validation, is void and redundant. Modern compression algorithms, which are also becoming increasingly common as part of relational databases, remove the challenge of redundancy in data storage. Average compression ratios of 90% or more cost less than the effort to split the data into tables to avoid redundancies. This provides immediate data set access to all data and disposes with the core paradigm of joining data from separate tables from the relational world. Document folders provide single-stop shopping for data.

The second major difference is the data format itself. The internet has long been using a format called Java Script Object Notation (JSON) to send data between applications. Utilizing the same JSON format as the top-level application for communication, MongoDB implements a conversion-free format from disk-based storage to transferral to the requesting applications. In comparison, relational databases store data in tables and then join and transform this data from an SQL table to the result set. This result set is often transferred using the JSON object (or BSON—Binary Jason Object Notation) format. MongoDB, on the other hand, reduces all these operations to a "grab data and send" procedure. Different data types that result in data conversion inside the database are not needed.

The beauty of MongoDB is clearly seen in a third defining factor when it comes to divergence of data. A relational database always requires a schema that defines EXACTLY which data is stored in each column. If data is broadly divergent, concepts like serialization can be used. However, this requires major work when it comes to schema management and upgrades. An example from the financial environment would be an option being represented by completely different fields than a savings account. In the relational world, each of these would be stored in their own structure by type. In a document-based database, this is not only unnecessary, but in contradiction to the usage pattern. The application recognizes what these instruments are, and they can be mixed anywhere inside the MongoDB data store. MongoDB itself has no use for the formats and can work with any document in any form. The rest is left to the applications. Consequentially, the applications automatically receive the data in the right format for their usage pattern and the overhead of database-type management is removed. For the FIS BSM solutions stack, the simplification provided by document-based

20 MongoDB: The Journey from a Relational to a Document-Based ... 375

databases has increased performance by five times, while reducing the hardware footprint by 50% in the database infrastructure.

4 From MongoDB to the Web

Here is an example of the new world of documents. The example in Table 1 represents a financial instrument including related secondary information. The same data was represented above using a schema of 26 tables optimized for a relational database. As the table shows, the data is not only user-readable but can now easily be expanded and annotated during processing. In our documents folder, this could represent changes made to the document or annotations. A typical set in BSM consists of editing a position for correction. In our example, this involves writing the new value in the "payment" field and adding the change info for user, date, and approval flow as new entries at the end of the document. In a subsequent step, data can be aggregated and summarized into larger positions to simplify the view and positions can be extended with additional metadata. All this can be easily and transparently achieved using the JSON format. The application simply represents the JSON document stored in MongoDB in a web page in the following example (Fig. 1).

The simplicity of the combination of data format and integration with web technologies impacts the speed of application development, application

Table 1 Example of a MongoDB representation of a financial position

⌄ ⊞ (3) ObjectId("5a3a5d90a4b36997a574c189")	{ 6 fields }	Object
☐ _id	ObjectId("5a3a5d90a4b36997a574c189")	ObjectId
⌄ ⊞ Snapshot	{ 6 fields }	Object
⊞ ReferenceDate	2011-12-30 23:00:00.000Z	Date
⊞ SnapshotName	ALM Sample Analysis	String
⊞ EntityCode		String
⊞ Evaluation		String
⊞ DataHubPoolName	null	Null
⊞ DataQueriedAt	null	Null
⌄ ⊞ Position	{ 5 fields }	Object
⊞ RootPositionKey	604009515	String
⊞ AggregationUnitKey	604009515	String
⊞ PositionType	Operational	String
⊞ PositionOriginGroup	Current Positions	String
⊞ AdditionalInformation	null	Null
⊞ SimulationScenario	Actual :: <none>	String
⌄ ⊞ Dimensions	{ 2 fields }	Object
⊞ GeneralLedger	Fixed Rate Loans	String
⊞ Currency	EUR	String
⌄ ⊞ Cashflows	[2 elements]	Array
⌄ ⊞ [0]	{ 5 fields }	Object
⊞ ResultsDate	2011-12-30 23:00:00.000Z	Date
⊞ PaymentDate	2012-01-14 23:00:00.000Z	Date
⊞ ContributionType	0	Int32
⊞ CashflowType	1	Int32
⊞ Payment	150000.0	Double
⌄ ⊞ [1]	{ 5 fields }	Object
⊞ ResultsDate	2011-12-30 23:00:00.000Z	Date
⊞ PaymentDate	2012-01-14 23:00:00.000Z	Date
⊞ ContributionType	0	Int32
⊞ CashflowType	2	Int32
⊞ Payment	4875.0	Double

Fig. 1 MongoDB web interface

complexity, and transparency. While, in the old model, each page had to be designed for each function, the presentation is now extracted directly from the object, embedded into Angular code and presented to the user. Changes to the data model have no impact on the code and are presented transparently. The cost savings for each page can be measured in person days when testing and quality assurance are considered.

5 Size Matters—Scaling MongoDB for Volume and Availability

Relational databases allowed for concepts of data sharing like Oracle RAC or function shipping in an MPP setup like DB2. There were also options for federating data. MongoDB breaks with both concepts and now allows for flexible scaling in both directions. The default MongoDB configuration is a three-instance setup including a primary instance for active production and two secondary instances. In case of failure, two copies are always available, which allows for usage of very inexpensive server hardware and storage. In the case of updates, the secondary instances are upgraded first, then the primary instance is "degraded" and one of the secondary instances takes over production while the original primary instance is updated. At no point in this process is a single instance operational alone and production is never interrupted. This differs from classic cluster solutions like Oracle RAC, which have to be taken down and upgraded in sync, thus risking negative press in case of failure.

The second direction of scaling consists of the concept of sharding data. This is roughly comparable to the MPP concept mentioned above, but has the distinct difference that shards can be positioned in different locations. Let's assume we have a bank with headquarters in New York and independent entities in Germany, Singapore, and Hong Kong. The regional entities can have shards of locally relevant data, which is in line with compliance requirements, and the headquarters can have copies of all data for consolidated reporting. The difference of data locality is invisible to the application but a comparable solution in heritage relational technology would have included federated setups, multiple database instances, and a lot of copied data.

6 Deployment in the Real World

FIS BSM utilizes MongoDB's intrinsic availability capabilities. For smaller implementations, it is sufficient to have a single instance and make file-based backups, as the recovery time is very short and the overhead in managing clusters is not always justified. FIS BSM uses MongoDB in a primary-secondary configuration in the examples below. As mentioned above, MongoDB can be scaled almost without limits and therefore a project team has to decide from among endless models. The described environment can handle data up to 50 TB, which is almost always enough for initial steps.

6.1 Basic Single Machine/Image Setup

In the basic setup for FIS BSM deployment, all components can reside on a single physical or virtual server. MongoDB can manage multiple data stores equally to the concept of a single instance with multiple databases in Microsoft SQL Server. The very minimum deployment includes two distinct independent database instances, which are referred to in these examples as PRD and DEV. Each one can have multiple data stores, which in turn have MongoDB collections that could be interpreted as something comparable to the relational schema from the hierarchical level (Fig. 2).

This very small setup naturally provides no availability and, in case of failure, the instance has to be recovered. That said, in a world of redundancy and virtual servers the "restart" option may be fully sufficient for a smaller project and the lack of log recovery that makes relational databases so painful to recover does not exist with MongoDB.

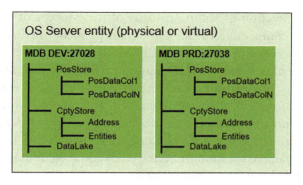

Fig. 2 OS server entity

6.2 Simple Replicated Setup—Two Data Bearing Nodes

Clustering provides additional operational security through data duplication on separate machines/images. Memory and usage are managed inside the MongoDB engine and fewer resources are consumed. This matches the behavior of Microsoft SQL Server. Now the most logical setup would consist of adding a production failover instance to the development server and keeping the development instance local only (Fig. 3).

Production is executed on the PRDA instance. It has a secondary failover copy on the development machine. In the case of PRDA failure, the PRDB instance immediately takes over with simple automatic reconnection through the application. The failover concept introduces the MongoDB arbiter, which prevents the classic "split brain" effect for failover solutions. The arbiter is the tiebreaker instance and is only needed for two-node setup. Any larger scenario obviously has a quorum for the larger number of machines. The arbiter can be installed on any machine as long as it is in the

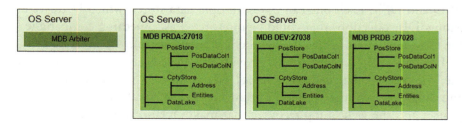

Fig. 3 Server overview

same logical network as the cluster nodes. For best practices, the FIS team uses the central application server as an arbiter machine.

6.3 Other Scenarios

The two basic scenarios described can now be extended with additional nodes for replication, e.g., disaster recovery data centers, nodes utilized for backup, or reporting purposes. However, the underlying mechanism always remains the same and nodes can also be added at a later stage.

7 MongoDB Product Options

As with many open-source products, MongoDB is available as an open-source "community edition", as a commercial product under the label "MongoDB Enterprise Advanced" and as a MongoDB cloud product called MongoDB ATLAS, which is hosted in co-location on AWS, Azure, or Google. As usual there are pros and cons for the usage of the various flavors. A brief summary of the differences is provided below.

The MongoDB Community Edition code is identical to the MongoDB Enterprise Advanced Edition. Both products function with the FIS stack in the same way and no different performance or operational characteristics have been seen thus far. Both versions are available as binary code and can be directly deployed without compilation or assembly of pieces. The excellent installer cannot be compared to that of some other big data products, which often involves a complex procedure of installing 20 or more packages.

Compared to the community license, the commercial license additionally provides a set of tools and service level that many "production" clients appreciate.

1. 24×7 support, warranty and indemnification,
2. Integration in LDAP, PKI, and advanced encryption,
3. Compass GUI tool for managing the database,
4. Emergency patches are automatically provided (versus self-monitoring and downloading when available in the community edition),
5. Ops Manager tool for automating operational tasks and monitoring.

At the time of writing, the price for the MongoDB Enterprise Advanced was priced at around \$14,000 [with some deviations per country depending on currency exchange rates (MongoDB, Inc., 2019b)]. This is a license for one server with an unlimited number of cores, 256 GB RAM maximum memory and unlimited usage not limited to Ambit Focus. This can be deployed in multiple virtual machines on the same physical server.

The third option for deploying a MongoDB database is as a cloud service called MongoDB ATLAS directly from MongoDB (see MongoDB, Inc., 2019a). Assuming the solution stack is deployed on a cloud-based infrastructure anyway, the FIS technical team suggests MongoDB ATLAS as the deployment of choice, as it removes any need for patching, security management and the like. It integrates into the stack in co-location and provides true utility computing. For self-deployment on a cloud infrastructure, MongoDB is naturally available as default component in the Docker Hub.

Literature

MongoDB, Inc. (2019a, January 28). *MongoDB—Atlas*. Retrieved January 28, 2019, from MongoDB https://www.mongodb.com/cloud/atlas.

MongoDB, Inc. (2019b, January 28). *MongoDB enterprise advanced*. Retrieved January 28, 2019, from MongoDB https://www.mongodb.com/products/mongodb-enterprise-advanced.

21

Summary and Outlook

Volker Liermann and Claus Stegmann

The book covers a large cross section of the digitalization story with a focus on the financial sector. The introduction highlighted several major digitalization and fintech trends. The first part dealt with some of the most interesting aspects such as process automation, distributed ledgers and client-related innovative approaches. Part 2 was broken down into three domains (a) bank management aspects of planning and forecasting using machine learning, (b) applications for financial risk management followed by (c) a look at future prospects. It also described interesting applications of the new methods for prediction and pattern recognition. Regulation and how technology can help better meet the demands were discussed in part 3. The fourth part described some of the important methods and designs for architecture.

The required push to achieve efficiencies is inevitable. Technology adaption and innovation must be transformed to help the business model. The transformation challenge is exacerbated by a business model, which is itself shifting, adapting and transforming. An adaptive or agile change process or project management framework like scrum are the only ways to

---

V. Liermann (✉)
ifb AG, Grünwald, Germany
e-mail: volker.liermann@ifb-group.com

C. Stegmann
ifb Americas, Inc., Charlotte, NC, USA
e-mail: claus.stegmann@ifb-group.com

© The Author(s) 2019
V. Liermann and C. Stegmann (eds.), *The Impact of Digital Transformation and FinTech on the Finance Professional*, https://doi.org/10.1007/978-3-030-23719-6_21

handle these challenges. When everything happens simultaneously, organizations, management, employees and worst of all, customers get lost.

The financial industry is at a crossroads and traditional players are in the process of deciding how to approach the challenges at hand. Many companies in the financial sector are in the process of adapting the best ideas and designs from new players[1] in various dimensions (e.g., organizational, technology, adoption of client-orientation). This new mindset of being open for change is important and ensures the adaptability demanded by clients and regulatory instances.

Amara's law[2] hints at what happens when the scaling effect of digital business models strikes. While some see Amara's law as an example of the hype cycle,[3] they might underestimate the level that can be achieved with the digital framework on the "plateau of productivity". When the dot-com bubble burst in 2000, everyone laughed at dog food sold online, but only a few saw the potential of Amazon.

The most important thing is to remain engaged with change after the hype starts cooling down. It is hard to tell where we stand now in the curve of digitalization hype. We may be on the peak or behind it. If not already, it could soon be time to sort the diamonds from the stones and then transform the rough diamonds into cut gems.

What are the rough diamonds of digitalization in the financial sector? Or, in other words, what is the "teenage sex" (Ariely, 6 January 2013) and what are the things you need to be involved in or not? RPA and all process-driven improvements including automated decisions are certainly rough diamonds. Machine learning and deep learning applications in the client context (NBO and NBA) including positioning in the customer journey must also be rated as such. The distributed ledger technology offers a superior instrument for tracking and sharing approved information (e.g., Everledger for diamonds), which can easily be extended to any other asset class (e.g., real estate). In the area of private distributed ledgers (i.e., by a consortium lead with restricted access), there are more applications to come. Private blockchains (like bitcoin, Etherium and all the other token-based blockchains) have a future, but

---

[1] Fintech and technology companies (GAFA).

[2] "We tend to overestimate the effect of a technology in the short run and underestimate the effect in the long run" (2016).

[3] The hype cycle is a branded graphical presentation developed and used by Gardner. It provides a graphical and conceptual presentation of the maturity of emerging technologies through five phases (Technology Trigger, Peak of Inflated Expectations, Trough of Disillusionment, Slope of Enlightenment, Plateau of Productivity).

the associated speculative investment potential (i.e., sanction-free transfer of value) casts a shadow over the basic concept. Nonetheless, the idea of peer-to-peer payments still has disruptive potential, as it removes banks from the equation.

Technology and new infrastructure patterns are more like diamond deposits than actual rough diamonds. Certainly, machine learning and deep learning are the most important methods for improving the prediction and forecasting process as well as the risk control and management processes. The methodology and technological improvements can push this field to the next level. ABM is a good example of technology enabling methods.[4]

To emphasize this point again, some rough diamonds are easy to identify, but the competitive advantage over fintech companies, GAFA and other traditional market participants is achieved by finding such diamonds before everyone else does. This can only be achieved by continuously questioning and challenging the things commonly agreed on in the community and identified as best practices. Questioning and challenging these things can be best achieved by gaining a deep and practical understanding of the methods and infrastructure.

Literature

Ariely, D. (2013, January 6). *Big data is like teenage sex …* [Twitter].
"Roy Amara 1925–2007, American futurologist" [book auth.] (2016). Susan Ratcliffe. *Oxford essential quotations* (4th ed.). Oxford: Oxford University Press.

---

[4]The affordable cluster structure offered by Hadoop clusters enables this technology to make the required computation.

Notes on Contributors

Volker Liermann worked in the banking industry for over two decades, primarily focusing on financial risk management. Throughout his career, he has focused on developing integrated and comprehensive frameworks to help organizations correctly project risk at a strategic and tactical line of business and departmental level. He has also focused on developing frameworks to integrate stress testing and regulatory stress tests. In recent years, his focus has shifted to digitalization, machine learning and other improvements to classical financial risk management. He has a background in economics and a degree in mathematics from the University of Bonn.

Claus Stegmann, Partner and Member of the Board, has acquired extensive know-how over the last two decades regarding topics including SAP Bank Analyzer, risk management for banks, accounting, regulatory compliance (Basel III, CRR/CRD IV, Solvency II) and managing complex projects in the financial industry. He has also co-authored books on stress tests in banks and Basel III. He graduated from business school at the University of Passau.

Eljar Akhgarnush, Implementation Consultant at ifb since April 2018, gained knowledge in software and financial sector topics during his studies as well as the various positions he has since held. Starting out with a focus on financial supervision & regulation as well as project management issues, he soon shifted his attention to the technical side, using tools like SAP WEB IDE, PowerDesigner and Cloudera. After having received his B.Sc. in Business Administration at CAU Kiel, he studied International Economics and Policy Consulting at OvGU in Magdeburg. He has since remained keen on exchanging knowledge.

Noah Bellon, Research Analyst at BearingPoint, has gathered extensive knowledge in the area of finance in the past few years. He collected experience in process digitalization in managerial accounting, accounting and treasury. Most recently, his focus has shifted to blockchain and distributed ledger technology as well as the possible use cases in the area of regulatory technology. He studied business administration and economics at the University of Hohenheim.

Dr. Martina Bettio is working as a senior consultant at ifb group for the banking sector since 2016. She is currently working in SAP Bank Analyzer, SAP Business Warehouse and SAS related topics, with focus on Project Management and Business Analysis. She joined the ifb Blockchain Team in 2018 due to her personal interest in new technologies. In the group, she focused her work mainly on Hyperledger Fabric. She has a Ph.D. in Molecular Biomedicine from the University of Bonn.

Notes on Contributors

Boris Bialek, Head of Development at FIS Ambit Risk products, leads the global development teams for the various banking risk applications. He spends a lot of his time with innovating new concepts for large scale solution stacks and data infrastructures. Before joining FIS, he worked for many years with IBM, Dell and Compaq Computers. He was one of the founding members of the SAP LinuxLab, implemented the first ever Linux client with SAP and held many SAP benchmarks. Boris obtained an MS degree from the Karlsruhe Institute of Technology.

Dr. Lars Broeckers has been working in the field of IT and consulting since 2014. He started out with system administration for clients and data center infrastructures. Since entering the finance industry, he has continually deepened his knowledge in the field of databases, data warehouses infrastructure and data management. He has also focused on SAP Bank Analyzer and SAP BW implementation regarding IFRS9 and project management. He has a B.Sc. and M.Sc. in physics and completed his Ph.D. in chemistry at the Heinrich Heine University in Düsseldorf.

Fabian Bruse, Managing Consultant, has worked at ifb group since 2011. He started his career in the regulatory reporting sector (Basel III, CRR/CRD IV) as a software tester and later moved on to SAP BW and SAP Bank Analyzer development with a particular focus on IRR and CRA modules for customers in Germany and Luxembourg. His most recent projects include HANA and HADOOP ETL processes. Since 2017, he has coordinated the technical part of the ifb Hyperledger team and administrated the ifb blockchain system on Kubernetes. Fabian has a degree in physics from the University of Bonn.

Notes on Contributors

Dr. Gereon Dahmen is Director Business Consulting Accounting at ifb Lux S.A. He possesses in-depth knowledge of IFRS valuation, balancing, accounting logic, chart of accounts, reporting, impairment, hedge management and hedge accounting of financial instruments. He is also an expert in process architecture, functional and technical data modeling and software architecture. Throughout his career, he has managed many software implementation projects in the financial industry and served as a leading consultant for analysis, design, conception and implementation of business requirements in numerous projects. His academic background includes a degree in physics and a Ph.D. in astronomy.

Florian Dinges, Consultant at ifb group, studied mathematics and physics at the Goethe University in Frankfurt along with management studies. His interests include risk management, machine learning and digitalization.

Dr. Harro Dittmar, Consultant at ifb AG, focused his academic career on statistical research and the development of program code for pattern recognition in high-performance computer simulations. He has several years of experience in analytic writing and teaching. As a consultant, he has specialized in credit risk modeling, strategic approaches to data architecture and data management in the context of BCBS239, and assisted in the development of various IDVs for data collection and reporting. He has a background in programming and statistics and a Ph.D. in chemistry from the University of Calgary.

Notes on Contributors

Victoria Dobryashkina, Consultant at ifb International AG, primarily specializes in quantitative methods in financial risk management such as risk modeling with a particular focus on credit and liquidity risk modeling. She is particularly skilled in the area of statistics and has most recently put this to use developing the new exposure at default model for credit risk management at one of the leading banks in Austria. Victoria holds a Master's degree in quantitative finance from the Vienna University of Economics and Business.

Philipp Enzinger, Senior Consultant at ifb, has been working in banking and insurance for over five years covering the business and implementation side of risk in topics such as securitization, stress testing and IFRS 17/9. His recent focus has shifted toward how to integrate open source software like R or Python, which is typically used in machine learning and risk modeling, into traditional system architectures. His academic background in business and economics and he holds an M.Sc. degree in economics from the University of Cologne with a focus on statistics and financial econometrics.

Dr. Sascha Florin, Director at ifb group, has been working in the IT Consulting and Banking Industry for over fifteen years with a primary focus on business warehousing, data management and harmonization of data storage in central data repositories. Over the last few years, he has also worked more intensively on developing IT landscapes in a future-oriented manner with in-memory databases to reunite transactional and analytical driven parts. He has been a co-author for articles concerning reverse stress tests in banks. He has a degree and doctorate in physics from the University of Bonn.

Achim Franke, Senior Consultant at ifb group, has been working as a consultant in the banking and insurance industry for over three years in several projects involving IFRS9 and IFRS17. He has extensive knowledge of SAP products including SAP Bank Analyzer and SAP FPSL. He has been interested in blockchain and DLT since 2016 and has since developed in-depth knowledge of Hyperledger Fabric and other public and private blockchains. He holds an M.Sc. in physics from the University of Vienna.

Stefan Grossmann, Senior Director at ifb Canada, has been working in the banking and insurance industry in Europe and North America for more than twenty years. He has focused on the architectural design and implementation of solutions for a broad range of topics in enterprise management, risk and compliance as well as the financial controlling and accounting domains including Basel II/III and IFRS 9/17 with a keen interest in recent developments in data science and digital transformation. He has co-authored books on stress tests and Basel III and has a background in statistics, stochastics and physics including a degree in mathematics from the University of Bonn and studies at the University of Warwick.

Dr. Richard L. Harmon is Managing Director—Financial Services at Cloudera and has been working in the financial industry for more than three decades. He started his post-academic career at the Federal Reserve Bank of New York followed by leading fixed income and mortgage research teams at Citibank, Bankers Trust, JP Morgan and Bank of America. He is the co-founder of a GMAC funded Risk Management & Analytics start-up called Risk Monitors, which was acquired by BlackRock, where he was an MD & Partner in the

Risk Management Group. Richard left BlackRock to start and manage the North American business for Norkom Technologies, which was later sold to BAE Systems. Starting in 2010, he served as Director of SAP's EMEA Capital Markets group for six years, where he helped grow the business across the EMEA region. Dr. Harmon holds a Ph.D. in economics with specialization in econometrics from Georgetown University.

Thorsten Jakoby, Senior Consultant at ifb, gathered experience in AnaCredit including the different implementations of several national banks. He works on blockchain-related topics and in big data projects. He has most recently worked in a Hadoop project including HDFS, Hive, Spark, Sqoop, Oozie, HBase and Kafka. He has been working for the ifb AG for two years, within which he has installed and supervised some parts of ifb AG's big data infrastructure. He studied mathematics at RWTH Aachen with a focus on discrete mathematics and graph theory in particular. He took part in a one-year research project on distributed algorithms in Osaka, Japan.

Eva Kopic has been working as a Consultant for ifb since January 2018. She holds a Master's degree in biophysics and worked for 3 years at the University of Würzburg as a research associate. Her current focus consists of data modeling and business analysis. She also gained experience using modern SAP technologies in the banking context during a 7-month stay at SAP, where she took part in the development of a demo case including SAP Data Hub, SAP FSDP and SAP Analytics Cloud among others.

Iosif Levant, Senior Engineer at BearingPoint, gained experience in areas such as regulatory compliance (Basel III, CRR/CRD IV, MiFID II and Solvency II), stock markets, digitalization of processes in the financial industry and the architecture of regulatory reporting software. In recent years his primary focus has been on AI, machine learning and the application of these technologies in the financial markets. He has an academic background in mathematics.

Sangmeng Li started her career as a Consultant at ifb group at the beginning of 2017. She has primarily worked on quantitative risk management in the financial industry with a focus on risk modeling, model validation and technical implementation. She received her doctorate in mathematics from the University of Münster, having conducted research on stochastic modeling and numerical simulation as part of her Ph.D.

Constantin Lisson is an economist and financial econometrician by training. Prior to joining LIQID, he gained experience at the European Central Bank's Directorate Monetary Policy and as a research assistant at EBS. At LIQID, he is responsible for quantitative modeling and investment product development. He also specializes in ESG integration and innovative approaches to sustainable investment.

Uwe May is Co-Founder and Managing Director Sales/Marketing at maihiro, a company specialized in CRM, Customer Experience (CX) and Commerce. The consultancy offers support ranging from strategic advice and organizational development, to process optimization and implementation, right through to the management of SAP Customer Experience solutions. Its own product add-ons complete its range. Before founding maihiro, Uwe May acquired extensive know-how in the banking industry, worked as a project manager at CSC Ploenzke and assumed responsibility as for an international bank as Global Account Manager at Oracle. He has an economics background with a degree in business administration from the University of Passau.

Alexa Philo has worked in financial services for over twenty years as a banker, advisor and regulator. At Deutsche Bank, she led the Market Risk Management unit's Regulatory and Governance team, managing regulatory interactions, assessing the impacts of new and changing regulations, and overseeing modifications to DB's US MRM framework. At Ernst & Young, she advised clients on the financial, operational and legal impacts associated with the Dodd-Frank Act of 2010. In this capacity, she led engagements resolution plans for and established a Swap Dealer regulatory framework. During her eleven years as a regulator, Ms. Philo represented the Federal Reserve Bank of New York as the Examiner-in-Charge for two large European banks with a US presence. She also led the Secretariat of the Senior Supervisors Group, coordinating the collaborative efforts of supervisors from seven countries to publish the report Risk Management Lessons from the Global Banking Crisis of 2008.

Moritz Plenk is a Manager at BearingPoint, where he is responsible for RegTech DLT solutions. He has long-term experience in consulting for the financial services industry with a focus on regulatory topics. His goal consists of creating value for his clients in an ever-changing regulatory environment with solid, flexible and sustainable consulting services. The primary focus of his work is on regulatory software implementation projects, credit risk mitigation and DLT use cases. As head of RegTech DLT, he is responsible for the blockchain product strategy. His work aims at bringing technology and business for RegTech DLT use cases together. His academic background is in business informatics as well as banking & finance.

Dr. Daniel Schärf, Senior Consultant at ifb, has been working in the banking industry for over three years. He focuses on risk management and SAP products such as SAP Bank Analyzer and SAP FPSL. He has been using Bitcoin since 2012, long before working in the finance sector, based on his strong belief in the possibilities of this technology. His interest in this topic has since broadened and he now focuses on the many possible applications of blockchain technology. He has a background in theoretical chemistry with a specific focus on simulating and predicting crystal structures under extreme conditions.

Thomas Schneider has worked in the banking IT industry for over eight years. He acquired extensive knowledge in business topics like regulatory risk management, particularly with regard to credit risk, as well as technological systems and frameworks including SAP Bank Analyzer and SAP HANA. Since its first release, he has focused on the development of SAP's in-memory database

SAP HANA and its applications in the banking sector, as well as on the recently evolved HANA-based platforms and management suites like SAP FRDP, FSDP and FSDM. He studied applied mathematics, minoring in computer science, at the Universities of Bonn and Cologne and has a degree in mathematics from the latter.

Norbert Schaudinnus has been working in consulting for over two years with a focus on financial risk management. Within this field and related topics, he seeks out efficient AI and machine learning algorithms to tackle current challenges. His interests include neural network tailoring, kaggle competing and dockerizing applications. To balance this, he has spent much time climbing and riding his mountain bike through the black forest, where he also obtained a Ph.D. in physics from the University of Freiburg.

Ralph Steurer, Director of Engineering at ifb group, has been working in the financial services industry for over 10 years. Through his experience as architect and technical project manager for many different SAP implementation projects, he became an expert in designing innovative and scalable software applications. Ralph is currently leading the global development of finance and risk solutions for external as well as internal customers. His focus is on SAP HANA XSA, Kafka, Node.js and Spring Boot. Before joining ifb, he worked at SAP as developer and senior HANA consultant. His academic background includes a bachelor's degree in computer science from the Zurich University of Applied Sciences as well as continuing studies in big data and information retrieval at Swiss Federal Institute of Technology.

Dr. Bezu Teschome has been working in the IT consulting and banking industry for two years. His work primarily focuses on the design and implementation of data flows in the SAP businesses warehouse. He also provides assistance in transforming the existing classical business warehouse into the next-generation data warehouse, which is based entirely on an in-memory database system. He holds a doctorate in physics from the University of Dresden.

Markus Thiele has been working as a consultant in the banking industry for over 15 years with a focus on financial risk management and regulatory reporting. He has in-depth experience both in advising business departments and in implementing standard software. In addition to this, he possesses thorough enterprise architecture knowledge and implements the methodology in the project context. One of his keen interests is applying machine learning to financial risk management. He studied physics and holds a doctoral degree in this field.

Simon Valjanow is Director at ifb, where he is responsible for controlling and management accounting practice for banks. As a project manager and subject matter expert, he has been advising financial institutions on financial controlling topics for over ten years. He has most recently been developing solutions for the optimization of planning processes and integrated reporting. In addition to this, he has advised within the framework of transformation projects as well as change processes regarding the implementation of business cases and user stories. His holds a degree in business and law.

Nikolas Viets, CFA, heads ifb group's Treasury & Portfolio Management unit. He has been working as a consultant for the CRO/CFO agenda for over 13 years. His work experience includes a wide variety of industries, from large utilities and e-commerce companies to investment managers, with a primary focus on financial institutions. Nikolas holds degrees both in business administration and political economics and is a Certified Corporate Treasurer VDT®.

Index

A

ABM. *See* Agent-based model; Agent-based modeling
ACID principle 365
Activation functions 311
Active learning 274
Adjusted rand index 301
Agent based model 121, 128, 179, 234
Agent-based modeling 97, 205, 213, 214, 383
  interbank lending system 215
  systemic risk 204
AI. *See* Artificial intelligence
AIC. *See* Akaike information criterion
AIDA 72
Akaike information criterion 108
Alignment path 286, 287
ALM. *See* Asset liability management
4AMLD. *See* The Fourth EU Anti Money Laundering Directive
Alphago 277
Alternative scenario 103
Amara's law 31, 382
Amazon 382
AML. *See* Anti-money laundery

AMPLab 342
AnaCredit 241, 242
Analytical data 364
Analytics platform 225
Android 33
Angular 68
Anomaly detections 318
Anti-money laundery 30, 95, 251, 253, 254, 256
Apache
  Hadoop 225, 226, 373
  Hive 346, 348
  Mesos 349
  Software foundation 348
  Spark 348
  Sqoop 353
Appraisals capture 180
Architecture 381
Area under the curve 169, 172
Arima-models 302
Artificial intelligence 14, 225, 242, 249, 256, 272, 306
  black box 251
Artificial neural networks 169, 175
Asset liability management 203

© The Editor(s) (if applicable) and The Author(s), under exclusive license
to Springer Nature Switzerland AG, part of Springer Nature 2019
V. Liermann and C. Stegmann (eds.), *The Impact of Digital Transformation
and FinTech on the Finance Professional*, https://doi.org/10.1007/978-3-030-23719-6

400 Index

AUC. *See* Area under the curve
AuRep. *See* Austrian reporting
    company
Austrian reporting company 243
Autoencoder 16, 19, 23, 318, 328
    reconstruction error 23
Automated machine learning 273
AutoML. *See* Automated machine
    learning
Avro 347

B

Back propagation 313
Bagging and pasting 295
Bank management
    further development 99
Bank of Canada 8
Basel Committee on Banking
    Supervision 140, 232
Batch process 13, 15, 27
    pattern recognition 13
Bayesian information criterion 108
Bayesian network 16, 19, 20, 276, 289
    parameter learning 293
    selection and training 21
    structure learning 292
    training 291
BCBS. *See* Basel Committee on
    Banking Supervision
    interest rate shock scenarios 367
BCBS 239 106
BCBS 248 140
Behavioral responses 234
BIC. *See* Bayesian information criterion
Big data 225, 242, 249, 256
    architecture 229
    revolution 226
Bigram model 333
Bill Gates 7
Bitcoin 10, 30, 45
Black-box 164
Black swans 141

Blankfein, Lloyd C. 3
Blockchain 2, 45
    coins and tokens 29
    data-technology 30
    functional-technology 30
    Public 30
Blocktolive 41
Bnlearn 20
Board and senior management over-
    sight 262
Bohr, Niels 130
Boltzmann machines 320
BPM. *See* Business process modeling
BSON 374
Budgeting and planning 100
Bundesbank. *See* German central bank
Business model 104
Business process modeling 209
Business strategy 199, 234

C

C++ 367
CA. *See* Certificate authorities
Caffe 336
Calinski-harabasz index 301
CAMELS rating system 203
Capital planning/funding 263
Capital requirements directive 117
Capital requirements regulation 117
Cash Flow Generator 270, 367
Cash flow generator on HANA 366
Cassandra 348, 373
Causal relationships 102, 104,
    106–108
CBOW. *See* Continuous bag-of-words
CCAR. *See* Comprehensive Capital
    Analysis and Review
CDD. *See* Customer Due Diligence
CECL. *See* Current Expected Credit
    Loss
Center of Excellence 232
Certificate authorities 38

CFG. *See* Cash Flow Generator
Chief risk officer 97, 225
Chukwan 341
Citigroup 250
CLAR. *See* Comprehensive Liquidity
    Assessment and Review
Classification 274
Client-orientation 382
Climate risk 124
Cloud 225
   computing 225, 229
   strategies 4
Cloudera 4, 225, 373
Cluster analysis 298
Cluster evaluation 298
Clustering 277, 280
   centroid-based models 281
   connectivity-based models 281
   density-based model 283
   distribution-based model 283
   time series specific 283
Clustering analysis 147, 153
Cluster validity indices 299
   external 299
   internal 299
CNN. *See* Convolutional neural
   network
CoE. *See* Center of excellence
Collateral value 128, 134
Comprehensive Capital Analysis and
   Review 118, 135
Comprehensive Liquidity Assessment
   and Review 118, 135
Concerto 34
Conditional independence 291
Conditional probability 290
Conditional random field 330
Consensus protocol
   proof of elapsed time 33
   proof of Work 37
Contagion effects 194
Contagion mechanism 233
Contagion processes

credit-based 235
Continuous bag-of-words 331, 334
Continuous skip-gram 331
Convector 55
Convolutional neural network 254
Corda 11, 31, 47, 247
CoreNLP toolkit 330
Correlations 107
Cost and risk scenarios 101
Couchbase 373
Counterparty risk model
   agent-based 235
Counter terrorist financing 30, 95
CRD. *See* Capital requirements
   directive
Credit conversion factor 167
   model 168
Credit risk 120, 133
Credit risk model
   calibration 166
   development 166
   validation 166
Credit risk parameters
   estimation 163
Credit
   Value at risk 121
CRFClassifier 330
CRF. *See* Conditional random field
Crisp partitions 299
   adjusted rand index 299
   Folkes–mallows 299
   Jaccard index 299
   rand index 299
   variation of information 299
CRO. *See* Chief risk officer
Cross-border payments 31
Cross-correlation
   NCC 289
   with coefficient normalization 288
Cross-validation 297
   exhaustive 297
   non-exhaustive 297

CRR. *See* Capital requirements regulation
Cryptocurrency 31
Cumulative flow 144
Current Expected Credit Loss 118
Customer Due Diligence 253
Customer journey 7, 72
Customer relationship management 95
CV. *See* Collateral value
CVI. *See* Cluster validity indices
Cybercrime 95

D

DA. *See* Denoising auto encoder
DAG. *See* Directed acyclic graph
Daimler Benz 8
Dan Ariely 4
Danske Bank 250
Dashboard 140, 153
Data lake 269, 341
Data lineage 101
Data
  quality controls 225
  structured and unstructured 227
Dataset partition 172
Data warehouse
  modern 227
  traditional 226
Davies–bouldin index 301
DBN. *See* Deep belief networks
DBSCAN. *See* Density-based spacial clustering of applications with noise
DCIGN. *See* Deep convolutional inverse graphics network
DCN. *See* Deep Convolutional Network
Debt service coverage ratio 127, 179
Decision tree 276, 294
Deconvolutional network 171, 322
Deep belief networks 321

Deep convolutional inverse graphics network 323
Deep Convolutional Network 322
Deep feedforward 314
Deep learning 178, 269, 274
Deep residual network 326
Default event 165
Default risk 165
DeLi-Clu. *See* Density-link-clustering
Denoising auto encoder 318
Density-based spacial clustering of applications with noise 283
Density-link-clustering 283
Dependent variables 279
Design Thinking 4
Deutsche Bank 250, 253
DFF. *See* Deep feed forward
DGSE. *See* Dynamic Stochastic General Equilibrium
Digital asset 33
Digitalization
  of business models 2
  trade-off 198
Digital risk
  Framework 226
  transformation 226, 229
Digital transformation 220
  impact to finance and risk manager 220
  impact to IT manager 220
  impact to regulator 220
Directed acyclic graph 342, 349
Discretized Stream 351
Disruptive innovations of digitalization 99
Distance metric
  times series specified 285
Distributed computing 164
Distributed ledger 29, 45, 381
Distributed ledger technology 242, 244, 256
  cryptography 245
  decentralization 244

immutability 244
implications for banks and regulatory authorities 248
programmability 245
regulatory reporting network based on 246
single point of truth 244
transparency 244
Distributed representations 332
DL. *See* Deep learning
DLT. *See* Distributed ledger technology
DN. *See* Deconvolutional network
DNNClassifier 171
Docker 32
Document based databases 372
definition 373
Dodd-Frank Act 117
stress test 118, 135
Driver
forecast 105
forecast 105
granularity 104
number of 104
DRN. *See* Deep residual network
DSCR. *See* Debt service coverage ratio
Dstream. *See* Discretized Stream
Dtwcluster 147
DTW. *See* Dynamic time wrapping distance
Dunn index 301
Dynamic Stochastic General Equilibrium 214
Dynamic time wrapping distance 285, 287
alignment path 286

E

EAD. *See* Exposure at default
EBA. *See* European Banking Authority
ECB. *See* European central bank
Echo state machine 325
EDA. *See* Exploratory data analysis
ELM. *See* Extreme learning machine

Elu 312
EMIR. *See* European Market Infrastructure Regulation
EMIR II. *See* European Market Infrastructure Regulation II
Endogenous component 107
Endorser 36
Enterprise data
cloud 229
infrastructure 229
Enterprise risk function 226
Enterprise risk management 225, 230, 263
ERC-20 tokens 30
Error
analysis 13, 15
log 13
sources 27
Error-term 278
Erwarteter Verlust. *See* Expected loss
ESM. *See* Echo state machine
Ethereum 10, 30, 45, 46
ETL/data integration 353
ETL. *See* Extract transform load
European Banking Authority 118, 141, 252
European Central Bank 118, 252
European Market Infrastructure Regulation 117
European Market Infrastructure Regulation II 241, 247, 256
Everledger 8
EV. *See* Erwarteter verlust; Expected loss
Exogenous component 107
Exogenous variable 107
Expected loss 118
one year 128
Expert estimates 102
Expert judgment 128
Explanatory variables 279
Exploratory data analysis 169
Exponential linear unit 312
Exposure at default 128, 165

404 Index

Extended application services, advanced module 366
Extensible markup language 347
External driver 103
External value-driver 106, 108
Extract transform load 360
Extreme learning machine 324

F
Fabric 29
Facebook 270, 342
FASB. *See* Financial Accounting Standards Board
FATCA. *See* Foreign Account Tax Compliance Act
FCA. *See* Financial Conduct Authority
FDIC. *See* Federal Deposit Insurance Corporation
Features 169
Federal Deposit Insurance Corporation 118
Federal Reserve 118, 252
FED. *See* Federal Reserve
Feedforward network 307
Feedforward neural network 308
    training 312
Fiat-money 30
Figo 3
Financial Accounting Standards Board 118
Financial Conduct Authority 239
Financial crisis 225
Financial planning 120
Financial risk management 381
Financial Services Data Management 366
Financial Services Data Platform 366
FINMA. *See* Swiss Financial Markets Authority
Fintech 1, 2, 194
Fire sales contagion 234
FIS 270
FIS BSM 371

Flink 341
Folkes–mallows index 301
Forecast 101
Forecasting 155
Forecast the drivers 105
Foreign Account Tax Compliance Act 253
Forward-rate curves 131
The Fourth EU Anti Money Laundering Directive 253
Fragmented IT landscape 226
Franz Kafka 96
Fraud detection 294, 328
FSDM. *See* Financial Services Data Management
FSDP. *See* Financial Services Data Platform
Functional relationship 102
Further development
    controlling concepts 99
Future market potential
    mortgage loans 100
Future of stress testing 226, 232
Future result 101
Future risk profile 133
Fuzzy partitions 299
    soft adjusted rand index 299
    soft normalized mutual information based on max entropy 299
    soft rand index 299
    soft variation of information 299

G
GAFA 1, 4
GAK. *See* Global alignment kernel distance
GAN. *See* Generative Adversarial Network
Gardner 382
Gartner magic quadrant
    For data science and machine learning platforms 336
Gated recurrent unit 316
    memory cell 316

GATE. *See* General Architecture for
    Text Engineering
Gatekeeper 35
Gaussian kernel 288
GDA. *See* Gradient Descent
    Algorithms
GDP. *See* Gross Domestic Product
GDPR. *See* General Data Protection
    Regulation
General Architecture for Text
    Engineering 330
General Data Protection Regulation 39,
    231, 250, 254
    Article 16 255
    Article 22 254
    Article 32(1)(a) 255
Generalized linear models 279
Generative Adversarial Network 129,
    251, 253, 324
German Bundesbank 8
German Central Bank 124
GLM. *See* Generalized linear models
Global alignment kernel distance 287
Goldman Sachs 3
Google 269, 342
    Google automl 274
Go
    programming language 33
GPU. *See* Graphics processing unit
Gradient Descent Algorithms 313
Graphical user interface 186
Graphics processing unit 250
Green finance 124
    Definition 125
Gross Domestic Product 107
Grow-shrink algorithm 292
GRU. *See* Gated recurrent unit
GS. *See* Grow-shrink algorithm
GUI. *See* Graphical user interface

H
H2O.ai 336
H2O 23

Automl 274
Driverless 274
H2O framework 23
Hadoop 6, 226, 251, 270, 341, 366
    DataNodes 344
    Editlogs 344
    Fsimage 344
    introduction to 343
    NameNode 344
    Sap 353
    YARN 349
Hasso Plattner 362
HBase 341
HDFS 343, 348
Hidden layer 308
Hierarchical learning 274
High performance computing 229
Hive 341
    QL. *See* Hive query language
    query language 342, 346
HLF. *See* Hyperledger, fabric
Hopfield network 320
Horizon
    one year 135
Hortonworks 347, 373
HPC. *See* High performance
    computing
HQL. *See* Hive query language
Hype cycle 382
Hyperledger 11
    Caliper 34
    Cello 34
    Composer 11, 54
        access data 55
        assets 56
        Assets 56
        business network archive 58
        composer playground 59
        consensus algorithms 58
        events 57
        modeling language 11, 55
        participants 56
        permissions 57
        queries 57

406 **Index**

transactions 55–57
Explorer 34
Fabric 32, 35, 47
certificates 38
channels 35, 37, 39
consensus mechanism 37
endorsement policy 38
endorsing peers 37
membership service provider 35, 36
orderer 35–37
organizations 35, 36
peers 35
privacy methods 39
private transactions 40
SideDB 40
Fabric version 1.4 34
Indy 33
Iroha 33
Long term support 34
Quilt 34
Sawtooth 33

I

Iamb. *See* Incremental association markov blanket algorithm
IBM 33, 337, 361
DB2 361
In-memory Columnstore 361
IBM Cloudant database 373
ICAAP. *See* Internal Capital Adequacy Assessment Process
Identity mixer 41
ifb
Modern ALM 368
IFRS 9 252
impairment regime 118
Ignite 341
ILAAP. *See* Internal liquidity adequacy assessment process
Incremental association algorithm 292
Incremental Association Markov Blanket Algorithm 292

Independent variables 279
Inflow 144
In-memory database 164, 270, 360, 368
Concept 360
In-memory HANA database 362
Input layer 308
InsurTech 194
Integrated value driver-oriented planning 100
Intel 33
Interactive analysis 353
Interest rate curve 16
Interest rate risk in the banking book 118
Internal Capital Adequacy Assessment Process 123, 141
Internal Liquidity Adequacy Assessment Process 123, 141
Intraday liquidity 139
blockwise aggregation 156
forecast 151
pattern recognition 147
regular reporting to supervisors 145
regulatorical requirements 145
stress tests 145
subclustering 148
Intraday risk monitoring 225, 227
Investment temperament 88
Investor utility function 84
iOS 33

J

Jaccard index 301
Java 33, 342, 352, 367
JavaScript 33, 367
Joint probability distribution 291
JSON 64, 374

K

Keras 336
Auto keras 274

Key performance indicators 13
Key risk indicators 13, 132
K-folds cross-validation 297
KM. *See* Kohonen machine
K-Nearest Neighbor 351
Know Your Customer 30, 95, 251, 253
Kohonen machine 326
KRI. *See* Key risk indicators
KYC. *See* Know Your Customer

L

Landscape
    classical system 359
Large-value payment system 142
Layer configuration 174
LBBW 8
LCR. *See* Liquidity, coverage ratio
Learning
    reinforcement 277
    semi-supervised 274
    supervised 274
    unsupervised 274
Least-squares estimation 279
LECL. *See* Life-time expected credit
        loss
Lemmatizers 184
LGD. *See* Loss given default
LHS. *See* Variables, left hand side
Life-time expected credit loss 118
Linear classification 275
Linear regression 111, 278
    multivariate 278
Linear weighting of probabilities 85
Linux 33
Linux foundation 32
LIQID 79
    onboarding process 90
    risk test 89
Liquidity
    covarage ratio 142
    intraday 142
    risk 141, 168

intraday 142
management 141
short-term 142
strategic 142
structural 118, 142
the general idea 141
Liquidity/funds management 264
Liquid state machine 325
Litecoin 30
Logistic function 311
Logistic regression 165, 171, 175
Long/short term memory 316
Loss aversion 88
Loss given default 119, 128, 133, 165
LSM. *See* Liquid state machine
LSTM. *See* Long/short term memory
LTS. *See* Long term support
LVPS. *See* Large-value payment system

M

Machine learning 128, 140, 178, 225,
        251, 269, 353, 381
    abstraction 167
    algorithms 175
    automation 167
    availability 167
    classic 19
    components 273
    domains of 272
Machine learning frameworks 335
Macroeconomic data 105
Macroeconomic factors 134
Macroeconomic parameters 100
MapReduce 342, 344
Market data 120, 130
    scenarios 130
Market parameters 100
Market share 107
    prediction 113
Markets in Financial Instruments
        Directive II 241, 250, 254,
        256

408 Index

Article16(6) 255
Markov blanket discovery algorithms
    292
MAS. *See* Monetary Authority of
    Singapore
Mathworks 337
McKay 3
Mean 284
Mean-variance portfolio selection para-
    digm 88
Medium-term planning 104
MemDB 373
Micro-location 109
Microsoft 337, 361
    in-memory Columnstore 361
    in-memory OLTP 361
    SQL Server 346
    SQL server 361
MIFID II. *See* Markets in Financial
    Instruments Directive II
Minority report 358
ML. *See* Machine learning
Model configuration 171
Model parameter 130
Model validation 296, 314
    K-folds cross-validation 297
Monetary Authority of Singapore 8, 253
Mongo DB 270, 348, 372
    Atlas 380
    Community edition 379
    Docker hub 380
    Enterprise advanced 379
    web interface 376
Mortgage market development 113
MPP 376
MSP. *See* yperledger:Fabric:
    Membership service provider
MTAR. *See* Multi-target archive
Multi-cloud deployments 229
Multi-layered network 205
Multi-target archive 367
Multivariate linear regression 278
MySQL 346

N
N26 7
Named entity recognition 97, 186, 329
Natural intelligence 272
Natural Language Processing 97, 182,
    184, 251, 254–256
Natural language tool kit 184
NBA 71
NBO 71
    And Forecasting 76
    application 73
    in the banking sector 73
    Other industries 74
NCC. *See* Cross-correlation, with coef-
    ficient normalization
The nearest cluster 151
NER. *See* Named entity recognition
Net interest margin 101
    contribution 101
Network 97, 193
    collaboration network 193
    complex networks 214
    employee management 193
    external network 194
    internal network 196
    manage complex networks 199
    Network modeling 197, 199
    network modeling
        components 196
    network models of systemic risk
        194
    network topology 197
    real life network 204
Neural network 200, 276
    input layer 203
    monitor systemic risk 199
    output layer 202
Neural Turing machine 327
New business volume 107
Next best action 71
Next best offer 7, 11, 71
NIM. *See* Net interest margin
NLP. *See* Natural Language Processing

Nltk. *See* Natural language tool kit
NMD. *See* Non maturing deposits
Node.js 33
Nominal value 16
Nonlinear regression 279
Non maturing deposits 142
Normalization of time series 284
NoSQL 348
NOSQL databases 373
NSFR. *See* Net stable funding ratio
NTM. *See* Neural turing machine

O

Objective function 276
Observation
  scope of observation 75
Observation time 75
OCC. *See* Office of the Comptroller of
  the Currency
OCR. *See* Optical character recognition
OFAC. *See* Office of Foreign Assets
  Control
Office of Foreign Assets Control 253
Office of the Comptroller of the
  Currency 240
OLAP 353
OLTP. *See* Online transactional
  processing
On-demand risk aggregation 227
One-hot vectors 170
Online analytical processing 353
Online transactional processing 360
OpenNLP 330
Optical character recognition 183, 186
OPTICS. *See* Ordering points to iden-
  tify the clustering structure
Optimized RC files 347
Oracle 346, 361
  SQL Optimizer 361
ORC. *See* Optimized RC files
Ordering points to identify the cluster-
  ing structure 283
Output layer 308

P

P&L result 101
PaaS. *See* Platform as a service
Packaged retail and insurance-based
  investment products - regula-
  tion 255
Parameter learning 293
Parameter transformation 131
Parquet files 347
Parsing 182
Pattern recognition 19, 147, 381
  apply model 25
  General process 14
  Illustrative example 16
  Model comparison 25
  System architecture 15
Payment services directive 2 220
PayPal 250
PDFMiner 183
PD. *See* Probability of default
Perceptron 307
Performance measures 172
Petasort 342
Pig 341
Planning
  process 105
  Value driver
    oriented 100
Plan variables
  modeling 106
Platform as a service 363
Plausibility checks 13
Portfolio compositions 234
Portfolio credit risk 120
PoW. *See* Proof of Work
Power blackout 365
Prediction 381
Predictive analytics 99, 105
Predictive risk analysis
  Framework of 134
  The big picture 134
PRIIP. *See* Packaged retail and insur-
  ance-based investment prod-
  ucts - regulation

410 Index

Private blockchains 11
Probability of default 119, 127, 133, 165
Process automation 381
Process industrialization 9
Process mining 206
   methodology 207
Process monitoring 13
Projection of risk situation 120
Project Jasper 8
Project Ubin 8
Proof of elapsed time 33
Proof of Work 37
Property
   as a collateral 178
   as an investment 178
Prospect theory 79
   Case study 88
PSD2. *See* Payment services directive
Public blockchains 10
Pytesseract 183
Python 169, 183, 342, 352
   script 169
   version 3.6.0 169

Q

Qe. *See* Quantification error
Quality checks 13
Quantification error 203

R

R 23, 100, 111, 183, 342, 352
   Dtwcluster 147
   Shiny 153
   Tsclust 148
R3 47
Radial basis function neural networks 311
RAM
   non-volatile 365
Rand index 300

Random forest 276, 295
   algorithm 295
RBF. *See* Radial basis function neural networks
RBM. *See* Restricted Boltzmann machines
RC. *See* Record columnar files
RDBS. *See* relational database system
RDD. *See* Resilient distributed data
Real estate 177
   dynamic data 181
   substance data 181
Real estate risk 97, 126
Real estate risk management
   micro-based 178
   value driver oriented 178, 179
Real-time analysis of data streams 353
Receiver operating characteristic 169
Recommendation algorithm 75
Record columnar files 347
Rectified linear unit 312
Recurrent neural network 129, 251, 253, 315
Regression 278
Regression model 107
RegTech 194, 239
   in a narrowed sense 239
   in a wider sense 239
Regulation 381
Regulatory reporting
   Automation 246
Reinforcement learning 274, 277
Relu 312
Repayment types 367
   annuities 367
   fixed principal 367
   interest only 367
REPO. *See* Repurchase agreement
Representational state transfer 367
Repurchase agreement 142
Resilient distributed data 349
RESTful. *See* Representational state transfer

Restricted Boltzmann machines 320
Rest server 68
Return on investment
  AI 27
Rhs. *See* Variables, right hand side
Right to be forgotten 39
Ripple 31
Risk 3.0. *See* Future of stress testing
Risk assessment 263
Risk
  communication 135
  Real estate 126
  transversal 120
Risk horizon
  one-year 133
Risk management
  evolution of 135
  landscape 231
  multi-period perspective 120
  Pyramid 119
  traditional 135
Risk modeling 225
Risk parameters 120
Risk profile 129
Risk projections 129
Risk strategy
  quantitative 120
Risk-weighted-assets 118
RNN. *See* Recurrent neural network
Robert Solow 4
Robo advisor 7, 11
Robotic process automation 8
Robotics process automatisation 382
ROC-curve. *See* Receiver operating
    characteristic
RPA. *See* Robotic process automation
RWA. *See* Risk-weighted-assets

S

SAE. *See* Spare Autoencoder
SAP 337, 361
  ABAP 367
  Hadoop 366

Hybris 363
  as a service 363
Predicitive analysis library 364
Predictive analytics library 337
Smart Data Integration 366
WebIDE 366
SAP business suite 4 SAP HANA 363
SAP cloud platform 363
SAP HANA 6, 270, 337, 353, 362,
    364
  2.0 363
  2.0 database 367
  advantages 364
  Cash flow generator on 366
  cloud microservices 363
  Cockpit 365
  Database 362
  Dynamic tiering 365
  encryption technology 365
  Evolution 362
  Vora 353
  XSA 366
SAP S/4HANA. *See* SAP business suite
    4 SAP HANA
SAS 337
Scala 342, 349, 352
Scalar response variable 279
Scaling out 376
Scenario-based planning 120
SDA. *See* Smart data access
SDI. *See* Smart data integration
SEC. *See* U.S. Securities and Exchange
    Commission
Security-token 8
Self-organizing map 97, 129, 200, 201
Semi-supervised learning 274
Several sparse categories 170
SG. *See* Continuous skip-gram
SGD. *See* Stochastic gradient descent
Shaped-based distance 288
Sharding data 377
Sigmoid 311
Silhouette index 301
Size on disk 343

412 Index

Skip-gram model 334
  architecture 334
Smart contracts 29
Smart data access 366
Softplus 311
SOM. *See* Self-organizing map
Soramitsu 33
Sovrin foundation 33
SpaCy 330
Spare auto encoder 319
Spark 164, 270, 341
  Architecture 349
  Context 349
  Core 349
  GraphX 352
  ML 350, 351
  MLlib 350, 351
  R 351
  SQL 342, 346, 350, 351, 353
    ANSI 346
  streaming 350
SPNB 259
SQLScript 364
Sqoop 341, 353
SREP. *See* Supervisory review and eval-
  uation process
Standardized processes 9
Standard variation 284
Stanford NER 330
Stanford University 362
Stemmers 184
Stochastic gradient descent 171
Stop words 185
Stress scenarios 264
  value-driver based 120
Stress test
  EBA 135
  multi-period view 118
  value-driver oriented 120
Stress testing 256
  capabilities 225
  dynamic 234
  internal 225
  regulatory 225

static 233
Structured query language. *See*
  SQL
Structure learning 274, 292
Subclustering 148
Supervised learning 15
Supervisory review and evaluation
  process 141
Supply and demand calculus 129
Support-vector machines 276, 280
Support vector network 327
SVN. *See* Support vector network
Swiss Financial Markets Authority
  118
Syndicated loan 32, 46
  Best-effort syndication 50
  Business
    initiation 51
    origin 49
    process domains 50
    processing 51
  cash flows 61
  co-lead managers 48
  collateral 61
  introduction 48
  Involved parties 49
  joint lead manager 48
  lead arranger 48
  loan conditions 61
  process requirements 46
  sole-lead manager 49
  types of syndicated loans 50
  underwriting 50
Systematic risk
  contribution of the players 200
System breakdown 365
Systemic risk
  models recently studied 195

T

Table 2Vec 188
Target/actual comparisons 104
Target variable 169

TensorFlow 169, 336
  library 169, 171, 175
  quick start guide 171
Tensor processing unit 336
Term frequency-inverse document
      frequency 185
Testing set 297
TE. *See* Topological error
Tf-idf. *See* Term Frequency-Inverse
      Document Frequency
Throughput 144
Time series specified clustering 283
Times series specified distance metric 285
Time transformation 131
Tokenization 184
Topological error 203
Torch 336
TPU. *See* Tensor processing unit
Traditional database system 360
Traditional data warehouse 226
  architecture 227
Traditional disc-based database 360
Training set 297
Training
  size 173
  step 175
Trait recognition 201
Transactional data 364
Transaction scenarios 131
Transformation 132
  temporal 132
  transactional 133
Transversal risk 120, 121
  concept of 122
  definition 122
Trevni project 347
Tsclust 148

U

UI5 GUI 367
Uncertainty aversion on gains 88
UNIX 343
Unsupervised learning 277

Unweighted pair group method with
      arithmetic mean 281
UPGMA. *See* Unweighted pair group
      method with arithmetic mean
Ursa 35
U.S. Securities and Exchange
      Commission 252
US treasury
  Office of financial research 235
Utility function 84

V

VAE. *See* Variational AE
Validation system chaincode 38
Value at Risk 118, 121, 134, 233
Value-driver 128, 134
  based
    approach 114
    planning 99
  based perspective 128
  candidate 109
  design 121, 127
  external 107
  identification of 120
  internal 107
  model
    concept and design 102
  modeling 129
  oriented planning
    idea behind 106
    integrated 100
  planning 102
    real estate market—use case 109
    statistical methodology and appli-
      cation 106
    use cases 106
  tree 102, 103, 114
Variables
  dependent 273
  explanatory 279
  independent 273, 279
  left-hand-side 273
  right-hand-side 273

414 Index

Variational AE 318
VaR. *See* Value at Risk
Virtual machines 33
Von-Neumann-Morgenstern
  utility theorem 81
    axiom, completeness 82
    axiom, continuity 84
    axiom, independence 84
    axiom, transitivity 83
    axiom 82
VSCC. *See* Validation system chaincode

W
we.trade 8
Windows 33, 343
Word2Vec 97, 186, 188, 331

Word analogies 331
Word embedding model 331
Workforce automation 8

X
XML. *See* Extensible markup
  language
XSA. *See* Extended application services,
  advanced module

Z
Zero-knowledge proof 41
Zettabyte Era 2
Z-normalization 285
ZooKeeper 341